D1489421

GEORGIA vs. GEORGIA TECH

GRIDIRON GRUDGE SINCE 1893

JOHN CHANDLER GRIFFIN

HILL STREET PRESS **d** ATHENS, GEORGIA

A HILL STREET PRESS BOOK

Published in the United States of America by
Hill Street Press LLC
191 East Broad Street, Suite 209   Athens, Georgia 30601-2848 USA
706-613-7200
info@hillstreetpress.com   www.hillstreetpress.com

Hill Street Press is committed to preserving the written word. Every effort is made to print books on acid-free paper with a significant amount of post-consumer recycled content.

We have made every effort to make the information in this book as accurate as possible. If you have a correction to this book please write to us so that we can correct future editions.

Hill Street Press books are available in bulk purchase and customized editions to institutions and corporate accounts. Please contact us for more information.

Printed in the United States of America.

Library of Congress Cataloging-in-Publication Data

Griffin, John Chandler, 1936-
    Georgia vs. Georgia Tech : gridiron grudge since 1893 / by John Chandler Griffin.
        p.   c.
    ISBN 1-892514-96-6
        1. University of Georgia—Football. 2. Georgia Institute of Technology—Football. 3. Georgia Bulldogs
(Football team). 4. Georgia Tech Yellow Jackets (Football team). I. Title: Georgia versus Georgia Tech. II. Title

GV958.U524 G75 2000
796.332'63'09758—dc 21   00-059773

ISBN # 1-892514-96-6

10   9   8   7   6   5   4   3   2   1

First printing

Introduction

The greatest thing in the world is to compete and win.
The second greatest is to compete and lose.

—Bobby Riggs

Over the past few years I've compiled several college football histories similar to this one, but I can honestly say that not one of those books gave me the pleasure that doing this one has. Truly, researching and writing about the excellent football programs offered by Georgia Tech and the University of Georgia was a most gratifying experience, one I'll never forget. Writing this book and feeling that I have contributed in some small way to the sports history of two of the nation's greatest institutions is a tremendous honor for me.

I spent many weeks in the archives at both schools, greedily digging through their musty old sports records as though I'd uncovered the secrets of the universe. And of course I've tried to communicate as much of what I found to the reader as possible, though space limitations have forced me to omit certain important materials. (For the same reason, I must omit the photos of some truly great players.)

There is a wealth of data available at both institutions concerning the teams of the modern era of college football (1965–the present). But in all honesty I have to say that it was the early era of the game (1893–1964) that truly fascinated me and was the most fun to research and write about.

(Many sportswriters arbitrarily choose 1945, the first season following Word War II, as the beginning of the modern era in college football. But I feel it is more accurate to say that the year 1965 marks the beginning of this era. For that was the year that the NCAA approved the Unlimited Substitution Rule, the most significant rule change in the history of college football. Indeed, football players of 1964 were playing essentially the same game their grandfathers had played back in 1892. But after the rule change, young men were no longer expected to play sixty minutes of every game, specialists emerged, and coaches were free to run entire teams in and out of the game at will. For these reasons, I feel 1965 truly marks the beginning of the modern era of college football.)

The reader will be struck by the air of informality, the naïve innocence, that characterized the game and the players in the early era. There was a tremendous amount of personality and individuality in the game back then. The players were called Iron Men and were expected to play sixty minutes of every contest. They looked like real people in those days and most of them were saddled with distinctive nicknames (Froggie Morrison and Big Six Carpenter come immediately to mind). Nor were they in the least shy when it came to making disparaging remarks about their opponents to sportswriters. As for their losses, they generally attributed these to either crooked game officials or to inclement weather. Yep, judged by today's standards, the boys (and coaches) of this bygone era were most naïve and innocent.

They were also extremely honest. Back then, a man's word was his bond, and the boys sincerely believed that old cliché about how you play the game being more important than whether you win or lose. In fact, while conducting research at another institution several years ago I came across a poem in a 1903 student publication that well illustrates the heroic attitudes of the young men of yesteryear. It was written by a student named W. W. Stephens and says that the most important thing, in life as in football, is not whether you win or lose, but how you play the game.

THE GREATEST GAME

The gridirons are deserted now, and gone the season's strife,
But the game for us has just begun on the football field of life.

Never an intermission there the weary ones shall know,
Nor a time out call for the men that fall, nor the blessed whistle blow.

Never a sub can take your place, and never a man must yield,
For the game is o'er forevermore for the men who leave the field.

Perhaps the world shall see you win, and the pennants wave for you,
And your feet will tear the trampled turf as you drive the touchdown through.

Or perhaps upon your very goal the plunging bodies meet,
And the dusty lime of the last white line is crushed beneath your feet.

Perhaps the twilight wind is cold, and the goalposts shadows long,
And the victors swarm upon the field to chant their triumph song.

But if you play the losing game as but a hero can,
The men that buck your line will know they played against a MAN.

Dedication

*I humbly dedicate this book
to the memory of my late father,
John C. Griffin Sr., of Midway, Georgia
and
to my granddaughter, Emmalee Grace Ballard,
whose birth on December 23, 1999,
delayed work on this book for three whole days!*

Acknowledgments

This book truly represents a massive (but very enjoyable) undertaking on my part, one that consumed over a year of my life. It was the sort of project that involved a great deal of research and the gathering of a great many photographs, and thus required the assistance and cooperation of a great many people.

In particular, I would like to mention all the good folks at both the University of Georgia and Georgia Tech. I literally walked in off the street one morning (and numerous mornings thereafter), heavily laden with strange looking equipment and breathing heavily. But once I convinced shocked staff members that I was not the Mad Bomber, that my reasons for being there were totally legitimate, those good folks were more than eager to become involved.

In particular, I would like to mention Claude Felton, sports information director at the University of Georgia, and his staff members Steve Colquitt and Karen Huff who were most generous and helpful. And also Mike Finn, director of communications at Georgia Tech, and his very competent staff members. Those sports info folks have a wealth of material going back to 1892, and they were quick to make it available.

I also did a great deal of research in the archives at both institutions. I am deeply appreciative to everyone at the Hargrett Rare Books and Manuscript Room of the Ila Dunlap Little Library at the University of Georgia for all their help, in particular Nelson Morgan, who successfully tracked down several photos that I thought were lost forever.

And also to Michael Branch, Ann Salters, and Ruth Hale in the Library Archives at Georgia Tech. Not only did they make available all the obvious materials but they also thought of several private collections that I'd never heard of, and brought that material out for my perusal. I'm extremely grateful for their help.

I would also like to mention several excellent photographers from these two institutions: Travis Hatfield, Michael Bass, Meredith Page, Eric McCall, and Dwayne Bass.

All these people were most patient and were most cordial on every occasion. I will miss my associations with them.

Closer to home, what would I have done without my good friend and dean at the University of South Carolina at Lancaster, Dr. Joe Pappin? Joe is a confirmed Oklahoma Sooner who honestly believes that Bud Wilkinson's retirement in 1964 marked the end of civilization as we had always known it. But Joe put all the facilities of USC-Lancaster at my disposal and cooperated in every way in making this project possible. In fact, Joe seemed as enthusiastic about it as I was. So who knows? Maybe he's right about Bud Wilkinson and civilization after all.

And I would certainly be remiss if I didn't mention Ben Robertson, anthropology professor at USC-Lancaster and, oddly enough, the world's foremost authority on anything even remotely related to computers. Ben always had the solution to whatever my particular problem happened to be at the moment, and cheerfully came to my rescue on numerous occasions.

Truly, without the help of these and numerous other individuals I could only dream of doing a Georgia-Georgia Tech football book.

I should also mention my liberal use of old football articles from three of the South's most outstanding newspapers, the *Athens Banner,* the *Atlanta Constitution,* and the *Savannah Morning News.* The sports writers at these newspapers have always been excellent, and I gleaned much of my information from them.

In closing, I would like to mention Bill Cromarties's book, *Clean Old Fashioned Hate* which I found most helpful in my research. His book is chock full of interesting facts, and he approaches the whole Georgia-Georgia Tech thing with a terrific sense of humor, which makes it a very readable book.

So, to all of you, THANKS A MILLION! As I pointed out, this book truly represents a cooperative effort on the part of a great many people, and I hope you like the results of our labors.

1892: In the Beginning . . .

Both Georgia and Georgia Tech organized their first football teams in 1892 and completed the year with a combined won-loss record of 1-4, hardly an auspicious beginning for what would become two of the nation's most outstanding football programs.

The 1892 Georgia Tech team: They called themselves the Blacksmiths and lost to Mercer, Vanderbilt and Auburn. (Lineup): LE: Murdock McRae; LT: Ed Werner, E. E. West, Will Hunter; LG: F. O. Spain, Haralson; C: George Forrest; RG: Gavan; RT: Joe Little; RE: Ed Whitney; QB: Stafford Nash, Harry Miles; RHB: Will Hunter; FB: Hardin Jones: LHB: John Kimball.

The 1892 University of Georgia team: They called themselves the Wildcats, and beat Mercer while losing to Auburn. (Bottom, L-R): Julian R. Lane, Frank "Si" Herty, William W. Gramling, Henry C. Brown, John Kimball, L. D. Fricks. (Top, L-R): A. O. Halsey, Park Howell, E. W. Frey, George Shackelford, Rufus Ben Nalley.

1893: Tech Wins Game, Loses Brawl

It was the afternoon of November 4, 1893, a beautiful day for college football, as exuberant fans began to gather to watch this historical first meeting between the Wildcats of the University of Georgia and the Blacksmiths of Georgia Tech. The game was to be played in Athens on a large open field known as Herty Field located just to the rear of Georgia's New College. (The field was named for Dr. Charles H. Herty, the father of athletics at the University of Georgia.)

Georgia fans were especially lighthearted, for they had played two games in '92, losing to Auburn but beating Mercer, while their upstart foe from Atlanta, whom they referred to derisively as the Teckity-Techs, had played three games in 1892, losing to Mercer, Vanderbilt and Auburn by convincing scores. And since 1-1 is better than 0-3, the outcome of today's contest could hardly be in doubt. Indeed, it was widely stated that today's contest with Tech was nothing more than a warmup for next week's big game with Vanderbilt.

Georgia fans, unfortunately, were unaware that the Tech team now had a secret weapon in their possession, a young man by the name of Lt. Leonard Wood, who would make the Wildcats pay dearly for their arrogance.

Wood was an army officer stationed at Ft. McPherson near Atlanta, and when he learned that Tech was fielding a football team, he immediately volunteered to lead the way. He had previously played for four years at Harvard and another two years with his post team, so the Techs were more than happy to accept his services as both a player and a coach.

He played fullback on offense and guard on defense, and following the game the *Atlanta Constitution* reported that Wood "could handle his opposing guard, who was a much lighter man, almost as if he were a child."

The first half ended with Tech holding the big end of an 18-0 score (TDs counted 4 points, PATs 2 points). Wood, by the way, had scored two of Tech's TDs at this point, Nourse the other, and both were already becoming the target of angry taunts from the Athens sidelines.

As for the second half, Dr. Park Howell scored for the Techs and the score became 22-0. Georgia did manage to drive across a score with eleven minutes left in the game on what was called "the turtleback" play. Henry Brown

The 1893 Georgia Wildcats. (Bottom L-R): Crane, Fender, Ezelle, Halsey, George Butler, George Shackelford, Barrow, and Murphy. (Middle L-R): Fricks, Henry Brown, Fleming, Coach Ernest Brown, McCutcheon, and Wrigley. (Top L-R): Stubbs, Warren, Smith, Nalley, Black, Fleming and Mooreno.

These young men went 2-2-1 on the season with wins over the Augusta Athletic Club and Furman, losses to Georgia Tech and Vanderbilt, and a tie with the Savannah Athletic Club.

kicked the point and the score became 22-6. But then minutes later Tech came back with six more points when Leonard Wood again crossed the goal line. And thus the game finally ended, a 28-6 win for the Blacksmiths.

Outstanding for Tech that day, in addition to Wood who scored three touchdowns, was quarterback John Kimball, who had played for Georgia in 1892, and halfback Dr. Park Howell, an Atlanta physician who had also played for Georgia in 1892.

Throughout this encounter much physical activity was transpiring on the sidelines. It was known, for example, that the "umpire" that day was the brother of Tech's team trainer (a Mr. Nourse), and some 150 Georgia students led the fans in chanting:

Well, well, well,

Who can tell,

Tech's umpire has cheated like hell.

As though losing the game weren't terrible enough, the Georgia boys had to live with the humiliating fact that the Tech boys had persuaded some 200 girls from the Lucy Cobb Institute, which stood next door to the University of Georgia, to don gold and white ribbons for this contest and to cheer the Tech team on to victory.

As the game ended, scuffling broke out between Georgia and Tech fans, and soon the scuffling became a full blown brawl that spilled out onto the playing field. Rocks began to fly and it was then that Leonard Wood and his Blacksmiths, aware that discretion is the better part of valor, very expeditiously exited the field and didn't pause until they'd barricaded themselves aboard their waiting pullman at the railroad station.

Nor was that the end of the matter. For a week following the game local newspapers carried charges and counter charges of cheating from both institutions. Georgia claimed that the game's umpire was the brother of Tech's trainer and therefore obviously prejudiced in favor of the Blacksmiths, and that Tech had broken the rules by playing Leonard Wood and Dr. Park Howell. Wrote the *Athens Banner*: "Everyone who knows the personnel of the Tech team knows that many of them make no pretense of pursuing courses at the Technological school, and if this policy in athletics is pursued by that institution, its athletic record will soon be looked upon with disdain by the college world."

The 1893 Blacksmiths of Georgia Tech. (Standing, L-R): Werner, Nourse, Forrest, Spain, McRae, Ogletree, Holmes and Heidt. (Seated, L-R): E. L. Whitney, Hunter, John Kimball, Dr. Park Howell, Haskell, Raoul and Leonard Wood. (Both Howell and Kimball had played for Georgia in 1892.)

These young men went 2-1-1 on the season with wins over Georgia and Mercer, a loss to St. Albans and a tie with Auburn.

And the *Atlanta Journal* self-righteously responded:

"When the Tech team went to Athens they had an idea that they were to play Athens men, but they found a professional paid trainer playing at half back, which is against intercollegiate rules, and when they play Vanderbilt next, he will probably be ruled out. Every team that is beaten always has an excuse to offer, and Athens is no exception to the rule. The umpiring was just on both sides."

"The treatment the Techs received was not what they expected. Rocking the players, and threatening them was something never before witnessed on a football gridiron."

There was one other event of special note on that fateful day in 1893, one that would have far reaching results. As the happy Tech team and their delighted fans returned to Atlanta aboard their special train late that evening, they suddenly rear-ended a freight train stopped on the tracks ahead of them just west of Lawrenceville. No one was injured but the special train was severely damaged and all the Tech folks thus boarded the freight train for the rest of their journey to Atlanta. It is said that this unfortunate experience led to Tech's nickname, the Rambling Wrecks.

The University of Georgia chapter of Sigma Nu fraternity, 1893

TOP:
Ernest Brown, a graduate student who served as coach of the Red and Blacks in 1893. (He played half-back vs. Georgia Tech.)

MIDDLE:
Captain George Butler, Georgia's quarterback in 1893. (Note the rubber nose guard hanging from Butler's neck. Few players of this era wore helmets but they would not be caught dead without their nose guards.)

BOTTOM:
Lt. Leonard Wood, who led Tech to a win over Georgia in their first meeting ever. He would later become General Leonard Wood and in 1900 was named Military Governor of Cuba. Wood is a member of the Georgia Tech Athletic Hall of Fame (GT AHF).

1897: Georgia's Superior Size Tells the Tale

Captain William B. Kent, tackle for Georgia in 1897.

Charles McCarthy, a former player for Brown University who succeeded the great Pop Warner as Georgia's coach following the 1896 season.

Four years following the riot of 1893, school officials felt it was finally safe for Georgia and Tech to resume their series, and thus on October 23, 1897, these two hated rivals went at it once again.

The boys from Tech had organized a team and rented Brisbine Park at their own expense in order to have a place to play. Then they proudly announced that they planned to "sweep the Southern university field." Which might have been something of an exaggeration, since they went 0-3 in '94, had no team at all in '95, and lost to Auburn, and beat and tied Mercer in '96.

(In '94 Tech lost to Auburn by a score of 94-0. This remains their worst loss in history.)

As for Georgia, they had enjoyed a 5-1 season in '94, then fell to 3-4 in '95, and then rebounded with an unbeaten 4-0 record in '96.

This would the the initial contest of the '97 season for Tech, though Georgia had smashed Clemson 24-0 two weeks earlier. Optimism, it was said, was rampant on both sides, and the press reported that fully 600 fans turned out for today's game at Herty Field in Athens.

Tech took the opening kickoff and marched to the Red and Blacks's 45, but then came a fumble and suddenly Georgia was in business. Three plays netted Georgia nothing and they attempted to punt, but the kick was blocked and picked up by Hart who appeared headed for a TD when he was tackled by Reynolds Tichenor near the Georgia goal.

But Georgia held and Tech's efforts went for naught. There then followed an exchange of punts, and finally Georgia found themselves with the ball at their own 45.

Behind the running of William Kent, John Moore, Richard Von Albade Gammon, H. S. Walden, and A. C. Jones, Georgia went in for a TD, Jones getting the credit. The PAT failed, but Georgia led 4-0.

Then, just before half time, Georgia blocked a Tech punt, and two plays later Arthur Clark went in for the TD. Tichenor kicked the point, and Georgia led 10-0.

As for the second half, Georgia's size was beginning to tell, as the smaller Tech boys began to crumple under the repeated assaults of the big Georgia running backs.

And thirty minutes into it Kent was credited with two TDs, John McIntyre with another, and Tichenor with three PATs, giving Georgia a big 28-0 win.

And the game was played without incident. It was reported that

Tichenor and Newman exchanged a few hot words following the game, but cooler heads prevailed and the boys shook hands and departed.

But then tragedy struck the next week as Georgia went up against Virginia. During that contest Richard Von Albade Gammon, a sophomore halfback from Rome, Georgia, was killed on the playing field. As a result, Tech, Mercer, and Georgia cancelled their remaining schedules.

The Techs of 1897 had neither a coach nor a captain and played only a single game, losing 28-0 to Georgia.

The Red and Blacks of 1897 went 2-1-0 on the season, with wins over Clemson and Georgia Tech and a loss to Virginia.

Richard Von Albade Gammon

The University of Virginia presented this commemorative bronze plaque to the University of Georgia following the tragic death of Richard Von Albade Gammon who was fatally injured during the Georgia-Virginia game of 1897 played at Brisbane Park in Atlanta. Only a plea from Gammon's mother prevented the governor from signing a bill outlawing football in the state of Georgia forever.

The Georgia Drama Club of 1897.

1898: Georgia's McCutcheon Runs 105 Yards for a TD

Possibly as a result of Richard Von Gammons's death in 1897 the 1898 meeting between Georgia and Georgia Tech must go down as one of the quietest games ever played between these two institutions. Indeed, local newspapers did not even report the game until Monday morning, and then they published only a few paragraphs.

But the Blacksmiths at this point had lost to both Auburn and Clemson and were eager to show what they could do against undefeated Georgia which had wins over both Clemson and the Atlanta Athletic Club.

The game was played in Athens and had been in progress for less than five minutes when Georgia's H. S. Walden pushed across for a touchdown (which then counted five points). The PAT (which then counted one point) was missed and Georgia began celebrating their 5-0 lead.

They then kicked off to Tech and the Blacksmiths began a drive which the Georgia boys appeared unable to halt. Now, with a first down at the Georgia five, Tech seemed on the verge of a big score.

But then came one of the most bizarre plays in the history of this long series. Tech's halfback took the snap from center and dove straight ahead, disappearing into a big pile of bodies at the line of scrimmage.

Was it a touchdown?

NO! For now, out of that human conglomeration, there suddenly emerged Georgia end Frank McCutcheon, and he had the football tucked firmly beneath his right arm. And he began to run.

And run. And run. Running wildly, as though his very life depended on it.

Indeed, by now the entire Tech team was at his heels, but McCutcheon didn't pause until he'd crossed the goal line some 105 yards away (for reasons that remain obscure, football fields at that early date were 110 yards long).

William Ritchie also scored for Georgia in the second half, and the Red and Black walked away with a 15-0 win, their second in three outings against the Blacksmiths.

The Red and Blacks of 1898 enjoyed a winning 4-2-0 season, beating Clemson, the Atlanta AC, Georgia Tech, and Vanderbilt, while losing to UNC and Auburn.

H. S. Walden, Georgia halfback and team captain in 1898.

The 1898 Georgia track team.

With the Spanish-American War raging in 1898, military training assumed a new significance at the University of Georgia.

1899: Georgia Takes Another One, 33-0

It was October 28, 1899, and fully a thousand fans filled the stands at Herty Field in Athens to see if Georgia could extend their win streak over the Blacksmiths of Georgia Tech.

At this point the Red and Blacks had beaten Clemson while losing to mighty Sewanee. The Blacksmiths, on the other hand, had lost to both Auburn and Clemson. Indeed, Tech would go 0-5 in '99, scoring only once during the entire season (their five opponents scored 173 points against them). Indeed, Tech had not won a game now since October 31, 1896, when they beat Mercer 6-4.

And today, unfortunately for the Blacksmiths, would be no better.

Georgia took the opening kickoff and marched straight down the field for a touchdown, Emory Shannon getting the call. When the two teams went to the sidelines twenty minutes later (they played two halves of twenty-five minutes each) the Red and Blacks held a commanding 22-0 lead.

As for the second half, it was about the same as the first, only worse.

Twice Tech held Georgia inside their own five-yard line. But on both occasions Tech was forced to punt from behind their goal line. Both punts were blocked for Georgia touchdowns.

The final whistle finally blew and Georgia walked away with a big 33-0 victory, their third consecutive win over Tech.

Following today's game Tech would go on to lose to both Nashville and Clemson to close out a 0-5 season.

Georgia would lose to Tennessee and North Carolina while tying Auburn.

Georgia Tech suffered through an 0-5-0 season in 1899, with losses to Auburn, Sewanee, Georgia, Nashville, and Clemson. In fact, their only touchdown of the season came in their final contest vs. Clemson.

The Red and Blacks of 1899 went 2-3-1 on the season, with wins over Clemson and Georgia Tech, losses to Sewanee, Tennessee and UNC, and a tie with Auburn.

The University of Georgia chapter of Kappa Alpha fraternity of 1899.

1900: Tech and Georgia Struggle Just to Play the Game

It was October 12, 1900, the final year of the nineteenth century, and both Georgia and Georgia Tech were struggling just to get through a long season. The Red and Black squeaked by Tech and South Carolina in their first two games, then lost the next four by a whopping 159-11 margin. As for Georgia Tech, who had not won a game since 1896, the year 1900 saw them extend their winless streak by four more games (they were 0-13 over the past four years), scoring only a single touchdown, and that in their final game of the season against Davidson.

The year 1900 also marked the first time in history that this game would be played in Atlanta, and some 1,500 fans filed into Piedmont Park wondering if these two teams were really as poorly prepared as they were rumored to be. Well, they soon found out.

According to the *Atlanta Constitution*:

With rare exceptions there were no brilliant features brought out in the work of the game. The teams of both Tech and Georgia are yet in that formative state that gives little indication of relative merit, with only the few days' hard training both have received. It is clear that the university has now the advantage.

On account of the poor physical condition of the men, the two halves were cut down to fifteen minutes each. Had the full limit of thirty minutes been attempted it is more than likely that the Techs would at least have scored, since the Georgia boys were badly in need of wind. In the first half Georgia kept the oval moving continually in Tech territory. Rush after rush at the Tech center with an occasional swing around the ends was kept up with telling effect and at the close of the first half, with the score 12-0, the university men let up for the remainder of the game

Georgia suffered through another losing season in 1900, beating Georgia Tech and South Carolina while losing to Sewanee, Clemson, North Carolina and Auburn. (Note the young man on the second row wearing a helmet of sorts.)

Captain F. K. McCutcheon, quarter-back for Georgia in 1900. He ran for 105 yards and a TD in 1894.

This caricature of a Georgia Tech football bum appeared in a 1900 UGA student publication.

and only tried to prevent their opponents scoring.

Once with the oval tucked under his arm, Captain McCutcheon of Georgia cut a red and black streak through forty yards of the surrounding atmosphere, and in addition to scoring a touchdown did much to improve the looks of the game. Of the twenty-two men on the field, McCutcheon was in decidedly the best form, and to his fast work in the first half, Georgia owes the two touchdowns that gave her the victory.

The work of Dorsey, for the visitors, was splendid. It is seldom that the place of quarterback is acceptably filled so early in the season, but the youngster who essayed to pass the ball for Georgia had his head with him in a way that will mean much for the university during the season.

Georgia's baseball team of 1900 was declared champion of the Southern Intercollegiate Athletic Association (SIAA).

1902: Tech Ties Georgia 0-0

hanks to Dr. Steadman V. Sanford, who would later serve as president of the University of Georgia, 1902 saw the formation of the Southern Conference, a huge confederation of colleges that stretched across the South, all the way from Washington, D.C. down through Louisiana. Both Georgia and Georgia Tech would remain charter members of the Southern Conference until the formation of the Southeastern Conference in 1933.

For this particular Georgia-Georgia Tech game, the first of the twentieth century, the Red and Blacks arrived in Atlanta the night before the game and were quartered at the Aragon Hotel. The following morning 150 students arrived from Athens and the *Constitution* reported that a festive atmosphere pervaded the city.

As for Tech, at this point they had beaten Georgia only once, and that way back in 1893, and they were itching for revenge. Unfortunately for the Blacksmiths, they had played Auburn and Clemson this season and had lost both games rather handily. Thus the oddsmakers had Georgia favored by a 5-1 margin at kickoff.

Which may not have been good judgment. Georgia was undefeated, yes, but their only game of the season had been played against Furman (an 11-0 Georgia win), thus comparisons were difficult to make. And if ever a team had something to prove, it was Tech in 1902. They had gone undefeated in 1901, but Georgia wasn't on their schedule. Indeed, not only had they not beaten Georgia now since 1893, they had not even scored on Georgia since 1893.

Coach Billy Reynolds (1901–1902), a former star player for Princeton. He was determined to turn Georgia into a winner.

Captain Bully Young, a tackle on the 1902 Tech team.

F. M. Ridley, team captain and an All-Southern end for Georgia in 1902.

In 1902 Georgia Tech suffered through another winless season, losing to Auburn, Clemson, St. Albans, Davidson, Tennessee and Alabama, while tying both Georgia and Furman.

Kenneth Thrash (T) was named to the All-Southern Football Team in 1902, the first Tech player ever to be so honored.

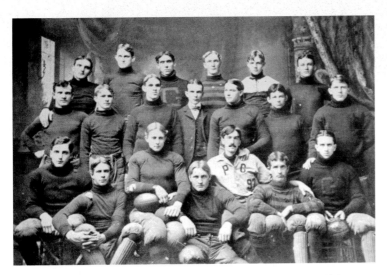

This 1902 Georgia team won four of seven games, beating Furman, Alabama, Davidson and Auburn, while losing to Clemson and Sewanee and tying Georgia Tech.

Harold Ketron (C), Sandy Beaver (G), Frank Ridley (E) and Marvin Dickinson (HB) were all named All-Southern in 1902, the first Georgia players ever to be so honored.

The game was played on October 25, a beautiful fall day, at Brisbane Park in Atlanta, and it was obvious from the opening whistle that the Techs were in far better shape than their Athens counterparts and that the Red and Blacks were in for the fight of their lives.

Indeed, Georgia took the opening kick-off and then, instead of cramming the ball down Tech's throat, they began running a series of timid line bucks which resulted in small gains. As the game continued and Georgia's heavy backs failed to overwhelm Tech's thin line, fans could see the momentum beginning to shift Tech's way.

Before the first half had ended the truth had become obvious to all. Neither team could score against the other. And that was indeed the case, and a final score of 0-0 was recorded for this contest.

Outstanding for Georgia in this game were quarterback Garmon, Captain Frank Ridley, and fullback Frank McIntire.

Players from Tech receiving prominent mention were backs McDaniel, Cannon and Lycett, and linemen Captain Bully Young, Wagner, Thrash, and Brinson.

Following the game, Georgia's Captain F. M. Ridley was quoted as saying, "Georgia never played so poorly in a practice game. I can only account for her work by the fact that we have recently changed our system of signals and the men had not learned the new system thoroughly. Tech has a strong team and played good football throughout the game."

And Captain Bully Young of Tech responded, "I consider it a victory for us. I am satisfied. It was a pretty game, and hard fought on both sides."

UGA All-Southern in 1902:
Harold Ketron (C), Sandy Beavers (G), Frank Ridley (E), and Marvin Dickinson (HB).
Tech All-Southern in 1902:
Ken Thrash (T).

1903: How 'Bout Them Apples

Georgia Tech kicked off the '03 season in grand fashion, losing 73-0 to Clemson at Piedmont Park. If folks were puzzled as to how Clemson could run up such a score, they had only to ask the University of Georgia.

It seems that the Bulldogs had lost to Clemson by a score of 29-0 on October 10. The next week, the week before Tech would tangle with the Tigers, Georgia promised Clemson a bushel of apples for every point over 29 they beat Tech. Clemson of course accepted the deal, and sure enough Georgia delivered 44 bushels of apples to Clemson on October 19.

But it's likely Tech would have gone down anyway, apples or no apples, for they beat only two opponents in '03 (Howard of Alabama and Florida State College), while losing to Clemson, Auburn, Tennessee and South Carolina.

As for Georgia, they weren't doing a great deal better. In addition to Tech, they also beat Tennessee and Auburn, while losing to Clemson, South Carolina, the Savannah Athletic Club and Vanderbilt.

Still, fully 1,200 fans showed up at Atlanta's Piedmont Park to see if this so-so Georgia team could revenge themselves for the embarrassing 0-0 tie administered by Tech in '02. But for reasons that remain a mystery, the Red and Blacks began play that afternoon with no real enthusiasm.

The *Constitution* reported:

Instead of keeping up an aggressive, steady, hit-smash, crash game, the Red and Black would send some man around end for 20 yards and then someone would call the men behind the line for a private conversation before giving the signal. Whether the Georgia men told jokes during the interval or whether they devoted it to writing letters home telling the results of the game to their families is uncertain.

Captain Harold Ketron, Georgia halfback, scored three TDs vs. Tech in '03. In '02 he became one of Georgia's first players ever to be named All-Southern.

M. M. Dickenson, Georgia coach in '03. Dickenson had been named All-Southern in '02.

Virlyn Moore, an outstanding Georgia halfback (1903–04). Moore is a member of the Georgia Sports Hall of Fame (UGA SHF).

Still, despite their relaxed approach to the task at hand, Georgia was far more than the Techs could handle. Only two minutes into the contest Harry Woodruff raced around end 75 yards for a Georgia score, then kicked the PAT, and Georgia led 6-0. Tech fumbled the ensuing kickoff and the Red and Black recovered at the Tech thirty. Three plays later John Bower scored from the six. The kick failed and the score became 11-0.

Three minutes later it became 16-0 when Captain Harold Ketron bucked across from the two. Then, just prior to half time, the score became 21-0 when Joe Killorin went in from the ten.

The second half saw more of the same. Georgia marched 74 yards for a score when Ketron again went in, this time from the twenty, and the score became 26-0. Later, both Bower and Ketron would add more touchdowns to their stats, and Georgia walked away with a 38-0 win.

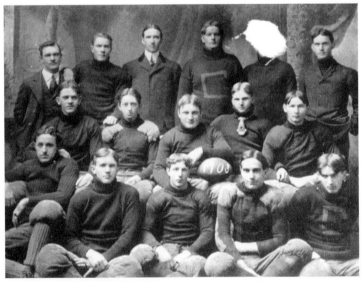

Tech All-Southern in 1903:
Jesse Thrash (T).

The Red and Blacks of '03 won three of seven games, beating Georgia Tech, Tennessee and Auburn, while losing to Clemson, South Carolina, Vanderbilt and the Savannah Athletic Club.

Georgia Tech would finish the season with a mediocre 2-5 record in '03, with wins over Howard (of Alabama) and Florida State College, and losses to Clemson, Georgia, Auburn, Tennessee and South Carolina.

1904: John Heisman Makes the Difference

Lured away from Clemson by promises of an annual salary of $2,250 (plus thirty percent of the gate receipts), John Heisman arrived on the Tech scene in 1904, and things would never again be quite the same.

That season, for example, Tech would win eight games (they had won only ten since 1892) including a 23-6 victory over Georgia, their first since 1893. They scored an impressive 287 points to their opponents' 34. Also in '04 they recorded a 12-0 loss to Auburn and an 11-11 tie with Clemson.

As for Georgia, they suffered through a 1-5 season in '04, their only win coming at the expense of Florida (52-0) in the first game of the season. (They would score only three TDs in their final five games.)

The legendary Coach John Heisman, for whom the Heisman Trophy is named, became head coach at Georgia Tech following the 1903 season. It is said that he was the first paid coach in America, with an annual salary of $2,250 (plus thirty percent of the gate receipts). It would be a gross understatement to say that his tenure at Tech was successful. Whereas they had a poor 2-5 record in 1903, they went 8-1-1 in 1904, and the race was on. Over the next sixteen years (1904–1919), under Heisman's guidance, Tech would compile an excellent 102-29-7 record, including a National Championship in 1917.

It might be noted that Heisman had acting ambitions and much of his spare time was spent performing in little theater productions in the Atlanta area.

Coach John Heisman puts his first Tech team through their paces.

The 1904 Blacksmiths of Georgia Tech, John Heisman's first Tech team, were wildly successful, enjoying an 8-1-1 record, including their first win over Georgia since 1893.

In 1904 Georgia beat only Florida while losing to Clemson, South Carolina, Alabama, Georgia Tech and Auburn.

Tech All-Southern in 1904:
Lob Brown (T).
Named to the Georgia Sports Hall of Fame in 1904:
Virlyn Moore.

Today's game was played at Piedmont Park in Atlanta, and some 1,200 fans braved the cold and heavy rain to see what difference, if any, John Heisman would make for Tech.

The game got off with a bang. On their first possession Tech took the lead when Lewis Clark scored on a 12-yard end sweep. The kick failed but Tech led 5-0.

It was then that one of the strangest plays ever seen in a football game occurred. After holding Tech at the Georgia one-foot line, the Red and Blacks attemped to punt from their own end zone. But the snap from center hit the crossbar and bounced over the high 12-foot wooden fence that surrounded the playing field. Players from both teams made a dash for that fence. Should Georgia come up with the ball, it would mean a safety and two points for Tech. But if Tech came up with the ball, it would mean a touchdown and five points for Tech.

The fight to scale that slippery, rain-soaked fence became intense. No sooner would a muddy player manage to reach the top than he would immediately be pulled down by a player from the other team.

Finally, Red Wilson of Tech and Arthur Sullivan of Georgia both reached the top and dived over (with the ref hot on their heels). For the next two minutes then the two boys engaged in an Easter egg hunt of sorts, searching vainly in the high brush for the ball. But finally Wilson came up with it. He held it aloft victoriously, the referee signaled a touchdown, and the Tech stands went wild.

J. C. Brown kicked the PAT and Tech went to the sidelines holding an 11-6 lead.

In the second half, Red Wilson and Craig Day scored more TDs for Tech, and the Blacksmiths walked away with a hard-earned 23-6 win over Georgia.

Georgia coach Charles L. Bernard, had been an outstanding player at Harvard and was hired in '04 to install the Harvard system at Georgia.

1905: Craig Day Runs 110 Yards for a Touchdown

It was November 18, 1905, a cool but cloudless day in Atlanta as some 1,500 fans filled the stands and stood around the playing field at what was then called The Flats (or Tech Park), which would eventually become Grant Field. Georgia at this point, under Coach M. M. Dickinson, had only a single win in four games, a shakey 16-12 triumph over Dahlonega. As for today's game with Tech, it was said that the Red and Blacks were ten pounds per man smaller than the Tech team, but still the Athens boys were ready to play.

In Atlanta, meanwhile, Coach John Heisman was in his second year at the helm, and he was ready to prove that his fine 1904 record was no fluke. Indeed, the Techs were sporting a 4-0-1 record when they went up against Georgia, an 18-18 tie with mighty Sewanee the only blemish on an otherwise perfect season.

From Tech's standpoint, 1905 is memorable for another reason. Earlier in the season a most bizarre event occurred as Tech went up against Sewanee the week prior to their big game with Georgia. At that point, seeking a better nickname, the Blacksmiths decided to call themselves the Bulldogs.

They even went out and purchased just such a dog. They outfitted him in an expensive gold collar adorned with gold and white streamers. He was a very handsome animal and the proud Tech boys took him to The Flats where he could inspire them as they went up against Sewanee.

Unfortunately for Tech, however, just prior to halftime a stray tabby cat ran across the playing field, as cats will do, and their alert mascot immediately spied him, gave a throaty growl, broke free of his handler, dashed across the playing field, streamers flying in his wake, and vanished into a little patch of woods to the east of the field. He has not been heard from since. And that was the end of the Bulldogs.

Still, we can only wonder. Had it not been for that stray cat, would the Yellow Jackets be known today as the Georgia Tech Bulldogs? (In 1906 Tech would become the Golden Tornadoes. As for Georgia, they would not become the Bulldogs until 1921.)

As for today's game, Georgia took the opening kickoff, ran several plays, then attempted a field goal from the Tech forty. It fell short and was caught by Tech's Craig Day. Day then ran 110 yards for a touchdown, the longest TD run on record for Georgia Tech, and the Blacksmiths were up 6-0.

Captain Don Sage, Georgia halfback.

According to the rules of 1905, Georgia then kicked off to Tech. On this play Red Wilson (who scored the over-the-fence TD for Tech in '04) took the ball at the 20-yard line. He didn't pause until he'd crossed Georgia's goal some 90 yards away.

Thus in only two plays Tech had run 200 yards and scored two touchdowns. But from Tech's standpoint, the fun had just begun.

Indeed, by the time intermission rolled around, Lewis Clark had scored two more TDs, Billy Wilson, Joe McCarthy and George Butler one each, and Lob Brown had kicked four PATs and Tech then led by a score of 34-0.

As for the second half, Billy Wilson, George Butler and Joe McCarthy scored more TDs for Tech before the game was mercifully called because of darkness.

And the Blacksmiths walked away with a whopping 46-0 win. (In 1943 Tech would win by a score of 48-0, the largest margin of victory ever in this series.)

Tech would enjoy a super year in 1905 with a 6-0-1 record. Over the previous two years now, under Coach Heisman, they had compiled a 14-1-1 record. And things would only get better.

As for Georgia, 1905 was not a good year. With a 1-5 record, they scored a total of only 36 points (they were blanked by Alabama, Tech and Auburn), while giving up a whopping 197 points. Indeed, Georgia's battle cry in '05 became "Thank God for Dahlonega!"

Named to the GT AHF in 1905:
Lob Brown and Lewis Clark.

The 1905 Blacksmiths of Georgia Tech enjoyed a super year under the legendary Coach John Heisman, winning six of seven games (including a 46-0 trouncing of Georgia) and tying mighty Sewanee. Lewis Clark, team captain, is standing at the top, far right.

The 1905 Red and Blacks stumbled through a miserable season, beating only Dahlonega among six opponents. Note that the players are now wearing padding sewn inside their jerseys.

In 1905-06, Georgia decided to give basketball a try.

The Georgia marching band of 1905.

1906: Tech Becomes the Golden Tornadoes

The University of Georgia, having suffered through a 1-5 season in 1905, did little better in 1906, despite the presence of their sixth new head coach since 1900, W. S. Whitney. In a seven-game schedule, they managed wins over Mercer and Auburn and a tie with Tennessee, while losing to Davidson, the Savannah Athletic Club, Clemson and Georgia Tech. Indeed, their only scores of the season came against their two victims, Mercer and Auburn. All in all, a rather poor season for the Red and Black.

Back in Atlanta, things were still humming along under Coach Heisman, though not quite as loudly as over the past two years. The Golden Tornadoes (for so they now called themselves) would go 5-3-1 on the season, with wins over Dahlonega, Grant University (Tenn.), Davidson, Auburn and Georgia, losses to Sewanee, Vanderbilt and Clemson, and a tie with Maryville.

November 10, 1906, was a cool day with plenty of sunshine, and the 1,500 fans who showed up at The Flats were in a festive mood. For what had once been a mere football game had by now become a grand annual event and a much-anticipated social occasion. Indeed, it was said that almost half the fans seated in the stands for this game were female, and all dressed to the nines in their favorite school colors and waving flags of red and black or white and gold.

Following the kickoff the two teams exchanged several punts before Georgia's Richard Graves fumbled at his own five-yard line. It was just the break Tech had waited for.

On the first play Harrison Hightower scored on a line buck straight up the middle. Tech missed the PAT but took a 5-0 lead.

A few minutes later Tech recovered another Georgia fumble, but the Red and Black held and Tech's Lob Brown missed his field goal try.

Georgia ran three plays which netted them nothing and they were again forced to punt. Tech then did the same and Lob Brown got off a magnificent 60-yard kick which the Tornadoes recovered at the Georgia five (back then punts could be covered by either team).

F. C. Davies ran for three yards, then Charles

The week prior to Tech's Thanksgiving 1906 meeting with Clemson at Ponce de Leon Park, this student cartoon suggested for the first time that the Tornadoes might someday become known as the Yellow Jackets. (Clemson won 10-0.)

Adamson went to the one on a sweep. Davies went the final yard on the next play, Brown kicked the point, and Tech lead 11-0.

The second half consisted of missed opportunities for both teams, though Charles Sweet did score again for the Tornadoes. Again Brown was true with his kick and Tech walked away with a 17-0 win.

Since 1893 Georgia still led the series 5-4-1.

Named to the UGA SHF in 1906:
Morton Hodgson.
Tech All-Southern in 1906:
Lob Brown (E).

W. S. "Bull" Whitney, Georgia's coach in 1906, had starred at Syracuse before coaching NC A&M to an undefeated season in 1905. In 1906 he became the first Georgia coach to try the forward pass.

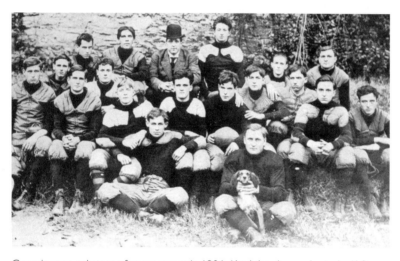

Georgia won only two of seven games in 1906. (And they have adopted a K-9 mascot of sorts, though he's a far cry from Uga.)

Captain J. C. Lowndes, Georgia quarterback.

The Georgia Military Training Unit of 1906.

1907: Georgia's Ringers Lose a Close One

As the 1907 season got underway the Red and Blacks blistered tiny Dahlonega 57-0, but then came a 15-0 loss to Tennessee, then a 26-6 win over Mercer and a 0-0 tie with Alabama. This had become, in other words, a season of peaks and valleys, and fans were puzzled as to just how good (or bad) Georgia really was.

And the same was true of Tech. After going 19-4-3 over the past three years, the 1907 Tornadoes showed signs of weakening. By the time the Georgia game rolled around, Tech had bombed Gordon (51-0) and Dahlonega (70-0), then edged out Tennessee (6-4) before losing to Auburn (12-6). In other words, this was not a typical John Heisman football team. Still, hoped fans, they would be good enough to beat Georgia.

The game was played on November 2, 1907, at Ponce de Leon Park in Atlanta before some 6,000 fans, the largest crowd ever to witness an athletic event in Georgia.

The game's first score came late in the first half when Tech's quarterback Carliss Buchanon drop-kicked a field goal of twenty yards squarely between Georgia's goal posts, giving the Tornadoes a 4-0 half time lead. (Yes, at that early date field goals counted four points.)

Then to open the second half, Georgia kicked off to the Tornadoes. Buchanon took the kick and ran it back 40 yards, down to the Georgia seven. On the next play, with the Red and Blacks bunched up over center to stop the line buck, Buchanon pitched out to J. R. Davis who was hit in the backfield but managed to stagger on into the end zone, half of Georgia's team hanging around his neck.

Buchanon was injured on this play and was replaced by Hightower who kicked the PAT, giving Tech a 10-0 lead.

Following a succession of punts, Tech ran three plays and was forced to kick the ball away. Hightower's kick was blocked and Georgia took over on the Tech twenty. Then

Kyle Smith, Georgia halfback and team captain in 1907.

The 1907 Red and Blacks won four of seven games, including a good 6-0 win over Auburn. (Georgia was suspended from the SIAA in 1907 for using "ringers" or paid players.)

came runs by McGee, Joe Rossiter and McDuffey. McDuffey finally carried the ball over for a touchdown, Captain Kyle Smith kicked the point, and Tech's lead was cut to 10-6. But then darkness closed in and the rest of this contest was called, Tech the winner by a score of 10-6.

Two weeks following this game famed sports writer Grantland Rice accused Georgia of using "ringers" (players who were paid for their services) on their 1907 team. Georgia initially denied the charge, but then admitted it was true. As a result they were suspended from the Southern Intercollegiate Athletic Association. Three days later Tech was also suspended for paying several of its players. Then Rice accused a great many other Southern team of irregularities. All but Georgia denied their guilt.

Several weeks later Tech was cleared of all charges and was re-admitted to the SIAA. Georgia's suspension was also lifted. Still, Coach Whitney was fired and prohibited from ever again coaching in the South.

As a result of all this, Tech very rightously refused to play Georgia in 1908.

Named to the UGA SHF in 1907: Rankin Smith. **Tech All-Southern in 1907:** John Davis (T).

Captain C. A. Sweet, halfback for Georgia Tech.

The 1907 Tornadoes finished the season with a 4-4-0 record, the worst they would have during Coach Heisman's sixteen year tenure.

Push Ball, played between two opposing teams who tried to push the ball across their opponent's goal line, was a popular sport at Georgia earlier in the century. (To date, it still hasn't replaced football as the Bulldogs' number one spectator sport.)

The Georgia Senior Parade of 1907.

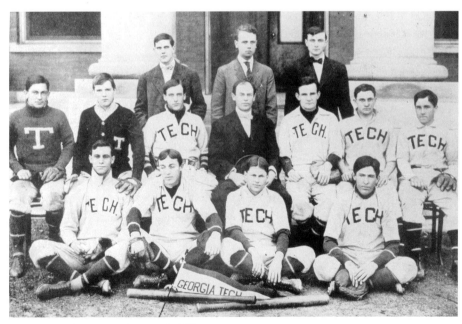

The Georgia Tech baseball team of 1907.

1909: Tech Fumbles Their Way to a Great Win

After a cooling off period Tech and Georgia resumed their series in 1909. By now, after five years as head coach of the Tornadoes, John Heisman had compiled a 36-13-3 record, and was 5-0 against the Red and Black. As for the current year, Heisman's boys were 5-2 as they prepared to meet Georgia, with wins over Gordon (18-6), the Mooney School (35-6), South Carolina (59-0), Tennessee (29-0), and Mercer (35-0), and losses to Sewanee (15-0) and Auburn (8-0). Following their win over Georgia they would beat Clemson (29-3) on Thanksgiving Day at the Flats, giving them a 7-2 record for the season.

At Georgia things were not going quite so well. They were still changing coaches the way most people change socks, and the current year was no exception. Branch Bocock replaced W. S. Whitney in 1908, then in 1909 came James Coulter, at least for the early part of the season. But by the time the Tech game rolled around Georgia was 1-4 on the season, their only score a field goal kicked in their 3-0 win over Tennessee. Thus in came Frank Dobson, another new head coach.

Earlier in the season Dobson had coached at Stone Mountain High School, and he knew his business. Indeed, the *Atlanta Constitution* commented that Georgia's progress was remarkable under Dobson and that it was a shame he couldn't have been with the Red and Black all season.

As for this game, on November 20, 1909, at Ponce de Leon Park, everyone remarked what a hard but cleanly fought contest it had been, with the players helping their opponents up after knocking them down.

Georgia kicked off to open the game, and Tech fumbled on the first play at their own seven-yard line. Georgia recovered and their halfbacks Hugh Bostick and Clifford Hatcher ran the ball down to the one, but they could go no further and Tech took over on downs.

Georgia and Georgia Tech (wearing striped jerseys) go at it tooth and nail at Ponce de Leon Park in Atlanta. (This is the earliest photo known to exist of a Georgia-Georgia Tech football game.)

Four plays later Georgia recovered another Tech fumble. The Red and Black then missed on a field goal and Tech took over at the 25. Again they fumbled on first down and again Georgia recovered. Then Georgia fumbled it right back.

Following an exchange of punts, Tech fumbled for the fourth time and again the ball went over to Georgia. Again Georgia ran three plays and was forced to punt. Tech's T. S. "Doc" Wilson took the kick and, showing some fine broken field running, took it back 50 yards to the Georgia 25.

Then, believe it or not, Tech fumbled for the fifth time. And so it went until just before half time. But now, with the ball on their own 40, Tech unveiled their new secret weapon, the forward pass.

Quarterback Doc Wilson amazed the crowd (and Georgia) when he drew back and heaved the ball downfield to a waiting A. T. Artley, good for 25 yards. Three plays later Wayne Patterson crossed Georgia's goal, Wilson kicked the PAT and Tech was up 6-0.

Georgia kicked off and for the sixth time Tech fumbled, this time at their own 15-yard line. Now Georgia showed what they could do with the forward pass as E. J. Robertson tossed the ball to Herbert Hatcher good for 11 yards. Then on the next play Arthur Maddox scored, Robertson kicked the PAT and the game was tied 6-6.

In the second half Tech ran back a punt to the Georgia 39. Wilson scored five plays later, then kicked the PAT and Tech won once again, 12-6.

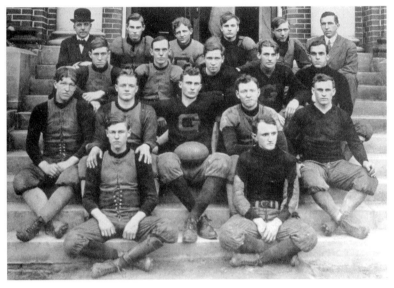

The Red and Blacks of 1909 would experience another losing season, going 1-4-2 on the year. But this would be their last losing season until 1914.

The Georgia Tech team of 1909 would enjoy a good season, losing only to Sewanee and Auburn.

Named to the GT AHF in 1909:
Harrison Hightower (QB).
UGA All-Southern in 1909:
J. E. Lucas (C).

Captain John Davis, tackle for Tech in 1909.

Quarterback Harrison Hightower, a devastating runner for Tech, and a member of the GT AHF.

James Coulter, Georgia's coach in 1909. Lacking experience, Coulter hired Frank Dobson, Heisman's assistant at Tech, as his special advisor. But Dobson soon overshadowed Coulter and became a favorite with Georgia fans.

Another shot of the Georgia-Georgia Tech game of 1909.

1910: Georgia's McWhorter Ends Drought

With new head coach W. A. Cunningham at the helm, Georgia seemed to be headed in the right direction. Indeed, in their first seven games of the 1910 season, prior to their meeting with Georgia Tech, they beat Locust Grove 101-0, Gordon 79-0, Alabama 22-0, Tennessee 35-5, Mercer 21-0, then lost a squeaker to mighty Sewanee 15-12, and tied Clemson 0-0—a most impressive effort.

As for John Heisman and his Tornadoes, they had gotten the season off well enough, beating Gordon 57-0, Chattanooga 18-0, Mercer 46-0, Alabama 36-0, but then losing to both Auburn (16-0) and Vanderbilt (23-0). They would lose to Georgia today, but then come back the next week with a 34-0 win over Clemson.

The game was played on November 19, a bitterly cold, rainy day in Atlanta. Yet fully 5,500 fans showed up for the contest at Ponce de Leon Park, a thousand of those brought up by special train from Athens. Again, Georgia was hopeful that this was the year they'd end the drought and beat those Heisman Tornadoes.

George Woodruff kicked off for Georgia. The ball was taken by Tech's Dean Hill and the game was underway, the players running around in mud up to their ankles.

Six minutes later, following several punt exchanges, Tech had a first down at the Georgia 42. Courtney Lewis gained 10 yards, and Hill ran for 15 more. Then it was Wayne Patterson carrying down to the Georgia five. Hill went over on the next play, Patterson kicked the point, and Tech took the lead 6-0.

And Georgia fans exchanged those "Well, Here We Go Again" looks.

This is Herty Field at the University of Georgia where the Red and Black and Tech played their first game in 1893. In the above photo Georgia and Tennessee lock horns in 1910, a game won by Georgia 35-5.

This was the first Georgia-Georgia Tech game that was divided into quarters. And it was early in the second quarter when Tech drove to Georgia's 15-yard line but could go no further. At that point Georgia's all-time great running back, Bob McWhorter, took a pitchout and raced 95 yards for what everyone thought was a TD, but then the referee said that McWhorter had stepped out of bounds at the 45, and thus a great run was nullified.

The third quarter came to a close and Tech still clung to their narrow 6-0 lead. But then, two minutes later Tech punted to mid-field where Woodruff took it on the fly and returned it 30 yards to the Tech 20. On first down McWhorter raced around end, bowling over opposing players as he went, and crossed the Tech goal line. Hafford Hayes kicked the point and the score was tied 6-6.

As the seconds ticked away it appeared that the game would end in a tie, but then, with Georgia backed up to their own five-yard line, Clifford Hatcher broke off tackle and ran for what appeared to be a TD. But again the referee said he'd stepped out of bound at the four. So McWhorter tried it, and this time he went in standing up. The PAT missed, but at this point no one cared. The final score was 11-6, Georgia's favor. At last, the drought had been broken.

UGA All-Southern in 1910:
Bob McWhorter (HB).
Tech All-Southern in 1910:
Pat Patterson (T).
Named to the GT AHF in 1910:
J.W. Davis.

The 1910 Golden Tornadoes enjoyed a winning 5-3 season but lost to Georgia 11-6.

Coach W. A. Cunningham played for Michigan, coached at Vanderbilt, and would lead Georgia to winning seasons seven out of the next eight years.

Dean Hill, team captain of the 1910 Tornadoes.

Omer W. Franklin, team captain and an outstanding Georgia guard.

The Georgia baseball team of 1910 had an excellent season and was crowned champion of the Southern Conference.

1911: McWhorter 5, Tech 0

It was November 18, 1911, a great autumn day for football, and fully 15,000 fans streamed into Ponce de Leon Park to watch what had by now become an event of special note to the entire state of Geogia. The *Constitution* reported the spectacle this way:

The illustrious Bob McWhorter, still one of Georgia's most memorable players of all time.

It was the most picturesque assemblage ever gathered in Ponce de Leon Park. In personnel, enthusiasm, and dynamic force, it was perhaps the finest gathering ever seen at a Southern sporting event.

It was more than a sporting event. It was a classic state affair. It was an occasion when persons stopped being ordinary humans and became impassioned beings who once more returned to their primal state, forgot customs and precedents and acted on natural impulse, regardless of position in business, worldly wealth, or any other mortal environment.

Millionaires slapped humble clerks on the back. Society belles smilingly waved at enthusiastic rough necks. Dignified business men shouted. Austere club women screamed. The entire audience was back to nature.

Yep! It was your typical run-of-the-mill Georgia-Georgia Tech football game, a madhouse shootout.

Tech was 5-1-1 coming into the game with five shutouts to their credit, their only loss a close 11-6 decision to Auburn.

Georgia, on the other hand, was 6-1 at this point, their only loss a 17-0 decision to national power Vanderbilt. (Vandy's overall record at this point, by the way, was an incredible 86-14!) And much of Georgia's success could be attributed to their great halfback Bob McWhorter. Here's the *Constitution*'s description of McWhorter as he warmed up for the 1911 contest with Tech:

The feeling seemed unanimous that on his broad shoulders the game would rest, and they figured well. His stocky build could be quickly recognized. His muscular neck and chest, his sturdy legs, his fighting face, all made him the most noticeable man on the field.

Bill Patterson, an early kicking specialist, boots a 23-yard field goal as Tech upended Mercer by a score of 17-0.

Following the opening kickoff the game rocked back and forth with neither team able to get the best of the other. Run three plays and punt seemed to be the order of the day. Midway the first quarter Tech did recover a fumble at the Georgia 15-yard line, but nothing came of that either. And the first half ended, a 0-0 tie.

Tech kicked off to open the second half. But then, after three plays, Georgia punted. Tech fumbled the punt at the 43-yard line and Georgia recovered.

On first down McWhorter took a handoff and raced through the entire Tech team 43 yards for a touchdown. The PAT missed, but in the end it made no difference. Georgia took the lead and the game 5-0.

McWhorter carred the ball 14 times that afternoon, gaining 122 yards and scoring the game's only touchdown. He would become Georgia's first All-American in 1913.

Sanford Field, 1911.

Coach Cunningham kicks that "dawg" around. This somewhat puzzling cartoon lampooning Coach John Heisman and his Georgia Tech football team appeared in a 1911 Georgia student publication. (Tech had not referred to themselves as the Bulldogs since 1905. Georgia would not become the Bulldogs until 1921.)

The Golden Tornadoes of 1911 lost to only Georgia and Auburn while playing a nine-game schedule, another excellent season for Coach Heisman and his team.

W. H. Patterson, team captain and an All-Southern tackle for Georgia Tech.

1912: McWhorter Again Leads Georgia Win

It was November 16, 1912, and at this point Georgia Tech could boast of wins over The Citadel, Alabama, Florida and Mercer, a tie with the U. S. 11th Cavalry, and losses to the two biggies on their schedule, Auburn and Sewanee. In other words, 1912 was something of an off season for the Tornadoes.

Georgia, on the other hand, under the very successful Coach W. A. Cunningham, had wins over Chattanooga, The Citadel, Alabama, and Clemson, a tie with mighty Sewanee, and a loss to the annual Champions of the South, Vanderbilt. Now they were more than eager to show what they could do against their old antagonists from Atlanta.

Indeed, Coach Cunningham had now led the Red and Black to a 17-3-3 record since his arrival in Athens, and the good folks in Atlanta knew they'd have a fight on their hands this afternoon. The *Constitution* remarked:

> Atlanta is football mad. It matters not whether a Democratic President has been elected, the Balkan allies are winning or the price of coal is beyond the reach of the poor man. There is but one major topic of discussion today: THE GEORGIA-GEORGIA TECH FOOTBALL GAME!

From the opening kickoff the story of Georgia was Bob McWhorter who was carrying the ball three out of every four plays. Still, not even he could crack that small but dedicated Tech defense.

The Golden Tornadoes of 1912 experienced another winning season, losing only to Georgia, Auburn and Sewanee while beating the likes of Alabama, Florida, Mercer and Clemson.

The second quarter had just begun and Georgia faced a fourth down at their 38-yard line. David Paddock went back as though to punt the ball, but then with several blockers out in front, he took off around right end and dashed down the right sideline all the way to the Tech five.

From there McWhorter smashed into the Tech line on four straight plays but got only a single yard to show for his troubles. But then Tech was penalized down to the two. Again McWhorter smashed into the line. This time he pushed on into the end zone. John Henderson kicked the PAT and Georgia went up 7-0. (Touchdowns now counted six points, PATs one point, and the length of the field reduced to 100 yards.)

Georgia now kicked off and Tech star Frank McDonald returned the ball to midfield. Then it was McDonald for 23 yards, down to the Georgia 26. Three plays later Tech had the ball at the seven, first and goal to go.

Then McDonald took a handoff and appeared to have scored, but W. M. Lucas gave him a terrific hit just as he crossed the goal line, the ball popped free and Georgia recovered in the end zone.

Late in the third period Georgia began a drive from their own nine-yard line, one that finally ended with McWhorter going in for another touchdown. Henderson converted and the Red and Black took a 14-0 lead over the Tornadoes.

Henderson scored again for Georgia late in the game, but by then the contest had been decided. Georgia and Bob McWhorter took it 20-0.

Georgia fans and students make their way from the train station in Atlanta to the big game at The Flats.

Named to the GT AHF in 1912:
Roy Goree and Pat Patterson.
UGA All-Southern in 1912:
Bob McWhorter (HB).

Timon Bowden, Georgia halfback.

J. E. Lucas, an All-Southern center for the Red and Black.

John Henderson, Georgia end.

Captain D. R. Peacock, an All-Southern guard.

Tech's offense on the move as they lost to a powerful Auburn team by a score of 27-7 in 1912. The ball carrier appears to be wearing a face mask of sorts.

1913: Historic Grant Field Becomes a Reality

The 1913 season again saw Georgia off to a roaring start. Before their big game with Tech on November 15, they had wins over Alabama Presbyterian (108-0, their largest margin of victory in history), Dahlonega (51-0), Alabama (20-0), UNC (19-6) and Clemson (18-15), plus a 13-6 loss to Virginia. By season's end they would add Auburn to their list of losses (21-7) and finish with a good 6-2 record.

Bob McWhorter was named to the All-Southern Team for four consecutive years, and then in 1913 he became the first Georgia player ever named to the All-American team.

According to Early Era records, McWhorter scored 61 touchdowns during his career, a record never approached by any other player. (By comparison, the great Herschel Walker scored 52 touchdowns during his career at Georgia.)

Doubtlessly Georgia would have retired his jersey years ago, but players of his era did not wear numerals on their jerseys.

It might also be noted that he was the first of eight members of the McWhorter family to letter at Georgia between 1910 and 1973. He went on to become a professor of law at the university and later mayor of Athens.

He is a member of the College Football Hall of Fame and the Georgia Sports Hall of Fame.

At Tech, meanwhile, they too were having a super year. They had opened the season with wins over Ft. McPherson (19-0), The Citadel (47-0), Chattanooga (71-6), Mercer (33-0), and a loss to Auburn (20-0). By season's end they would add Clemson to their list of wins (34-0) and finish with a good 7-2 record.

This year, for the first time in history, the two teams would play at Tech's brand new Grant Field. Georgia at first demanded that the game be played at Ponce de Leon Park, a neutral site, but then relented and agreed to play at Grant Field under the condition that Tech students not be allowed to perform their snake dance around the stadium at half time.

Tech officials agreed to Georgia's conditions and the game was on. The *Constitution* described that gala event:

> The new Grant Field of Tech may never again hold such a crowd, yelling wildly throughout the afternoon of play, a gay, carefree football assemblage.
>
> The stands, the sidelines and the bands were a riot of color. An automobile load of pretty girls flaunting Red and Black colors were lined alongside a bunch of undergrads showing their Old Gold and White pennants.
>
> It was a happy crowd, a good natured crowd and there were few if any squabbles throughout the battle. The student bodies and their bands were on hand. They cheered each other, the rival teams, they cheered everyone that the energetic cheer leaders could think of to cheer.

Georgia kicked off and Tech's E. K. Thompson fumbled on first down. Georgia recovered and after nine attempts Steve Crump went over for a touchdown from the three. John Henderson kicked the point and Georgia was up 7-0.

Minutes later Tech's Wayne Patterson punted to Bob McWhorter who returned the ball 12 yards to the Tech 49. Georgia then began a sustained drive of 12 plays, one that culminated in Crump's second touchdown of the afternoon when he went over from the three. Again Henderson was good with the PAT and Georgia led 14-0.

Georgia scored twice more before game's end, but both were nullified by penalties. As for Tech, they mounted no serious threat all afternoon. And the game ended, a 14-0 win for the Red and Black, their fourth consecutive win over Tech.

UGA All-American in 1913:
Bob McWhorter (HB).
Named to the UGA SHF for 1913:
Bob McWhorter.

Homer Cook, team captain and a great halfback for Georgia Tech.

The Golden Tornadoes of 1913 won seven games while losing to Georgia and Auburn.

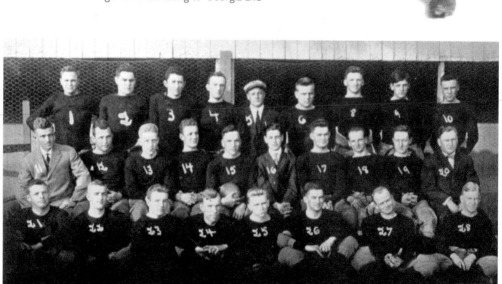

The University of Georgia enjoyed a good 6-2 season in 1913, losing only to Virginia and Auburn. (Georgia defeated Locust Grove by a score of 101-0.) Coach Cunningham's Georgia teams were now 25-6-3 over the past four years.

1914: Mud and Fielder Carry Tech to 7-0 Win

It was November 14, 1914, and already World War I had enveloped Europe in the greatest conflagration the world had ever known, one that would soon involve the United States. But at the moment folks in Georgia were concerned only with what Georgia and Tech would do to one another this afternoon at Grant Field.

Tech had not beaten the Red and Black since 1909, but it looked like this would be the year Heisman and his young charges would break the string.

They were 6-2 at this point, including a 20-0 win over perennial Southern power Sewanee, and a whopping 105-0 beating of cross-city rival Mercer University.

For the first time in history, Tech was calling themselves the Yellow Jackets.

As for Georgia, in 1914 they would suffer through their first losing season since 1909, going 3-5-1 on the year. Indeed, prior to the day's game they had suffered defeats in their last four outings, losing big to UNC (41-6), Virginia (28-0), Clemson (35-13) and Mississippi A&M (9-0).

The greatest thing in Georgia's favor today--perhaps the only thing--was the weather. It had been raining in Atlanta for several days prior to the game, and on game day the rain was still coming down with no signs of letting up. Grant Field had become Mud Field, and Red and Black fans were hoping that the bigger and faster Tech team would be slowed down by all this.

Captain K. J. "Wooch" Fielder, an All-Southern halfback for the Yellow Jackets and a member of the GT AHF. It was Fielder's touchdown that brought Tech a win over Georgia in 1914.

And they were. But not by much. This was their best chance to beat Georgia since 1909, and they were not going to let that chance slip away.

Early in the first quarter Georgia fans were given hope when the big Red and Black drove to Tech's 10-yard line. But then Georgia fumbled the wet ball, Tech recovered, and that was the end of that threat.

Then, later in the quarter Tech took the ball at their own 35-yard line following a Georgia punt. They began a long, sustained drive at that point, D. E. "Froggy" Morrison banging into the Georgia line on carry after carry. Than came a great 30-yard end sweep by Gene Patten. Finally, with a first down at the Georgia two, Wooch Fielder plunged through the line for a touchdown. He then kicked the point and Tech led 7-0.

It might be remarked that this was Tech's first score against Georgia since 1910, and it couldn't have come at a better time, since the weather became so bad at that point that fans began

The Yellow Jackets of 1914 went 6-2 on the season, including a 105-0 win over Mercer and a 7-0 win over Georgia.

scurrying for the exits in droves, and players on the sidelines sought shelter under blankets. The game continued, of course, but the following two quarters, for understandable reasons, were scoreless. Fielder's touchdown was the only score of this contest and it carried a highly favored Tech team to their first win over Georgia since 1909. As the *Constitution* remarked:

Dave Paddock, an All-American quarterback for the 1914 Red and Blacks.

> Fighting desperately on a muddy field and with the wind and rain adding to the general discomfiture of everyone present, especially the spectators, the Tech Yellow Jackets defeated the University of Georgia in their annual battle yesterday.
>
> No more stubborn game has ever been fought on the local gridiron, the ball seesawing back and forth throughout the entire game, with no marked advantage for either side. The final count was Tech 7, Georgia 0.
>
> This verdict was considerably closer than the general dope in advance of the game, when predictions ranged as high as Tech to win by four or five touchdowns.
>
> The Red and Black deserve credit for their wonderful fight in the face of tremendous odds. They were defeated, but not disgraced. They fought nobly for the glory of the Red and Black and their fighting spirit is to be commended.

Tech All-Southern in 1914:
Jim Senter (E).
Named to the GT AHF in 1914:
Wooch Fielder and Al Loeb.
UGA All-American in 1914:
David Paddock (QB).

Georgia Tech beat Sewanee 20-0 on their way to a 6-2 season in 1914.

It was a cold grim day in November as the Red and Black fell to Clemson 35-13 at Sanford Field. (Fans pulled their vehicles right up to the playing field at this early date.)

1915: Another 0-0 Deadlock

George "Pup" Phillips, an outstanding center, became Tech's first All-American in 1916. He was also named to the All-American team in 1917.

It was November 13, 1915, and a million young men had been slaughtered in the trenches of France since Tech had battled to a 7-0 win over Georgia in 1914. Many attributed that low scoring duel to the inclement weather, and today would be no different. It was a cold, dreary day with the rain coming down in torrents as the Red and Black made ready to meet the Yellow Jackets at Grant Field.

Georgia at this point was 4-2-1 on the year, with wins over Newberry, Dahlonega, The Citadel and Florida, and losses to Virginia and Auburn and a tie with Chattanooga. Following today's game with Tech they would beat Clemson. Not a bad season, but not one to get real excited about either.

As for Tech, they were going great guns at this point, with wins over Mercer, Davidson, Transylvania, LSU, UNC, and Alabama. Following today's tie with Georgia, they would beat mighty Auburn on Thanksgiving Day to complete a fine 7-0-1 undefeated season and become Champions of the Southern Conference. (Tech was now 2-19 vs. Auburn.)

Despite the nasty weather, a record crowd of some 8,000 hearty souls turned out at Grant Field to witness this eighteenth meeting between Georgia's two strongest state institutions.

And from the beginning it became a classic defensive contest, with neither team able to move, let alone score, against the other. Indeed, 60 minutes later the two teams were still locked in a 0-0 tie. (Georgia and Tech had last fought to a tie in 1902, and that game also ended in a 0-0 deadlock.)

As for line plunges, reported the press at the time, both teams were distinctly disappointing, while end sweeps were a total failure. Said the *Constitution*:

> The field prohibited fleet running, though occasionally Dave Paddock of Georgia, or Strupper of Tech, would sweep end, but always were smothered under a squad of tacklers before they had reeled off any great amount of territory.

Indeed, offensive stars in this game were hard to find, again because of the muddy conditions, though the *Atlanta Constitution* was most complimentary of Tech's Froggie Morrison:

It was November 13, 1915, and for the second time in history Georgia and Georgia Tech battled to a 0-0 tie. (Here Tech's highly touted offense is butting heads with Georgia's hardnosed defense.)

In our opinion, Froggie Morrison, taking every department of play into consideration, is the best quarterback of the year in the South, offensively and defensively. He can kick, throw forward passes, can buck the line as no quarter of the year can, and on defense is without an equal backing up the line.

Georgia's Coach Cunningham, over the previous six years, had compiled a 33-13-6 record, including a 4-1-1 record against Tech. The legendary Coach John Heisman, on the other hand, had compiled an enviable 72-25-6 record at Tech since 1904, including a 6-4-1 record against Georgia.

In 1915 Bill Fincher, Tech's placekicker, fashioned a big homemade numeral for his jersey, a first for Southern football.

UGA All-Southern in 1915:
Tom Thrash (T).
Tech All-Southern in 1915:
Wooch Fielder (QB), Jim Senter (E) and Froggie Morrison (HB).

Walker "Big Six" Carpenter was named an All-American center for Tech in 1917.

Jim Senter, All-Southern end for Tech in 1915.

Tommy Spence, Tech's All-Southern halfback, was killed in France in 1918.

Georgia Tech, with a 7-0-1 record, was crowned Champions of the Southern Conference in 1915. During an eight-game schedule, they had only a 0-0 tie with Georgia to mar their record.

John W. Powell, Georgia quarterback in 1915.

Captain John G. Henderson, Georgia center.

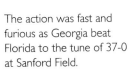

The action was fast and furious as Georgia beat Florida to the tune of 37-0 at Sanford Field.

The undefeated Yellow Jackets of 1915.

1916: Undefeated Tech Takes Georgia

Georgia Tech, which had gone undefeated in 1915, repeated the same trick in 1916. By season's end they had beaten Mercer, Cumberland, Davidson, Auburn, Tulane, UNC, Alabama, and Georgia. Indeed, the only blemish on their 1916 record was a 7-7 tie with Washington and Lee, and for the first time national recognition was beginning to come their way. Still, they would not receive the recognition they truly deserved until 1917 when they would go 9-0 on the season and be declared national champions. (Between 1915 and 1918 Tech would compile an incredible 30-1-2 record, and John Heisman would become the Dean of American Coaches.)

Tech defeated Cumberland 222-0, the biggest score ever recorded in an American football game.

Everette Strupper returned a punt 92 yards for a TD vs. Mercer, still number two in the GT record book.

As for Georgia, they were experiencing an up-and-down year in 1916, with wins over The Citadel, Clemson, Florida, Virginia, Furman and Alabama, and losses to Navy, Auburn and Georgia Tech. Not a bad year, but not the sort of season Georgia had come to expect under Coach Cunningham.

As for the Georgia-Georgia Tech game of 1916, fans were startled to learn that something new had been added. This year, for the only time ever, the game would be played not in Atlanta but at Sanford Field in Athens. (Sanford Field was located at what is today the parking lot at the main entrance to Sanford Stadium.)

Some 10,000 fans turned out for this festive occasion, noting with glee the "Georgia Welcomes Tech" banners strung from posts and store windows all over Athens. This was the first time these two teams had met in Athens since 1906, and city fathers were pulling out all the stops. Indeed, when the Tech players arrived by special car at the train station, they were met there by Georgia students, faculty, citizens and the college band. Which was quite a change from 1893 when furious rock-throwing Georgia fans chased the Tech team out of town.

And the weather could not have been finer--a bright, sunshiny day with just a hint of autumn in the air. A perfect day for football all around.

As for the game itself, the first quarter was scoreless, and Tech had the ball on their own 47 when the second began. On first down Tally Johnson dashed 20 yards, down to the Georgia 33. Three plays later Tommy Spence scored from the one on a line buck. Bill Fincher converted and Tech led by a score of 7-0, the half time score.

In the third quarter Spence inter-

In 1916 Georgia Tech defeated Cumberland College 222-0, the highest score ever recorded in any American football game. (The above photo is the only shot known to exist of this game.) Everette "Strup" Strupper, Tech's All-Southern halfback, scored eight touchdowns in this game.

cepted a Georgia pass in the end zone. Tech then marched 80 yards in 12 plays, Spence going in for his second TD of the day. The PAT was good and Tech was up 14-0.

In the final period Everette "Strupp" Strupper went over from the six, the PAT was good, and Tech walked away from this gala event with a good 21-0 win under their belts.

Tech All-American in 1916:
George "Pup" Phillips (C).
Tech All-Southern in 1916:
Tommy Spence (B), Bob Lang (G), Everette Strupper (B), Walker "Big Six" Carpenter (T).

The Yellow Jackets of Georgia Tech, with an 8-0-1 record, were declared Champions of the Southern Conference in 1916.

This photo is from the Georgia-Georgia Tech game of 1916. They would not meet on the gridiron again until 1925. (For the first time ever, the game was played at Sanford Field.)

W. G. Germany,
Georgia's captain-elect
for 1917.

Team captains meet for the coin toss just prior to kickoff of the big Georgia-Georgia Tech
game of 1916 at Sanford Field.

Three all-time Georgia Tech greats: Captain Tally Johnson, Walker "Big Six"
Carpenter and Froggie Morrison.

Captain Tom Thrash,
an All-Southern
Georgia tackle.

1917–1924: The Great Interregnum

Fans streaming from Sanford Field in 1916 were unaware that Georgia and Georgia Tech, these natural rivals who were developing two of the nation's most successful football programs, would not meet on the gridiron again for some nine years, or until 1925.

What happened was this: with America's entry into World War I in 1917, the University of Georgia, as a symbolic show of patrotism, discontinued football in 1917 and 1918.

Georgia Tech, on the other hand, insisting that to drop football would not make the war end one day sooner, refused to discontinue their program. Indeed, in 1917 the Golden Tornadoes easily ran undefeated through a nine-game schedule and won not only the Southern Conference crown but the national championship as well.

Tech's attitude did not sit well with the University of Georgia, who charged their Atlanta friends with being less than patriotic. Tech poo-pooed such charges, retorting that to drop football was a stupid measure which served only to deprive students of the right to participate in an extracurricular activity.

Relations between the two schools, which had never been particularly warm to start with, went from bad to worse, with each institution questioning the sanity of the other.

Georgia Tech and the Atlanta skyline in 1917.

But Georgia again cranked up their football program in 1919 and were scheduled to meet Georgia Tech. But such a game was not to be. The bone of contention this time was this: it was May 9, 1919, a Friday afternoon, and Georgia and Tech were embroiled in the first game of a baseball doubleheader at Grant Field. And things were not looking good for the Tornadoes. It was the bottom of the ninth inning and Georgia was leading 2-1. Tech was at bat, one out, with the tying run on second.

At that point, Tech's band members arose from the stands and quickly trotted down to the first base line, instruments blaring, drums pounding, just making as much racket as possible in hopes of rattling Georgia's pitcher. But it didn't work, and Tech's final two batters struck out.

Following the game students from both colleges began ranging up and down Peachtree Street, engaging in rowdy behavior for the rest of the afternoon and far into the night.

The following afternoon some 7,000 fans turned out to watch the second game of this Georgia-Georgia Tech doubleheader (and to witness the fun once the students from Georgia and Tech began razzing one another.)

As luck would have it, Georgia pitcher Tommy Philpot would pick this very day to hurl the only no-hitter of his career, and the Red and Black took the game 8-0.

Coming on top of having heard their patrotism questioned over the past two years, losing this doubleheader to Georgia was a bitter pill for the Tornadoes to swallow.

And again the students from both colleges, who were suffering from spring fever anyway, engaged in riotous behavior far into the night, with fist fights the order of the day.

On May 14, officials from both colleges, hoping to somehow soften the hard feelings that existed between their student bodies, decided to defuse the situation by sending student representatives to meet and discuss the situation.

The *Constitution* described (somewhat tongue-in-cheek) their meetings:

At two meetings held in Atlanta and Athens Wednesday, the old enemies joined hands and declared that in the future all the battling would be on the athletic field.

Tech sent B. B. Williams and Tommy Semmes to attend the conference in Athens and Georgia sent Wallace Zachry to Atlanta. A big attendance of the Tech student body gathered on Grant Field. The Tech band played "Glory, Glory to Old Georgia" and the Tech students cheered the Georgia representative.

Among the terms of the treaty, the following were the most important:

Both student bodies agreed not to put laxatives in the water bucket of the opposing team.

Both student bodies agreed not to use shotguns on any members of the opposing teams during the progress of the game.

It was agreed that after each baseball game this week in Athens, the winners were to be given the freedom of the city and the losers were to retire gracefully.

The Tech and Georgia freshmen agreed not to steal any more caps from each other, and also agreed not to exhibit any such caps stolen during the late Tech-Georgia baseball series.

Both student bodies agreed unanimously that the former German Kaiser should be hung.

The floats insinuated that while UGA boys were fighting in the trenches of France...

But the following week, after all the heartwarming hoopla, Tech played another two-game series with their Georgia cousins, this one in Athens. It was a series that aroused much interest in the state. The *Constitution* reported:

The Tech delegation arrived here at 10 o'clock and at once proceeded to raise well-known bedlam. At all the towns en route, the band got off and played "Rambling Wreck" for the edification of the natives. From all sections of Georgia, where Tech and Georgia alumni struggle for a livelihood against the high cost of living, there have been motor parties. The only thing that exceeds the auto population of Georgia today is the human population. Every make of auto from the Ford to the high falutin' Packard is here and very well represented.

On Friday, Georgia again beat the Tornadoes, which meant that they were now 3-0 against Tech, and the clear winners of their four-game series. It was then that the real trouble started.

On Saturday morning, prior to Georgia's fourth game of the series with Tech (to be played that afternoon), Georgia staged what they called their Annual Senior Parade.

And in that parade, for all the world to see, especially Tech fans, Georgia students were pulling a plywood replica of a World War I tank. A big banner strung across the turret read "1917 Georgia In France 1918." It was obviously intended to celebrate Georgia's participation in World War I.

...the Tech boys were living it up in Atlanta.

And then came the Great Insult. Just behind the tank Georgia students were pulling a Model A Ford which bore a huge banner reading "Tech in Atlanta 1917-18."

The inference was clear to even the dullest among the crowds lining the sidewalks. While Georgia students were very patriotically giving their all in the trenches of France, the boys of Georgia Tech were living it up in Atlanta.

(As an aside, it might be noted that some 10,000 fans turned out that afternoon to watch Georgia again defeat Tech, this time by a score of 5-2, to sweep the series.)

Monday morning Tech students and alumni were still seething over the insult hurled at them in the Senior Parade. Indeed, Dr. J. B. Crenshaw, Tech's Athletic Director, stated that he would demand a public apology from Georgia's senior class, or athletic relations between the two schools would be severed forever.

Georgia responded that they had no intention of apologizing and couldn't care less whether Tech wanted to continue their athletic relations with Georgia.

Soon officials from the two schools and newspapers throughout the state became embroiled in the controversy. The *Constitution* commented:

> If the boys can't agree to conduct their sports in a friendly manner—more than that, in a sportsmanlike manner—then it is time to sever athletic relations and for the two schools to look elsewhere for rivals on the gridiron, the field and diamond.

And the *Athens Banner* responded:

> We are compelled to criticize such unfair, cruel and false insinuations the senior class of Georgia made against the patrotism of fellow Americans, fellow Southerners and fellow Georgians.
>
> There is no college in this country that has a monopoly on patriotism. Men went to war from every college in the land. Georgia may not remember many of the Tech athletes who served their country in the late war. But surely Georgia remembers Tommy Spence, the Tech fullback who carried the entire Georgia football team on his shoulders up and down Sanford Field in 1916. And Tommy Spence died in France.

Responding to all this, from the University of Georgia came A. M. Thornton, president of the senior class, who wrote in the *Constitution*:

Day by day we have been taunted by Tech students and supporters because we did not play football in 1917. They said we showed a "yellow streak" by not having our team play them. While the war raged, the Golden Tornadoes ran wild over its opponents in Atlanta. Georgia was held up to ridicule because its athletic authorities refused to permit football to be played. The senior who carried the offending banner in the parade has a brother at Tech and only a wide stretch of the imagination can enable Tech to be angry at a prank that was purely boyish.

Tech's complaints are based purely on that school's inability to accept defeat gracefully. Four defeats leaves one's sensibilities on the quiver.

In the final analysis Tech demanded an apology and Georgia refused to grant one. Thus the two schools had reached an impasse. They would not meet again until 1925.

Georgia Football, 1919–1924: An Update

Georgia 1919

Captain Arthur Pew, All-Southern tackle for Georgia in 1919.

UGA All-Southern in 1919: Owen Reynolds (E).

1919: Georgia, of course, had discontinued football during the 1917-18 seasons. But then came the end of the war and they were back on the gridiron in 1919. Considering that they had not fielded a team for the past two years, they enjoyed a remarkably fine season in 1919, posting a 4-2-3 record. They had good wins over The Citadel, South Carolina, Sewanee and Florida, close losses to Auburn (7-0) and Alabama (6-0), and ties with Virginia, Tulane and Clemson. Indeed, in nine games their defense gave up a total of only 27 points.

Coach W. A. Cunningham would resign following the 1919 season, having compiled an enviable 43-18-9 record, and in his place would come H. J. Stegman, who would remain at the university for the next four years.

The Red and Blacks defeated Florida 16-0 in 1919. (Note that the Florida players are wearing numerals on their jerseys.)

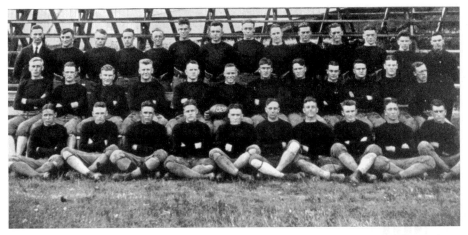

1920: In fact, Stegman got off to a roaring start as his 1920 Georgia Wildcats went 8-0-1 on the season, a 0-0 tie with Virginia the only blemish on their record, and claimed the Southern Conference championship. Again, as in 1919, Georgia's defensive team was extremely strong, blanking seven opponents and giving up only 17 points to the two others.

In 1920 Buck Cheeves returned a punt 87 yards for a TD vs. Alabama, still number four in the UGA record book.

Georgia
1920

UGA All-Southern in 1920:
Owen Reynolds (E), Bum Day (C), and Art Pew (T).
Named to the UGA SHF:
James "Doc" Harper and James "Buck" Cheeves.

Captain A. M. "Bum" Day, an All-Southern center for Georgia in 1920.

Coach H. J. Stegeman, a star player for Alonzo Stagg at the University of Chicago, produced outstanding teams at Georgia (1920–22), winning the Southern Conference in 1920.

Georgia
1921

1921: This season remains extremely important in the history of Georgia football, for this was the year that they adopted the bulldog as their namesake and their mascot. From this date forward they would become known throughout the nation as the Georgia Bulldogs, and for the following reason: it seems that Dr. Steadman V. Sanford, a professor and later president of the University of Georgia, was a graduate of Yale University, and he always maintained close ties with Yale. It is said that he persuaded the Georgia athletic department to select the name Bulldogs because of his fondness for the Yale Bulldogs. Indeed, in 1929, upon Sanford Stadium's completion, the dedication game was played against none other than the Yale Bulldogs. (Georgia won in an upset, 15-0.)

The 1921 Bulldogs enjoyed another good season, going 7-2-1 against some of the toughest teams in the nation. They defeated Mercer, Furman, Oglethorpe, Auburn, Virginia, Alabama and Clemson, tied Vanderbilt, and lost to Harvard and Dartmouth, the two big Eastern schools on their schedule.

UGA All-Southern in 1921:
Owen Reynolds (for the third time), Bum Day, Art Pew and Hugh Whelchel.

A 1921 shot of Georgia in action against one of the most powerful teams in the country, Harvard University, in a game played at Cambridge, Massachusetts. Here Jim Reynolds, Dan Bennett and team captain Hugh Whelchel put the stop on a Crimson runner. Harvard took this one in a hard fought contest, 10-7.

1922: The Bulldogs began well enough, but then lost three of their last four games to complete a 5-4-1 season. They had wins over Newberry, Mercer, Furman, Tennessee and Oglethorpe, and losses to Chicago, Auburn, Vanderbilt and Alabama, and a tie with Virginia.

UGA All-Southern in 1922:
Hugh Whelchel (G), Joe Bennett (T) and John Fletcher (FB).

Georgia
1922

John Fletcher runs off the weak side of the Furman line as Georgia won a close one from the Hurricanes, 7-0. (Fletcher would serve as team captain in 1924.)

1923: The 5-3-1 Bulldogs of 1923 were highly unpredictable. They defeated such teams as Tennessee (17-0), Auburn (7-0), Virginia (13-0), Mercer (7-0), and Oglethorpe (20-6), tied powerful Centre (3-3), while losing to Yale (40-0), Vanderbilt (35-7) and Alabama (36-0).

UGA All-American in 1923:
Joe Bennett (T).
Named to the UGA SHF:
Andy Johnson.

Georgia
1923

All-Southern fullback John Fletcher bulldozes his way into the Virginia secondary as the Bulldogs took this one 13-0 at Sanford Field in 1923.

1924: Here Georgia wins a close one from Vanderbilt by a score of 27-24. This season was significantly better for the Bulldogs as they won seven games while losing three. They beat Mercer, South Carolina, Furman, Vanderbilt, Tennessee, Virginia and Auburn, while losing to Yale, Alabama and Centre.

Georgia
1924

All-Southern in 1924:
Jim Taylor and Ralph Thompson.

Dr. Steadman Vincent Sanford, president of the University of Georgia and founder of the Southern Conference. Sanford Stadium is named in his honor.

Coach Cecil "Kid" Woodruff became head coach of the Bulldogs in 1923. He installed Knute Rockne's famous Notre Dame Box Formation, and compiled a fine 32-16-1 record during his five year tenure, including a conference championship in 1927.

Captain John Fletcher, an All-Southern fullback for the '24 Bulldogs.

Georgia Tech Football, 1917–1924: An Update

1917, An Undefeated Season and the National Championship: Tech, of course, did not drop football during the World War I years, and though they didn't play Georgia in 1917, they did play some of the strongest teams in the nation, and beat them all. Beat them handily, in fact. It is revealing to take a look at their record for that great undefeated season: Furman (25- 0), Wake Forest (33-0), Penn (41-0), Davidson (32-10), Washington & Lee (63-0), Vanderbilt (83-0), Tulane (48-0), Carlisle (98-0) and Auburn (68-7).

Tech's defense gave up only 17 points all season while blanking seven opponents. Tech's offense, on the other hand, scored 491 points, an average of 54.5 points per game. Indeed, this 1917 Tech team was declared National Champions, and they obviously deserved it.

Tech 1917

On October 6, 1917, Tech surprised the football world when they defeated Penn, the pride of the Big East, by a score of 41-0.

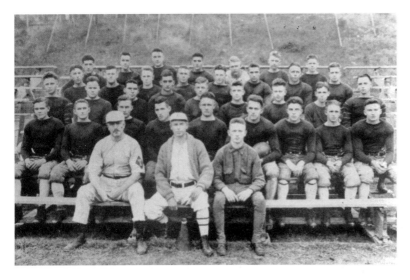

1918: This was another great season for John Heisman and his Golden Tornadoes. Not quite as good as 1917, but good enough to win the Southern Conference Championship. They went 6-1 on the season, with wins over Clemson (28-0), Furman (118-0), the 11th Cavalry (123-0), Auburn (41-0), Camp Gordon (28-0) and NC State (128-0). Their lone loss came at the hands of Pitt (32-0), the only team to score against Tech.

Before losing to Pitt on November 23, 1918, Tech had last lost to Auburn on November 7, 1914, a winning streak of thirty-three games, still their longest win streak on record. (Tech lost only three games during the entire World War I period, 1914-18.)

Walker "Big Six" Carpenter, Tech's All-American tackle in 1917, is a member of the College Football Hall of Fame.

Everette Strupper, All-American halfback for Tech in 1917, is a member of the College Football Hall of Fame. (Strupper scored eight TDs vs. Cumberland College in 1916, still an all-time Tech single-game scoring record.)

Tech
1918

Tech All-American in 1918:
Ashel "Bum" Phillips, Bill Fincher, Ralph "Buck" Flowers and Joe Guyon.
Named to the GT AHF:
Walker "Big Six" Carpenter, Bum Day and Joe Guyon.

1919: The Tornadoes slipped just a bit in 1919, recording a 7-3 season, with wins over the 5th Division, Furman, Wake Forest, Clemson, Vanderbilt, Davidson and Georgetown, and losses to Pitt, Washington and Lee and Auburn. Dewey Scarboro returned a kickoff 102 yards for a TD vs. Georgetown, still an all-time GT record. Hollywood movie star Randolph Scott is standing on the back row, third from left.

But the big news of 1919 concerned the resignation of Coach John Heisman following his divorce from his wife (she wished to remain in Atlanta, so he moved on).

Tech
1919

Tech All-Southern in 1919: Judy Harlan, Buck Flowers, Red Barron, Albert Staton, Dummy LeBey and George "Pup" Phillips.
Named to the GT AHF: Pup Phillips and Coach John Heisman.

Captain Bill Fincher, Tech's All-American end in 1918, is a member of the Helms Football Hall of Fame.

Coach John Heisman resigned at Tech following the 1919 season, having compiled a most enviable 102-29-7 record. He is a member of the College Football Hall of Fame.

Joe "Chief" Guyon, an All-American halfback for Tech in 1918, is a member of the College Football Hall of Fame.

1920: This season saw the arrival at Tech of Bill Alexander, an excellent coach who would remain with the Tornadoes for the next 25 years, or until 1944. His 1928 team would defeat California in the Rose Bowl and win the National Championship.

This season would see Alexander off to a good start as his Tornadoes posted a great 8-1 record and were declared Southern Conference champions. Indeed, they moved easily through eight of their nine opponents, beating Centre (24-0), Wake Forest (44-0), Oglethorpe (55-0), Davidson (66-0), Vanderbilt (44-0), Clemson (7-0), Georgetown (35-6) and Auburn (34-0). Their only loss came at the hands of Pitt, their old nemesis, by a score of 10-3.

Tech
1920

Tech All-American in 1920:
Bill Fincher and Buck Flowers.
Tech All-Southern in 1920:
Red Barron.
Named to the GT AHF:
Bill Fincher and Buck Flowers.

Buck Flowers carries the ball in Tech's 35-6 win over Georgetown. (He had an 82-yard TD run in this game, still the fifth longest such run in the GT record book. He also had an 85-yard punt vs. Davidson in 1920, still the second longest punt in the GT record book.) He is a member of the College FOotball Hall of Fame.

Coach Bill Alexander would become a mainstay at Tech over the next 25 years, compiling a 134-95-15 record.

1921: This year was a re-play of 1920 with Tech again going 8-1 on the season and being crowned champions of the Southern Conference. They moved easily through their schedule, beating Wake Forest (42-0), Oglethorpe (41-0), Georgetown (21-7), Davidson (70-0), Furman (69-0), Rutgers (48-14), Clemson (48-7) and Auburn (14-0). Their lone loss came at the hands of Penn State (28-7) in a game played at the Polo Grounds in New York.

(Coach Alexander's record over the previous two seasons stood at 16-2. Plus he'd garnered two conference championships. Not a bad average.)

Tech
1921

All-American in 1921:
Red Barron and Judy Harlan.
All-Southern in 1921:
Albert Staton.

Judy Harland and Red Barron in action as Tech beat Clemson 48-7 in 1921. Harland and Barron were both named All-American that year.

1922: This season saw Tech fall to 7-2 with wins over NC State, Oglethorpe, Davidson, Alabama, Clemson, Georgetown and Auburn. Their losses came at the hands of their two new opponents, Navy and Notre Dame.

All-American in 1922:
Red Barron (for the second time).
All-Southern in 1922:
Oscar Davis and Claire Frye.

Georgia Tech won the Southern Conference Championship with their 14-6 win over Auburn in 1922. Here Auburn's captain presents the championship trophy to Tech's Captain Red Barron.

In 1921, Red Barron, Tech's All-American halfback, set a single-season rushing record that would stand for the next 56 years, until broken by Eddie Lee Ivery in 1977.

1923: This team would suffer through a losing season, one of the few they'd have under Coach Alexander. They went 3-2-4 on the year with wins over Oglethorpe, VMI, and Georgetown, losses to Penn State and Notre Dame, and ties with Florida, Alabama, Kentucky, and Auburn. Indeed, 1923 was Tech's worst year since they'd gone 2-5 in 1903.

Tech All-Southern in 1923:
Doug Wycoff and John Staton.

Tech
1923

J. F. McIntyre, team captain of the Tornadoes in 1923.

Tech All-American Doug Wycoff moves for yardage as Tech defeated Oglethorpe 28-13 in '23.

1924: Tech improved their record in 1924, going 5-3-1 on the season, with wins over Oglethorpe, VMI, LSU, Auburn and a big upset of Penn State. They lost to Alabama, Notre Dame and Vanderbilt, and tied Florida.

Tech All-American in 1924:
Walter Godwin and Doug Wycoff.

Tech 1924

The Tornadoes close in on this Auburn receiver as Tech upset the Tigers 7-0 on Thanksgiving Day, 1924.

1925: Time Begins Once Again

I t was November14, 1925, a bright but chilly day in Atlanta as a crowd of some 35,000 eager fans (the largest crowd ever to witness an athletic event south of the Mason-Dixon Line) streamed into Grant Field.

At this point the Bulldogs, under Coach George Woodruff, were 4-3 on the season with wins over Mercer, Furman, Vanderbilt and Auburn, and losses to Virginia, Yale and Tennessee.Following today's game with Tech, they would also lose to Alabama to finish the year with a 4-5 record, their first losing season since 1914.

As for Tech, to date they had wins over Oglethorpe, VMI, Penn State, Florida and Vanderbilt, and losses to Alabama and Notre Dame.Following today's contest they would tie Auburn to finish the season with a good 6-2-1 record.

Georgia's Tom Kain kicked off,the ball was taken by Doug Wycoff, and this old series was off and running once again.On first down Tech fumbled at their own 30, Georgia recovered and tried two running plays at the right side of the Tech line.They lost two yards,bringing up a third and twelve.At that point George Morton threw to Roy Estes, down to the Tech 17 for a first down.Three stabs at the line netted them nothing, so Howell Hollis attempted a field goal.The kick was blocked and Tech took over at their own 20.

For the next twenty-five minutes then this game became a defensive duel, with neither team able to move against the other.

Then, just before the first half ended, fans witnessed one of those official misunderstandings that can truly affect the outcome of a football game.This one probably cost Georgia Tech a touchdown.

Ike Williams kicks the winning field goal as the Tornadoes beat Georgia 3-0 at Grant Field.

What happened was this:Tech had a first down at the Georgia six yard line. At that point, Tech captain, Doug Wycoff, asked the referee how much time was left in the half.

The referee then ran to the sideline to ask the time of the official timekeeper.The timekeeper responded that one minute and fifteen seconds remained.

The referee, unfortunately, misunderstood the timekeeper and reported to Wycoff that only fifteen seconds remained.

So, instead of trying to push the ball over for a touchdown, Tech's Ike Williams immediately lined up to attempt a field goal.His kick sailed wide to the right and the score remained tied, 0-0. Georgia then ran off four plays before the half finally ended, and Tech went wild with anger. Whose side was the timekeeper on anyway?

In the third quarter Ike Williams did manage to kick a 27-yard field goal, the game's only score, and Georgia Tech walked away with a hard-earned 3-0 victory.

Tech All-American in 1925:
Walter Godwin (G) and Doug Wycoff (FB).
Tech All-Southern in 1925:
Owen Poole (C) and Mark Tharpe (T).
Named to the GT AHF for 1925:
Doug Wycoff and George Gardner.

Joe Bennett, an All-American tackle for the Bulldogs.

Ike Williams kicks a PAT as Georgia Tech defeated VMI 33-0 in 1925.

Bulldog coach George "Kid" Woodruff (1923-1927), captain of the 1911 Georgia team, introduced the Notre Dame Box Formation to the South. He was a wealthy businessman and coached the team for one dollar per year.

Ralph "Smack" Thompson, All-Southern end and captain of the 1925 Bulldogs.

Doug Wycoff a '25 All-American and a member of the GT AHF.

Gus Merkle, a member of the GT AHF.

Mercer "Mack" Tharpe, Tech's All-Southern tackle and a member of the GT AHF.

The Georgia Tech team of 1925 went 6-2-1 on the season, losing to only Alabama and Notre Dame.

Tech All-Southern Carter Barron skirts end as Tech beat Florida 23-7.

1926: Both Teams Go Airborne

It was November 13, 1926, and Coach Woodruff was now in his third year as head coach of the Bulldogs and fans were beginning to feel that by now he'd had time to get all the kinks out. Still, at this point the Bulldogs were 4-3 on the year with wins over Mercer, Virginia, Florida and Auburn, and losses to Yale, Furman and Vanderbilt, which indicated that the Bulldogs were still trying to find themselves. Fans (and Coach Woodruff) hoped they'd hurry and do so.

The Golden Tornadoes were also experiencing something of an off season, and at this point were struggling along with wins over VMI, Tulane and Washington and Lee. What really upset Tech fans was the Jackets' loss to little Oglethorpe (7-6) in their opening game of the season. And then there were also losses to Alabama, Notre Dame and Vanderbilt. (This would be Tech's first losing season since 1903.)

As for today's game, Tech felt if they were to have a chance at all against Georgia's bigger eleven, they'd have no choice but to unwind their passing game, a ploy that had proven singularly unsuccessful at that point.

As for the game itself, towards the end of the first quarter, with the score tied 0-0, fans witnessed a play that has been seen neither before nor since. With the ball on their own ten, Tech's Bob Parham punted from his own end zone. The ball, aided by a stiff breeze, did not come to rest until it had crossed Georgia's goal line over a hundred yards away.

Tom Nash, an All-American and member of the UGA Sports Hall of Fame

In the Tech record book this kick went down as a 90-yard punt, but in reality the ball traveled much further than that, and remains the longest punt in Tech history.

The ball was brought out to the Georgia 20 where it was put into play. Two plays later there was a fumble and John Marshall recovered for Tech at the 23. Sam Murray then hit Marshall with a pass, down to the Georgia six. Then Bob Horn went in for the touchdown, Murray converted and Tech led 7-0.

Following an exchange of punts, Murray intercepted a Georgia pass and returned it to the Bulldog 46. Three plays later Murray passed 21 yards to Bob Horn, down to the Georgia 25. On the next play, Murray threw complete to John Brewer running all alone in the end zone for a touchdown. But then Chick Shiver blocked Murray's kick and the score became 13-0.

In the third quarter Tech's Parham

Team captains George Morton of Georgia and Owen Poole of Tech, both named to the All-Southern team of 1926, meet for the coin toss just prior to kickoff at Grant Field.

bobbled a punt, Bob Morris recovered for Georgia, and the Bulldogs were on the comeback trail. On first down George Morton threw to Cecil Sherlock for 13 yards, to the Tech 36. Two plays later Herdis McCrary darted through a big hole and dashed 23 yards for a Georgia touchdown. Roy Johnson's PAT was good and Tech's lead was cut to 13-7.

The game then seesawed back and forth until early in the fourth quarter when Tech punted out of bounds at mid-field. Three plays later, with a first down at the Tech 35, George Morton calmly unleashed a long throw to Jack Curran who caught the ball at the eight, then trotted on into the end zone.

Johnson's kick was good and Georgia took this one 14-13.

UGA All-Southern in 1926:
Curtis Luckey (T) and George Morton (HB).
Named to the UGA SHF in 1926:
Howell T. Hollis.
Named to the GT AHF in 1926:
Gus Merkle and Mack Tharpe.

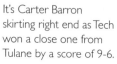

Robert Parham had a 90-yard punt in Tech's game with Georgia in 1926, still an all-time record in the GT record book.

It's Carter Barron skirting right end as Tech won a close one from Tulane by a score of 9-6.

Georgia's Cecil Sherlock took this George Morton pass for a first down before being wrestled to the ground as Georgia took a squeaker from Tech, 14-13.

Tech flappers whoop it up for the Tornadoes just prior to kickoff versus the University of Georgia in 1926.

The famous Arches at the entrance to the University of Georgia in 1926. These Arches have been standing since 1864.

Tech on the move against Georgia in a thriller won by the Bulldogs 14-13.

Fans stream from Grant Field following the big game in 1926.

1927: Georgia Loses to Tech, Wins National Championship

It was December 3, 1927, and both Georgia and Tech had enjoyed banner seasons. Indeed, the Bulldogs, with a great 9-0 record, were ranked number one in the nation. A trip to the Rose Bowl and the National Championship was theirs for the taking. All they had to do was bump off Georgia Tech. No big thing, considering the Bulldogs' performance to date.

They had easily run through their schedule, beating Virginia (32-0), Yale (14-10), Furman (32-0), Auburn (33-0), Tulane (31-0), Florida (28-0), Clemson (32-0), Mercer (26-0) and Alabama (20-6). If anyone ever deserved a National Championship, Georgia obviously did. And all they had to do was beat Georgia Tech.

Unfortunately for Georgia, Tech wasn't exactly a pushover in '27. At this point they were 7-1-1 on the season, with wins over VMI, Tulane, Alabama, UNC, LSU, Oglethorpe and Auburn, a loss to Notre Dame, and a tie with Vanderbilt. A pretty tough team in anybody's book. And to say that they badly wanted the day's game is an understatement.

Some 38,000 fans turned out on a cold, rainy day in December to watch this memorable encounter at Grant Field, to see if Tech could really pull off the upset of the decade.

By kickoff time Grant Field was a sea of mud. And the first quarter ended in a 0-0 deadlock. Indeed, there were eleven punts in the first quarter alone.

Early in the second quarter the Bulldogs took the ball at the Tech 32. Herdis McCrary slogged for three yards, then Roy Estes hit Frank Dudley with a 12-yard pass, down to Tech's 17. Dudley picked up eight yards on two carries, then it was Estes for two, and Georgia faced a fourth down and inches at the Tech seven. The Bulldogs called on their big fullback Herdis McCrary to ram it across, but McCrary slipped down in the mud, and that was the end of Georgia's big chance.

The crowd was brought to its feet late in the second quarter when Tech's Warner Mizell, standing at midfield, threw a 50-yarder to Bob Durant who had gotten behind the Bulldog defenders. Durant took the pass over his shoulder and waltzed into the end zone. The PAT was no good but Tech led 6-0.

Later, with only minutes left in the third quarter, Tech's Stumpy Thomason intercepted an Estes pass and returned it 58 yards, down to the Georgia 23. Three plays later Thomason circled Georgia's end for

TOP:
Captain Chick Shiver, a Georgia All-American end, and a member of the UGA SHF. (It was Shiver who blocked Tech's PAT in 1926.)

MIDDLE:
Captain Edgar Crowley, Tech's All-Southern end.

BOTTOM:
"Stumpy" Thomason, an All-Southern halfback, and the hero of Tech's upset win over Georgia in 1927.

another Tech touchdown. The PAT again failed, but it didn't matter. Tech took this game 12-0.

Today's contest proved one of the most satisfying wins in history for this 8-1-1 Tech team. Not only had they upset a heavier (and more talented) opponent, they had knocked the hated Bulldogs out of a Rose Bowl bid and won the Southern Conference championship for themselves in the bargain. Still, despite the day's loss and being deprived of a Rose Bowl bid, the 9-1 Bulldogs were declared national champions.

TOP:
John Brodnax, UGA QB.

SECOND:
Roy Estes signed with the Greenbay Packers, the first Bulldog to play pro football.

THIRD:
Bob McTigue, UGA HB.

BOTTOM:
Harvey Hill, UGA HB.

UGA All-American in 1927:
I. M. "Chick" Shiver (E) and Tom Nash (E).
UGA All-Southern in 1927:
Gene Smith (G) and Herdis McCrary (FB).
Named to the UGA SHF for 1927:
I. M. "Chick" Shiver and Tom Nash.
Tech All-Southern in 1927:
John Griffin "Stumpy" Thomason (HB), Peter Pund (C), Frank Speer (T) and Edgar Crowley (E).

It was December 3, 1927, as these Georgia fans alighted from the train at the Seaboard depot in Atlanta. They had only to beat Tech this afternoon to finish the season with a great 10-0 record and a national championship. Tech, unfortunately for the Bulldogs, refused to cooperate.

Bulldog All-American end Tom Nash snags a Brodnax pass good for 22 yards as Georgia fell to Tech by a score of 12-0 on a cold December day at Grant Field.

Coach Bill Alexander who coached at Tech for twenty-five years (1920–44) and finished with a 134-95-15 record.

Frank Speer, Georgia Tech All-Southern tackle.

Peter Pund, Tech All-American center, is a member of the College Football Hall of Fame.

Frank Dudley goes out at the five to set up Georgia's 14-10 win over Yale in their second game of the season. This was considered a tremendous upset, and propelled Georgia to a number one national ranking.

Frank Dudley, Georgia halfback.

Herdis McCrary, Georgia All-Southern halfback.

Gene Smith, Georgia All-Southern tackle.

1928: Tech Wins Rose Bowl and National Championship

Turnabout is fair play, or so they say, but what sane person would have thought that such fairness would descend upon the great state of Georgia in 1927-28? But such was indeed the case.

Coach Bill Alexander and his 1928 Yellow Jackets breezed through nine regular season opponents before beating California 8-7 in the 1929 Rose Bowl. At that point, with a 10-0 record, they were declared national champions.

There was the University of Georgia, national champions and only a heartbeat away from a bid to play in the Rose Bowl in 1927, and now, a year later, here comes the Tornadoes of Georgia Tech with an 8-0 record and an invitation to play California in the 1929 Rose Bowl, whether they beat Georgia or not. At this point the football world was their oyster.

Tech had already demolished eight quality opponents, beating VMI, Tulane, Notre Dame, Oglethorpe, UNC, Vanderbilt, Alabama and Auburn, and beating them by convincing scores.

Georgia, on the other hand, had suffered a relapse of sorts since '27 and was sporting a mediocre 4-4 record under new head coach Harry Mehre coming into the day's game.

Some 38,000 fans, a new record for this game, turned out on December 8 at Grant Field to see which team could pull off the greatest miracle. If Georgia won it would be a miracle that they'd upset such a fine team as Georgia Tech. On the other hand, if Tech won, it would be a miracle that they'd run through nine such tough opponents without a single loss.

For several minutes it looked as though Georgia might just get their miracle. Late in the first quarter, after several punt exchanges, Tech's Warner Mizell was kicking from his own 28 when the snap from center sailed over his head. Georgia's Henry Palmer grabbed the ball and dashed down to the Tech 12 before being pulled down by Bob Durant. Three plays later Herdis McCrary took the snap and lateralled to Harvey Hill, who then threw to Herbert Maffett for a score. The PAT missed but Georgia was up 6-0.

Tech fans sat stunned. But then in the second quarter Tech punted to Georgia's 18. The receiver bobbled the ball and C. C. "Coot" Watkins recovered for the Yellow Jackets. Three plays later the Jackets had a first down at the Georgia four. Then Roy "Father" Lumpkin bulled his way in for a touchdown, Thomason kicked the point and Tech led 7-6.

In the third quarter "Stumpy" Thomason returned a punt 42 yards, down to the Georgia 15. Three plays later Lumpkin went in for his second score of the day, Thomason converted and Tech led 14-6.

John Leach, equipment manager for Tech, seems to have stepped right out of an F. Scott Fitzgerald novel.

Following a Georgia punt Tech destroyed whatever hopes the Bulldogs might have had of an upset when they drove 55 yards in 14 plays, down to the Georgia two-yard line. Thomason scored from there, but missed the PAT, and Tech took this game 20-6.

Next stop Pasadena, where they'd beat California 8-7 in the '29 Rose Bowl, complete a great undefeated season and be crowned national champions.

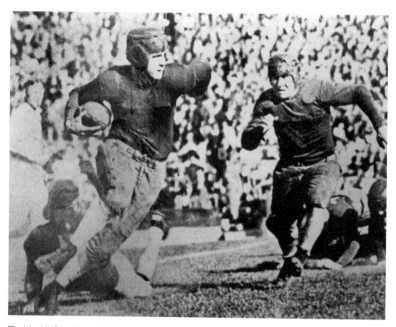

Tech's All-Southern halfback, John Griffin "Stumpy" Thomason, shows the speed that made him great as he skirts end in Tech's 13-0 win over Notre Dame. Tech went on to an 10-0 season and a national championship.

Warner Mizell, an All-American halfback and a member of the GT AHF.

Captain Peter Pund, an All-American center for Georgia Tech.

Raleigh Drennon, an All-Southern guard for Georgia Tech.

Ken Thrash, an All-Southern tackle for Georgia Tech.

Roy "Father" Lumpkin, Tech's All-American fullback in '28.

Coach Harry Mehre spent eleven very prosperous years with the Bulldogs, winning Conference championships four of those years.

Co-captain Glenn Lautzenhiser, center for the '28 Bulldogs.

Co-captain Roy Jacobson, halfback for the '28 Bulldogs.

Georgia's All-Southern end, Herbert Maffett, scores Georgia's only TD of the day as they fell to Tech 20-6.

Roy "Father" Lumpkin runs the final yards for a touchdown to give Tech a 7-6 lead over Georgia. Following this game Tech, with a great 9-0 record, would go on to defeat California in the '29 Rose Bowl and be declared national champions.

Tech's Great
Rose Bowl Win of 1929
One of the Strangest Bowl Games Ever Played

Following Georgia Tech's win over Georgia to cap an undefeated season, they traveled to Pasadena to tangle with the other great national power in '28, the University of California. In fact, few experts gave Tech much of a chance against what was considered the class of the West. But those experts reckoned without the knowledge of the help the Yellow Jackets would receive from California's Captain Roy Riegels.

Before this game ended, fans would witness one of the strangest plays ever performed in a college football game.

What happened was this: early in the second quarter, with the score tied at 0-0, Tech's "Stumpy" Thomason was hit at his own 36-yard line. The ball popped high in the air and was snagged on the fly by an alert Roy Riegels. Surrounded by Tech defenders, Riegels spun first this way, then that. Again he was hit, and again he spun away. Then, suddenly, finding himself free of all those pesky white jerseys, he dashed for daylight. He could see the goal line ahead, only moments away, and not a white jersey in sight. He was in the clear. He had only to make sure he didn't trip over his own feet and soon he'd cross that goal line and Cal would take the lead.

TOP:
"Wrong Way" Roy Riegels, pursued by his own team-mates, mistakenly makes a dash for his own goal line. He was finally wrestled to the turf at the California 4-yard line.

BOTTOM:
"Wrong Way" Roy Riegels walks dejectedly to the side-lines after his 64-yard wrong way run into immortality.

It was then that he heard a teammate, Bennie Lom, yell, "Stop, Roy, you're running the wrong way."

But with the blood pounding in his ears, Riegels failed to understand what Lom was trying to tell him. Later, he explained that he thought Lom was yelling for him to lateral the ball.

Thus Riegels turned his head just long enough to reply,

"Get away from me, Bennie. This is my touchdown."

Lom finally caught up with Riegels at the Cal 10 and grabbed him by the arm. But Riegels, thinking Lom had lost his mind, shook free. Still Lom hung on, and finally dragged Riegels to the turf at the Cal 4-yard line.

Riegels had made a fine 64-yard run. Unfortunately for Cal (and himself) he'd run the wrong way.

But the Golden Bears still had the ball, and on first down they attempted to punt from their own end zone, Riegels snapping to Lom. It was then that Tech's Vance Maree broke through and blocked the kick. The ball rolled out of bounds and Tech took a 2-0 lead.

Cal and Tech traded touchdowns in the second half, and thus it was this 2-point safety that proved the margin of victory for Tech. When the final gun sounded they held an 8-7 lead, which was the final score, a great win for the Yellow Jackets.

Now, with a 10-0 record they were the undisputed national champions, their second such honor.

As for Roy Riegels, he was quoted after the game as saying, "Now why did I do something like that?"

His run made every headline in America, and he became known throughout the land as "Wrong Way" Riegels. (In 1929 he would again serve as captain of the Golden Bears and would be named to several All-American teams.)

1929: The Stock Market Crashes (and So Does Tech)

It was December 7, 1929, a cold, rainy day in Athens as the Bulldogs and Yellow Jackets squared off for this twenty-fourth meeting between the two schools. (Tech at this point led in the series 11-10-2.) And for the first time ever these two teams would meet at Georgia's new Sanford Stadium, and fans were eager to see what difference a change of scene might make.

Coach Bill Alexander's Tornadoes were coming off a great 1928 season, but 1929 had proven something of a disappointment. To date they'd beaten Mississippi A&M, Florida and Auburn, while losing to UNC, Tulane, Notre Dame, Vanderbilt and Alabama. In other words, they were 3-5 going into the Georgia game and hoping for the best against an average Bulldog team. (Georgia lost their opening game of the season to little Oglethorpe, 13-6, which did nothing to encourage the Red and Black faithful.)

Indeed, Coach Harry Mehre's Bulldogs were 5-4 coming into today's contest, having defeated Furman, Yale, UNC, Auburn and Alabama, while losing to (in addition to Oglethorpe), Florida, Tulane and NYU. Their win over Yale, the class of the East, was considered a tremendous upset, and did much to make fans forget the Oglethorpe fiasco.

Today they too were hoping for the best against a mediocre Tech team.

Only 20,000 fans turned out on what proved to be one of the most miserable days in recent memory, with the temperature in the low thirties and the rain coming down in sheets at Sanford Stadium.

The Bulldogs returned the opening kickoff to their own 35-yard line. Four plays later Spurgeon Chandler flipped a 29-yard pass to Herbert Maffett at the Tech 20, and Maffett then outran Tornado defenders the remaining distance for a touchdown. The PAT missed, but Georgia still led, 6-0.

The two teams battled each other and the unfortunate elements for the rest of the half. But early in the third quarter Tech's Tom Jones blocked a Chandler punt. The ball rolled back behind Georgia's goal line and Jim Brooke immediately pounced upon it for a Tech touchdown. Again the PAT missed, and the score stood tied at 6-6.

It was Saturday, December 7, 1929, (just a few weeks after the stock market crash), a dark, gloomy day in Athens, but Georgia fans were sitting on top of the world as they watched the Bulldogs take the Tornadoes by a score of 12-6. Here Spud Chandler throws 35 yards to All-American Herb Maffett for Georgia's first touchdown of the afternoon in the midst of a rainstorm.

It was in the fourth period that one of the most memorable plays in this long series occurred when Vernon Bryant blocked a Tech punt, and ran it in 45 yards for Georgia's winning touchdown.

Ralph McGill of the *Constitution,* in an article entitled "Bryant Made World Safe for All Fat Men," explained it this way:

> With a slanting rain leaning against the brown turf of Sanford Field, solemn-faced "Fats" Bryant broke through the Georgia Tech line, blocked a punt, caught it as it wobbled crazily in the air, and raced 45 yards to a touchdown and a 12-to-6 victory for Georgia Saturday afternoon.
>
> Mr. Bryant made the world safe for fat men. No longer will fat men be pointed out as objects of scorn. For Mr. Bryant is of comfortable girth. He likes his pancakes covered with butter and drowned in maple syrup. He likes hot biscuits and gravy. He dotes on mashed potatoes covered with melted butter.
>
> Tomorrow the sons of Georgia will be hanging the picture of "Fats" Bryant on the wall along with those of Woodrow Wilson and Robert E. Lee. He administered the first defeat to Georgia Tech since 1926. It was also a defeat for diets and lettuce salad. Steak and potatoes won by a touchdown from calories and grapefruit.

Named to the GT AHF for 1929:
Raleigh Drennon and Warner Mizell.
UGA All-Southern in 1929:
Vernon "Catfish" Smith (E).

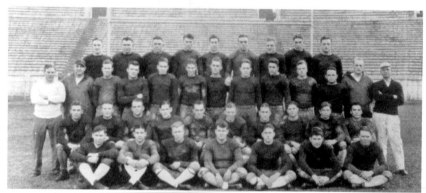

The Golden Tornadoes of 1929.

Tech's All-Southern end Tom Jones takes this Sam Colvin pass for a first down as the Golden Tornadoes defeated Mississippi A&M 27-13.

TOP:
George Maree, an All-American tackle for the Tornadoes.

MIDDLE:
Captain Harold Rusk, Tech quarterback.

BOTTOM:
Fred Holt, tackle for the Tornadoes.

Captain Joe Boland, Georgia center.

Spurgeon "Spud" Chandler, a fierce runner and a member of the UGA SHF.

Herbert Maffett, All-American end and a member of the UGA SHF.

Guard Vernon "Fats" Bryant scored on a fumble recovery and won the game for Georgia over Tech in 1929.

These beautiful young Georgia coeds from the Phi Mu sorority ("good girls all") are in a festive mood just prior to kickoff on October 12, 1929, a sunny day in Athens, as they await the arrival of the Yale and Georgia Bulldogs down on the playing field.

The dedication of Sanford Stadium. Here Dr. Sanford, president of the University of Georgia, for whom Sanford Stadium is named, receives an award just prior to kickoff with the Yale Bulldogs on October 12, 1929.

Georgia scheduled the Yale Bulldogs for their dedication of Sanford Stadium in 1929. This aerial shot of Sanford Stadium shows the two teams in action. (Yale is huddling in this photo.) Yale lost to Georgia this afternoon by a score of 15-0. This game is still remembered as a tremendous upset for the Georgia team.

Vernon "Catfish" Smith again scores in this hard fought game with Yale. (Smith scored all 15 of Georgia's points this afternoon.)

1930: A Terrible Fight (Before, During and After the Game)

Nineteen thirty got off with a bang for the University of Georgia as in quick order they marched undefeated through Oglethorpe, Mercer, Yale, UNC, Auburn and NYU. And there was also a scoreless tie with Florida. But then the 6-0-1 Bulldogs ran into trouble, losing to both Tulane and Alabama prior to their meeting with Georgia Tech on December 6 at Grant Field.

As for the 2-5-1 Yellow Jackets, this was their second off-season in a row and fans were beginning to look askance at Coach Alexander. To date they'd beaten only USC and Auburn, while tying UNC and losing to Carnegie Tech, Tulane, Vanderbilt, Penn and Florida. Indeed, Tech came into the encounter with their worst record since 1902.

And Tech was very much aware that Georgia had beaten both Yale and NYU (an incredible upset), which indicated that the Bulldogs could be tough to deal with, given the right circumstances.

Some 22,000 fans showed up at Grant Field, shivering in the cold and shaking their heads at the sight of the muddy field.

Just prior to kickoff a group of Tech freshmen emerged from the north end of the stadium leading an old milk cow bearing a sign which read "THIS AIN'T NO BULL. WE ARE GOING TO BEAT GEORGIA." Then the cow broke away from the startled freshmen and began lumbering down the field, slipping and sliding in the mud. The freshmen finally caught her and led her back to the north end where they were met by a contingent of angry Georgia students. But then a dozen cops arrived on the scene and ended the fun—for the moment.

Georgia's Marion Dickens goes for a first down as the Bulldogs downed Tech 13-0.

As for the game, Georgia got the break they'd been waiting for just before halftime when Tech punted to Austin Downes Jr., who ran it back 13 yards to the Tech 47. After five plays, including a 13-yard pass from Spud Chandler to Catfish Smith, the Bulldogs were on the Tech 9-yard line. Downes took it in on the next play, the PAT missed, and Georgia went in at halftime leading 6-0.

During intermission a delightful riot erupted between the students from the competing colleges, sparked by the earlier cow incident. Police rushed down onto the field but were quickly brushed aside by the swinging students.

Then again the game resumed. But it was midway the fourth quarter when the action truly began. Tech's M. J. Flowers attempted to punt but was rushed so hard that he had no choice but to run the ball. He fumbled and the ball was recovered by Georgia's Spero Tassapoulis at the Tech 47. Then Bulldogs Marion Dickens and Jack Roberts alternated carries until they reached the Tech 12-yard line. At that point Dickens began a sweep left, suddenly halted and fired a perfect strike to Catfish Smith standing in the end zone. Smith then kicked the point and Georgia won this twenty-fifth game of the series. (Georgia now led 12-11-2).

At game's end the riot that had begun at halftime continued in earnest just outside the stadium with some 500 participants beating hell out of one another. Many were treated to a free night's lodging in the city jail. Ralph McGill of the *Constitution* wrote:

> Black eyes were so numerous that one kept thinking of black-eyed peas . . .

Captain Herbert Maffett, an All-American Georgia end.

UGA All-American in 1930:
Herbert Maffett (E) and Ralph "Red" Maddox (G).
UGA All-Southern in 1930:
Vernon "Catfish" Smith (E), Milton Leathers (G) and Jack Roberts (FB).
Named to the UGA SHF for 1930:
Herb Maffett.
Tech All-American in 1930:
Vance Maree (T).
Named to the GT AHF for 1930:
Frank Speer.

Milton Leathers, an All-Southern guard for the Bulldogs.

Jack Roberts, an All-Southern fullback for the Bulldogs.

Ralph "Red" Maddox, an All-American Georgia guard.

FUMBLE! Earl Dunlap separates this Auburn runner from the ball as Tech went on to win, 14-12. Though some teams are now wearing numerals on their jerseys, many of the players still refuse to wear helmets.

Georgia Tech's Pat Barron gives a shoulder to this Penn defender.

Vance Maree, an All-American tackle for Tech in '30.

Frank Speer, All-American tackle for the Yellow Jackets.

Sam Fincher, Tech's great All-Southern tackle.

In '31 Pat Barron returned a punt 92 yards for a TD vs. Penn, still number two in the GT record book.

1931: Both Georgia and Tech Play One Game Too Many

It was November 28, 1931, and the mighty Bulldogs were 7-1 as they prepared for their annual conflict with Georgia Tech. The only blemish on their record was a 20-7 loss to national power Tulane who would go on to play Southern Cal in the Rose Bowl. Indeed, at this point Georgia had beaten both Yale and NYU (for the second year in a row) and were considered one of the top teams in America.

As for Tech, they were suffering through another mediocre season, their third consecutive losing season since winning the national championship in 1928. At this point they were 2-5-1, with wins over USC and Florida, a tie with UNC, and losses to Carnegie Tech, Auburn, Tulane, Vanderbilt and Penn. A win over Georgia today would do much to brighten a dismal season.

Some 22,000 fans showed up at Sanford Stadium to watch as Tech's hopes of salvaging something from a disastrous season quickly went down the drain. Georgia had scored only four touchdowns in their past three games, but they would make up for that scoring drought this afternoon.

Georgia's scoring parade started early in the first quarter when "Spud" Chandler recovered a fumble at the Tech 36. Seven plays later Chandler went in from the one, "Catfish" Smith kicked the PAT (the first of five he'd kick this afternoon) and Georgia took the lead, 7-0.

Tech took the ensuing kickoff, ran three plays and punted to the Georgia 35. Six plays later the Bulldogs were at the Tech 29. From there Lloyd Gilmore took a pitch and raced all the way for another touchdown, and the Bulldogs stretched their lead to 14-0.

But the outgunned Yellow Jackets fought doggedly and held the Bulldogs scoreless for the rest of the half. But then to open the third quarter Georgia took the kickoff back to their own 37. Seven plays later, with Homer Key, Buster Mott and Gilmore carrying the

Lloyd Gilmore goes 29 yards for another TD to make the score Georgia 14, Georgia Tech 0.

mail, they had a first down at the Tech 12. Key then ran it in from there, Smith kicked the point, and Georgia's lead became 21-0.

The most sensational play of the game occurred on Georgia's next possession when "Spud" Chandler broke off tackle and raced 76 yards for another Bulldog score, and Georgia stretched their lead to 28-0.

Early in the fourth period Georgia concluded their scoring parade when Wendall Sullivan tossed a 40-yard pass to Marion Dickens standing all alone in the Tech end zone, making the score 35-0.

But Tech didn't quit. Late in the final period they drove 75 yards for their lone score. Roy

TOP:
Vernon "Catfish" Smith, Georgia All-American end, is a member of the College Football Hall of Fame.

MIDDLE:
Captain Austin Downes Jr., quarterback for the Bulldogs.

BOTTOM:
Homer Key, an All-Southern Georgia halfback.

McArthur completed four passes for 64 yards in this drive, including a 7-yard TD throw to Wink Davis. The PAT was blocked and Georgia walked away with a big 35-6 win.

A week following this game, this 8-1 Georgia team took a train to Los Angeles to take on Southern California.

In 1931 the Bulldogs lost 60-0 to Southern Cal, their worst loss in history. As for Tech, on December 26, the day after Christmas, they played California at Grant Field and lost 21-6.

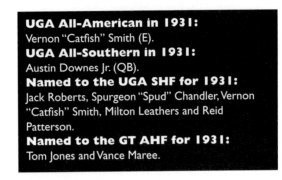

UGA All-American in 1931:
Vernon "Catfish" Smith (E).
UGA All-Southern in 1931:
Austin Downes Jr. (QB).
Named to the UGA SHF for 1931:
Jack Roberts, Spurgeon "Spud" Chandler, Vernon "Catfish" Smith, Milton Leathers and Reid Patterson.
Named to the GT AHF for 1931:
Tom Jones and Vance Maree.

It was December 10, 1931, and jubilant Georgia fans rode the Bulldog Special to Los Angeles where the 8-1 Bulldogs would take on Southern Cal. Two days later, the Trojans won by a whopping 60-0 score.

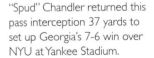

"Spud" Chandler returned this pass interception 37 yards to set up Georgia's 7-6 win over NYU at Yankee Stadium.

Tech's Pat Barron, despite the blindfold, returned this punt 92 yards for a touchdown vs. Penn, still number two in the GT record book.

Georgia's Milton Leathers comes up fast to hold this Tech runner to no gain on the play.

Bill Petersen,
Tech's All-Southern receiver.

In 1931 Tech hired a new assistant coach fresh out of Tennessee named Bobby Dodd.

1932: Eleanor Roosevelt Roots Georgia and Tech to 0-0 Tie

Tech and Georgia met on November 26, 1932, with the wind howling and a cold rain coming down in sheets. Another miserable day at Grant Field. To make things even worse, special guets for this game included Eleanor Roosevelt, Governor Richard Russell, and retired coaching legends Amos Alonzo Stagg and John Heisman. They were just four of the crowd of 18,000 who braved the elements to witness this contest. (By 1932 the nation was in the grip of the Great Depression, and to have 18,000 people show up for anything, short of a free bowl of soup, was considered a major achievement.)

But both teams were having their problems in 1932. Georgia was sporting a 2-5-1 record at this point, with wins over Florida and Clemson, a tie with UNC, and losses to VPI, Tulane, Vanderbilt, NYU and Auburn.

Tech, on the other hand, had also lost four games, but they had also won four, twice as many as Georgia. They had defeated Clemson, UNC, Alabama and Florida, while losing to Kentucky, Auburn, Vanderbilt and Tulane. Following the day's game they would travel all the way to Berkeley where they would lose 27-7 to California.

Georgia's Captain Vason McWhorter and Tech's Captain Howard "Monk" Neblett meet for the coin toss just prior to kickoff at Grant Field in 1932.

As had so frequently been the case in the past, Grant Field was a sea of mud at kickoff time.

Tech won the toss, glanced around at the muddy field and elected to let Georgia have the ball. Eddie Laws then kicked off to George "Buck" Chapman who ran it back to the Georgia 25-yard line.

And as Tech had hoped, on first down Chapman fumbled and Dave Wilcox recovered for the Tornadoes at the Georgia 26.

On first down Tech lost 14 yards, then Georgia's Byron Griffith intercepted a pass and Tech's big threat ended.

Later in the first quarter Tech had another chance to score when they took a punt back to the Georgia 45. In seven plays they had a first down at the 21. But then Marion Gaston intercepted a Tech pass and that was the end of that threat.

Still later, now in the third quarter, Tech had another golden opportunity to score when they fielded a Georgia punt at the Bulldog 30-yard line. But they fumbled on first down, Georgia recovered and thus escaped without harm.

Georgia's big chance came midway the fourth quarter when Vason McWhorter recovered a D. J. Phillips fumble at the Tech 36. Chapman carried the ball on three straight dives off tackle and gained 11 yards, down to the Tech 25 for a first down.

(This was Georgia's only earned first down of the game, the other one coming as the result of a penalty.) But then Tech held at their 20, and took possession of the ball.

Minutes later this game ended, a 0-0 tie. This was the third tie of the series, all by 0-0 scores.

Georgia had two first downs, 24 yards rushing and 0 yards passing. Tech had four first downs, 61 yards rushing, and one completed pass. Georgia punted 17 times, Tech 15 times.

What Eleanor Roosevelt thought about all this was not recorded.

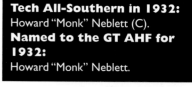

Tech All-Southern in 1932:
Howard "Monk" Neblett (C).
Named to the GT AHF for 1932:
Howard "Monk" Neblett.

Tech on the move as the Tornadoes defeated Clemson 32-14 in '32.

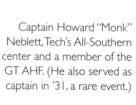

Captain Howard "Monk" Neblett, Tech's All-Southern center and a member of the GT AHF. (He also served as captain in '31, a rare event.)

Cy Grant, Georgia All-SEC halfback in '33.

R. H. Tharpe, an All-Southern tackle for Tech in '32.

Captain Vason McWhorter, center for the '32 Bulldogs.

LeRoy Moorehead, Georgia All-SEC guard.

The Bulldogs move the ball in their 13-6 losss to NYU in a game played in New York City.

Georgia and North Carolina battled to a 6-6 tie in '32.

This Tulane runner goes down but not before dropping the ball. Georgia lost this one 34-25 in a game played in New Orleans.

1933: The SEC Becomes a Reality

It was November 25, 1933, as the 7-1 Bulldogs prepared to meet the 4-4 Yellow Jackets at Grant Field. The experts gave Tech little chance in this contest, for this Georgia team was tough by anyone's standards. In fact, just the week prior to the Tech game they had been 7-0 on the season and were ranked second in the nation behind Michigan. But then came the big upset at the hands of Auburn (14-6), and Georgia's record had fallen to 7-1. Still, they were heavily favored to beat Tech.

As for the Jackets, they had beaten Clemson, Auburn, UNC and Florida at this point, while losing to Kentucky, Tulane, Vanderbilt and Alabama. Following the Georgia game they would beat a good Duke team (6-0) to complete their 5-5 season.

The year 1933 saw the formation of the Southeastern Conference, the most powerful conference in America, and Georgia had been a shoo-in to win the first SEC title ever, but then came pesky Auburn, and the rest is history.

The Jackets were heavy underdogs, but they played Georgia to a standstill throughout the first quarter.

But then with only moments left in the first period the Bulldogs had a first down at their own 21. At that point Homer Key took the snap from center, faded back to the 11, leaped high in the air and fired a pass to a wide-open Cy Grant at the 35.

Georgia Tech missed the PAT, and Georgia then hung on to win a close one, 7-6 at Grant Field.

Grant caught the ball on the run and didn't slow down until he'd crossed Tech's goal line some 65 yards away. It was a 79-yard pass play, still the longest pass play in the history of this long series. Grant then kicked the PAT and Georgia led 7-0.

The second period had just begun when Tech drove from their own 35 to the Georgia 9, but the Bulldogs held and that was the end of that threat.

Then, following an exchange of punts, Tech took the ball at the Georgia 46. After two running plays they were facing a third and 11. At that point D. J. Phillips threw a 19-yard completion to Jerry Perkerson, and the Jackets had a first down at the Georgia 28. A running play netted three yards, then Charles Galloway tossed an 18-yard completion to Tom Sprading and Tech had a first down at the Georgia 7.

Captain Graham Batchelor, an All-SEC end for Georgia in '33.

On first down W. S. Martin swept right end for the score and Davis Wilcox lined up to try for the tying PAT. But the holder on this play, C. H. Roberts, bobbled the snap from center, and Georgia still led 7-6.

Late in the game Tech took the ball at their own one-yard line, and it looked as though the game were over. But then Phillips went to the air and passed the Jackets down to the Bulldog four-yard line. There, facing a fourth down, Tech called time-out.

Coach Bill Alexander called on Wilcox to kick a field goal at that point. Initially, his

Chick Galloway,
Tech back.

kick appeared to be good but then it sailed wide right, and the Bulldogs were lucky to walk away with a hard earned 7-6 win.

On Sunday morning Morgan Blake wrote in the *Journal*: "This last ditch performance of Tech's courageous eleven was one of the finest drives any team ever made. Out of the deep valley of defeat, the Golden Tornadoes came storming."

UGA All-SEC in 1933:
Graham Batchelor (E), LeRoy Moorhead (G), Cy Grant (HB), Homer Key (HB) and George Chapman.
Named to the UGA SHF for 1933:
Graham Batchelor.
Tech All-SEC in 1933:
Bob Tharpe (T), Jimmy Slocum (E), Jack Phillips (FB), Clyde Williams (T) and Dave Wilcox (G).
Named to the GT AHF for 1933:
Jimmy Slocum and Wink Davis.

Clyde "Pee Wee" Williams,
All-SEC tackle for Tech.

Ed Laws and Bob Tharpe,
co-captains of the '33
Tornadoes.

Bill Martin scoots in for a touchdown to narrow Georgia's lead to 7-6, which would be the final score.

Georgia defender Joe Grant breaks up this Tech pass in the end zone to preserve a 7-6 Bulldog win.

1934: Tech Fights the Good Fight but Loses 7-0

It was December 1, 1934, a bright, sunlit afternoon at Sanford Stadium, as some 22,000 fans turned out to see what would happen when these two old rivals went head-on in their twenty-ninth meeting. At this point Georgia held a 14-11-3 lead in the series with every intention of adding one more game to their win column this afternoon. Indeed, Tech had not beaten Georgia since 1928 and the experts were giving them little chance in '34.

Georgia was enjoying a fairly good 6-3 season at that point with wins over Stetson, Furman, Florida, Yale, NC State and Auburn, and losses to UNC, Tulane and Alabama. Over the past month, however, Georgia had totally destroyed four opponent, giving up only seven points in the process. They seemed to be getting stronger as the season progressed.

As for Tech, they were suffering through a 1-8 season at this point. They had a good 12-7 win over Clemson in their season opener, but then the injury-laden Jackets had reeled off eight consecutive losses—to Vanderbilt, Duke, Michigan, Tulane, UNC, Auburn, Alabama and Florida. Indeed, Tech would not experience a worse season until 1981 when they went 1-10 on the season.

And the experts were right about today's game. Georgia would take it--but they'd have to work like the dickens to do it.

Midway the first quarter Georgia had the ball deep in Tech territory, but then Charley Preston intercepted a pass and returned it to the Tech 41. Over the next three minutes Tech's Shorty Roberts would rip off runs of eight and ten yards, toss a pass of 19 yards to Jerry Perkerson, and suddenly the Jackets were at the Georgia eight-yard line.

However, Tech couldn't ram the ball over in four attempts, and Georgia dodged the bullet.

The rest of the first half was spent in pretty much the same way, with Georgia being held deep in their own territory, then punting out to midfield where Tech would put the ball in play. But the Jackets could put no points on the board.

The middle of the fourth quarter found these two teams still locked in a scoreless defensive duel. Then, with eight minutes left to play, Georgia took the ball at their own 45.

Four plays later Maurice Green scooted off-tackle for 13 yards and a first down at the Tech 30. Glenn Johnson then ran for 9 yards and

Georgia end Henry Wagnon has just taken a pitch from fullback Maurice Green on an end-around play as the Bulldogs edged Georgia Tech 7-0 on a sunny December day in Athens.

Green for two, then came a 5-yard penalty against Tech, and Georgia had the ball at the Tech 19.

On the next play Alf Anderson skirted left end for 14 yards, down to the Tech 5. And by this time it was obvious to everyone in the stadium that the Tech boys were totally exhausted. But still they didn't quit.

Georgia ran the ball twice and gained nothing. They then tried a pass which was batted down by Jack Phillips.

There were now four minutes left to play, and Georgia was looking at a fourth and goal from the Tech five. At that point Henry Wagnon informed quarterback Maurice Green that on the previous play no one was covering him as he ran into the end zone. Green called the same pass play. And sure enough, Green took the snap from center, looked downfield, and there, standing all alone in the end zone, was Henry Wagon. Green fired the ball, Wagnon made the catch, and Georgia took the lead 6-0. Cy Grant then kicked the point, and Georgia won this viciously fought contest 7-0.

Al Minot, Georgia halfback.

Georgia QB Jack Griffith.

George Chapman,
All-SEC Georgia halfback.

John Brown,
All-SEC Georgia guard.

John McKnight,
All-SEC Georgia center.

Team captain Charlie Turbyville takes this pass for a 14-yard gain as the Bulldogs went down 14-0 to the UNC Tarheels.

Clyde Williams, Tech All-SEC tackle.

Tech Coach
Bill Alexander.

L. C. Hayes,
Tech halfback.

Tech's L. C. Hayes
sweeps left end as
the Tornadoes fell
to Duke 20-0.

1935: Tech Breaks Long Losing Streak

It was November 30, 1935, and Tech had not beaten Georgia since 1928, and fans were beginning to shake their heads. Over the previous six years, since their great national championship team of '28, Bill Alexander and his Tornadoes had won a total of only 17 games. What was going on up there?

As for 1935, Tech had started well enough, with wins over both Presbyterian College and Sewanee, but then they'd lost to Kentucky. Then they'd come back with a big win over a strong Duke team, but then they'd suffered consecutive losses to UNC, Vanderbilt, Auburn and Alabama. Then they'd beaten Florida the week before the day's biggie with Georgia. It was truly difficult to predict just what Tech was going to do in '35.

As for Georgia, they appeared to have their feet planted a little more firmly on solid ground. To open the '35 season they'd reeled off wins over Mercer, Chattanooga, Furman and NC State before losing to Alabama. Then came wins over Florida and Tulane. At that point they were 6-1 and looking forward to an excellent season, but they'd lost to both LSU and Auburn and were carrying a so-so 6-3 record into the Tech game.

Some 26,000 fans turned out at Grant Field for this thirtieth encounter between these two schools (Georgia led in the series 15-11-3), and once it was over most of them walked away well pleased that they'd gotten their money's worth.

Tech held their own throughout the first period and even drove to the Georgia three before giving the ball over to the Bulldogs.

At that point Georgia went on the offensive, with Paul Causey dashing for 24 yards on one play and Al Minot for 46 yards on another, down to the Tech 13. Ward Holland bulled his way down to the 9, then Alf Anderson tossed the ball to Otis Maffett for the touchdown. Anderson kicked the point, and Georgia led 7-0.

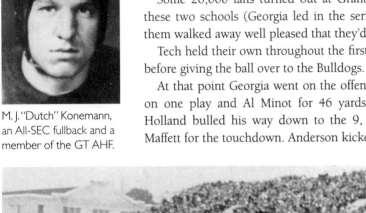

M. J. "Dutch" Konemann, an All-SEC fullback and a member of the GT AHF.

An exchange of punts later, Georgia was again on the move, with a first down at the Tech 34-yard line. But then Charles Preston intercepted an Anderson pass and Tech had possession at their own 21. Four plays later, from the Tech 41, Dutch Konemann took a pitch and raced 54 yards, down to the Georgia 5. L. C. Hayes scored on the next play, the PAT missed, and Tech now trailed 7-6.

Dutch Konemann streaks 54 yards to set up Tech's first TD of the day as the Jackets went on to defeat Georgia 19-7.

Then, midway through the third quarter, Tech scored again following an 11-play drive when Konemann went over from the 2. Fletcher Sims again missed the point, but Tech still led, 12-7.

Early in the fourth period Tech recovered a fumble at the Georgia 28. After two running plays had gained little, Fletcher Sims passed complete to A. E. Jones down to the Georgia four. George Edwards scored on the next play, Konemann kicked the point, and Tech beat Georgia 19-7, their first win over the Bulldogs since 1928.

Tech All-SEC in 1935:
J. M. FitzSimmons (G) and Dutch Konemann (HB).
UGA All-American in 1935:
John Bond (G).
UGA All-SEC in 1935:
Frank Johnson (G) and Otis Maffett (E).
UGA SHF in 1935:
Henry Wagnon and John Bond.

Captain R. W. Eubanks, Tech center.

J. M. FitzSimmons, All-SEC guard.

H. H. Appleby, Tech fullback.

George Edwards, Tech halfback.

Tech's H. H. Appleby breaks into the Georgia secondary as Tech went on to defeat the Bulldogs 19-7 at Grant Field.

Fletcher Sims, Tech's All-SEC QB.

L. C. Hayes makes a timely interception to stop a Georgia march.

1936: Georgia's Rugged Defense Tells the Story

I t would be an understatement to call the 1936 season an odd one for the University of Georgia. They opened with wins over Mercer and Furman, then reeled off losses to LSU, Rice, Auburn and Tennessee before beating both Florida and Tulane. But oddest of all, perhaps, is the way this so-so Georgia team went to New York and played unbeaten and unscored on Fordham to a shocking 7-7 tie. Playing in the line that year for Fordham were the famous Seven Blocks of Granite (including Vince Lombardi), and they were a shoo-in for the Rose Bowl. But this day the 4-4 Bulldogs played like world beaters as they upended the Rams and any hopes they might have had of a big post-season bowl game. Now the 4-4-1 Bulldogs were thinking of the Yellow Jackets and licking their chops.

As for Tech, they had not enjoyed a winning season now since they'd won the national championship in 1928. At this point in 1936 they had beaten Presbyterian College, in their first night game ever, by a score of 55-0. Then they dispatched both Sewanee (58-0) and Kentucky (38-0) before losing to Duke. Then came a 0-0 tie with Vandy, followed by one-point losses to both Clemson and Auburn and a 20-16 loss to Alabama. Then they beat Florida, and were 4-4-1 as they began preparing for Georgia.

On November 28, some 23,000 fans streamed into Sanford Stadium to watch these two 4-4-1 teams slug it out.

Following the opening kickoff Georgia moved to Tech's 15-yard line. But then L. C. Hayes intercepted Bill Hartman in the end zone and the ball was brought out to the 20.

First down for the Jackets. But the center snapped the ball over everyone's head and the ball bounded into the Tech end zone. Marion Konemann desperately gave chase and picked up the ball, but Quinton Lumpkin and Otis Maffet nailed him behind the goal line and the score became 2-0, Georgia's favor.

Tech's Dutch Konemann, Jack Chivington and C. R. Wood close in on Georgia's Jim Fordham in a game played at Sanford Stadium.

Later, early in the third quarter, with Georgia still holding their slim 2-0 lead, Tech took the ball at the Bulldog 44. Harry Appleby, Konemann, and Fletcher Sims then alternated runs and Tech quickly found themselves at the Georgia 28. Sims then threw passes of seven and eleven yards to Konemann and Georgia was backed up to their own eight. Then Sims took it in on the next play, but missed the PAT, and Tech led 6-2.

Following an exchange of punts, Tech fumbled at their own 19, and Maffett recovered for Georgia. Eight plays later Glenn Johnson scored from the five, Lew Johnson's kick was good, and Georgia led 9-6.

Later, with only five minutes left in the contest, Georgia began a drive from their own 26. Nine plays later Alf Anderson tossed a short pass to Lew Johnson who waltzed into the end zone from the five. Young kicked the point, and Georgia walked away with a 16-6 victory.

So Georgia finished the season with a 5-4-1 record, while Georgia Tech would go on to defeat mighty California 13-7 at Grant Field to finish with a 5-5-1 record. (This was Tech's first 11-game schedule in history.)

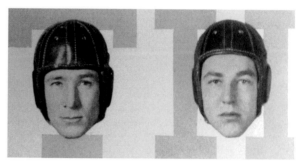

James Hall and Harry Harmon, co-captains of the 1936 Georgia Bulldogs.

Glenn Johnson breaks into Tech's secondary, setting up another Georgia score at Sanford Stadium.

Team captain James Hall intercepts Tech's L. C. Hayes as the Bulldogs beat the Tornadoes 16-6.

Tech's All-American halfback J. L. Chivington puts the stop on a Blue Devil running back as the Jackets lost to Duke 19-6 in a game played in Durham.

Bill Jordan, All-American end and a member of the GT AHF.

Tech All-American and GT AHF member Bill Jordan, pursued here by an eager defender, takes another pass as the Jackets beat Sewanee 58-0 in '36. (As late as 1936 some players still refused to wear helmets.)

Middleton FitzSimmons, team captain and an All-SEC guard for the '36 Yellow Jackets.

Dutch Konemann catches this Fletcher Sims pass on a grim day at Grant Field as the Jackets upended California 13-7 to conclude a 5-5-1 season.

1937: Hartman and Sims Battle to 6-6 Tie

It was November 27, 1937, and the stands at Grant Field were crammed to the rafters as 30,000 fans turned out to watch this 32nd encounter between the Georgia Bulldogs and the Georgia Tech Yellow Jackets.

The Bulldogs at this point were 5-3-1 on the season, with wins over Oglethorpe, USC, Clemson, Mercer and Tulane, and losses to Holy Cross, Tennessee and Florida, and a tie with Auburn. Georgia's offense had begun to sputter as the season progressed, and they'd scored but one touchdown in their past four games. Indeed, many fans doubted they'd even be able to score against Tech's stingy defense.

Indeed, Tech had given up but one touchdown in their past four games, and were sporting a good 6-3 record as they prepared for Georgia, with wins over Presbyterian College, Mercer, Kentucky, Vanderbilt, Clemson and Florida. They had lost by one point to Duke (20-19) and by one touchdown to Alabama (7-0), and were blown out by Auburn (21-0). All in all, not a bad season.

Those fans who love to consider all the dark intangibles when picking a favorite pointed out that today would mark Coach Harry Mehre's final game against Tech. After ten years he would soon be leaving, and thus the Bulldogs would be pulling out all the stops when they took the field this afternoon.

Again, as had happened so often in the past, the rain had been falling throughout the day and by game time the field was ankle-deep in mud.

The first quarter was scoreless, a defensive duel, with both teams punting on first and second downs.

Indeed, Georgia's Bill Hartman punted 15 times in this game, averaging a phenomenal 42 yards per kick.

The first half ended, a 0-0 tie. But then Tech kicked off to open the second half, and that's when the fireworks started. Bill Hartman took the ball at his own seven, fumbled it, picked it up, then ran 93 yards straight down the field for a touchdown. Hartman missed the PAT, but Georgia held a big 6-0 lead.

Then late in the third quarter Tech got their big opportunity when Jim Fordham fumbled at the Georgia 17 and Dutch Konemann recovered for the Yellow Jackets. Three plays later they were at the Bulldog eight, but then Harry Appleby was thrown for an 11-yard loss and Georgia had dodged another bullet.

But on first down Oliver Honeycutt fumbled and Charles Wood recovered for the Jackets at the 17. On first down Sims threw to Konemann down to the one.

Captain Fletcher Sims, All-SEC quarterback, scored Tech's lone touchdown vs. Georgia in 1937.

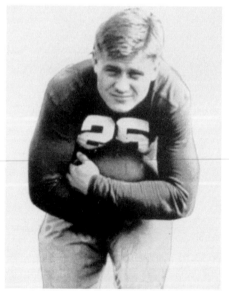

Bill Hartman, Georgia's All-American fullback, is a member of the College Football Hall of Fame. (He had an 82-yard punt vs. Tulane, still number two in the UGA record book.

Sims went over on the next play. Quinton Lumpkin blocked the PAT, to the relief of Georgia fans everywhere, and the game ended, a 6-6 tie.

On December 10 the Bulldogs would defeat Miami 26-8 in their final game to conclude a 6-3-2 season.

Lewis Young, Georgia quarterback, takes it to the Tigers as the Bulldogs beat Clemson 14-0 in a game played at Sanford Stadium.

Captain Bill Hartman of Georgia and his Miami counterpart meet just prior to kickoff as part of the gala celebration to dedicate Miami's new Roddey Burdine Stadium (it cost almost $325,000 to construct). Despite the festivities, the Bulldogs overwhelmed their hosts by a score of 26-8 in Georgia's first night game ever. This was Coach Harry Mehre's final game with the Bulldogs.

All-American fullback Bill Hartman carries for a nice gain as Georgia lost to Florida 6-0.

Jack Nixon makes a hard tackle as Tech beat Florida 12-0 in 1937.

J. S. Bartlett picked up 26 yards on this end sweep as the Jackets beat Kentucky 32-0.

The Georgia Tech marching band of 1937.

1938: Another 0-0 Tie!

Coach Joel Hunt would work with the Bulldogs for only the 1938 season. Today he is best remembered for having brought aboard a young assistant named Wally Butts.

But on November 27, the date of the Tech game, Georgia was rolling along with a mediocre 5-3 record, having beaten The Citadel, USC, Furman, Mercer and Florida, and lost to Holy Cross, Tulane and Auburn.

Georgia's Bill Mims is brought down by Tom Allen's one-handed tackle as the Bulldogs and Jackets tied 0-0 in 1938.

Tech halfback Bobby Beers seems to be having the time of his life as he eludes this Georgia defensive back for a good gain.

As for Tech, Bill Alexander was now in his eighteenth season as head coach of the Yellow Jackets and suffering through a poor 3-3-2 season, with wins over Mercer, Auburn and Kentucky, and losses to Notre Dame, Duke and Vanderbilt. Plus there were ties with Alabama and Florida.

And even though Georgia's won-loss record was better than Tech's, the experts pointed out that Tech had played a significantly tougher schedule.

It might also be pointed out that Coach Alexander's wife was critically ill in an Atlanta hospital and thus he did not accompany the team to the game, turning over his responsibilities to his assistants Bobby Dodd and Mack Tharpe.

The weather for today's game, believe it or not, was truly excellent, pleasantly cool with plenty of sunshine, as some 28,000 fans streamed into Sanford Stadium. And they all came to their feet as Tech's Howard Ector kicked off to Georgia's Earl Hise.

The first 25 minutes saw this game become the usual Georgia-Georgia Tech stalemate, with neither team able to make much headway against the other.

But then Tech took the ball at their own 30, and on first down Bobby Beers streaked 32 yards on an end sweep, down to the Georgia 38. Seven plays later the Jackets were at the 20, facing a fourth and one. Howard Ector took a handoff and struggled down to the Georgia ten. Three plays later and Tech was knocking at the door from the two. It was fourth down and two, and Tech sent in their place-kicker Alex Shaw.

Shaw faked the kick and passed to Ector, but Billy Mims broke up the play and Georgia escaped with no harm done.

Then, midway the fourth period, Tech again threatened when Ector intercepted a pass and returned it 23 yards to the Tech 43. On first down Joe Bartlette passed to George Smith who lateralled to Jack Chivington, good for eight yards. Then Ector ran for another eight, down to the Georgia 47. Then came Bartlette for 15, Gay Thrash for five, and Bartlette again for 18, and Tech had a first down at the Georgia nine-yard line.

Then it was Bartlette again, first to the five and then to the two. On third down he was stopped for no gain, and Tech was once more looking at a fourth down at the Georgia two.

Again Alex Shaw entered the game. Only this was no fake. Standing at the 14, he took the snap from center, dropped back three steps and drop-kicked the ball towards the uprights. Unfortunately, his kick was inches short, and again Georgia had twisted off the bullseye.

Just prior to the final whistle Tech again moved to the Georgia 24, then Beers ran it down to the eight. But a holding penalty moved the ball back to the 39. And that was the old ball game, a 0-0 tie, the fourth 0-0 tie in this series.

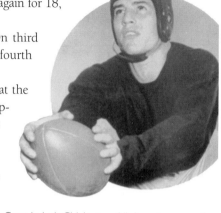

Captain Jack Chivington, All-American guard and a member of the GT AHF.

UGA All-SEC in 1938:
Quinton Lumpkin (C), Jim Fordham (FB).
Named to the UGA SHF:
Quinton Lumpkin.
Tech All-American in 1938:
Jack Chivington (G).
Tech All-SEC in 1938:
J. L. Brooks (G).
Named to the GT AHF:
Bill Jordan.

Tech end, George Smith, makes a super catch of this TD pass to beat Auburn 7-6.

Tech's All-SEC halfback Howard Ector, vaults in for a score as the Jackets lost to Notre Dame 14-6.

Howard Ector, an All-American back and a member of the GT AHF.

Accompanied by Governor Rivers, UGA Chancellor Sanford, President Caldwell (and Secret Service agents), President Franklin D. Roosevelt is presented an honorary doctorate of law by the University of Georgia in October, 1938.

Earl Hise took a short pass good for five yards as Georgia beat Furman 38-7.

Playing in downtown Athens on November 27, 1938 was Spring Madness, starring Maureen O'Sullivan, Lew Aires and Ruth Hussey.

Coach Joel Hunt, a former Texas A&M star, is best known for having brought Wallace Butts in as his assistant coach.

1939: Bowl Bound Tech Won't Be Denied

It was December 2, 1939, but Adolph Hitler and his war in Europe was a world away as Coach Wally Butts wound up his first season as head coach of the Georgia Bulldogs. It had not been a terrible season, but then it hadn't been a particularly good one either. Indeed the Bulldogs were 4-5 as they prepared to go up against Tech this afternoon, with wins over The Citadel, Mercer, Florida and USC, and losses to Furman, Holy Cross, Kentucky, NYU and Auburn. (Furman beat Georgia 20-0 in 1939, a loss Bulldog fans found most disturbing.) They would end the season with a good 13-0 win over Miami on December 8.

But the Yellow Jackets were romping-stomping in 1939 and could hardly wait to get their hands on those stumbling Bulldogs. Indeed, Tech was 6-2 coming into this game, their two close losses coming at the hands of national powers Notre Dame (17-14) and Duke (7-6).

They would complete the season with a 7-2 record, be declared SEC champions, then go on to defeat Missouri in the 1940 Orange Bowl. Quite a year!

Some 30,000 fans turned out at Grant Field to see if Tech could live up to their advanced billing as the clear favorites to take this game today. Georgia had promised that, win or lose, Tech would know they'd been in a football game, and they were telling the truth. Sports writers at the time described this contest as one of the most viciously fought in recent memory.

Following an exchange of punts in the first quarter, Tech moved to the Georgia 14 yard line. But then Jim Fordham intercepted a Johnny Bosch pass and that was the end of that threat.

Minutes later Tech's Howard Ector fumbled at the Tech 40 and James Skipworth recovered for the Bulldogs. Vassa Cate and Cliff Kimsey then alternated runs down to the Tech 18, but a holding penalty killed that drive and Tech was off the hook.

Then, on the final play of the first quarter, Georgia fumbled at their 40, and Eston Lackey recovered for Tech.

Four plays later Tech had moved to the 25, but then a 15-yard penalty moved the ball back to the 40, and Georgia fans breathed a sigh of relief.

For the first time ever, fans were treated to a look at Georgia sensation Frankie "Fireball" Sinkwich as the Baby Jackets and the Bullpups played their annual freshman game on Thanksgiving Day, 1939. Back in those days Georgia was running the single-wing formation, and Sinkwich was their tailback, the best in America.

But they breathed too early, for on the next play Earl Whelby ran for 16 yards, down to the 24, and the Yellow Jackets were back in business.

Then Joe Bartlett made a great catch of a Bosch pass at the Georgia 9. Bosch kept the ball on the next play and behind heavy blocking swung around right end and into the end zone for a Tech touchdown. C. P. Goree's kick failed, but Tech had a 6-0 lead. And that's how the first half ended.

With eight minutes elapsed in the third period Tech's Charles Wood blocked a punt and George Webb recovered for the Yellow Jackets at the Georgia 42. Tech then marched to the Bulldog 9, but Vassa Cate intercepted a Bosch pass at the four, ending another Tech threat.

Three plays later Cliff Kimsey punted out to the Georgia 40. With C. P. Goree, Bobby Beers, George Webb and Howard Ector alternating runs, Tech soon moved to the 23. Then, facing a second and nine, Beers pitched out to Bob Ison who ran it down to the 4. Goree scored on the next play, then kicked the point, and Tech took this game 13-0.

At this point the Yellow Jackets were 7-2 on the season, champions of the SEC, and on their way to Miami where they would defeat Missouri (champions of the Big Six Conference) 21-7 in the 1940 Orange Bowl.

At the conclusion of the 1939 season, with some 48 years of football under their belts, Georgia and Georgia Tech's overall won-loss records (which were among the best in the nation) stacked up this way: Georgia was 209-136-30 and Tech was 213-135-26. (Pretty darned good for both teams!)

TOP:
N. M. "Hawk" Cavette, Tech's All-SEC halfback. Cavette punted 21 times vs. Florida in 1938, still an all-time GT record.

MIDDLE:
Captain R. W. Murphy, Tech's All-SEC quarterback.

BOTTOM:
Bob Ison, All-American end and member of the GT AHF.

Tech's Howard Ector, an All-American halfback and a member of the GT AHF, carried the mail as the Tornadoes lost a close one to Duke 7-6.

It was New Year's Day in Miami, the Orange Bowl, and Tech upset favored Missouri 21-7. Here R. L. "Buck" Ison, an All-American end, gallops 59 yards for Tech's first TD of the afternoon. That's Neil Cavette getting ready to lower the boom on an inquisitive Tiger.

Coach James Wallace Butts, head coach of the Bulldogs for 21 years (1939–60), led Georgia to four SEC championships and eight bowl games.

Alternate captain Glenn Johnson, guard.

James Skipworth, a member of the UGA SHF.

Captain Vassa Cate, All-SEC halfback for the Bulldogs, had a 95-yard KO return vs. South Carolina in '39, still number three in the UGA record book.

Georgia's great backfield for 1939 (L-R): Vassa Cate, Bob Salisbury, Jim Fordham and Bill Mims.

1940: Sinkwich, Missed Kicks Give Georgia Hard Win

It was November 30, 1940, a beautiful day in late fall, as 28,000 fans streamed into Sanford Stadium for the 35th meeting between Georgia and Georgia Tech.

At this point Tech had not lived up to their pre-season billing, and were struggling along with a poor 2-6-1 record. They'd beaten only Howard College of Alabama and Vandy, while losing to Notre Dame, Auburn, Duke, Kentucky, Alabama and Florida. Following today's loss to Georgia, they'd go on to upset a good California team by a score of 13-0 to end the season with a 3-7 record.

As for Georgia, they weren't doing a great deal better. At this point in the season they were 3-4-1, with wins over Oglethorpe, USC and Auburn; losses to Ole Miss, Columbia, Florida and Tulane; and a tie with Kentucky. Following today's win over Tech, they would soundly beat Miami 28-7 to end the season with a 5-4-1 record.

Still, Georgia now had on hand a secret weapon by the name of Frankie Sinkwich, a young sophomore quarterback who had already begun to stun the football world with his incredible gridiron exploits.

For the first time ever, Tech's players were wearing navy blue jerseys, a break from their usual mustard-colored tops.

Tech took the opening kickoff and surprised the crowd with the way they immediately began to move against the highly favored Bulldogs. Johnny Bosch ran the kickoff back to his own 27. Just four plays later (including a 27-yard pass from Johnny Bosch to Bobby Beers), Tech was at the Georgia 13.

Then on three straight plays, Ralph Plaster took cracks at that big Georgia line, taking the ball down to the three. Then Beers went in for the TD, Plaster kicked the point and Tech led 7-0.

Then, late in the second quarter, Georgia had the ball at their own eight when Heyward Allen started to toss a short pass but dropped the ball. Charles Sanders recovered for Tech at the four, and the Jackets were again in business.

Three plays later Plaster went in for the score, missed the PAT, and Tech led 13-0.

Georgia then took the kickoff and in six plays moved to the Tech 19. From there, facing fourth and 10, Heyward Allen threw incomplete, but Tech was called for interference, and Georgia had a first down at the 11. James Todd then threw to Carl Grate in the end zone, Leo Costa kicked the point, and Tech's lead was cut to 13-7 as the half came to a close.

It was in the second half, then, that Frankie Sinkwich began to assert himself. Georgia took the opening kickoff back to their 35. Sinkwich passed to Lamar "Race Horse" Davis for 12 yards, then he himself ran for 12 yards. Cliff Kimsey carried to the

In many ways the story of Georgia football between 1940 and 1942 is the story of Frankie Sinkwich. Today, after more than half a century, many still consider the 1942 Heisman Trophy winner to be the finest all-around backs ever to play for the Bulldogs.

Tech 34, then Sinkwich ran for another 11, down to the 23. Then Sinkwich threw to James Skipworth for 12 yards, and the Dogs had a first down at the 11. On first down Sinkwich fired a scoring strike to Paul Kluk. Costa's PAT was good and Georgia was up 14-13.

Moments later Tom Witt intercepted Bosch and returned it to the Jackets 27. Sinkwich ran for six yards and Kimsey for three. Sinkwich scored on the next play, but a penalty brought the ball back. But two plays later, quite undaunted, Sinkwich threw a TD pass to Skipworth, Will Burt kicked the PAT and Georgia took the lead at 21-13.

Late in the game Tech scored again when Bosch threw a 17-yard strike to Webb in the end zone, but the PAT missed and Georgia was up 21-19.

With only moments left Tech tried a field goal from the 32, but the ball fell short and Georgia walked away with a hard earned 21-19 victory.

As for Sinkwich, he had 127 yards rushing on 28 carries, and 12 pass completions for another 106 yards and two TDs.

Sinkwich and Coach Butts during an evening game with Oglethorpe at Atlanta's Ponce de Leon Park. (Georgia won, 53-0.)

Tech All-American in 1940:
Bob Ison (E).
Tech All-SEC in 1940:
Johnny Bosch (QB).
Named to the GT AHF:
Bob Ison and Charlie Wood.
Named to the UGA SHF:
James Skipworth, Jr.

The Yellow Jackets missed two PATs and a field goal and fell 21-19 to Georgia.

Bulldog co-captains for 1940, James Skipworth and Bobby Nowell.

All-SEC halfback Lamar "Race Horse" Davis goes around end for a score as Georgia smothered South Carolina 33-2. Davis had a 96-yard KO return vs. Tulane in 1940, still number two in the UGA record book.

G. C. Wilkins and J. E. Nettles put the stop on this Vandy runner as Tech won 19-0.

John Bosch, Tech's All-SEC QB.

The starting lineup for the Yellow Jackets of 1940.

Bobby Beers lunging forward for a first down as Tech lost to Florida 16-7.

1941: Sinkwich Leads Georgia to a Big Win

As the '41 season rolled to a close Wally Butts and his Georgia Bulldogs were having a great year. In fact, they'd finish the season with a 9-1-1 record, their best since they'd won the national championship with a 9-1 record in 1927. And much of their success could be attributed to their junior All-American tailback, Frankie Sinkwich. He entered the Tech game with 1,038 yards rushing, just 84 yards shy of the all-time NCAA single-season rushing record. Aided and abetted by a bevy of great teammates, he would lead Georgia to a number-six national ranking, and to their first bowl game ever. (Incredibly, Sinkwich performed his miracles in '41 while wearing an ungainly face mask because of a broken jaw.)

As for Tech, they were struggling in '41. As November 29 rolled around, they were 3-5 on the season with wins over Chattanooga, Auburn and Kentucky, and losses to Notre Dame, Vanderbilt, Duke, Alabama and Florida. They were heavy underdogs in today's game with Georgia.

It was an unusually warm fall day as some 32,000 fans packed Grant Field for this 32nd meeting between these two old rivals.

(Only eight days after the day's game the Japanese attacked Pearl Harbor and the world would never again be the same.)

As usual, the first quarter was scoreless. But late in the second, Tech punted to their own 49-yard line. Twelve plays later, after a 47-yard drive, Sinkwich tossed a 4-yard pass to George Poschner for the touchdown. Leo Costa's PAT was good, and Georgia went to the sideline leading 7-0.

Despite the fact that Georgia obviously had the superior team, Tech fought gallantly and turned away threat

Heyward Allen, halfback and captain of the '41 Bulldogs, meets his TCU counterpart just moments prior to kickoff in the '42 Orange Bowl. Georgia won this wild-scoring contest 40-26.

TOP:
Walter Ruark, All-SEC guard.

BOTTOM:
Georgia center Steve Hughes returned an interception 89 yards for a TD vs. The Citadel in '42, still number three in the UGA record book.

after threat to their goal line. Indeed, it was not until late in the third quarter that the Bulldogs were able to mount another scoring drive.

Georgia took the ball at the Tech 46. On first down Sinkwich passed 14 yards to Cliff Kimsey, then Poschner ran for another 6, down to the 26. Sinkwich then threw a bullet to Melvin Conger in the Tech end zone for another score. Costa's PAT was good and Georgia went up 14-0.

Fifteen minutes later, with only minutes left in the final quarter, Sinkwich drilled a 32-yard pass to Lamar "Racehorse" Davis for another touchdown. Costa's kick was again good, and Georgia took the lead, and the game, 21-0.

Sinkwich finished the game with 64 yards rushing, and completed 15 passes for another 197 yards and three touchdowns.

As for Georgia's performance in the '42 Orange Bowl (their first bowl appearance ever), the Bulldogs smothered TCU by a score of 40-26. Sinkwich rushed for 139 yards, including a 43-yard TD run, and passed for another 243 yards, including TD tosses of 60 and 61 yards—an Orange Bowl total offense record.

Heyward Allen (WB), Coach Butts, and Cliff Kimsey (BB).

And it's old number 21, Frankie Sinkwich, the Georgia Fireball, running wild as he led the Bulldogs to a big 40-26 win over TCU in the Orange Bowl. Sinkwich ran for 139 yards (including a 43-yard TD run) in this game and completed nine passes for another 243 yards and three TDs.

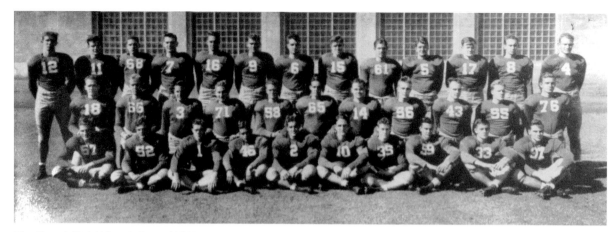

The Georgia Tech Yellow Jackets of 1941.

George Webb, Tech's All-SEC end.

John Bosch eludes this defender as Tech went on to defeat Chattanooga 20-0 to kickoff the '41 season.

George Webb nails this Moccasin runner as Tech beat Chattanooga.

1942: Georgia Again Wins the National Title

As Georgia and Tech prepared to meet each other on November 28, the Bulldogs were sporting a 9-1 record and ranked number 5 in the nation. Only a week before they had been 9-0 and ranked number one in the nation, but then came an incredible upset loss to a so-so Auburn team (27-13) and the Bulldogs fell to number five.

As for Georgia Tech, led by their All-American freshman tailback Clint Castleberry, they were enjoying a superb 9-0 season and ranked number two in the nation. Yes, only the week previous, the great state of Georgia boasted the top two football teams in America. But then came Auburn, and Boston College thereafter held the number one ranking.

Both colleges were aware of the rewards riding on the outcome of this contest. The winner had a chance to be named national champions. As though that weren't enough, two days prior to the day's game, the Rose Bowl Committee announced that the winner would be invited to Pasadena to play UCLA in the 1943 Rose Bowl.

It would be an understatement to say that interest in the day's contest was rampant. Thousands of extra seats were added to Sanford Stadium to accomodate fans who were coming from all over America. Dozens of panting sports writers from as far away as Seattle had applied for press passes.

Following the opening kickoff, the teams exchanged punts, and then from the Tech 37 Clint Castleberry, Tech's great All-American freshman tailback, tossed a short pass which was intercepted by Frankie Sinkwich. On first down Sinkwich dashed for 20 yards, down to the 17. Then, on second down, future All-American Charley Trippi passed 17 yards to Van Davis for a touchdown. Leo Costa's kick was good, and Georgia led 7-0.

On Tech's next possession they punted out of bounds at the Georgia 8. Jacket fans breathed a sigh of relief at that point, but nine plays later Georgia scored again when Van Davis went over from the four. Costa's kick was good and the score went to 14-0.

Then, just before halftime, Tech punted out at the Georgia 13. On first down Trippi drifted back to pass but changed his mind and began to run. He didn't stop until he'd crossed the goal line 87 yards downfield. (This remains the longest run ever in this series.) Georgia went in at halftime leading 20-0.

As for the third quarter, it too was all Georgia. The Bulldogs scored twice more, once when Trippi hit Van Davis

This handsome Tech freshman was known to his classmates simply as Jimmy. In later years he became known to the world as President Carter.

Frankie Sinkwich, an All-American tailback and winner of the Heisman Trophy in '42, slashes through the Tech line as Georgia defeated the Tornadoes 34-0.

with a 42-yard TD pass (Davis' third TD of the day), and later when Clyde Ehrhardt intercepted a pass and returned it 27 yards for a touchdown. And Georgia won this game 34-0.

Following their 9-0 win over UCLA in the '43 Rose Bowl, the Bulldogs would be declared national champions.

Georgia Tech, with a fine 9-1 record, would lose 14-7 to Texas in the

TOP:
Dick McPhee, fullback for the Bulldogs. McPhee would continue his career at Georgia in '46, following the Second World War.

SECOND:
George Poschner, Georgia All-American end. Poschner's three touchdown receptions vs. Florida in '42 is still a UGA record.

THIRD:
Lamar "Racehorse" Davis, an All-SEC halfback. Note: Davis averaged 28.5 yards per catch in '42, still number one in the UGA record book.

BOTTOM:
Charley Trippi, who would become an All-American tailback in '46, following World War II.

TOP:
Gene Ellenson, an All-SEC Georgia tackle.

BOTTOM:
Ardie McClure, fullback.

Fireball Sinkwich slices through the Jackets' line as Georgia went on to beat an excellent Tech team by a score of 34-0.

TOP:
Captain Jack Marshall, Tech's All-SEC end.

SECOND:
Harvey Hardy, Tech's All-American guard.

THIRD:
George Manning, All-SEC center for Georgia Tech.

BOTTOM:
Co-captain R. A. Plaster.

R. A. Plaster zips through the Notre Dame defense for a touchdown as Tech upset the Mighty Irish 13-6.

The amazing Clint Castleberry outruns the entire Alabama defensive unit for a TD as Tech went on to a 7-0 win on their way to a great 9-1-0 season, a number five national ranking and a Cotton Bowl bid versus the University of Texas. His tragic death in World War II is still remembered.

Georgia cheerleaders Ann Findley, Kathryn Rice and Martha Sullivan were on hand in Pasadena to root the boys on.

Frankie Sinkwich, Coach Wally Butts and All-SEC guard Walt Ruark pose for the press just before leaving for Pasadena and their big meeting with UCLA in the '43 Rose Bowl.

The Bulldog dream backfield of '42: Frankie Sinkwich, Charley Trippi, Dick McPhee and Lamar "Racehorse" Davis.

Georgia defeated UCLA in the '43 Rose Bowl by a score of 9-0. Charley Trippi, filling in for the injured Sinkwich, gained 118 yards in this game and received the game's MVP Award. Trippi was recently named to the All-Time Rose Bowl Team.

Lamar Davis returned the opening kickoff 78 yards before being pulled down by the Bruins in the '43 Rose Bowl. The Bulldogs would win this one to complete a great 11-1-0 season and be declared national champions.

It's Frankie Sinkwich going over for the fourth quarter touchdown that would seal the fate of UCLA.

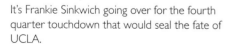

Gridiron Immortals

Frankie Sinkwich

After the passage of almost 60 years, Frankie "Fireball" Sinkwich continues to personify the very best in Georgia football. A native of Youngstown, Ohio, he was a great fellow off the field and was without peer on the field. He ran a 9.8 second 100-yard dash and still holds numerous offensive records for the Bulldogs.

For example:

- In 1942 he scored 16 touchdowns and 96 total points. These single-season figures for a running back stood for forty-four years in the UGA record book.
- He averaged 7.9 yards per carry in '42, still number-one in the UGA record book.
- He completed 14 TD passes in '41, still number five in the UGA record book.
- He threw 30 TD passes during his career, still number five in the UGA record book.
- He accounted for five touchdowns vs. Cincinnati in '42 (three running, two passing), still number one in the UGA record book.
- He accounted for 59 touchdowns during his career, still number two in the UGA record book.
- He was named All-SEC for three seasons, All-American in '41 and '42, and was awarded the Heisman Trophy in '42.
- He is a member of the College Football Hall of Fame.
- His is one of only four jerseys ever retired by the University of Georgia.

Clint Castleberry

Due to World War II, Clint Castleberry, a native of Rome, Georgia, was never allowed to truly realize his potential as one of America's finest athletes. But while he was here, he set the football world on its ear.

Indeed one well-known sports writer said that "for one fleeting season in 1942, Clint Castleberry blazed across the football field like a crazed jackrabbit. Some said he could have been the greatest Tech player in history—if it weren't for World War II and a plane that disappeared off the West African coast without a trace."

As a freshman at Tech, his only season of college football, he finished third in the Heisman Trophy balloting. He was, in other words, judged to be the third best college football player in America after only his freshman year of play.

Until his own death in 1988, Coach Bobby Dodd claimed that Castleberry would have been the greatest runner in Tech history, and a sure bet to win the Heisman.

But what happened was this: some six weeks after playing in the '43 Cotton Bowl, Caslteberry joined the Army Air Corps. (Ten members of Tech's 1939 team were killed in World War II.)

On November 7, 1944, Castleberry, a co-pilot of a B-26 bomber, took off along with another plane from a field in Nigeria for Dakar, Senegal. It was just a short, routine run, one he made on a regular basis.

They have not been heard from since. Despite extensive Air Corps searches, their fate remains a mystery.

His is the only jersey Georgia Tech has ever retired.

1943: Tech, SEC Champs, Swamps Georgia 48-0

It was November 27, 1943, and the Yellow Jackets could boast a 6-3 record and a good chance to take the SEC championship—if they could just beat Georgia. At that point they'd defeated UNC, Georgia Navy Pre-Flight, Ft. Benning, LSU, Tulane and Clemson, and lost to such national powers as Notre Dame, Navy and Duke. Not a bad record considering their rugged schedule.

As for Georgia, defending national champions, gone now were Frankie Sinkwich and all their other great players from '42, most now serving in the U.S. Army. Yet the Bulldogs were also sporting a 6-3 record coming into the day's game, with wins over Presbyterian College (UGA beat them twice in '43), Tennessee Tech, Wake Forest, Howard (Alabama), and VMI, and losses to LSU (lost to them twice in '43) and Daniel Field.

The big difference in Georgia and Tech in '43 concerned what was called the Navy V-12 Program. Students who signed up for this program were allowed to remain in college. Tech offered this program but Georgia did not. Thus Tech's athletes were allowed to finish their educations (and play football), while those at Georgia were not. Indeed, dozens of colleges across the country dropped football during the war years because they could not find enough men to field a team. (Of the twelve SEC teams in '43, only four—Georgia, Tech, LSU and Tulane—fielded football teams.) Tech also was the site of a Navy flight school which drew students—many of them fine athletes—from other universities. For this reason many Georgia fans do not count the '43 and '44 games in the rivalry's total.

November 27 was a gray, cloudly day as 28,000 fans gathered at Sanford Stadium to watch this 38th encounter between Georgia and Tech. The Bulldogs, by the way, had abandoned their old single-wing formation and for the first time ever were going with the new T-formation.

Tech took the opening kickoff and immediately fumbled deep in their own territory. Georgia recovered, but on third down John Cook threw a pass which was intercepted by Frank Broyles, who dashed 79 yards to the Georgia 12. On first down Broyles threw a TD pass to Mickey Logan, Eddie Prokop kicked the PAT, and Tech led 7-0.

Tech fullback Tom Carpenter makes a leap over the Georgia line only to be met by Bill Chonko and Junior Meeks.

Tech kicked off. Three plays later Georgia punted, and Prokop returned it 37 yards to the Bulldog 23. Four plays later Prokop went in from four yards out for another touchdown. He then kicked the PAT and Tech led 14-0.

Then came another Georgia punt, which Prokop fielded at the 45. He then lateralled to Mickey Logan, who dashed 40 yards for another score. The PAT was no good, but Tech led 20-0 as the first quarter ended.

In the second quarter Tech's Bill Ritter passed 9 yards to Bobby Gaston for another TD, then just before halftime Prokop returned an interception 63 yards for another TD, both PATs were good, and Tech led 34-0 at the half.

In the third period Frank Broyles scored from six yards out. Then, with moments left in the game, Tech got their final score of the afternoon when Prokop went over from the three. Eddie Prokop scored three touchdowns and kicked six PATs in this contest, giving him 24 points on the day.

Tech's 48-0 win is still the largest margin of victory ever recorded in this series.

Tech would go on to beat Tulsa in the Sugar Bowl, and finish the season with an 8-3 record.

TOP:
Captain George Manning, Tech's All-American center.

MIDDLE:
Tech's Captain John Steber, an All-American guard.

BOTTOM:
Eddie Prokop, Tech's All-American back and a member of the GT AHF. In '43 Prokop threw four TD passes vs. Tulane, still number two in the Tech record book.

The Georgia Tech College Inn, "Where Tech Fellows Get Together," in 1943. With the war in full swing, everyone is in uniform.

All-American Eddie Prokop hauls in a Frank Broyles pass good for a first down as Tech, in a great comeback, beat Tulsa 20-18 in the '44 Sugar Bowl. Prokop set a new Sugar Bowl record when he rushed for 198 yards on the afternoon.

The Georgia Bulldogs of 1943.

Georgia's starting lineup for 1943.

Tech's Ed Scharfschwerdt is stopped by Georgia's John Cook and Bill Rutland. But it helped little as the Jackets won by a whopping 48-0 score.

1944: Frank Broyles Passes Tech to Big Win

America was suffering through her third year of World War II, and the sports situations at Georgia and Georgia Tech remained the same as in '43. Tech still had its V-12 Program while Georgia did not. And that made all the difference.

Actually, the Bulldogs were doing pretty well. They came into the Tech game with wins over Presbyterian College, Kentucky, Daniel Field, Alabama, Florida, Auburn and Clemson. They had lost only to Wake Forest and LSU, and were enjoying an enviable 7-2 record.

Tech's All-SEC halfback Allen "Dinky" Bowen charges through the UGA line for a first down as the Tornadoes rolled the Bulldogs 44-0 at Grant Field.

Coach Bill Alexander, Phil Tinsley, Mickey Logan and Tech's assistant coach, Bobby Dodd. Alexander would resign following the '44 season with an overall record of 134-95-15, including eight conference championsips and one national championship (1928).

As for Tech, they had an identical 7-2 record, with wins over Clemson, UNC, Auburn, Navy, Georgia Navy Pre-Flight, Tulane and LSU, and losses to only Duke and Notre Dame, both considered national powers at the time.

Still, despite their identical records, Tech was considered a heavy favorite that afternoon because they'd played a much tougher schedule.

Sadly, a week prior to the day's game, the great Clint Castleberry's wife and parents were officially notified that he had been killed in action in the Mediterranean theater.

This game was played on December 2, a bright but very cold day at Sanford Stadium, before 28,000 shivering fans.

Following the opening kickoff, Georgia punted out at the Tech 40. Five plays later George Mathews threw 19 yards to George Murdock for Tech's first TD of the day. Allen "Dinky" Bowen kicked the point and Tech was up 7-0.

Georgia again took the ball. But this time Dinky Bowen intercepted Ken McCall at the Bulldog 45. Six plays later Frank Broyles threw 21 yards to George Mathews for another score. The PAT missed but Tech was on top 13-0 as the first quarter came to a close.

Four plays into the second quarter Georgia punted to their own 48. Six plays later Broyles went in from the five on a keeper, Phil Tinsley kicked the point and Tech was up 20-0.

Twelve minutes later Broyles again found Mathews in the end zone, hit him with an eight-yard pass, and Tech led 26-0.

Tech scored again in the third quarter when Broyles went over on a one-yard sneak. The PAT missed, but with a 32-0 lead, the Yellow Jackets were beginning to make a runaway of the game.

Later, in the fourth period, Tech again got on the board when Broyles threw short to C. H. Murdock for a touchdown, stretching Tech's lead to 38-0. Then, just before the final whistle, with frozen fans streaming from the stands by the thousands, Tech's Charlie Nixon intercepted a pass and returned it 37 yards for another touchdown and a final score of 44-0.

Frank Broyles was the hero of this contest. He completed 28 passes for 343 yards and three TDs. He ran for two more.

Now, with a great 8-2 record and ranked 10th in the nation, Georgia Tech accepted a bid to play Tulsa in the '45 Orange Bowl. They thus became America's first team ever to play in all four major bowls—the Rose, Sugar, Cotton and Orange.

Tech's game against Tulsa would be Coach Bill Alexander's final game with the Yellow Jackets. After 25 years, and a 134-95-15 record, he was stepping aside. He would be replaced by a gentleman named Bobby Dodd.

UGA All-SEC in 1944:
Herb St. John (G), Andy Perhach (T), Reid Mosely (E) and Mike Castronis (T).
Tech All-American in 1944:
Phil Tinsley (E), Frank Broyles (QB).
Tech All-SEC in 1944:
Maurice Furchgott (G), Allen Bowen (HB), Roland Phillips (G) and George Mathews (FB).
Named to the GT AHF:
Bill Chambers and Coach Bill Alexander.

Andy Perhach, Georgia's All-SEC tackle.

Herb St. John, Georgia's All-SEC guard.

Captain Billy Rutland.

Charles "Rabbit" Smith, All-SEC halfback.

An early Uga surrounded by Georgia cheerleaders in 1944.

Ken McCall shows his form as he leaps high in the air to deliver this pass to Reid Mosely in Georgia's 44-0 loss to Georgia Tech.

The '44 Yellow Jackets prepare to meet Navy. (Backs, L-R): Allen Bowen, Ed Holtsinger, John McIntosh and Frank Broyles. (Linemen, L-R): Deane Gaines, Bill Chambers, Phil Tinsley and Jim Daniel. Tech beat Navy 17-15.

Frank Broyles, Tech All-American quarterback, threw four TD passes vs. Tulane, still number two in the Tech record book.

Charlie Helzer leads the interference for Dinky Bowen in Tech's 27-0 win over Auburn.

Phil Tinsley, Tech All-American end.

George Mathews takes this Broyles pass in Tech's rematch with Tulsa in the '45 Orange Bowl. The Tornadoes lost this time, 26-12.

Dinky Bowen, George Mathews (both Tech All-SEC halfbacks) and Coach Bobby Dodd meet Vernell Bush, Queen of the 1945 Orange Bowl.

1945: Trippi 33, Tech 0

It was the fall of 1945, the war had finally ended, and a sense of normalcy was returning to the nation and to college football, with many of the old veterans from '41 and '42 returning to continue their careers.

Following their fine '44 season, the Yellow Jackets of '45, Bobby Dodd's first year as head coach, suffered a relapse of sorts, managing only four wins in a ten-game schedule. As their date with Georgia rolled around they had beaten UNC, Howard (Alabama), Auburn and Tulane, while losing to Notre Dame, Navy, Duke, LSU and Clemson.

Just up the road in Athens, the Georgia Bulldogs were going great guns. They were 7-2 coming into the day's game, with wins over Murray State, Clemson, Miami, Kentucky, Chattanooga, Florida and Auburn, and mid-season losses to only LSU and Alabama. Indeed, Georgia's defense blanked five opponents in '45, while their offense, led by All-American Charley Trippi, was averaging 29 points per contest.

Georgia's longest win streak in history, 17 games, would begin with their 34-7 win over Chattanooga in '45 and end with their 14-7 losss to UNC in 1947.

The experts picked Georgia as heavy favorites in this game, and the Bulldogs quickly proved the experts right.

35,000 fans crammed into Grant Field on December 1, a cold day in Atlanta, to watch this contest.

Midway the first quarter, after the teams had already exchanged several punts, Tech quick-kicked to the Georgia 29. Two plays later Charles "Rabbit" Smith ran a fly pattern down the right sideline. At the Tech 30 he looked up and there was the ball. He didn't break stride as he made the catch and dashed on into the end zone, a 61-yard TD pass from Charley Trippi. George Jernigan kicked the PAT and Georgia led 7-0.

Ten minutes later, in the second quarter, Johnny Rauch broke through Tech's offensive line and tipped a George Mathews's pass. Floyd "Breezy" Reid, a 17-year old freshman, made the interception and ran 43 yards for a touchdown. The PAT missed, but Georgia went to the sidelines leading 13-0.

Tech kicked off to open the second half. On first down Trippi threw to Reid Moseley, the nation's number one pass receiver in '45, who had gotten behind the Yellow Jacket defense. Moseley took the ball over his right shoulder and dashed on into the end zone,

Coach Bobby Dodd retired in 1966 with a 165-64-8 record, including a national championship in '52. His name is still synonymous with Georgia Tech football.

The great Charley Trippi returned from WW II in '45 and was immediately named to the All-SEC team. Here Trippi goes high in the air to shoot a short one to Joe Tereshinski as Georgia beat Tech 33-0. Trippi threw for 321 yards and three touchdowns in this game.

a 67-yard TD completion. Jernigan kicked the point and Georgia went up 20-0.

Minutes later a Tech drive deep into Bulldog territory was stopped when Moseley intercepted a pass at the 15. On first down Trippi threw a 37-yard completion to John Donaldson. On the next play he threw a 41-yard TD pass to Johnny Rauch. The PAT was good and Georgia was up 27-0.

In the final quarter Georgia added another touchdown to their collection when Trippi himself scored from the one. That made the score 33-0, which was the final score, Georgia's 20th win in this series. (Tech had 15 wins, and there had been five ties.)

Trippi carried the ball 42 times during this game and accounted for 517 total yards, an average of 12 yards per carry.

He rushed for 61 yards, completed 12 passes for 321 yards and three TDs, and returned six punts for 114 yards.

Rabbit Smith gained 193 yards on 19 attempts, and John Donaldson 91 yards on only five attempts.

TOP:
Captain Paul Duke, Tech All-American center.

SECOND:
Bob Davis, Tech All-SEC tackle.

THIRD:
George Mathews, Tech All-SEC halfback.

BOTTOM:
Walt Kilzer, Tech All-SEC end.

George Mathews runs for Tech's only TD of the day as they fell to Notre Dame 40-7.

Hatcher quick-kicks on second down to get the Yellow Jackets out of a deep hole. They went on to lose to Georgia 33-0.

Bulldog starters in '45. (Front, L-R): Frank Plant, Joe Tereshinski, J. P. Miller. (Rear, L-R): Dan Edwards, Gene Frank, Sam Bailey, Joe Chesna, Alton Davis. (Tereshinski's son, Joe Jr., would star for Georgia, 1974–1976.)

John Rauch, All-SEC quarterback, started for Georgia at the age of 17.

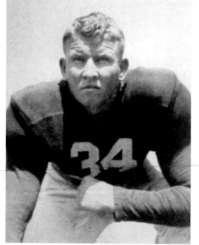

Co-captain Charles Eaves, Georgia guard.

Co-captain J. P. Miller, Georgia tackle. A company commander during World War II, he won a Purple Heart in Europe.

Here a grinning Charley Trippi skirts right end vs. Tulsa in the '46 Oil Bowl. Trailing Tulsa 7-6 in the fourth quarter, Trippi threw 65 yards to John Donaldson for one TD, then returned a punt 68 yards for another in a great Georgia comeback.

1946: 11-0-0 Georgia Wins National Championship

For Georgia this was the year that was, the year that Wally Butts and his Bulldogs would prance undefeated through a 10-game schedule and be declared national champions. As they prepared to meet Georgia Tech on November 28, they had beaten Clemson (35-12), Temple (35-12), Kentucky (28-13), Oklahoma A&M (35-13), Furman (70-7), Alabama (14-0), Florida (33-14), Auburn (41-0) and Chattanooga (48-27). At that point Georgia was ranked number three in the nation, behind only Army and Notre Dame.

John Griffith ran 89 yards for a TD vs. Furman, still an all-time UGA record.

George Jernigan kicked 47 PATs in 1946, still an all-time UGA record. He also kicked ten PATs vs. Furman in 1946, another all-time UGA record.

As for Georgia Tech, they too were going great guns in '46. Following an opening game loss to Tennessee (13-9), the Yellow Jackets reeled off eight consecutive wins: VMI (32-6), Ole Miss (24-7), LSU (26-7), Auburn (27-6), Duke (14-0), Navy (28-20), Tulane (35-7) and Furman (41-7). Tech was ranked number seven in the nation at that point.

As though all this were not enough to pump up fans all over Georgia, the Sugar Bowl announced that the winner of this game would be invited to New Orleans to play UNC and the great Choo-Choo Justice on January 1.

Indeed, some 55,000 fans crammed every inch of space in, on and around Sanford Stadium for this contest.

Early in the first quarter Frank Broyles quick-kicked for Tech. Charley Trippi took the ball at his own goal line and ran it back to the 20. From there Georgia ran 19 consecutive plays, Trippi finally scoring from the four. George Jernigan's kick was good and Georgia led 7-0.

Then, in the second period, Georgia's Garland "Bulldog" Williams recovered a fumble at the Tech 42. Seven plays later Trippi passed nine yards to Johnny Rauch for another score, the PAT was good, and Georgia went in at halftime leading 14-0.

Following the second half kickoff, Trippi intercepted a Tech pass at midfield and returned it 21 yards to the 29. He then passed 13 yards to Dan Edwards to the 16. Two plays later Rauch found Trippi in the end zone, hit him with a 10-yard pass, the PAT was good, and Georgia was on top 21-0.

Six minutes later Georgia started from their own 18. They then ran 14 consecutive plays, finally scoring when Rauch hit Rabbit Smith with a nine-yard pass. The PAT was good and Georgia led 28-0.

Bobby Dodd on the first day of practice in 1946 with (L-R): Walt Kilzer, George Mathews, Bill Healy, Pat McHugh, Frank Broyles and Bobby Davis.

Georgia's great All-American tailback, Charley Trippi, is a member of the College Football Hall of Fame. He averaged 7.52 yards per play during his career, still number one in the UGA record book. His is one of only four jerseys ever retired by the University of Georgia.

But the spunky Tech team didn't quit. On the ensuing kickoff they drove 74 yards for a touchdown, scoring when Frank Broyles hit James Bowen with a 28-yard strike in the end zone. Bowen then kicked the PAT, and Georgia led 28-7.

Georgia took the kickoff back to their own 35. On first down Trippi took a pitchout and raced 65 yards down the right sideline for Georgia's final score of the afternoon.

Georgia then went on to defeat UNC 20-10 in the Sugar Bowl, while Tech defeated St. Mary's 41-19 in the Oil Bowl.

UGA All-American in 1946:
Charley Trippi (QB) and Herb St. John (G).
UGA All-SEC in 1946:
Joe Tereshinski (E), John Rauch (HB) and Jack Bush (T).
Named to the UGA SHF:
Charley Trippi and John Griffith.
Tech All-American in 1946:
Paul Duke (C).
Tech All-SEC in 1946:
Bill Healy (G), Louis Hook (C), George Brodnax (E) and Allen "Dinky" Bowen (HB).
Named to the GT AHF:
Bob Davis and George Mathews.

Trippi runs here against a great Tar Heel team as Georgia beat UNC and Choo-Choo Justice 20-10 in the Sugar Bowl.

Dan Edwards, Georgia All-American end.

Herbert St. John, Georgia All-American guard.

Trippi surprises UNC with a quick kick to get Georgia out of a deep hole.

The national champion Bulldogs and their dates enjoy a great evening at the St. Charles Hotel in New Orleans following their 20-10 win over UNC in the Sugar Bowl of 1947.

Joe Tereshinski blocks Luke Bowen as Charley Trippi runs 66 yards for a TD in Georgia's 35-7 win over Tech.

Allen "Dinky" Bowen squeezes through an opening as Tech whipped Auburn 27-6.

Bulldog Eli Maricich is nailed by a bevy of Yellow Jackets.

Pat McHugh returned this interception 73 yards for a TD as Tech beat St. Marys 41-19 in the '46 Oil bowl.

1947: Tech Takes Georgia, SEC Championship

It was November 29, 1947, and a banner year for both the Bulldogs and the Yellow Jackets. Georgia, after winning the national championship in '46, suffered something of a relapse in '47 but were still good enough to go 7-4 on the season and win a bid to play in the '48 Gator Bowl.

As for Georgia Tech, after a great 9-2 season in '46, they were doing even better in '47. They cruised to a 9-1 record, were awarded the SEC Championship, then defeated a good Kansas team in the '48 Orange Bowl.

Obviously the great state of Georgia was well represented by these two excellent institutions.

Georgia was 7-3 as they prepared to meet Tech at Grant Field, with wins over Furman, LSU, Oklahoma A&M, Clemson, Florida, Auburn and Chattanooga, and losses to UNC, Kentucky and Alabama. Georgia's 14-7 loss to UNC on September 27 ended their 17-game winning streak, their longest in history.

This great Tech team had beaten Tennessee, Tulane, VMI, Auburn, The Citadel, Duke, Navy, and Furman. Their only loss had come at the hands of Alabama in an upset. Indeed, Tech had blanked five of their opponents and given up a total of only 41 points, and were ranked number six in the nation when they went up against Georgia.

Bob Davis, Tech's All-American tackle, is a member of the College Football Hall of Fame.

Some 38,000 wildly enthusiastic fans turned out for this encounter, the 42nd meeting between these two old rivals on a sunny fall afternoon at Grant Field.

As had happened so often in the past, this game quickly settled into a defensive struggle, with neither team able to seriously threaten the other's goal.

They went in at halftime tied 0-0 and Georgia fans were beginning to hope that the Bulldogs might pull off a big upset that afternoon. Tech fans were just as hopeful that their Yellow Jackets would unleash their big passing attack and bury Georgia just as they had done against eight other opponents.

Midway the third quarter, Tech got the big break they had been waiting for when Georgia's Bobby Walston intercepted a Jim Still pass and returned it to the Georgia 24. But then, on first down,

Tech's J. E. Brown throws a pass to George Brodnax for a 27-yard gain as the Jackets went on to defeat Georgia 7-0.

Johnny Rauch threw a short pass intended for Don Edwards and Tech's Jimmy Castleberry leaped high in the air, came down with the ball, and ran it down to the Georgia 13 before tripping over one of his own blockers.

On second down, following an incomplete pass, Jimmy Patton relieved Jim Still at quarterback. He took the snap from center, looked downfield, then fired a bullet to George Brodnax in the end zone. Robert Jordan kicked the point and Tech took the lead 7-0.

Later, with only minutes left in the final quarter, Johnny Rauch would pass the Bulldogs down to the Tech 25. But then he fired two incomplete passes, was thrown for a loss on third down, and missed with a pass on fourth down.

And that was the old ball game. Tech took it 7-0, their ninth win of the season. They would then be declared champions of the SEC, and go on to defeat Kansas 20-14 in the Orange Bowl. Their final 10-1 record was their best since their 10-0-0 team of 1928 won the national championship.

Georgia would meet a great Maryland team in the Gator Bowl on January 1, and come away with a 20-20 tie.

UGA All-American in 1947:
Dan Edwards (E).
UGA All-SEC in 1947:
Herb St. John (G) and John Rauch (QB).
Tech All-American in 1947:
Bob Davis (T).
Tech All-SEC in 1947:
Bill Healy (G), Louis Hook (C), George Brodnax (E) and Allen Bowen (HB).
Named to the GT AHF:
Bob Davis and George Mathews.

Jim Still threw three touchdown passes in this game, two to Jim Patton (above) and one to Billy Queen, as Tech defeated the Jayhawks 20-14.

TOP:
Captain Bill Healy, Tech's All-American guard.

SECOND:
Rollo Phillips, alternate captain of the Jackets.

THIRD:
Jim Still, Tech quarter-back.

BOTTOM:
George Brodnax, Tech's All-American end.

Tech, with a great 9-1 record, beat a good Kansas team today 20-14 in the '48 Orange Bowl. Here, Jim Still has just tossed a short pass to Jimmy Castleberry for a first down.

Georgia's All-American end Don Edwards and All-American quarterback John Rauch take time out for a photo session.

Eli Maricich picks up short yardage as Georgia lost to Tech 7-0.

Herb St. John, John Rauch and Breezy Reid find a fan in Jacksonville.

Breezy Reid picks up yardage as the 7-4-1 Bulldogs and Maryland tied 20-20 in the '48 Gator Bowl.

1948: Georgia Beats Tech, Wins SEC Crown

I t was another super season for both Georgia and Georgia Tech, though the Bulldogs, who came into their annual meeting with an 8-1 record, as opposed to Tech's 7-2, was given a slight edge.

At that point, Georgia had wins over Chattanooga, LSU, Kentucky, Miami, Alabama, Florida, Auburn and Furman, and a single loss, a 21-14 upset at the hands of UNC in the second game of the season. They were now ranked number eleven in America and had to beat Tech if they were to take the SEC crown and win a big bowl bid.

Georgia's Alvin Bodine (All-SEC back), Coach Butts and Porter Payne (All-SEC tackle).

All-American quarterback John Rauch completed four TD passes vs. Clemson in '46, still number one in the UGA record book. He completed 252 career passes for 4,044 yards, still number four in the UGA record book.

The Yellow Jackets at this point had wins over Vanderbilt, Tulane, Washington and Lee, Auburn, Florida, Duke and The Citadel, and losses to Tennessee and Alabama. Bob McCoy had an 87-yard TD run vs. The Citadel, still an all-time Tech record. Indeed, Tech had won their first six games of the season and were ranked number six in America before tough back-to-back losses to Tennessee (13-6) and Alabama (14-12).

Still, Tech's defense was the best in America. They were almost impossible to run against, and had given up only 48 points to nine opponents. Truly, this promised to be a real shootout between two of the finest teams in America.

Some 52,000 fans turned out on November 27, a cool, sunny day in Athens, to see if their team could pull it off and go on to bigger and better things.

Midway the first quarter, after feeling each other out for a few minutes, Georgia Tech had suffered two 15-yard penalties and were backed up to their own 7-yard line. Buster Humphries, standing in his own end zone, then got off a high spiraling punt that came down at the Georgia 36.

On first down John Rauch hit Gene Lorendo with a 38-yard completion, down to the Tech 26. Joe Geri gained 10 on the next play, then John Tillitski and Eli Maricich ran it down to the five. Breezy Reid ran it in from there for a touchdown, Geri's kick was good, and Georgia was on top 7-0.

Following an exchange of punts Georgia found themselves with a first down at their own seven. But Rauch then led the Bulldogs on a 93-yard scoring drive with Geri getting 46 of those on a scamper down to the Tech 47. Five plays later Tillitski took it in from the 4, the PAT was good and Georgia's lead went to 14-0, the halftime score.

Following the second half kickoff, Georgia's Geri went back to punt from his own 21. But George Mathews broke through and blocked the kick. The ball bounced back into the end zone where it was covered by Geoge Brodnax for a Tech TD. Dinky Bowen kicked the point and Georgia's lead was cut to 14-7.

But later in this period Tech punted to Ken McCall at the Georgia 46. He then zigged and zagged his way through the entire Yellow Jacket team 54 yards for another score. The PAT made it 21-7.

Later, only minutes into the final period, the Jackets took the ball at their own 39. Jimmy Southard then went to the air, hitting Jack Griffin for 22 yards and Jimmy Jordan for 10 yards. Bob McCoy ran for nine, then came Bowen on a scoring end sweep from the four. The PAT missed, and Georgia escaped with a hard-earned 21-13 victory over a fine Georgia Tech team.

Georgia won the SEC Championship and went on to lose to Texas in the '49 Orange Bowl.

UGA All-American in 1948: J John Rauch (QB).
UGA All-SEC in 1948: Porter Payne (T), Homer Hobbs (G) and Joe Geri (HB).
Named to the UGA SHF: John Rauch, John Donaldson, and Joe Geri.
Tech All-American in 1948: George Brodnax (E), Bill Healy (G).
Tech All-SEC in 1948: Frank Ziegler (HB), Jim Vurgin (G), Clay Mathews (G) and Bob McCoy (HB).

Eli Maricich and Gene Chandler have a brief confrontation with Tech's Morris Harrison.

Georgia All-SEC halfback Joe Geri finds an opening as Georgia beat Kentucky 35-12. Geri scored 90 points in '48.

Georgia captain Bernie Reid meets his Texas counterpart just prior to kickoff in the '49 Orange Bowl.

Eli Maricich is about to cut upfield for a short gain as Georgia crushed Alabama 35-0 on their way to a great 9-2 season and an SEC Championship.

Tech's co-captains for '48, All-American end George Brodnax and Jim Castleberry. (Castleberry is the younger brother of Tech's late, great Clint Castleberry.)

Jack Griffin, Tech end.

Frank Ziegler, Tech All-SEC fullback.

Morris Harrison gallops in for a TD as Tech lost to Georgia 21-13 in a hard-fought contest in Athens.

Jimmy Southard throws a completion to J. C. Anderson as Tech smashed Auburn 27-0.

1949: Tech Wins By Inches

1949 marked the first year since 1940 that neither Georgia nor Georgia Tech would go to a big bowl game on January 1.

As they prepared to meet one another on November 26, Georgia was suffering through a 4-5-1 season, with wins over Furman, Chattanooga, LSU and Duquesne, losses to UNC, Kentucky, Miami, Alabama and Florida, and a tie with Auburn. Indeed, six opponents had held Georgia's shaky offense to one TD or less. Not a season to get real excited about.

Things at Tech were somewhat better. The Yellow Jackets were 6-3 at this point, with wins over Vanderbilt, Auburn, Florida, Washington and Lee, Tennessee and South Carolina, and losses to Duke, Alabama and Tulane

Tech kicked off and the Bulldogs immediately brought 40,000 fans to their feet when Mal Cook threw to Eli Maricich for 19 yards, down to the Tech 45. Then Breezy Reid ran it down to the 33 on the next play. But Tech held at that point and that was the end of Georgia's first threat, and their fans sat back down.

With only a minute left in the first quarter, Tech moved to the Georgia 20. But then facing fourth and inches, the Bulldogs held and that was the end of Tech's first big threat.

With seven minutes elapsed in the second period Georgia's Pat Field punted into Tech's end zone and the Yellow Jackets took over at their own 20. In six plays they'd moved to the Georgia 46, but Bobby North fumbled at that point and Gene Chandler recovered for the Bulldogs.

On first down, after trying and failing all afternoon, Cook took the snap from center, faked to Floyd Reid, then faded back and threw long for Gene Lorendo who took the ball at the 25 and ran untouched the remaining distance for a touchdown. Bob Durand's PAT try was no good, but Georgia still had a big 6-0 lead.

Early in the third period it appeared that Georgia would pad their lead when they began a long drive from their own seven-yard line. On first down Floyd Reid took a handoff and raced 41 yards before Powell Sheffer knocked him out of bounds at the Georgia 48. Then Cook threw to Lorendo who was downed at the Tech 34. Three plays later, facing third and 10, Reid raced down close to the first down marker.

Georgia missed this PAT and Tech escaped with a 7-6 victory.

But a measurement showed he was a foot shy. On fourth down, then, Dick Raber banged straight into the line. But he too was inches short. Tech had held and would take over the football.

Three plays later, from their own 38, Tech quick-kicked on third down. The ball sailed all the way down to the Georgia 5-yard line.

From there the Bulldogs couldn't move. Field punted out to the 50 and J. A. Jordan returned it to the Georgia 39.

Buster Humphries ran for 10. Then two plays later he dashed for another 16, down to the Bulldog 11. Then it was Humphries for six. On the last three plays he'd accounted for 32 tough yards and was told to take a break. Three plays later Jim Southard went in for a one-yard touchdown on a quarterback sneak. Jim Patton kicked the PAT, and Tech walked away with a hard-earned 7-6 victory.

Captain Tom Coleman,
Tech All-SEC tackle.

Dick Harvin,
Tech All-SEC end.

Henry "Buster" Humphries, who sparked Tech's scoring drive against Georgia, is pushed out of bounds at the Bulldog 29-yard line.

Jimmy Jordan and Bob North,
Tech's All-SEC halfbacks.

Humphries follows good blocking for a first down as Tech edged Georgia 7-6 at Grant Field.

All-SEC back Jimmy Jordan sweeps right as Tech lost to Tulane 18-0 in New Orleans. (A crowd of 55,000 turned out for this game.) Jordan averaged 16.3 yards per punt return during his career, still number three in the Tech record book.

Floyd Reid, Georgia All-SEC halfback.

Marion Campbell, Georgia All-SEC tackle.

Eli Maricich had 12 career interceptions, still number four in the UGA record book.

Ed Filipovits, a fine Georgia lineman.

Alvin Bodine dashes for a 26-yard pickup as Georgia won a close one from LSU 7-0.

Bobby Walston, Georgia All-SEC end, averaged 21 yards per catch in '48, still number one in the UGA record book.

1950: Turnovers Kill Georgia's Hopes

Zeke Bratkoski, an all-time great Bulldog quarterback.

It was December 2, 1950, and a bloody war had been raging in Korea for the previous six months. But all that seemed far away as the Bulldogs and Yellow Jackets prepared for their 45th meeting. This one would be played in Athens where the Jackets had managed to win on only three occasions (1893, 1916 and 1944) out of fifteen attempts. But perhaps this year would be different.

The Yellow Jackets at this point were 4-6 on the season with wins over Florida, LSU, Auburn and Davidson, and losses to SMU, South Carolina, Kentucky, Duke, Alabama and VMI.

With their win over Davidson in 1950, Tech would begin an unbeaten streak that would not end until they were beaten by Notre Dame in '53, a streak of 31 games.

Up in Athens, meanwhile, the Bulldogs were having a fine year. At this point they were 6-1-3 on the season with wins over Maryland, Mississippi State, Boston College, Florida, Auburn and Furman, a 14-7 loss to Alabama, and ties with St. Mary's, UNC and LSU.

Some 50,000 fans turned out at Sanford Stadium to see what would happen when the Bulldogs (favored by three touchdowns) tangled with Bobby Dodd's Yellow Jackets.

Early in the first quarter Tech's Joe Salome tossed a short pass out in the flat, but an alert Claude Hipps made the interception and ran it back 21 yards, to the Tech 15. It was just the sort of play that Tech fans had been dreading.

Four plays later the Bulldogs were facing fourth down at the Tech 8. But the Yellow Jackets held at that point and Georgia was stymied.

Five minutes later the Bulldogs were again on the march. They moved 44 yards in six plays, down to the Tech 19. But quarterback Mal Cook fumbled on a keeper and Lamar Wheat recovered for the Yellow Jackets at the 26.

(Following this contest all the experts pointed to this as the one play that cost Georgia the game. Not only was Georgia deprived of a score, but Tech gained possession and seemed unstoppable as they moved the ball down the field.)

First, Bobby North ran for 6 yards, then a roughing penalty moved the chains another 15 yards, and the Yellow Jackets were at the 47. Then came

Tech captain Bob Bossons, an All-SEC center, meets with Georgia captain Mike Merola for the coin toss in 1950. (Note Tech's natty new navy blue jerseys.)

North again, followed by a pitchout to George Maloof, and Tech was at the Georgia 32. On the next play Salome passed to John Weigle to the 21.

Then came the big play. Salome went back to pass and was roughed by an ambitious Georgia lineman. That truly was the play of the day, and took the ball down to the Bulldog 6-yard line. First down for the Yellow Jackets.

Two plays later Darrell Crawford sneaked over for the touchdown, Jimmy Patton kicked the point, and Tech led 7-0. Georgia threatened constantly as this game progressed, but turnovers killed their efforts on every occasion, and Tech walked away with a big upset win.

Following this game Georgia would lose 40-20 to Texas A&M in the Presidential Cup Bowl at College Park, Md.

Tech All-American in 1950:
Bob Bossons (C), John Weigle (E) and Bob North (HB).
Named to the GT AHF:
Bob Bossons.
UGA All-SEC in 1950:
Rocco Principe (G), Marion Campbell (T) and Billy Mixon (HB).

Georgia co-captains Mike Merola and Dick Yelvington.

Zippy Morocco, a member of the UGA SHF, averaged 14.2 yards per punt return 1949–1951, still number one in the UGA record book.

Rocco Principe, Georgia All-SEC guard.

Bill Mixon, Georgia All-SEC halfback.

Anthony "Zippy" Morroco returned this punt down to the Tech 31-yard line, but the Yellow Jackets took it 7-0.

Captain Bob Bossons,
Tech's All-SEC center.

Chappell Rhino who threw a
TD pass vs. Georgia in '52.

Darrell Crawford,
Tech's All-SEC quarterback.

Darrell Crawford goes in for the TD that
upset a good Georgia team 7-0 in 1950 at
Sanford Stadium.

John Weigle, Tech's All-SEC end.

Ray Beck, Tech's
All-American guard,
is a member of the
College Football
Hall of Fame.

1951: The Golden Age of Georgia Tech Football

This was truly a great season for Bobby Dodd and his Georgia Tech Yellow Jackets. They could boast of a 9-0-1 record and a number six national ranking as they went out to face Georgia on December 1, 1951. To date they'd beaten SMU, Florida, Kentucky, LSU, Auburn, Vanderbilt, VMI, Alabama and Davidson, and did so by very convincing scores. Indeed, the only blemish on their record at this point was a 14-14 tie with Duke.

Darrell Crawford threw four TD passes vs. Auburn, still number two in the GT record book.

As for Georgia, 1951 was a rather mediocre season. To date the Bulldogs were 5-4 on the year with wins over George Washington, UNC, Boston College, Florida and Auburn, and losses to Mississippi State, Maryland, LSU and Alabama.

A crowd of some 40,000 fans showed up on a warm but cloudy day at Grant Field to watch this 46th meeting between the two institutions.

Tech kicked off and Georgia got a short return, only to their 13 yard line. On second down, Lauren Hargrove took a hard hit and fumbled the ball. Pete Ferris recovered for the Jackets. First came John Hicks, then Leon Hardeman, and the ball was at the three. From there George Maloof took it in for the score. Glenn Turner missed the PAT but Tech led 6-0.

Five minutes later Tech took a punt on the Georgia 46. Leon Hardeman carried for ten on first down, then for the remaining 36 on the next down. Turner kicked the PAT and Tech led 13-0.

Following an exchange of punts, Zeke Bratkowski, who broke all Georgia passing records during his career, fumbled the ball, and Tech's Ray Beck recovered at the 18. On first down Hardeman ran to the four, then Maloof went in on the next play. Pepper Rodgers kicked the PAT and Tech led 20-0.

Ten minutes into the second quarter Georgia punted out to their own 32. Four plays later Maloof went in from the one for his third TD of the afternoon. Rodgers kicked the PAT and Tech led 27-0.

With only three minutes left in the half, Georgia fumbled the kickoff at their own 48, and it was recovered by Tech's Ted Shuler. On first down Darrell Crawford bootlegged the ball around right end and dashed for 44 yards before he was caught from behind. He then lateralled the ball to Pete Brown, who then lateralled to Buck Martin, who went in for the TD. Rodgers kicked the PAT and Tech led 34-0 at the half.

Early in the third quarter Hardeman fumbled at the Tech 40 and the ball was covered by Georgia's Bobby Morris. Bratkowski then completed passes of 18 and 15 yards to Harry Babcock. Dick Raber scored from the seven, the PAT missed and Tech's lead was cut to 34-6.

George Maloof.

George Maloof scored four TDs vs. Georgia in '51, an all-time record for this series, as the Yellow Jackets romped over the Bulldogs 48-6.

Minutes later Bobby Moorhead intercepted Bratkowski at the Georgia 47. Three plays later George Maloof gained instant immortality when he scored from the four, his fourth TD of the day. The PAT was good, and Tech's lead went to 41-6.

Later, with only minutes left in the game, Larry Morris intercepted Bratkowski and returned it 55 yards for Tech's final TD of the day. The kick was good, and Tech beat Georgia by a smashing 48-6 score.

The 10-0-1 Yellow Jackets, now ranked number five in the nation, would then be crowned SEC champions and go on to defeat Baylor in the '52 Orange Bowl.

Over the next six years Tech's won-loss record would be an incredible 59-7-3, an average of almost 10 wins per season. This was the beginning of the Golden Age of Tech football.

Tech All-American in 1951:
Ray Beck (G), Lamar Wheat (DT).
Tech All-SEC in 1951:
Lum Snyder (G), Darrell Crawford (QB),
Buck Martin (E) and George Morris (LB).
Named to the GT AHF:
Pete Ferris.
UGA All-SEC in 1951:
Harry Babcock (E), Claude Hipps (DB), Zeke Bratkowski (QB) and Marion Campbell (DT).
Named to the UGA SHF:
Marion Campbell and Zippy Morocco.

A proud Bobby Dodd holding the '52 Orange Bowl trophy.

TOP:
George Morris, a '52 Tech All-American center and linebacker.

SECOND:
Pete Ferris, All-SEC end and a member of the GT AHF.

THIRD:
Lum Snyder, Tech's All-SEC tackle and a member of the GT AHF.

BOTTOM:
Ray Beck, an All-American guard for the Yellow Jackets.

There were two minutes left in the Orange Bowl and the score was tied 14-14 when Pepper Rodgers kicked this field goal to give Tech a great 17-14 win. Rodgers kicked 39 PATs in '52, still an all-time GT record.

The Yellow Jackets celebrate their great comeback win in the '52 Orange Bowl.

Coach Wally Butts and All-SEC defensive back Claude Hipps.

In '52 Jim Campagna returned a punt 100 yards for a TD vs. Vanderbilt, an all-time UGA record.

Dick Raber goes in from the seven to cut Tech's lead to 34-6. But it was too little too late.

Marion Campbell, Georgia All-SEC tackle and a member of the UGA SHF.

Zippy Morocco leads the charge as the Bulldogs smashed Auburn 46-14.

1952: 12-0-0 Yellow Jackets Win National Championship

It was November 29, 1952, and despite cold, overcast skies, things were beginning to heat up in Athens. The so-so Bulldogs were 6-3 at this point and about to go up against undefeated Georgia Tech, the number two team in America. To say that Georgia badly wanted this game would be a gross understatement.

Three all-time great Georgia All-Americans: Harry Babcock, Zeke Bratkowski and Johnny Carson.

To date they'd beaten Vanderbilt, Tulane, NC State, LSU, Penn and Auburn, while losing to Maryland, Florida and Alabama. According to the experts they'd have to fight like the dickens just to stay in the same stadium with Tech.

Tech, unfortunately for Georgia, had an unbeaten streak of 24 games going at this point and had no plans to lose. To this date they'd easily zipped through ten opponents—The Citadel, Florida, SMU, Tulane, Auburn, Vanderbilt, Duke, Army, Alabama (this was the same Alabama team that would destroy Syracuse 61-6 in the Orange Bowl several weeks later) and Florida State—and were ranked number two in the nation behind only Michigan State. They had blanked four opponents, and only Florida had scored more than one touchdown against them.

Dave Davis had an 80-yard punt vs. Army, still number two in the GT record book.

Fifty thousand fans turned out for this classic struggle between Georgia Tech and the underdog Bulldogs.

Following the opening kickoff, things got off with a bang. Starting from their own 25, Tech's Bill Brigman fumbled on first down and Babe Locke recovered for Georgia. Bratkowski passed 11 yards to Johnny Carson, down to the 14-yard line. Robert "Foots" Clemens ran for a first down at the three. Then Clemens bulled in for a touchdown, Sam Mrvos kicked the PAT, and Georgia led 7-0.

Ten minutes later Georgia punted to Bobby Moorhead who lateraled to Billy Teas. Teas ran it back 21 yards to the Georgia 35. Four plays later Tech was at the nine. But they stalled there and on fourth down Pepper Rodgers kicked a field goal to cut Georgia's lead to 7-3, the halftime score.

Early in the second half Tech took the ball at their own 33. After nine plays the Yellow Jackets had a first down at the Georgia 18. And by then Bulldog fans were beginning to cool down. Three plays later the Jackets were facing fourth and two at the ten. It was then that Coach Dodd sent in Chappel Rhino with a trick play. (Rhino is the father of Tech's great All-American Randy Rhino, 1971–1974.)

Glenn Turner blocks for Billy Teas as Tech beat Georia 23-9. (That's Georgia's Ron Williams giving pursuit.)

Brigman faked a handoff to Glenn Turner, then pitched to Rhino who started on a sweep right but then held up and tossed a pass to Buck Martin in the end zone. (This was Rhino's only play of the game.) Rodgers kicked the PAT and Tech took the lead 10-7.

Later, backed up deep in their own territory, Pepper Rodgers gave up a safety to Georgia, cutting Tech's lead to 10-9. At that point, Zeke Bratkowski went to the air and passed the Jackets silly, but still Tech's great defense would not yield.

With five minutes left, throwing from his own end zone, Bratkowski was intercepted by Moorhead who returned the ball to the one. Rodgers then sneaked over for the TD, missed the PAT, but Tech led 16-9.

With two minutes remaining, Georgia shanked a punt and Tech took the ball at the 19. Glenn Turner scored from there, Rodgers kicked the PAT and Tech escaped with a 23-9 win.

Tech went on to beat Ole Miss in the Sugar Bowl to complete a 12-0-0 season and win the national championship.

UGA All-American in 1952:
Harry Babcock (E).
UGA All-SEC in 1952:
Art DeCarlo (SAF), Joe O'Malley (DE) and Chris Filipkowski (DG).
Named to the UGA SHF:
Harry Babcock.
Tech All-American in 1952:
Reid Brown (G), Buck Martin (E), Leon Hardeman (HB), Hal Miller (T), Bob Moorhead (B) and George Morris (LB).
Tech All-SEC in 1952:
Sam Hensley (E), Larry Morris (LB), Orville Vereen (G) and Jake Shoemaker (G).
Named to the GT AHF:
Pete Brown, Bob Moorhead, Lum Snyder and George Morris.

Connie Manisera vaults the line for a first down as the Bulldogs fell to Florida 30-0.

John Carson, All-American end and a member of the UGA SHF, takes a short Bratkowski pass for a 23-yard gain vs. Georgia Tech.

Zeke Bratkowski fires a strike to John Carson in Georgia's 34-27 upset of Penn, again proving that the best college football in America is played in the state of Georgia. Bratkowski completed 360 passes during his career, still number three in the UGA record book. (Only Eric Zeier and Mike Bobo completed more.)

Coach Butts poses with Bob West and Frank Salerno.

The 1952 Yellow Jackets, possibly Georgia Tech's greatest football team in history, ran through eleven regular season opponents, then defeated Ole Miss in the Sugar Bowl and were crowned national champions. (During the 1951-56 seasons, Tech compiled an incredible 59-7-3 record.)

Leon Hardeman, All-American halfback and winner of the MVP Award in the '52 Sugar Bowl, rushed for 22 TDs during his career, still number two in the GT record book.

Coach Dodd and the team whoop it up following Tech's 28-7 win over a great Duke team in '52. The Yellow Jackets were well on their way to an amazing 12-0 record and a national championship.

Bill Brigman smashes through the Ole Miss line for a TD and a great 24-7 win for Georgia Tech in the '53 Sugar Bowl.

Tech captains, Hal Miller and George Morris. Both were All-American and both are members of the GT AHF. Morris is a member of the College Football Hall of Fame.

All-American defensive back Bobby Moorhead and All-SEC guard Orville Vereen, two of the stalwart team members that made the '52 Yellow Jackets click. Moorhead had 13 interceptions during his career, still number three in the GT record book.

Pete Brown, All-American center and a member of the GT AHF.

Tech's national championship team of '52 featured six first-team All-American players: Leon Hardeman (HB), George Morris (LB), Buck Martin (E), Bobby Moorhead (DB), Pete Brown (C) and Hal Miller (T).

Quarterback Bill Brigman who led Tech to a national championship.

Buck Martin, Tech's All-American end and a member of the GT AHF, had 14 TD receptions during his career, still number one in the GT record book.

1953: Powerful Jackets Glide Past Bulldogs

Georgia had not beaten Tech since 1948, a string of four games, and things were not looking real promising for 1953. As November 28 rolled around, the hapless Bulldogs, with a 3-7 record, were suffering through their worst season since 1932 when they were 2-5-2 under Coach Harry Mehre. To that date they'd managed to defeat Villanova, Tulane and UNC, but had lost to Texas A&M, Maryland, LSU, Alabama, Florida, Auburn and Mississippi Southern. And things would only get worse.

As for Tech, they weren't quite as potent as the previous year, but were still good enough to carry a 7-2-1 record into the day's game, with wins over Davidson, SMU, Tulane, Auburn, Vanderbilt, Clemson and Duke, losses to Notre Dame (the number one team in the nation) and Alabama, and a tie with Florida. (The loss to Notre Dame snapped their unbeaten streak at 31 games, still the second longest in Tech history.) They were currently ranked number ten in America and looking for a nice bowl bid.

Some 41,000 fans turned out at Grant Field, knowing that this game would be televised by WSB-TV in the Atlanta area.

Tech's Billy Teas hit Jim Durham with this scoring pass to defeat Georgia 28-12 at Grant Field. (This was Teas's only pass of the season.)

Tech kicked off and the game was underway. Both teams frittered away early scoring chances with turnovers, but then Georgia fumbled again and Tech's Jakie Shoemaker covered it at the Bulldog 14. Three plays later Pepper Rodgers sneaked over from the one, kicked the PAT, and Tech led 7-0.

Later in the first quarter, facing a third and six from their own 34, Rodgers threw to Henry Hair for a first down at the Georgia 47. Rodgers then ran for 17 more yards, down to the 30. He then threw to Jimmy Durham for 13 yards and another first down. Then came Buster Humphries bursting through the line all the way for a touchdown. Rodgers' kick made it 14-0, Tech's favor.

Early in the second quarter, Wade Mitchell fumbled and Bill Saye recovered for the Bulldogs at the Tech 25. Jimmy Campagna ran for 10, then came Clemens and Charlie Madison for six more and a first down at the four. Then Charlie Madison went in for the score, Mrvos missed the PAT but Tech's lead was cut to 14-6.

Minutes later Georgia took over at the Tech 46. Bratkowski then threw long to Madison who caught the ball at the 30 and took off down the sideline with nothing between him and the goal line. But at the five, for no apparent reason, he dropped the ball, and Ben Daugherty recovered for Tech.

Fifteen plays and 83 yards later Billy Teas threw his only pass of the year, a 12-yard wobbler to Jimmy Durham in the end zone for a touchdown. Rodgers kicked the PAT and Tech was up 21-6. That was all the scoring until the fourth quarter.

Then, from the Georgia 20, Rodgers threw to Henry Hair for the touchdown, then kicked the PAT and Tech led 28-6.

With only minutes remaining, Georgia had the ball at the Tech 34. Bratkowski threw for 17 yards to Madison, then Howard Kelly took the ball on five straight carries, scoring on his final try. Bratkowski missed the PAT and Tech walked away with a 28-12 win.

Georgia finished the year with a 3-8 record, the first time ever they'd lost eight games in a single season.

Tech would go on to defeat number ten West Virginia in the Sugar Bowl and a number six national ranking.

UGA All-American in 1953:
John Carson (E).
UGA All-SEC in 1953:
Zeke Bratkowski (QB).
Named to the UGA SHF:
John Carson and Zeke Bratkowski.
Tech All-American in 1953:
Larry Morris (C).
Tech All-SEC in 1953:
Glenn Turner (HB), Bob Sherman (T), Leon Hardeman (HB), Sam Hensley (E), Billy Teas (HB) and Orville Vereen (G).
Named to the GT AHF:
Glenn Turner, Ray Beck, Lamar Wheat, Hal Miller, Darrell Crawford, Harvey Hardy, Buck Martin, Leon Hardeman and Pepper Rodgers.

It was All-American Leon Hardeman slamming in for another score and Tech put the Sugar Bowl on ice.

TOP:
Henry Hair,
Tech All-SEC end.

SECOND:
Bob Sherman,
Tech All-SEC tackle.

THIRD:
Pepper Rodgers,
quarterback and
member of the
GT AHF.

BOTTOM:
Glenn Turner,
Tech All-American
halfback.

Tech captains for '53: Ed Gossage, Orville Vereen and Sam Hensley. All were named All-SEC and Vereen and Hensley are members of the GT AHF.

Zeke Bratkowski, named All-American in '52 and '53, finished his career at Georgia with 4,824 yards in total
offense, a new SEC record. (Here he fires a pass in
Georgia's 21-7 loss to Florida.)

Georgia team captains and their sponsor meet with their
Alabama counterparts for the coin toss just prior to kickoff on
Homecoming Day, 1953. (Georgia lost, 33-12.)

Jimmy Williams in pursuit of an enemy running back as
Georgia took a close one from Tulane 16-14.

The Georgia Bulldogs of 1953.

1954: Georgia Dominates Everything but the Score

It was November 27, 1954, and Georgia Tech had now won five consecutive games from the Bulldogs, a highly rare phenomenon which caused Georgia fans to look askance at one another. What was going on over there in Athens?

Still, Georgia was 6-2-1 going into the Tech game, with wins over Florida State, Clemson, UNC, Vanderbilt, Tulane and Florida, and losses to Texas A&M and Auburn, and a tie with Alabama. Indeed, with a couple of breaks, Georgia could have enjoyed a super year in '54.

As for the 6-3 Yellow Jackets, at this point they could show wins over Tulane, SMU, Auburn, Tennessee, Alabama and LSU, and losses to Florida, Kentucky and Duke. But they had lost by only one point to both Florida (13-12) and Duke (21-20), and could have been enjoying a super year themselves had they kicked those PATs. Still, despite Georgia's better won-loss record, Tech was picked to win by three touchdowns.

By game time it had been raining torrents for the previous twelve hours in Athens and would continue to rain throughout the contest. But that didn't stop the 50,000 chilled fans who showed up that day.

Georgia took the opening kickoff, ran three plays, then punted to the Tech 38. Paul Rotenberry ran for nine tough yards, but Georgia's Don Shea hit Wade Mitchell on the next play and the ball squirted free to be covered by Joe O'Malley at the Jackets' 42.

John Bell, Jimmy Harper and Bob Garrard alternated carries, down to the 17. Four plays later Joe Graff missed a 14-yard field goal and the Jackets took over.

After an exchange of punts, Tech's John Menger fumbled and Garrard recovered at the 11. Four plays later Georgia again called on Graff for a field goal. This one was good, and the Bulldogs went up by a score of 3-0. This was the first field goal Georgia ever kicked vs. Tech.

By halftime, as weather conditions worsened, Tech could not show a single first down for their efforts, while Georgia had eight.

On the first play of the second half, Georgia's Jimmy Harper fumbled at the Bulldog 19, and Franklin Brooks recovered for the Yellow Jackets. On first down Wade Mitchell faded back and threw long for Henry Hair waiting all alone in the Georgia end zone. This

Don Shea, Georgia's All-SEC guard, walks dejectedly from the field following Tech's 7-3 win in the '54 Mud Bowl. Everyone, winners and losers alike, was just glad it was over.

Tech's Billy Teas struggles just to hold onto that muddy ball as he's gripped by the Bulldog forward wall.

would be Tech's only pass completion of the afternoon, but it was enough. Mitchell then kicked the PAT and Tech took the lead, and the game, by a score of 7-3.

Tech had now won six consecutive games from Georgia, and this win evened the series at 22-22-5.

Tech would then go on to defeat Arkansas 14-6 in the 1955 Cotton Bowl.

UGA All-SEC in 1954:
Joe O'Malley (DE), Don Shea (G), Bobby Gerrard (FB) and Pud Mosteller (T).
Tech All-SEC in 1954:
Larry Morris (C), Frank Brooks (G), Henry Hair (E) and Jimmy Thompson (HB).
Named to the GT AHF:
Henry Hair, Billy Teas, Sam Hensley, Larry Morris and John Hunsinger.

Captain Joe O'Malley, All-SEC defensive end for the Bulldogs.

The Georgia Bulldogs of 1954 went 6-3-1 on the season.

In the final moments of the Vanderbilt game, with Georgia trailing 14-13, Joe Graff walked onto the field and calmly booted this 24 yard field goal to take the game for the Bulldogs, 16-14.

Georgia alternate captain, Robert "Foots" Clemens, fullback.

All-SEC halfback George Volkert stiff-arms this Hog as he breaks out for Tech's final TD of the day in the Yellow Jackets 14-6 win over Arkansas in the '55 Cotton Bowl.

TOP:
Tech's John Menger averaged 19.2 yards per punt return during his career, still an all-time Tech record.

SECOND:
George Humpries, a great Tech halfback.

THIRD:
Billy Teas, Tech All-SEC halfback.

BOTTOM:
Tech captain Larry Morris, an All-American center and a member of the College Football Hall of Fame.

Jubilant Yellow Jackets following their good win over Arkansas in the '55 Cotton Bowl.

1955: Tough Tech Takes Another

Same song, second verse. Tech was cruising along with a great 7-1-1 record as they prepared to meet the Bulldogs on November 26, 1955.

Georgia was suffering through a losing season with a 4-5 record at that point. They had wins over Vanderbilt, UNC, Florida State and Alabama, and losses to Ole Miss, Clemson, Tulane, Florida and Auburn. (This was their first loss to Clemson since 1914 when they went down 35-13.) As for today's contest with Georgia Tech, even Georgia fans didn't see much hope.

All-SEC Bulldog halfback Bobby Gerrard (minus his right shoe) breaks out for a 55-yard gain as Georgia lost to Tech 21-3 in '55 at Sanford Stadium.

Bobby Dodd huddles with his starting backfield for the '56 Sugar Bowl: George Humphreys, Paul Rotenberry, Johnny Menger and Wade Mitchell.

And they were right. At this point the Yellow Jackets had beaten Miami, Florida, SMU, LSU, Florida State, Duke and Alabama, lost a close one to Auburn (14-12), and tied Tennessee. By season's end they could boast a 9-1-1 record, a great 7-0 win over Pitt in the Sugar Bowl and a number seven national ranking.

Tech had the number one defense in the nation and had given up only 43 points to nine opponents as they trotted out to meet Georgia at Grant Field in this 50th meeting between the two schools. On hand were 42,000 fans.

The Bulldogs, eleven-point underdogs for this meeting, were pumped sky-high as they took the opening kickoff. Jimmy Harper returned it 27 yards to his own 33. It was on third down that Bobby Garrard broke out for what appeared to be a touchdown run, but then his right shoe flew off and he was finally caught by Wade Mitchell at the Tech 12.

Tech's stout defense held at that point, and Ken Cooper came in and booted a field goal to put the Bulldogs up 3-0.

Following an exchange of punts, Tech took the ball at their own 47. Twelve plays later, with the ball now at the six, quarterback Toppy Vann threw to Danny Bagwell in the end zone. Vann made a diving catch. But the ball popped loose and rolled out of bounds. Still, the referee ruled that Vann had possession long enough for a touchdown. Mitchell then kicked the PAT and Tech was up 7-3. (The Georgia stands roared their disapproval of the ref's call for a full five minutes.)

Three minutes later Jimmy Morris threw complete to Jimmy Harper, the ball bounced loose and was covered by Tech's Frank Brooks at the Georgia 17. On the next two plays George Volkert carried to the 4-yard line. Then Mitchell sneaked over from there, kicked the PAT, and Tech was up 14-3.

Tech took the second half kickoff, then marched 86 yards for their next score. Volkert carried five times on this drive, gaining a total of 61 yards, down to the Georgia 25. Then, as though that weren't enough, on the next play he swept off tackle and raced the remaining 25 yards for the score. Again Mitchell's kick was good and Tech took this contest 21-3.

Tech then went on to defeat Pitt 7-0 in the '56 Sugar Bowl and a number four national ranking.

UGA All-SEC in 1955:
Roy Wilkins (E).
Tech All-American in 1955:
Franklin Brooks (G).
Tech All-SEC in 1955:
Henry Hair (E), George Volkert (HB),
Jimmie Morris (C), Carl Vereen (T)
and Wade Mitchell (QB).
Named to the GT AHF:
Orville Vereen.

George Volkert, Tech All-SEC halfback.

Frank Brooks,
Tech All-American guard.

Little Jimmy Thompson (never mind the jersey) dashes for a TD as Tech smashed Tulane 40-0.

Don Ellis goes high for this Mitchell pass. Interference was called on Pitt at the one, Tech scored and won the Sugar Bowl 7-0.

Captain Jimmy Morris, with his wife Ann and daughter Marti. This marked the first time in history a Tech team captain was sponsored by his own daughter.

Dick Young,
quarterback for
the Bulldogs.

Roy Wilkins,
Georgia All-SEC end.

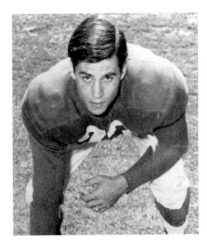

Wayne Dye, an outstanding Bulldog
lineman and the brother of Nat and
Pat Dye.

Captain
Robert Gerrard,
Georgia All-SEC
halfback.

A heated discussion broke out between Georgia and
Clemson players which necessitated the quick appearance of
Coach Quinton Lumpkin and others on the field. The Bulldogs
lost this game 26-7.

Co-captain Don Shea,
Georgia All-SEC guard.

1956: The Yellow Jackets Romp

December 1, 1956 dawned cold but sunny, a great day for football, as 50,000 fans crowded into Sanford Stadium to see if Georgia Tech could continue their incredible winning streak against the Bulldogs. Tech had won every contest now since 1948, and Georgia fans were beginning to seriously wonder if there was some strange curse at work.

Tech at this point was 8-1 on the season with wins over Kentucky, SMU, LSU, Auburn, Tulane, Duke, Alabama and Florida, and were ranked number four in the nation. Their only loss had come three weeks before at the hands of number three Tennesse (6-0). It was a close loss, but would prevent Tech's being named national champions. They had blanked five opponents and held the others to one TD or less.

As for Georgia, they were 3-5-1 at this point, with wins over Florida State, UNC and Alabama, losses to Vanderbilt, Mississippi State, Kentucky, Florida and Auburn, and a tie with Miami. They had scored a total of only 66 points all season, and would not better their stats in today's contest against the nation's number one defense.

In fact, the score was tied 0-0 at the end of the first quarter, and Georgia fans were beginning to hope. But then, with seven minutes remaining in the half, Tech took the ball at their own 16-yard line, and 13 plays later Paul Rotenberry scored on an 8-yard burst off left guard. Mitchell kicked the PAT and Tech went up 7-0, which was the half-time score.

Georgia kicked off to open the third period, and on first down Rotenberry took a pitchout and raced 53 yards, down to the Georgia 19, before being chased down by Marion Bush. Then little Jimmy Thompson sped to the 1. Mitchell took it in on the next play, kicked the point and Tech led 14-0.

Wade Mitchell, Tech's All-SEC QB, also intercepted 13 passes on defense during his career, still number three in the GT record book.

Tech had moved 72 yards in three plays and things would go downhill for the Bulldogs from there on.

As the fourth quarter got underway Georgia, which had obviously been playing on heart alone, began to show signs of exhaustion. They had held the mighty Yellow Jackets to only a two-touchdown lead, but now they were getting tired.

At that point the floodgates opened

Paul Rotenberry scores from the eight to put Tech up 7-0 over Georgia. Unfortunately for the Bulldogs, the Jackets would score another 28 points before the day was over.

and Tech moved for another three touchdowns in the final 15 minutes.

First, it was R. C. Mattison scoring on a 1-yard plunge. The PAT was good and Tech led 21-0. Then, only three minutes later, Stan Flowers slammed over from the two. Again the PAT was good, and Tech led 28-0.

But the game wasn't quite over. With only two minutes remaining, Toppy Vann surprised everyone when he started on a sweep, then paused and tossed a short pass to Flowers for another score. Final: Tech 35, Georgia 0.

Tech would go on to their sixth bowl win in six years, a 21-14 triumph over Pitt in the '56 Gator Bowl, and a number four national ranking (behind only Oklahoma, Tennessee and Iowa).

Between 1951-56 Tech had a phenomenal 59-7-3 won-loss record, one to be envied by fans across America. This had truly been the great Golden Age of Georgia Tech football.

Georgia co-captains in '56, Knox Culpepper and Laneair Roberts.

Tony Cushenberry, Georgia All-SEC guard.

Carl Manning, Georgia back.

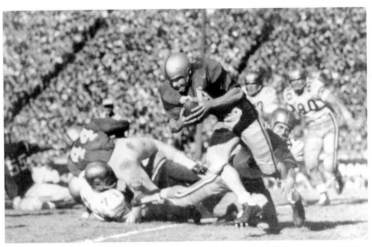

Carl Manning piles into the Tech line as Georgia lost to the Yellow Jackets 35-0.

Carl Manning kicks the clutch PAT that tied Kentucky at 7-7. Georgia lost this one 14-7.

Toppy Vann, Tech's All-SEC quarterback.

Don Stephenson, Tech's All-American center.

Paul Rotenberry, Tech's All-SEC halfback.

Ken Owen averaged 30.7 yards per kickoff return in '55, still number one in the Tech record book.

All-SEC halfback Paul Rotenberry, led by Dick Mattison and Wade Mitchell, dashes for a first down vs. Georgia.

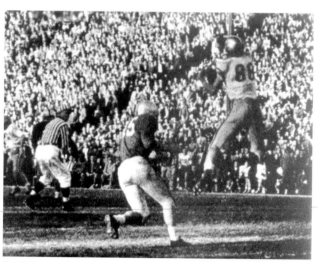

Paul Vickers takes a Mitchell pass for a 21-yard pickup as Tech smashed Georgia 35-0.

1957: Theron Sapp Zaps Tech

It was November 30, 1957, the year that Tech's dream finally came crashing down and they became just a regular football team again. Which isn't to say that they were a poor team. In fact, at that point they were 4-3-2 on the season, with wins over Kentucky, Tulane, Duke and Alabama, scoreless ties with SMU and Florida, and close losses to LSU (20-13) and Auburn (3-0), and a 21-6 loss to Tennessee. They were hurting offensively, but their defense had given up just 64 points. Indeed, just a few breaks and Tech could have been sporting another excellent record.

An hour up the road, in Athens, UGA was suffering through another losing season. After dropping their first three games, they finally got to ticking with wins over Tulane and Kentucky. But that was it. They also had losses to Texas, Vanderbilt, Michigan, Navy, Alabama, Florida and Auburn. And their prospects of beating Tech this afternoon were not good. But the experts had been wrong before.

The temperature was below freezing in Atlanta that afternoon with a stiff wind blowing out of the northeast as some 40,000 fans turned out at Grant Field to see if Tech could make it nine in a row over Georgia.

The Yellow Jackets kicked off, then after an exchange of punts Tech took the ball at their own 41. Larry Fonts carried for 26 yards on two carries and Cal James took it for 10 more, down to the Georgia 20. But on the next play Theron Sapp and Jimmy Vickers sacked Tech quarterback Fred Braselton for an 11-yard loss. The Bulldogs held at that point, ending Tech's first threat, and Jerry Nabors punted into the end zone.

Later in the first quarter Georgia's Ken Cooper got off a poor punt that went out at the Bulldog 39. On first down Tech's Taz Anderson dashed for 25 yards, down to the 14. Then came Les Simmerville and Floyd Faucette, taking the ball to the nine. But again Georgia held and another Tech threat was turned aside.

Jimmy Orr, Georgia's All-SEC receiver and member of the Baltimore Colts All-Time Football Team.

Early in the second quarter Tech recovered a fumble at the Georgia 24. But four plays gained them nothing, and again the Bulldogs took the ball.

Early in the second half, Faucette fumbled at midfield and Theron Sapp recoved for the Bulldogs. Several plays later, facing third and 12 at the Tech 39, Charlie Britt hit Jimmy Orr with a 13-yard pass for a first down at the Tech 26.

From there on it was all Theron Sapp. He carried on six consecutive plays, down to the Tech 1-yard line. At that point, facing third and goal, Britt tried a quarterback sneak that

Theron Sapp, Georgia's All-SEC fullback, goes in for a TD to upset Georgia Tech 7-0 in a game played at Grant Field. This was Georgia's first win over Tech since 1948.

failed to gain. Then on fourth down, Britt again handed off to Sapp who slammed off the right side and into the end zone. Ken Cooper kicked the PAT and Georgia was up 7-0. (This was Georgia's first touchdown vs. Tech since 1953.)

Some 15 minutes later, midway the fourth quarter, mainly on the passing arm of Fred Braselton, Tech moved from its 25 to the Georgia 16. But then, facing third and five, Cicero Lucas and Nat Dye broke through the Tech line and threw Braselton for an 11-yard loss. On fourth down he threw incomplete, and again Georgia had survived.

They had also established themselves as football champions of the great state of Georgia—at least for a year.

Don Stephenson, Tech's All-American center and member of the College Football Hall of Fame.

Bobby Dover, Tech guard.

Joe Delany, Tech halfback.

Jerry Nabors, Tech All-SEC end and member of the GT AHF.

Stan Flowers, an excellent Tech halfback.

The Bulldogs break up this pass to Tech's Jack Rudolph as Georgia won 7-0.

Fred Braselton, a first-rate Tech halfback.

Don Soberdash took this Tommy Lewis pass for a short gain as Georgia lost to Florida 22-0.

Charlie Britt lofted a long pass to Jimmy Orr for a TD as Georgia lost to Texas 26-7. Orr is a member of the UGA SHF.

TOP:
Captain J. B. Davis, Georgia halfback.

SECOND:
Travis Vinesett, Georgia guard.

THIRD:
Nat Dye, Georgia All-SEC tackle.

BOTTOM:
Theron Sapp, Georgia All-SEC halfback and hero of Georgia's '57 win over Tech.

1958: Tenacious Georgia Hangs On For Tough Win

After an eight year drought Georgia had finally beaten Tech in '57 and now they were hungry for another such miracle. The Bulldogs had a 3-6 record at this point with wins over Florida State, Kentucky and The Citadel, and losses to Texas, Vanderbilt, South Carolina, Alabama, Florida and Auburn.

As for Tech, whose great Dream Team came crashing down in '57, they were 5-3-1 at this point with wins over Florida State, Tulane, Tennessee, Duke and Clemson, and close losses to Kentucky, SMU and Alabama, and a tie with Auburn. A win today would give them a 6-3-1 record and a respectable season. Thus they were motivated.

Indeed, all the experts agreed that Tech was a far better team than their record indicated, and they were heavily favored to take Georgia this afternoon before 50,000 frozen fans at Sanford Stadium.

The first 25 minutes of this game was a defensive standoff, with neither team able to seriously threaten the other. Then Tech's Gerald Burch went back to punt from his own 30. But Larry Lanchester scrambled past blockers and blocked the kick. Jimmy Vickers scooped up the bouncing ball at the 20 and ran it in for a Bulldog touchdown. The PAT missed, but Georgia held a 6-0 lead.

Later, with only moments remaining in the half, Georgia took the ball at midfield. Theron Sapp, hero of the '57 game, then took the ball on three straight carries for a total of 34 yards, down to the Tech 16. Now, with only eight seconds on the clock, Dave Lloyd kicked a field goal and Georgia went in at halftime with a 9-0 lead.

Early in the second half Georgia fumbled at their own 24 and Floyd Faucette recovered for the Jackets. Faucette himself carried on first down and took such a hit that the ball squirted out of his hands and rolled all the way to the 11-yard line where Tech recovered for a nice gain. Then, following carries by Cal James and Faucette, the Jackets were facing a fourth-and-two at the 3. James tried the right side, but was thrown for a loss and the Bulldogs took over.

Again Georgia was forced to punt, and again the Jackets moved down to the Bulldogs 17. But a fourth down play was inches short of a first down and again Georgia moved off the bullseye.

But Georgia again fumbled and Gerald Burch recoverd at the 20. Cal James and Tommy Lewis alternated carries until they'd pushed down to the Georgia 2. At that point, facing a fourth and goal, Tommy Wells kicked a field goal and Georgia's lead was cut to 9-3.

Captain Theron Sapp, Georgia's all-time great fullback. His is one of only four jerseys ever retired by the Bulldogs.

Fred Brown, All-SEC halfback, scoots 34 yards for Georgia's clinching touchdown as they downed the Jackets 16-3 at Sanford Stadium.

Nat Dye, All-SEC tackle and brother of Wayne and Pat Dye.

Early in the fourth quarter Georgia's Bobby Walden, standing at his own 14, got the Bulldogs out of a deep hole when he kicked a booming punt that finally rolled dead at the Tech 8-yard line. It was a kick of 78 yards and put the Jackets in the hole for the first time in the second half.

Tech then drove to midfield and Delany punted out of bounds at the Georgia 7, and the Bulldogs were right back where they started.

Just as they'd done in '57, the Bulldogs then called on Theron Sapp. He ran for 16 yards to the 26, but four plays later Georgia was again forced to punt.

Tech took the ball at their 31. But on first down Tech made a fatal mistake. Walt Howard attempted a pass which Charlie Britt picked off and ran back to the Tech 34. Britt then handed off to Fred Brown who rocketed all the way for a touchdown. (Brown, by the way, is the nephew of famous Hollywood cowboy star Johnny Mack Brown.) Carl Manning kicked the PAT and Georgia won this 53rd meeting 16-3.

Fred Brown, All-SEC halfback for the Bulldogs.

UGA All-SEC in 1958:
Theron Sapp (FB) and Nat Dye (T).
Tech All-SEC in 1958:
Gerald Burch (HB), Maxie Baughan (C) and Floyd Fawcett (HB).

Dave Lloyd, Georgia back.

In '59 Charlie Britt returned an interception 100 yards for a TD vs. Florida, still number one in the UGA record book.

Two all-time Georgia greats: Theron Sapps follows Pat Dye around end as the Bulldogs whopped The Citadel 76-0 in '58.

TOP:
Frank Nix,
Tech back.

SECOND:
Captain Foster Watkins,
Tech halfback.

THIRD:
Gerald Burch,
Tech All-SEC halfback.

BOTTOM:
Floyd Faucette,
Tech All-SEC halfback.

Cal James dances away from a Georgia defender in a game won by the Bulldogs 16-3.

The Bulldogs block Gerald Burch's punt. It was a bad mistake for the Yellow Jackets.

1959: 10-1-0 Georgia Surprises Everybody

Over the previous six years, since 1953, Georgia had compiled an unenviable 23-36-2 won-loss record, and fans were beginning to yearn for the good ol' national championship days of Frankie Sinkwich and Racehorse Davis. Or at least for a winning season now and then.

What made it worse was the knowledge that over that same period of time Georgia Tech had compiled one of the finest won-loss records in the history of college football. Maybe Wally Butts was growing complacent. Maybe it was time for a coaching change.

O ye of little faith!

By the time of the Georgia Tech shootout, the Bulldogs were boasting a fine 8-1 record, with wins over Alabama, Vandy, Hardin-Simmons, Mississippi State, Kentucky, Florida State, Florida and Auburn. Indeed, their only loss was a tremendous 30-14 upset at the hands of South Carolina. And by then all the former sceptics were shaking their heads and saying, Ho-ho! I told you so!

Charlie Britt returned an interception 100 yards for a TD vs. Florida, still an all-time UGA record.

And Tech was also doing well. They were 6-3 at this point, with wins over Kentucky, SMU, Clemson, Tennessee, Tulane and mighty Notre Dame, and close losses to Auburn (7-6), Duke (10-7) and Alabama (9-7). With a few breaks Tech could have again been in the running for the national championship.

A bright but frigid afternoon greeted the 44,000 fans who turned out at Grant Field for this encounter.

Fred Brown dashes 58 yards with a Charlie Britt pass for a touchdown to down Tech 21-14.

For the first 10 minutes of this game both teams threatened, but untimely fumbles erased each threat. Then Tech's Ben Smith bobbled the ball and Fred Lawrence recovered at the Tech 33. Charlie Britt lost 7 yards on first down, but then Fred Brown took a pitchout and raced all the way to the Tech 2-yard line. On the next play Fran Tarkenton pitched to George Guisler who scored standing up. Durwood Pennington kicked the PAT and Georgia led 7-0.

Later, with less than three minutes remaining in the half, Georgia took the ball at the Tech 48. Tarkenton then completed passes of 12 yards to Brown and 22 yards to Guisler, and the Bulldogs were knocking at the door. Then Tarkenton came back with a 16-yarder to Bill Herron in the end zone, the PAT was good and Georgia was up 14-0.

Tech took the ensuing kickoff and, to the surprise of everyone, quick-kicked on first down—which was a mistake.

Georgia took the ball at their own 42. On first down Britt threw long for Brown racing down the sideline. Brown took the ball over his shoulder and danced on into the end zone, a 58-yard completion. The PAT was good and Georgia took a 21-0 lead in at halftime.

Later, with 12 seconds remaining in the third quarter, Tech got on the board when Marvin Tibbetts threw short to Gerald Burch who fought his way through the entire Georgia team, then ran 57 yards for a touchdown. Tommy Wells kicked the PAT and the score became 21-7. Later, with only three minutes remaining, Tibbetts hit Fred Murphy with a 38-yard pass good for another Tech score. The PAT was good, and Georgia led 21-14, which was the final score, Georgia's third straight win over the Jackets.

The Bulldogs went on to defeat Missouri 14-0 in the 1960 Orange Bowl, and a number five national ranking.

Tech accepted a bid to play in the Gator Bowl where they lost 14-7 to Frank Broyles and his Arkansas Razorbacks.

UGA All-American in 1959:
Pat Dye (G).
UGA All-SEC in 1959:
Jim Vickers (E), Fran Tarkenton (QB), Bobby Walden (HB), Billy Roland (G) and Charley Britt (QB).
Tech All-American in 1959:
Maxie Baughan (C).
Tech All-SEC in 1959:
Gerald Burch (HB), Toby Deese (C), Billy Shaw (T) and Taz Anderson (HB).
Named to the GT AHF:
Maxie Baughan and Billy Shaw.

Taz Anderson, Tech All-SEC back.

Toby Deese, Tech All-SEC tackle.

Billy Shaw, Tech All-SEC tackle, went on to star for the Buffalo Bills and is a member of the Pro Football Hall of Fame.

Tech's Captain Maxie Baughn, an All-American center and a member of the College Football Hall of Fame.

Chick Graning, behind Gerald Burch and Taz Anderson (all three were named All-SEC), sweeps Georgia's end as the Yellow Jackets fell by a score of 21-14 at Sanford Stadium.

Three all-time Georgia greats, Fran Tarkenton, Wally Butts, and Pat Dye.

SEC champions with a great 10-1 record, Georgia met and defeated Missouri 14-0 in the '60 Orange Bowl. Here Bill McKenney takes a Fran Tarkenton pass in for a touchdown and a 7-0 lead over the Tigers.

Bill Jackson runs for a first down as the Bulldogs fell to South Carolina 30-14 in a terrific upset, their only loss of the season.

Georgia co-captains Don Soberdash and Jim Vickers pose with their SEC championship trophy.

1960: Pat Dye's Dives Give Georgia a Close Win

It was November 26, 1960, and hopes were running high that a 5-4 Georgia team, defending SEC Champions, could beat Tech today and end a so-so season on a winning note. To date they'd beaten Vanderbilt, South Carolina, Mississippi State, Kentucky and Tulsa, while losing close games to Alabama, Southern Cal, Florida and Auburn.

Georgia Tech, on the other hand, had an identical 5-4 record coming into this contest, with wins over Kentucky, Rice, LSU, Tulane and Tennessee and losses to Florida (18-17), Auburn (9-7), Duke (6-0) and Alabama (16-15). They'd lost three of their games by a total of four points, in other words, which would suggest that Tech was truly better in '60 than their record indicated.

Neither team expected to be going to a bowl in '60, but still some 55,000 fans showed up for this game on a cool but sunny day in Athens. And it was a humdinger.

Georgia received the opening kickoff, ran off nine plays and were looking at a first down at the Tech 22. Fran Tarkenton then threw to Bobby Walden at the 12, but Walden was hit and bobbled the ball. Walter Howard recovered for Tech and the Jackets breathed a sigh of relief.

Fran Tarkenton, a Georgia All-American, is a member of the College Football Hall of Fame.

Later, with only minutes remaining in the second quarter, Tech had the ball at their own 45. Jimmy Nail, Billy Williamson and Stan Gann alternated carries down to the Georgia 42. Chick Graning picked up two, but a roughing penalty moved the ball to the 25. Three plays later, Tech had a first down at the Bulldog 12. Then came Marvin Tibbetts to the 1. Then it was Tibbetts bulling his way in for the score.

The two teams lined up for the extra point try, the ball was snapped, Tommy Wells stepped forward and gave the ball a good swift kick. But at that moment a red jersey appeared out of nowhere. It was Pat Dye and he was running wide open. He dove at the last moment and his outstretched hand just grazed the ball as it began its ascent.

The kick was blocked and Tech led 6-0.

Then, with only moments left in the half, Tech tried a field goal from the

Durward Pennington kicks the PAT that sunk Tech in '60, as Georgia won a squeaker 7-6, thanks to Pat Dye. (Fran Tarkenton is the holder.)

Georgia 28, but again Dye's outstretched hand deflected the ball and the field goal try was no good.

Most of the action in the third quarter consisted of the referees throwing penalty flags from one end of the field to the other as the players engaged in fist fights after almost every play.

In the fourth period Tech had a first down at their own 33. Then Gann threw short to Chick Graning, but Georgia's Bill McKenny picked it off and ran it back to the 13.

Five plays later David Godfrey went off right tackle from the one for the TD, Durwood Pennington kicked the PAT, and Georgia escaped with a close 7-6 win.

UGA All-American in 1960:
Pat Dye (G), Fran Tarkenton (QB)
UGA All-SEC in 1960:
Fred Brown (HB) and Pete Case (T).
Named to the UGA SHF:
Thomas Paris, Fran Tarkenton, Pat Dye and Coach Wally Butts.
Tech All-SEC in 1960:
Billy Shaw (T), Gerald Burch (E), Ed Nutting (G), Bill Williamson (HB) and Chick Graning (FB).
Named to the GT AHF:
Taz Anderson and Billy Shaw.

Pat Dye was successful in blocking this PAT try (and later a field goal try) vs. Tech which resulted in a Georgia win, 7-6.

Pat Dye, Georgia All-American guard.

Georgia's 1960 starting backfield: Bob Walden (#39), the SEC's leading punter; Fred Brown (#26), the SEC's leading receiver; David Godfrey (#42) who never lost a yard during his varsity career; and Fran Tarkenton, All-American quarterback. Quite a crew!

Fran Tarkenton bootlegs the ball for a first down as Georgia beat Vanderbilt 18-7.

Ed Nutting,
Tech All-SEC tackle.

Chick Graning,
Tech All-SEC fullback.

Harold Erickson,
Tech All-SEC guard.

Captain Gerald Burch, Tech
All-SEC halfback.

Tech's defense mobs Fran Tarkenton.

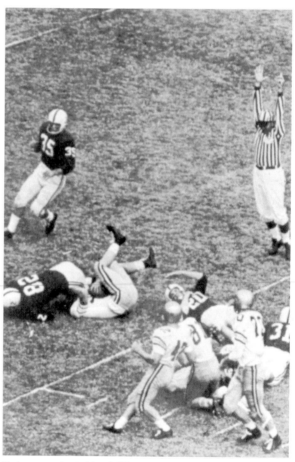

Tech quarterback Marvin Tibbetts slams in for a TD, but the
Jackets then missed the PAT and Georgia walked away with a
7-6 win.

1961: Tech's Tough Defense Makes the Difference

After 22 years as head coach of the Georgia Bulldogs, the great Wally Butts resigned following the 1960 season. During his tenure the Bulldogs compiled an excellent 140-86-9 record, won four SEC championships and made eight bowl appearances. He would be a tough man to replace.

The new coach was Johnny Griffith, a former player and freshman coach under Wally Butts.

As December 2 rolled around Georgia was stumbling along with a 3-6 record, showing wins over South Carolina, Mississippi State and Kentucky, and losses to Alabama, Vanderbilt, Florida State, Miami, Florida and Auburn. Obviously they would not be big favorites in this day's game.

At Tech, meanwhile, Bobby Dodd was now in his sixteenth year as head coach and his 6-3 Jackets were enjoying a fairly good season. In their opener they had a big upset victory over Southern Cal, the number nine team in the country, plus other wins over Rice, Duke, Auburn, Tulane and Florida, and losses to LSU, Tennessee and Alabama. As usual, Tech had a nationally ranked defense and none of their opponents had scored more than one touchdown against them.

Prior to this day's game Tech had already accepted a bid to play Penn State in the '61 Gator Bowl.

Bill Williamson averaged 24.8 yards per kickoff return during his career, still number two in the Tech record book.

December 2 was a warm sunny day at Grant Field as 47,000 fans streamed in to see if the Bulldogs could hold their own against the favored Yellow Jackets. Well, they didn't have long to wait. Following the opening kickoff, Georgia punted to the Tech 44. Eleven plays later the Jackets were at the Georgia 11. On first down, Stan Gann bootlegged the ball into the end zone, Billy Lothridge kicked the PAT, and Tech was up 7-0. And there were fans still streaming into the stadium.

Only minutes later, Georgia's punter received a bad snap from center, the ball sailed over his head, and Tech recovered at the Bulldog 16. Lothridge kicked a 26-yard field goal from there and Tech was up 10-0.

Early in the second quarter Tech took the ball at their own 19. Lothridge ran for 15, then came a 15-yard penalty, plus 10-yard runs by Billy Williamson

Stan Gann, pursued by John Paul Holmes, bootlegs the ball into the end zone to put the Yellow Jackets up 6-0 over Georgia. Tech would eventually win by a score of 22-7.

and Joe Auer, and the Jackets had a first down at the Georgia 30. On first down Lothridge ran to the 18 where he was hit hard but managed to lateral to Billy Williamson who then dashed the remaining yards for another Jacket touchdown. The PAT was no good but Tech increased their lead to 16-0.

In the third quarter Georgia took the ball at their own 33. Five plays later, from the Tech 30, Jake Saye passed to Billy Knowles in the end zone for a Bulldog touchdown. Durwood Pennington kicked the PAT and Georgia trailed 16-7.

Midway the final period Tech took the ball at their own 20, then scored 14 plays later when Williamson went in from the 6. The PAT missed, but Tech had a big 22-7 win under their belt, and a 7-3 record. They would go on then to lose to Penn State in the '61 Gator Bowl.

Dave Watson, Tech's All-American guard.

UGA All-SEC in 1961:
Pete Case (T) and Bill McKenney (HB).
Named to the UGA SHF:
Bobby Walden.
Tech All-American in 1961:
Rufus Guthrie (G).
Tech All-SEC in 1961:
Dave Watson (G), Harold Ericksen (G), Bill Williamson (HB).

Rufus Guthrie, Tech's All-American guard.

Mike McNames, Tech's All-American fullback.

Tech tri-captains for '61 (top to bottom): All-SEC back Bill Williamson, All-SEC back Chick Granning, and Willie McGaughey.

Larry Stallings, Tech All-SEC guard and a member of the GT AHF.

Bulldog captain and All-SEC halfback Bill McKenney, Coach John Griffith, and All-SEC tackle Pete Case.

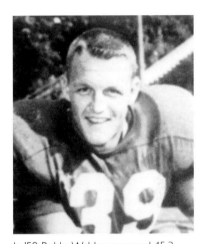

In '59 Bobby Walden averaged 45.3 yards per punt, still number two in the UGA record book.

All-SEC end Pat Hodgson took this Larry Rakestraw pass in for a touchdown as the Bulldogs beat Kentucky 16-15.

Bill McKenney slashes off the right side of the Vandy line as Georgia lost 21-0.

1962: Lothridge Sets Record, Whacks Bulldogs

The Yellow Jackets were 6-2-1 coming into the Georgia game, with wins over Clemson, Florida, Tennessee, Tulane, Duke and Alabama, and 3-point losses to LSU (10-7) and Auburn (17-14), and a tie with Florida State. In other words, with a couple of breaks Tech could have been in the running for the national championship. But such is football.

As for Georgia, they were limping along with a 3-3-3 record, with wins over Vanderbilt, Clemson, and Auburn, losses to Alabama, Florida State and Florida, and ties with South Carolina, Kentucky and NC State.

Joe Burson returned an interception 87 yards for a TD vs. Auburn, still number three in the UGA record book.

Both teams were idle on November 24, but a week prior to that date, on November 17, both teams had pulled off very memorable upsets, with Georgia upending a great 7-1 Auburn team by a score of 30-21, and Tech defeating Joe Namath and Alabama, the number one team in the nation, 7-6. This would be Alabama's only loss of the season.

So both schools were feeling pretty good about themselves as they squared off on December 1 before 55,000 fans at Sanford Stadium for their 57th meeting.

Following the opening kickoff, Georgia punted and Tech took the ball at their own 18. Twelve plays later they were at the Georgia 1. Mike McNames scored from there, Billy Lothridge kicked the point and Tech was up 7-0.

On the very next series Frank Sexton blocked a Georgia punt and Ray Mendheim recovered at the Bulldog 17. On first down Lothridge threw to John Wright at the 2. Then it was Lothridge sneaking in from there. He then kicked the PAT and Tech was up 14-0.

Georgia Tech's 1962 starting line which Bobby Dodd called "the greatest in Tech history." (L-R): All-American end Billy Martin, All-SEC tackle Larry Stallings, All-SEC guard Dave Watson, center Bobby Caldwell, All-American guard Rufus Guthrie, tackle Ed Griffin and All-SEC end Ted Davis.

Some 20 minutes later, to open the second half, Tech's Joe Auer ran the kickoff back 55 yards to the Georgia 39. Three plays later Lothridge hit Doug Cooper with a pass at the 5, then it was Joe Auer to the 1. Lothridge went in from there, his second TD of the day, kicked the PAT, and Tech was up 21-0.

Six minutes later, midway through the third period, with the ball at their own 14-yard line, Gerry Bussell took a pitch and raced 86 sensational yards for another Tech touchdown, still number two in their record book. Lothridge kicked the point and Tech led 28-0.

Georgia got on the board two minutes later when Larry Rakestraw tossed a 10-yard touchdown pass to Carl Guthrie. The Bulldogs 2-point conversion failed, and they trailed Tech 28-6.

Early in the final period Bussell picked off a Rakestraw pass and returned it to the Georgia 14. The Bulldogs held, however, so Lothridge kicked a 42-yard field goal, and Tech went up 31-6.

Eight minutes later Auer intercepted another Rakestraw pass at the Tech 33 and returned it 39 yards to the Georgia 28. Lothridge hit Steve Copeland with a pass at the 1, then he ran it in on the next play, and Tech was up 37-6. And that was the final score. With this win the Jackets tied up the series at 26-26-5.

Billy Lothridge finished the day with one of the finest performances ever seen during this long series. He scored three touchdowns, kicked four extra points, kicked a 42-yard field goal, scored a total of 25 points on the day (still a series record), and averaged 35 yards per kick on four punts.

Following this game Tech went on to lose 14-10 to Missouri in the the '62 Bluebonnet Bowl.

(Over the previous four years 14 of Tech's 17 losses had been by one touchdown or less.)

The players are congratulated after a long drive that resulted in a touchdown, but again it was too little too late as the Bulldogs wound up with a 7-7 tie with Kentucky.

It's Fred Barber going 37 yards for the touchdown that would sink Vanderbilt 10-0.

Richard Boykin returns a punt as the Bulldogs and South Carolina walked away with a 7-7 tie.

Carl Guthrie took this Larry Rakestraw pass in for a score, but Tech won this one by a whopping 37-6 margin.

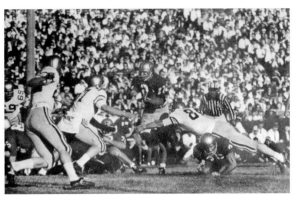

Bobby Dodd and All-American quarterback Billy Lothridge discuss strategy during the Georgia game.

Captain Tom Winingder and All-SEC guard Larry Stallings meet Sandra Dee prior to the '62 Bluebonnet Bowl.

Rufus Guthrie leads Gerry Bussell for a first down as Tech beat Georgia 37-6 to complete a solid 7-2-1 season.

Despondent Yellow Jackets take a moment to ponder the situation as they trail Missouri 14-10 with time running out in the '62 Bluebonnet Bowl.

1963: Bulldogs Bobble the Game Away

After their disappointing season of '62, the Bulldogs were hoping for better things in '63. Things did get better, but not by much. They were 4-4-1 as they prepard for Tech on November 30, with wins over Vanderbilt, South Carolina, Miami and Kentucky, losses to Alabama, UNC, Florida and Auburn, and a tie with Clemson.

As for Tech, they were clicking right along with a 6-3 record at this point, with wins over Florida, Clemson, Tennessee, Tulane, Duke and Florida State, losses to LSU (7-6), Auburn and Alabama. Of their ten opponents, only Auburn and Alabama had scored more than 7 points against the nationally ranked Yellow Jacket defense in '63.

The game originally had been scheduled to be played on November 23, but because of the assasination of President Kennedy on November 22, the annual contest was postponed until the following week.

Game day in Atlanta was bright but brutally cold as some 53,000 fans moved into Grant Field for this 58th meeting between the Yellow Jackets of Georgia Tech and the Bulldogs of the University of Georgia. Tech, as had been the case over the previous three years, was favored to take this one easily.

The first quarter, as had happened so often in the past, consisted of each team running three plays, then punting. With four minutes remaining in that period, Billy Lothridge kicked out of bounds at the Georgia 4-yard line. Two plays later Larry Rakestraw fumbled at his own 23 and Dave Simmons recovered for Tech.

Three plays later Ray Mendheim scored from the 1, Billy Lothridge kicked the point, and Tech was making the experts look good.

Later, with less than a minute remaining in the half, George Nowicki recovered a Tech fumble at the Yellow Jacket 32. But six plays later Georgia's drive stalled at the 10, and Bill McCullough kicked a field goal and the two teams went in at halftime, Tech leading 7-3.

Jim Mendheim slams into the Bulldog end zone as Tech went on to take a 14-3 win at Grant Field.

In the third period Georgia again threatened following Mickey Babb's recovery of a Tech fumble at the Jackets' 37-yard line. Rakestraw threw to Pat Hodgson at the 11-yard line. But on the next play Georgia fumbled and Joe Chapman recovered for Tech. For all practical purposes, this was Georgia's last big threat of the afternoon.

In the final quarter, with the temperature dropping and hands frozen stiff, fumbles became a dime a dozen.

But with only minutes remaining, Tech took the ball at their own 47. Six plays later they were at the Georgia 3. From there Lothridge fired a short pass to Frank Sexton in the end zone, kicked the point, and Tech went up 14-3.

Later in the game, Tech again marched to the Georgia 3, but then the clock ran out and Tech walked away with a tough 14-3 win.

Georgia thus finished their season with a 4-5-1 record. Johnny Griffith resigned at that point to be replaced by a gentleman named Vince Dooley.

As for Tech, they finished their season with a respectable 7-3 record, but no bowl invitations.

This was Tech's last game as a member of the SEC. In '64 they would become a Southern Independent.

Two all-time Georgia Tech greats, quarterback Billy Lothridge and receiver Bill Martin. Both were named All-American and both are members of Tech's All-Time Football Team. Lothridge came in runner-up for the Heisman Trophy in '63.

Joe Auer breaks free on a long TD run as Tech beat Florida 9-0.

Lothridge huddles his Tech team as they prepare to kick off their game with LSU, a game won by the Tigers 7-6.

In addition to his many other talents, Bill Lothridge kicked 12 field goals in '63, breaking the all-time NCAA record for field goals in a single season. Here he boots a 27-yarder as Tech beat Duke by a score of 30-6.

The Georgia Bulldogs of 1963.

Georgia tri-captains for 1963 (L-R): Mickey Babb, Bill Knowles, and Len Hauss. Babb was an All-SEC end, and Hauss is a member of the UGA SHF.

Larry Rakestraw, Georgia quarterback, twice named All-SEC.

Super soph quarterback Preston Ridlehuber, urged on by wildly enthusiastic Georgia cheerleaders, scrambles for big yardage as the Bulldogs whacked Vanderbilt.

1964: Dooley Dazzles Dogs

It was November 28, 1964, and already Georgia fans were beginning to marvel at the changes they could see in their Bulldogs. At this point they were 5-3-1 with wins over Vanderbilt, Clemson, Kentucky, UNC and Florida, losses to Alabama, Florida State and Auburn, and a tie with South Carolina. In '64 they would have their first winning season since 1960, and they would go to their first bowl game since 1959. It looked like the long drought was over.

As for Tech, despite the fact that they were Southern Independents, they were still playing an SEC schedule, and they were cruising along with an even better record than their country cousins from Athens. Indeed, at this point they were 7-2 on the season with wins over Vanderbilt, Miami, Clemson, Navy, Auburn, Tulane and Duke, and losses to Tennessee and Alabama. In fact, as of October 31, the Jackets were 7-0 and ranked number six in the nation. But then came back-to-back losses to Tennessee and Alabama (the Tide would become national champions in '64) and there went their national ranking.

But despite Tech's success to date, Georgia had given up only nine touchdowns in their last eight games, and thus the experts decided that this game would be too close to call.

Fifty-two thousand fans braved a cold rain to fill Sanford Stadium for this 59th meeting between these two old adversaries.

Georgia with a 5-3 record was playing strictly for pride at this point, but the 7-2 Jackets had been promised a trip to the Gator Bowl should they win.

The boys were playing on a muddy field and mounting any sort of offense was difficult for both teams. In fact, throughout the first two quarters this game appeared to be a punting contest between Tech's Jerry Priestly and Georgia's Mack Faircloth.

All-SEC Lynn Hughes lofts a long one to Pat Hodgson as the Bulldogs beat the Yellow Jackets 7-0 in a tough fight at Sanford Stadium.

And the same is true of most of the third quarter. But then the break that both teams had awaited finally came—and it went to the Bulldogs.

Tech's Jeff Davis was nailed at the line of scrimmage, fumbled the ball, and John Glass recovered at the Jackets' 22-yard line.

On second down Preston Ridlehuber threw complete to Leon Armbrester at the 5. Two plays later Ridlehuber kept the ball and followed Armbrester all the way into the end zone for a touchdown. Bobby Etter kicked the PAT and Georgia led 7-0, which was the final score.

The then 6-3-1 Georgia went on to a great 7-0 win over Texas Tech in the '64 Sun Bowl, while 7-3 Georgia Tech stayed home on New Year's Day.

UGA All-American in 1964:
Jim Wilson (T), Ray Rissmiller (T).
UGA All-SEC in 1964:
Wayne Swinford (DB), Barry Wilson (DE), George Patton (DT).
Tech All-American in 1964:
Gerald Bussell (DB), Bill Curry (C).
Named to the GT AHF:
Gerald Bussell, Bill Curry, Bill Martin.

Jerry Varnado, Bulldog defensive end, makes a great try at blocking this Georgia Tech punt.

Lynn Hughes options right, then cuts upfield as Georgia beat Texas Tech 7-0 in the '64 Sun Bowl.

Big Frank Lankewicz bulldozes his way for another Georgia first down on a warm afternoon in El Paso, Texas.

Coach Vince Dooley is given a free ride across the field as the Bulldogs celebrate their good win in the Sun Bowl. It was quite a day for a new head coach and his team.

Jeff Davis cracks into the Auburn line as Tech upended the Tigers 7-3.

Bill Paschal and Garrett Lee, Tech defenders, nail this Miami runner as the Yellow Jackets crushed the Hurricanes 20-0 at Grant Field.

Gerald Bussell, Tech's All-American corner back, returned this interception for 70 yards vs. Miami.

Jolting Jeff Davis had to leave the field with a slight injury.

1965: Georgia Upsets Bowl-Bound Georgia Tech

It was November 27, 1965, and Tech was cruising along with a good 6-2-1 record, having defeated Clemson, Tulane, Auburn, Navy, Duke and Virginia, while losing to Texas A&M and Tennessee, and tying Vanderbilt. They knew a win over Georgia this day would solidify their hopes for a big bowl game.

As for the Bulldogs, they were 5-4 at this point with wins over Alabama, Vanderbilt, Michigan, Clemson and UNC, and losses to Florida State, Kentucky, Florida and Auburn. Indeed, they had experienced a roller coaster season, winning the first four games on their schedule—including big upset victories over both national champion Alabama and Rose Bowl winner Michigan—and a number four national ranking. But then, largely because of injuries, they lost four games they might well have won under normal circumstances.

Kirby Moore threw a 92-yard TD pass to Randy Wheeler vs. Auburn, number three in the UGA record book.

It was a bright but cool day as some 52,000 fans filled Grant Field. Tech was favored by seven, but that didn't mean much once these two teams met on the playing field.

Linebacker Randall Edmunds (#50) and his defensive comrades wait for Georgia to break their huddle. The Bulldogs won this one 17-7 in a game played at Grant Field.

From the opening whistle, it became apparent that Tech's smaller offensive line was having problems blocking Georgia's big defensive linemen and linebackers. Indeed, on the fourth play of the game, Georgia's George Patton chased down Kim King, Tech's sophomore quarterback, and threw him for a big loss. The ball popped from King's hands as he was going down and John Glass recovered for Georgia at the Tech 22.

Preston Ridlehuber threw complete to Pat Hodgson for 9 yards, then Ridlehuber himself ran for nine more and Georgia had a first down at the 4.

Then came Kirby Moore on an end sweep all the way for a touchdown. Bobby Etter kicked the point, and Georgia was up 7-0.

Five minutes into the second quarter Lynn Hughes intercepted a Kim King pass at midfield and ran it back to the Tech 25. But Tech held, and on fourth down Etter kicked a 40-yard field goal, and Georgia's lead went to 10-0.

At halftime Georgia's defense had held Tech to 0 yards rushing, 49 yards passing.

The Bulldogs took the second half kickoff back to their own 39. Then Ridlehuber threw to Charles Wheeler for 14 yards, then again for another 31 yards, and Georgia had the ball at the Tech 28. Next came Pat Hodgson on a sweep down to the 6. Ridlehuber scored from there, Etter kicked the PAT and Georgia stretched their lead to 17-0.

But Tech held on. In the final quarter, with the ball at their own 25, Kim King threw completions to Gary Williams and Mike Fortier, and suddenly Tech was at the Georgia 13. Then Lenny Snow completed his only pass of the season, a wobbler to Gary Williams running all alone in the end zone, and Tech was on the board. Bunky Henry kicked the point and Georgia's lead was cut to 17-7. But that was as close as Tech could get, and Georgia walked away with a very satisfying upset win.

Still, despite their loss, this excellent Tech team received a bid to play Texas Tech in the '66 Gator Bowl.

Named to the GT AHF:
Johnny Gresham.
UGA All-American in 1965:
George Patton (DT).
UGA All-SEC in 1965:
Lynn Hughes (DB), Pat Hodgson (E).

Tech's All-American halfback, Lenny Snow, runs for yardage as the Yellow Jackets lost to Georgia 17-7.

Kim King, Tech quarterback who led Tech to a 7-3-1 season in '65, is still a leader in passing yardage and total offense.

In '65 Jimmy Brown averaged 22.6 yards per kickoff return, still an all-time Tech record. Here he outruns everybody for a 43-yard touchdown as the Yellow Jackets blasted Navy and their great Roger Staubach by a score of 37-16.

Lenny Snow rushed for 136 yards as Tech upended Texas Tech in the '66 Gator Bowl. He also won the Bowl MVP Award.

Preston Ridlehuber,
Georgia All-SEC
quarterback.

Lynn Hughes,
Georgia All-SEC back.

Bob Etter,
Georgia All-SEC PK.

George Patton,
Georgia All-American
tackle and a member
of the UGA SHF.

All-American tackle George Patton hit Tech's Kim King on this play, causing a costly fumble.

Defensive back Lynn Hughes intercepted this Tech pass which he returned to the Jackets' 25-yard line.

1966: Two Great Teams Punch It Out

It was November 26, 1966, and for the first time since 1946 both Georgia and Georgia Tech would complete the year with at least nine wins each. (In '46 Georgia was 11-0, Tech 9-2-0.)

But at this point the Bulldogs were boasting a great 8-1 record with wins over Mississippi State, VMI, South Carolina, Ole Miss, Kentucky, UNC, Florida and Auburn. Their only loss was a one-point defeat at the hands of a so-so Miami team (7-6). Indeed, had Georgia beaten Miami, they'd be in the running for another national championship.

Down the road in Atlanta, meanwhile, the Yellow Jackets were also beating the dickens out of everything that moved. At this point they were 9-0, ranked number five in the nation, and had an Orange Bowl bid in their pocket. To date they had very convincingly beat Texas A&M, Vanderbilt, Clemson, Tennessee (the number eight team in the country), Auburn, Tulane, Duke, Virginia and Penn State.

Sammy Burke averaged 16.8 yards per punt return during his career, still number two in the Tech record book.

Some 49,000 fans jammed Sanford Stadium to watch one of the most important games ever in this long series.

Early in the game, after an exchange of punts, Tech kicked to Kent Lawrence standing at his own 29-yard line. Lawrence took the punt, then didn't stop until he'd crossed the goal line 71 yards away. The PAT missed, but Georgia led 6-0.

Following another exchange of punts, Tech took the ball at their own 4-yard line. Kim King then moved the Jackets 96 yards in 18 plays for a touchdown Lenny Snow ran nine times for 53 of those yards. King took the ball in for the score, Bunky Henry kicked the point and Tech led 7-6.

With five minutes left in the half, Georgia and Kirby Moore came out throwing. Taking the ball at their own 46, the Bulldogs moved down for another score, Brad Johnson going in from the two. Moore then threw complete to Hardy King for the 2-point conversion and Georgia led 14-7.

Then, with only moments remaining in the half, Patton deflected a King pass and Larry Kohn returned it to the Tech 27. From there Bobby Etter kicked a 27-yard field goal and Georgia took a 17-7 lead in at halftime.

Later, in the final quarter, Etter kicked

The great Bobby Dodd retired following the '66 season with an amazing 165-64-8 record (.713).

Kirby Moore throws to Hardy King for a 2-point conversion as Georgia defeated Tech 23-14 to complete a great 9-1 season. They then went on to beat SMU in the '66 Cotton Bowl.

a 33-yard field goal and Georgia's lead went to 20-7.

On the next series Tech gambled and lost. Facing a fourth down at their own 26, Lenny snow went for it but was stopped. Georgia took the ball and four plays later Etter kicked his third field goal of the day and Georgia led 23-7.

Later, with only five seconds remaining, Tech's Larry Good scored from the 4, Henry converted, and that was it. Georgia walked away with a 23-14 win.

The Bulldogs completed the season with an excellent 10-1 record and a number four national ranking, won the SEC Championship, and defeated SMU in the Cotton Bowl.

Tech finished with a great 9-1 record, a number eight national ranking, and a loss to Florida in the Orange Bowl.

Kent Lawrence returns a punt 71 yards for a TD and a 6-0 Georgia lead over Tech. That's Doc Harvin attempting a tackle.

All-SEC flanker Kent Lawrence takes this Kirby Moore pass for a TD vs. Tech but a penalty nullified the play.

All-SEC place kicker Bob Etter kicks his third field goal of the day in Georgia's 23-14 win over Tech, making him the top scorer in the SEC.

Kirby Moore tosses a TD pass to Billy Payne as theBulldogs beat SMU 24-9.

Larry Good, subbing for the injured Kim King, runs 27 yards for a TD as Tech beat Tulane 35-17.

Bill Eastman returned this interception 100 yards for a TD vs. Tulane in '66, still number three in the Tech record book.

Tech All-American Lenny Snow following Tech's 38-3 win over Texas A&M.

Kim King was named National Back of the Week following Tech's win over Tennessee.

1967: Bulldogs Ruin Bud Carson's Debut

Coach Bud Carson paces the sideline with his Yellow Jackets trailing Georgia 14-0.

Since 1904 Georgia Tech had employed just three head football coaches: John Heisman (1904-1919), Bill Alexander (1920-1944) and Bobby Dodd (1945-1966). But now in 1967 a new face arrived on the scene. It was Bud Carson and he would remain with the Yellow Jackets for the next five years, compiling a 27-27 record.

As Tech prepared to meet Georgia on November 25, they were bogged down in a 4-5 season, with wins over Vanderbilt, TCU, Clemson and Duke, and losses to Tennessee, Auburn, Tulane, Miami and Notre Dame. Few gave them any chance at all against Georgia.

The 10-1 Bulldogs of '66 now sported a 6-3 record coming into the Tech game, with wins over Mississippi State, South Carolina, Clemson, VMI, Kentucky and Auburn, and losses to Ole Miss, Houston (15-14) and Florida (17-16). With a couple of breaks, Georgia could have been one of the top-ranked teams in America.

Spike Jones had an 87-yard punt vs. Auburn, still an all-time UGA record.

In addition to the 54,000 fans on hand at Grant Field, this game was being watched nationwide, thanks to ABC-TV. It began at 4 P.M. and didn't end until long after dark, the first Georgia-Georgia Tech game played under the lights.

On Georgia Tech's first series Tommy Chapman punted 55 yards to Jake Scott who ran the ball back 37 yards, down to the Tech 34. Six plays later Georgia was at the 13, then Kirby Moore ran to the 2. Ronnie Jenkins took it in for the touchdown, Jim McCullough kicked the PAT and the Bulldogs led 7-0.

With only minutes remaining in the first quarter Georgia took the ball at their own 5. Four plays later Moore spotted Dennis Hughes deep downfield and threw long. Hughes took the ball at the Tech 30 and ran all the way for another Georgia score. The kick was good and Georgia led 14-0. The Bulldogs had marched 95 yards in only five plays.

Early in the third quarter Tech took the ball at their own 44. Thirteen plays later quarterback Larry Good went in from the 1, Tommy Carmichael kicked the point and suddenly Tech was back in the game, trailing 14-7.

With only moments left in the third, Georgia took the ball at their own 32. Thirteen plays later Ronnie Jenkins took it in from the 1, the PAT was good and Georgia stretched their lead to 21-7.

With five minutes left to play, Tech recovered their fourth fumble of the evening, this one at their own 44. Eleven plays later Dennis James went over from the 3, the PAT was good and Georgia led 21-14.

Tech tailback Dennis James breaks away with the Bulldogs in close pursuit. Georgia would win this one by a score of 21-14 at Grant Field.

And that was the final score. This was Georgia's fourth straight win over Tech, and the Bulldogs now led in the series 30-27-5.

The Yellow Jackets finished the season with a 4-6 record, their worst since 1945.

The 7-3 Bulldogs would go on to lose to NC State in the '67 Liberty Bowl.

Named to the GT AHF:
Jim Breland, Bill Eastman, Lenny Snow.
UGA All-American in 1967:
Edgar Chandler (OG).
UGA All-SEC in 1967:
Bill Stanfill (DT), Ron Jenkins (FB), Jake Scott (SAF), Larry Kohn (DE), Don Hayes (G).
Named to the UGA SHF:
Edgar Chandler.

Coach Bud Carson and Kim King talk the situation over as Tech went on to beat Vanderbilt 17-10. King is now the color analyst on Georgia Tech radio.

Eric Wilcox made 28 tackles versus Georgia in '67, still an all-time Tech defensive record.

Eric Wilcox set to make just one of his 28 tackles vs. Georgia in '67.

Atop all those bodies Tech's Dennis James dives over for a score, but Georgia went on to win 21-14.

The Bulldogs line up, then went on to defeat Georgia Tech by a score of 21-14 in '67 at Grant Field.

In '68 All-American tackle Bill Stanfill won the Outland Trophy, awarded annually to America's most outstanding lineman. He went on to an all-pro career and is a member of the UGA SHF. He is also a member of the College Football Hall of Fame.

Quarterback Kirby Moore who led Georgia to an SEC championship in '66, ran 87 yards for a TD vs. South Carolina in '67, still number three in the UGA record book.

Jubilant Bulldogs celebrate their win over Auburn. They would go on to lose 14-7 to NC State in the Liberty Bowl.

Georgia's great All-American guard Edgar Chandler has just returned an interception for a TD. Here he talks it over with Coach Erk Russell.

1968: 8-1-2 Bulldogs Win SEC Championship

November 30 dawned cool and cloudy as Georgia and Georgia Tech squared off for their 63rd meeting. At this point the Bulldogs had run undefeated through a nine game schedule, with wins over Clemson, South Carolina, Ole Miss, Vanderbilt, Kentucky, Florida and Auburn, and ties with both Tennessee and Houston. They were SEC champions, ranked number four in the nation and had just accepted a Sugar Bowl bid.

Things were not going quite so well for the Yellow Jackets. At this point they were 4-5 on the year with wins over TCU, Clemson, Auburn and Tulane, and losses to Miami, Tennessee, Duke, Navy and Notre Dame. Worse, Tech's defense had given up more points than any Yellow Jacket team in history.

Tech took the opening kickoff, then punted out on the Georgia 2-yard line. Sixteen plays later, Mike Cavan took the ball in from the 1, Jim McCullough kicked the point and Georgia was up 7-0. This 98-yard drive remains the longest ever in this series.

Two minutes later Bill Stanfill deflected a Larry Good pass and Happy Dicks intercepted at the Tech 16. Four plays later Brad Johnson went in from the 3. The PAT was good and Georgia was up 14-0.

Two minutes later Georgia marched 89 yards but were halted at the Tech 5. McCullough kicked a field goal and the Bulldogs went up 17-0.

In the second quarter Georgia moved first to the Tech 4-yard line and later to their 7, but the Yellow Jackets held on both occasions, and Georgia went in at halftime holding a 17-0 lead.

Later, in the third quarter, Craig Elrod and Bruce Kemp both scored for Georgia and the Bulldogs stretched their lead to 31-0.

In the fourth period, trailing 31-0, the never-say-die Yellow Jackets marched 89 yards for a score, Kenny Bounds going over from the 3. Then Jim Person completed a 2-point conversion pass to Bounds, and Georgia led 31-8.

Minutes later Georgia increased their lead when Donnie Hampton scored from the 7 and McCullough kicked the PAT.

As though that were not enough, a minute later Stanfill nailed Person in the end zone for a safety, and Georgia's lead went to 40-8.

(At this point anyone entering Sanford Stadium would have had no trouble finding a seat!)

All-American safety Jake Scott intercepted this Larry Good pass as Georgia smothered Tech 47-8. In '68 Scott returned a punt 90 yards for a TD vs. Tennessee, number two in the UGA record book.

Quarterback Larry Good attempted 61 passes in Tech's 24-7 loss to Tennessee in '68, still an all-time Jacket record.

Then, with only a minute remaining, Hampton scored his second touchdown of the day and Georgia increased their lead to 47-8. Which was the final score.

The 8-0-2 Bulldogs then went on to lose to Arkansas by a score of 16-2 in the '69 Sugar Bowl.

All-SEC flanker Kent Lawrence took this Mike Cavan pass for a first down vs. Arkansas in the '69 Sugar Bowl.

Bill Payne walloped this Vandy quarterback just as he got off a pass. Georgia won 32-6.

Happy Dicks, an All-SEC linebacker and a member of the All-Time Georgia Football Team.

Coach Dooley, Steve Fernsworth and Steve Woodward show concern as they watch the Bulldogs fall to Arkansas by a score of 16-2 in the '69 Sugar Bowl.

Jeff Ford, an All-Southeren Independent defensive back, returned an interception 102 yards for a TD vs. Notre Dame in '69, the longest TD run in the Tech record book. He also returned four other interceptions for TDs during his career, another all-time Tech record.

In '68 Tech's All-SI end John Sias caught 14 passes vs. Navy. For the season he had 902 yards in receptions. Both figures remain all-time Tech records. He is a member of the GT AHF.

Chip Pallman leads the way for Gene Spiotta in Tech's 23-19 win over Tulane.

Steve Harkey puts the move on a Clemson defensive end.

1969: Turnovers Sink Bulldogs

It was November 29, 1969, and both Georgia and Georgia Tech had been struggling throughout much of the season. The Yellow Jackets at this point were 3-6, with wins over SMU, Baylor and Duke, and losses to Clemson, Tennessee, Auburn, Southern Cal, Tulane and Notre Dame.

As for the Bulldogs, the defending SEC Champions of 1968, their record was better than Tech's, but not one to really brag about. They were 5-3-1 at this point, with wins over Tulane, Clemson, South Carolina, Vanderbilt and Kentucky, and losses to Ole Miss, Tennessee and Auburn and a tie with Florida. After the first six games of the season Georgia was 5-1 and ranked number seven in the nation. But then they didn't win another game all year.

Yet, strangely enough, Georgia came into the Tech game a 10-point favorite. And, strangely enough, the experts were so sure Georgia was going to win today, that they had already extended them a bid to play a tough Nebraska team in the '69 Sun Bowl in El Paso, Texas. And, strangely enough, the Bulldogs had already accepted.

Still, those who know about the law of averages pointed out that Georgia had won the last five encounters between these two institutions and that Tech was past due for a big upset. They were right.

It was a warm sunny day at Grant Field as some 60,000 fans, the largest turnout ever for a Georgia-Georgia Tech football game, filled the stands to watch what would become a thriller before the afternoon finally ended.

Tech kicked off but Georgia couldn't move and punted out at the Jackets' 29-yard line. Tech then drove to the Georgia 11, but Bill Darby intercepted a Jack Williams' pass and ended that threat.

Later, in the second quarter, Georgia drove to Tech's 23. From there, on fourth down, the Bulldogs attempted a field goal, but the ball sailed wide to the left and Tech took over at the 20.

Georgia football fans of 1969.

Williams ran for 13 to the 33, then came back with another bootleg to the 39. Then Brent Cunningham caught a screen pass good for 16 yards, up to the 45. On the next play Williams threw complete to Gene Spiotta for 12 yards, down to the Georgia 33.

Williams then threw complete to Chip Pallman down at the Georgia 13. Cunningham ran it down to the eight before Williams threw complete to Steve Norris at the 1. Williams himself took it over for a touchdown on the next play. The PAT failed but the Yellow

Jackets were up 6-0. And that was both the halftime score and the final score.

The Bulldogs had sputtered on offense throughout the entire game, and in the second half they they suffered four pass interceptions (three by John Hoats) which further hampered their efforts.

All-SI safety Jeff Ford returned this interception 102 yards for a TD (an all-time Tech record) as Tech lost to Notre Dame 38-20. He returned three interceptions for TDs in '69, tying an all-time NCAA record.

Defensive back John Hoats did his share, intercepting three Georgia passes on the day.

The final second ticks away and Georgia Tech escapes with a close 6-0 win over Georgia at Grant Field. This was Tech's first win over Georgia since 1963.

All-SI Brent Cunningham gave the Bulldogs all they could handle as Tech won 6-0.

All-SEC halfback Jim McCollough coming on a sweep as Georgia beat South Carolina 7-0.

Captain Steve Greer, Georgia's All-American defensive guard.

Quarterback Mike Cavan gets one off as Georgia lost to Tennessee 17-3.

Chip Wisdom (#48), Wayne Byrd (#78) and Ronnie Huggins (#82) lead interference for Lee Daniel as he returns this interception in Georgia's 45-6 loss to Nebraska in the '69 Sun Bowl. Nebraska had won the Big Eight championship with a shocking 44-14 beating of Oklahoma.

1970: Experts All Wrong, Yellow Jackets <u>Can</u> Fly

I t was November 28, 1970, and Georgia Tech was still celebrating their close 6-0 win over Georgia in '69. At this point they were having a very good season, cruising along with a 7-3 record despite playing some of the strongest teams in the nation. They had beaten South Carolina, Florida State, Miami, Clemson, Tulane, Duke and Navy, while losing to Tennessee and Auburn, both ranked in the top ten. Plus the Jackets had lost a 10-7 squeaker to Notre Dame, the number one team in the nation.

As for Georgia, they were 5-4 at this point, with wins over Clemson, Vanderbilt, Kentucky, South Carolina and Auburn, and losses to Tulane, Mississippi State, Ole Miss and Florida. Still, Georgia had proven they could get the job done when they upset number seven Auburn by a score of 31-17 just a week prior to the Tech game.

Tech had already accepted a bid to play Texas Tech in the Sun Bowl, while Georgia would be offered a bid to play in the Peach Bowl should they beat Tech.

And Georgia, for reasons known only to the experts, was favored to beat Tech this afternoon.

Steve Harkey slices through the Bulldog defense for a first down as the Yellow Jackets went on to defeat Georgia 17-7.

Five minutes into the first quarter Georgia quarterback Paul Gilbert was intercepted by Gary Carden at the Bulldog 46. Three plays later Jack Williams threw long for Mike Wysong in the end zone for a Tech touchdown. Bobby Thigpen's PAT was good and Tech took a 7-0 lead.

Tech then kicked off and Georgia ran it back to their own 38-yard line. Thirteen plays later they scored when Gilbert sneaked over from the 1. Kim Braswell's kick was good and the ball game was all tied up at 7-7.

And that was the halftime score. But in the third quarter Georgia tried a little razzle-dazzle, a flea-flicker play which didn't go well. Gilbert pitched out to Jack Montgomery who was supposed to toss the ball back to Gilbert who would then throw deep to some receiver. Unfortunately for the Bulldogs, Tech's Smylie Gebhart intercepted Montgomery's toss and ran the ball back to the Georgia 18-yard line.

On second down from the 14, Williams threw a completion to Larry Studdard for another Tech touchdown. Thigpen kicked the PAT and Tech led 14-7.

Early in the fourth period Montgomery recovered a Wysong fumble at the Tech 17, and Georgia fans began going wild with excitement. But then, facing third and goal from the Tech 10, Gilbert fumbled and the ball was quickly covered by Tech's Rock Perdoni. And that was the final big Georgia threat of the afternoon.

Later, with only seven minutes remaining, Richard Lewis intercepted a Gilbert pass at the Georgia 31. Eddie McAshan then threw complete to Steve Harkey at the 13. Four plays later, facing fourth and goal from the 8, Bill Moore came in and booted a field goal which boosted Tech's lead to 17-7.

And that was the ball game.

This was the 65th meeting between these two old rivals, and although Georgia had lost the last two encounters, they still led in the series 31-29-5.

Oddly enough, this game marked the 700th game played by both Georgia and Georgia Tech. Georgia's overall record since 1892 now stood at 400-253-47 (.605), while Tech's was a little better at 426-240-34 (.633).

Tech went on to defeat Texas Tech (17-9) in the Sun Bowl to complete a good 9-3 season.

Georgia's stout defense: Larry Brasher (#76), Phil Sullivan (#15), Chuck Heard (#91) and Dave Sage (#71).

Royce Smith, Georgia All-American guard, and Erk Russell, Georgia's famous defensive coach, talk it over.

Were you there? A sober look at the Georgia-Georgia Tech game of 1970.

Ricky Lake seems to have the Tech defense pretty well surrounded on this play as Georgia lost to the Yellow Jackets 17-7.

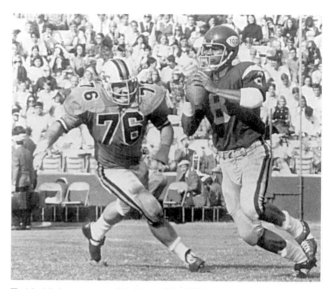

Tech's All-American tackle Renso "Rock" Perdoni was a finalist for the Lombardi Award in 1970.

Tech's Eddie McAshen, a member of the GT AHF, was the greatest passer in Tech history, with 4,080 yards to his credit. He was also the first Tech player to gain over 1,000 yards each of his three varsity seasons.

Here freshman McAshen is seen in action as Tech lost to a great Tennessee team, 17-6.

Georgia crosses Tech's goal line for 6, but Tech went on to win 17-7 in Athens.

The Bulldogs and Yellow Jackets take a moment to discuss one of the finer points of the game.

1971: Bulldogs Win a Real Thriller

It was Thanksgiving night, November 25, 1971, as the Georgia Bulldogs prepared to meet the Yellow Jackets at Grant Field. At this point Georgia had an excellent 9-1 record with wins over Oregon State, Tulane, Clemson, Mississippi State, Ole Miss, Vanderbilt, Kentucky, South Carolina and Florida. Of these, only Oregon State had scored more than 7 points against the Bulldogs (56-25), while they themselves were averaging 33 points per game, and were ranked number seven in the nation. The only blemish on their record was a 35-20 loss to fifth-ranked Auburn two weeks before.

As for Georgia Tech, they were 6-4 at this point with wins over Michigan State, Clemson, Tulane, Duke, Navy and Florida State, and losses to South Carolina, Tennessee, Army and Auburn. They had won their last four games of the season, however, and were eager to show what they could do against the favored Bulldogs.

Jeff Ford had 14 career interceptons, still number two in the Tech record book.

Before this game ended fans would say it was the finest, most exciting game ever played between Georgia and Tech.

Georgia kicked off and Tech's Eddie McAshan immediately led the underdog Jackets on a 65-yard touchdown drive, which concluded with McAshan zipping a 31-yard pass to Jim Owings in the Georgia end zone for a touchdown. Bobby Thigpen kicked the point and Tech went up 7-0.

Minutes later Tech drove 80 yards for another touchdown. Rob Healy went in from the 11, and the PAT made it 14-0. The experts were beginning to scratch their collective heads.

The late great Uga II.

Later in the quarter Georgia began a drive from their 18-yard line. With Jimmy Poulos and Andy Johnson leading the charge, the Bulldogs moved to the Tech 1. Johnson went in on the next play, Kim Braswell kicked the point and Tech's lead was cut to 14-7.

Following the kickoff, Tech took the ball all the way to the Georgia 24 but there they stalled and Cam Bonifay kicked a field goal to stretch the Jackets' lead to 17-7.

But Georgia came right back. Johnson hit Jimmy Shirer with a 23-yard strike for another Bulldog touchdown, Braswell's kick was good and Tech went in at halftime leading 17-14.

The third quarter was scoreless, but early in the fourth Georgia finally took the lead at 21-17 when Johnson scored his second TD of the day on a 1-yard sneak.

Tech then returned the ensuing kickoff to their own 33. Five plays later Healy ran it in for another Tech TD. The PAT was good, and Tech regained the lead at 24-21.

Tech stopped Georgia's next drive at their own 9-

The Rambling Wreck made its first appearance in 1961.

yard line. At that point there was 3:38 showing on the clock. Tech's Dick Bowley punted from his own end zone—a great 70-yard kick that finally came to rest at the Georgia 30.

There was 1:29 showing on the clock at this point. On second down Johnson ran 22 yards to the Tech 43. Four plays later Georgia faced a fourth-and-ten with 0:53 remaining. Johnson hit Mike Green with an 18-yard pass for a first down at the Tech 25. Three plays later with the ball at the Tech 9, Georgia called their last time-out.

Johnson then hit Shirer at the 1. Shirer stepped out of bounds with 18 seconds showing on the clock.

Then Johnson handed off to Poulos who hurdled the line for a Georgia touchdown. The PAT was good, but it really didn't matter. This was the last play of the game and Georgia had won it 28-24 in a real Hollywood finish.

Georgia would go on to beat UNC 7-3 in the Gator Bowl, while Tech would lose 41-18 to Ole Miss in the Peach Bowl.

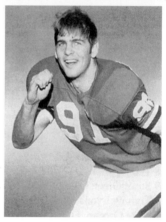

UGA All-American in 1971:
Royce Smith (OG).
UGA All-SEC in 1971:
Ken Keith (C), Buzy Rosenberg (DB), Tom Nash (T) and Chip Wisdom (LB). Named to the UGA SHF: Royce Smith.
Tech All-American in 1971:
Smylie Gebhart (DE).
Tech All-SI in 1971:
Rick Lantz (OT), Brad Bourne (DT), Mike Oven (TE), Jeff Ford (DB).
Named to the GT AHF:
Brent Cunningham, Jeff Ford, Smylie Gebhart.

Chuck Heard, Georgia All-SEC tackle.

Buzy Rosenberg, All-SEC safety, returns a punt as Georgia smashed Oregon State to open the '71 season.

Jim Shirer went all the way for a TD as Georgia whopped Tulane 27-7.

Jim Shirer picked up 18 yards on this play as Georgia beat Tech 28-24.

Greg Horne bulls his way in for a touchdown in Tech's 24-14 win over Clemson.

Tech quarterback Bill Stevens gets off a completion to Larry Stoddard as the Yellow Jackets lost to Georgia 28-24 in '71.

Larry Stoddard took this Eddie McAshan pass all the way for a touchdown in Tech's 10-0 upset win over a good Michigan State team.

Rob Healy slogs his way through the mud as Tech lost to Ole Miss by a score of 41-18 in the '71 Peach Bowl.

1972: Tech Loses Game, Wins Bowl Bid

Bud Carson resigned as head coach of the Yellow Jackets following the '71 season and in his place came Bill Fulcher who had played for Tech back in the early fifties. To date Coach Fulcher's team was doing well, sporting a 6-3-1 record with wins over South Carolina, Michigan State, Clemson, Tulane, Boston College and Navy, and losses to Auburn, Tennessee and Duke and a tie with Rice.

Eddie McAshan threw five TD passes vs. Rice, still an all-time Tech record.

Vince Dooley's Bulldogs had a similar record. They were 6-4 at this point, with wins over Baylor, NC State, Ole Miss, Vanderbilt, Kentucky and Florida, and losses to Tulane, Alabama, Tennessee and Auburn.

Still, the experts were so sure that Tech would take this one, that the Liberty Bowl had already invited the Jackets to meet Iowa State on December 18. Tech had accepted.

What the experts didn't know, however, was that Tech's super quarterback Eddie McAshan would not play in this game. In his place came Jim Stevens who had taken just three snaps all season. And that made all the difference.

Following the opening kickoff, the two teams exchanged several punts. Then with seven minutes remaining in the first quarter Georgia's Kim Braswell kicked a 29-yard field goal and the Bulldogs took the lead 3-0.

In the second period, Tech stopped Georgia on their 21-yard line, but a roughing penalty gave the Bulldogs new life and a first down at the Tech 11. Horace King scored four plays later, Braswell kicked the point, and Georgia led 10-0.

After an exchange of punts Georgia was again in business at midfield. Three plays later James Ray threw 37 yards to Rex Putnal for a another Bulldog touchdown. The PAT was good and Georgia led 17-0.

Then, with only moments left in the half, Braswell kicked a 40-yard field goal and Georgia went in at halftime with a big 20-0 lead.

At this point Tech fans and Liberty Bowl officials were noticeably quiet.

But in the third period Tech made a comeback of sorts when Randy Rhino intercepted a pass at the Georgia 19. Greg Horne then ran for 15 yards on the first play, then in for the TD on the next and Tech was on the board. Bobby Thigpen kicked the PAT and Georgia's lead was cut to 20-7.

Later in the quarter Jim Stevens led Tech on an 84-yard march, down to the Georgia 14, but then Buzy Rosenburg intercepted an errant pass and that was the end of that.

In the fourth quarter Georgia took the ball at the Tech 31. Horace King

James Ray throws to halfback Rex Putnall who takes it into the end zone for another Georgia score as the Bulldogs beat Tech 27-7 at Sanford Stadium.

ran for 30 yards, down to the 1, then he took it in for the score. The PAT was good and Georgia led 27-7, which was the final score.

This game was the end of the road for 7-4 Georgia, though 6-4-1 Tech would go on to score a great come-from-behind 31-30 win over Iowa State in the Liberty Bowl.

Jimmy Robinson catches his ninth TD pass of the '72 season, a record that still stands at Tech, as the Yellow Jackets beat Navy 30-7.

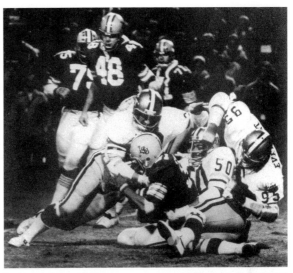

Tech smothers this Cyclone runner in the Yellow Jackets 31-30 win over Iowa State in the '72 Liberty Bowl

Fumbles were the story all day as Tech fell to Georgia 27-7.

Quarterback Bill Stevens and Coach Bill Fulcher celebrate Tech's win in the '72 Liberty Bowl.

Lenny Ellspermann, Milton Bruce, Jim Cagle, Dan Jones, Dennis Hester and other Bulldog defenders make life hard for this Vandy halfback who failed to make the first down. Georgia won 21-3.

All-SEC quarterback Andy Johnson hands off to Jimmy Poulos as the Bulldogs beat Florida 10-7.

Erk Russell can't bear to watch as his beloved Bulldogs fell to Tulane 24-13.

James Ray calls signals as Georgia rolled Florida 10-7 in '72.

1973: Late Hit Leads to a Georgia Win

It was December 1, 1973, a warm sunny day in Atlanta as Tech and Georgia prepared for their 68th meeting since 1893. The big news was that Bill Fulcher, who had compiled a 12-10-1 record over the past two years, had tendered his resignation as head coach of the Yellow Jackets. This season they were 5-5, with wins over Clemson, Army, Duke, VMI and Navy, and losses to South Carolina, Southern Cal, Tennessee, Auburn and Tulane. Thus the situation at Tech was again unsettled just as it had been in '72 when Eddie McAshan suddenly disappeared from the Tech lineup.

Ed Whealler booted a 55-yard field goal vs. VMI, still an all-time Tech record.

Randy Rhino is the only Tech player ever named All-American for three consecutive years. Among his numerous other records, he also returned a punt 92 yards for a TD vs. USC, still the longest punt return in the Tech record book.

The Bulldogs, on the other hand, were in about the same boat at this point with a mediocre 5-4-1 record. They had beaten Clemson, NC State, Ole Miss, Tennessee and Auburn, while losing to Alabama, Vanderbilt, Kentucky and Florida, and tying Pitt.

Don Golden had an 80-yard punt vs. Kentucky, the third longest punt in the UGA record book.

Still, the Peach Bowl committee informed Georgia that they were invited to play at Atlanta Stadium on December 28 if they beat Tech.

Some 60,316 fans jammed Grant Field this afternoon, the largest crowd ever to witness an athletic event in the state of Georgia.

Tech kicked off to Georgia, and on third down at their own 19, Jimmy Poulos fumbled the ball. Randy Rhino recovered for the Jackets and Tech was suddenly in business. On first down Jim Stevens passed complete to Mark Fields at the 1. Then came a handoff to Greg Horne who smashed into the big Bulldog line. Horne went one way, the ball the other, and Steve Taylor recovered for Georgia.

Several plays later Georgia punted out on the Tech 14-yard line. Pat Moriarty got off a dazzling 31-yard run, and then there was a 15-yard roughing penalty, and suddenly Tech found themselves at the Georgia 8. Four plays later Cam Bonifay came in and booted a field goal and Tech led 3-0.

Late in the half the Bulldogs, led by quarterback

Jim Owings runs for a first down vs. the Bulldogs. But Georgia's tough defense rose to the occasion all afternoon to keep Tech out of the end zone as the Bulldogs went on to win 10-3.

Andy Johnson, moved to the Tech 9-yard line. But following a big holding penalty, and a loss on a running play, Georgia was set back to the 24. Then, on the last play of the half, Alan Leavitt kicked a 42-yard field goal and the score was tied at 3-3.

To open the third quarter Georgia began play at their own 6. Three plays later they had moved just 3 yards, but a late hit on Horace King cost the Jackets 15 yards and gave Georgia new life at the 24. Poulis then ran 19 yards to the 43. Two plays later Johnson scrambled 28 yards, down to the Tech 15. Then, three plays later, Johnson hit Bob Burns with a bullet pass in the end zone for a touchdown. Leavitt kicked the PAT and Georgia led 10-3.

It was a 94-yard drive that should never have happened, and would never have happened had it not been for the late hit penalty some minutes before. But that's football, and Georgia walked away with a 10-3 win and a trip to the '73 Peach Bowl.

In that contest Georgia edged a tough Maryland team by a score of 17-16 to finish the season with a 7-4-1 record.

Tech All-American in 1973:
Randy Rhino (DB).
Tech All-SI in 1973:
Mark Fields (TE), Don Robinson (OG).
UGA All-SEC in 1973:
Mac McWhorter (G), Danny Jones (DG).

Andy Johnson moves out behind good blocking as the Bulldogs sank the Yellow Jackets at Grant Field.

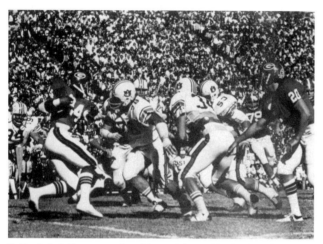

Fullback Bob Burns runs into big trouble on this play but Georgia would still beat Auburn by a score of 28-14.

Jimmy Poulos breaks away for the deciding TD in Georgia's 20-0 win over Ole Miss.

When the final whistle blew Georgia held a 10-3 lead over Tech.

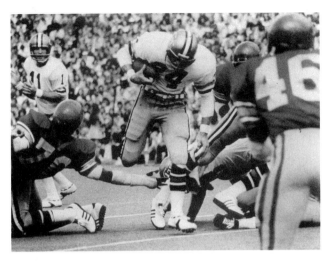

Jim Stevens hands off to Greg Horne as Tech fell to Southern Cal 23-6 at Grant Field.

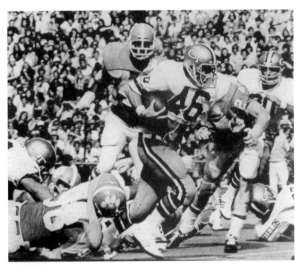

Bruce Southall breaks into the secondary as Tech beat Clemson 29-21.

Jimmy Owings congratulates Greg Horne on a TD catch as Tech beat Army 14-10 at Grant Field.

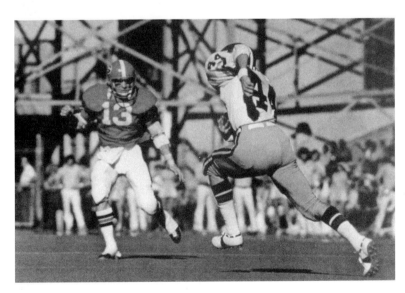

This Tech runner means business, but he was nailed short of Georgia's goal line.

1974: Underdogs Whip Bulldogs—Bad

The big news in Georgia in '74 concerned the hiring of Pepper Rodgers as Tech's new head football coach. He had enjoyed great success as head coach at UCLA, one of the top offensive teams in America, and now he brought with him plans to install the wishbone formation at Georgia Tech.

But things had not gone as well as Rodgers might have hoped. As of November 30, the Jackets were 5-5 on the season, with wins over South Carolina, Virginia, UNC, Tulane and Navy, and losses to Notre Dame, Pitt, Clemson, Auburn and Duke. Certainly not a season to get excited about.

In Athens, meanwhile, the so-so Bulldogs were 6-4 on the season, with wins over Oregon State, South Carolina, Ole Miss, Vanderbilt, Kentucky and Florida, and losses to Mississippi State, Clemson, Houston and Auburn.

Some 47,500 tickets were sold for this day's game, but it was said that about half those chose to remain at home rather than face the gale-like winds and frozen rain that swept Athens that afternoon. Old timers claimed it was the worst weather they'd ever seen for a Georgia-Georgia Tech football game.

Georgia kicked off and Tech took the ball at their own 12. Sixteen plays and 88 yards later, the Jackets got on the board when Adrian Rucker slogged his way in from the 17. Richard Smith kicked the PAT and Tech led 7-0.

Early in the second quarter Tech took the ball on the Georgia 47. Five plays later, facing a fouth down at the 30, Tech threw their only pass of the day, a 6-yarder from Danny Myers to Steve Raible, for a first down. Three plays later Tech scored again when Myers sneaked over from the 1.

The PAT missed, but Tech led 13-0.

Just before halftime Tech recovered a dropped pitchout at the Georgia 23. David Sims, the game's leading rusher, scored from the 10, Smith kicked the point, and Tech led 20-0.

At halftime many frozen fans who were brave enough to show up earlier began to scurry for the exits. Indeed, the stands were nearly bare.

But in the third period Georgia's Jim Baker blocked a Tech punt at the Jackets' 48. Three plays later Glynn Harrison dashed 30 yards, down to the 1. Matt Robinson sneaked over on the next play, Alan Leavitt kicked the PAT, and Tech's lead was cut to 20-7.

Tech took the kickoff to their own

Tech is on the move offensively, which was the story all afternoon, plowing through ankle deep mud, as they beat Georgia 34-14 on a dark, miserable November afternoon in Athens.

Tech All-American in 1974:
Randy Rhino (DB).
Tech All-SI in 1974:
Joe Harris (LB), Billy Shields (OT), David Sims (RB).
Named to the GT AHF:
Randy Rhino, Billy Shields, David Sims.
UGA All-American in 1974:
Craig Hertwig (OT).
UGA All-SEC in 1974:
Glynn Harrison (RB), Randy Johnson (G), Gene Washington (FL), Richard Appleby (TE), Horace King (RB), Allan Leavitt (PK), David McKnight (DE), Syl Boler (T).

30. Twelve plays later they were again on the board when David Sims went in from the 3. The PAT made it 27-7.

In the final quarter Georgia scored again when James Ray took a pitch at his own 38 and dashed 62 yards down the right sideline all the way into the end zone. Leavitt's kick was good, and Tech lead became 27-14.

Late in the game, starting from their own 37, Tech mounted a 63-yard drive which culminated with Myers scoring from 6 yards out. The PAT was good, and Tech walked away with a 34-14 win. Most folks were just glad it was over with.

This 6-5 Georgia team then went on to lose to Miami of Ohio (21-10) in the Tangerine Bowl. Tech, also 6-5, stayed at home and watched it all on TV.

Tech's alert defense stops this Panther runner in his tracks, but Pitt went on to win 27-17.

Highflying Danny Myers rushed for 921 yards during his career, still number one among Tech quarterbacks.

Now everyone—the players, the coaches, the crowd—get into the act in celebration of Tech's come from behind 29-28 win over UNC.

It was November 30, 1974, a dark, dismal day in Athens, as the Yellow Jackets slog through the muck for another TD in a game won by Tech 34-14.

Captain Glynn Harrison, an All-SEC halfback and workhorse of the '75 Bulldogs.

Joe Tereshinski, All-SEC tackle whose father had been a Bulldog star thirty years before.

All-American guard Randy Johnson won the Georgia MVP Award in '75.

All-SEC halfback Glynn Harrison averaged an amazing 6.37 yards per carry during his career, still number two in the UGA record book. Here he bowls over an Ole Miss defender in Georgia's 49-0 win.

All-SEC tight end Richard Appleby stretches to take this Matt Robinson pass as Georgia beat Vandy 38-31.

1975: Georgia Blasts Tech, Wins Cotton Bowl Bid

I t was November 27, Thanksgiving Day, as the Bulldogs and the Yellow Jackets prepared to butt heads at Grant Field.

This was the year that Georgia surprised all the experts by not finishing in the SEC cellar as predicted. Indeed, they were 8-2 at this point, with wins over Mississippi State, South Carolina, Clemson, Vanderbilt, Kentucky, Richmond, Florida and Auburn. As for defeats, there were only two of those, a 19-9 season opening loss to Pitt, and a 28-13 loss to Ole Miss a month later. They were going into the Tech game ranked number fifteen in the nation.

Alan Leavitt set a new SEC record when he kicked his 61st consecutive PAT vs. Georgia Tech.

Pepper Rodgers, who had served successful coaching stints at both Utah State and UCLA before returning to his alma mater, had enjoyed a respectable 6-5 record in '74 and was doing even better in '75 with a 7-3 record coming into the Georgia game. To date the Jackets had beaten VMI, Miami, Clemson, Florida State, Tulane, Duke and Navy. They had suffered a big upset loss to South Carolina in their opening game, and also lost to national powers Auburn and Notre Dame. On offense, they were America's number one team.

The temperature was just below freezing as over 55,000 chilled fans crowded into Grant Field for the 70th clash between Tech and Georgia. The game was considered a tossup.

Ray Goff hands off to Kevin McLee as Georgia won 42-26 on Thanksgiving Day in Atlanta.

On the first play of the game, Georgia's Bobby Thompson intercepted Danny Myers at the Tech 29 and returned it to the 12. Five plays later Ray Goff sneaked in from the 2, Alan Leavitt kicked the point, and Georgia led 7-0.

Later in the quarter Tech's Bucky Shamburger took a handoff at his own 7-yard line, burst off tackle and raced 68 yards before being pulled down at the Georgia 25. But on the next play Georgia recovered a Tech fumble—which ended that threat.

With only moments left in the first quarter Georgia had the ball at their own 3. Goff ran for 19 yards to the 22. Then on the next play Glynn Harrison ripped off an amazing 78-yard gallop for a TD and Georgia led 14-0.

To open the second quarter Georgia's Lawrence Craft grabbed a David Sims fumble and raced 20 yards for another Bulldog score. The PAT was good and Georgia led 21-0.

Just before halftime Georgia scored again when Bill Krug blocked a punt at the Jackets' 37. Three plays later Al Pollard went in from the 1, and Georgia led 28-0 at the half.

In the third quarter Georgia's lead went to 42-0 after a 13-yard scoring run by Mark Wilson and a 3-yard burst by Al Pollard.

By this time most of the frozen Tech fans on hand had long departed Grant Field for the comforts of home. But the Tech football team, to their lasting credit, didn't quit.

During the fourth quarter they scored four touchdowns, three of those coming from Rudy Allen on runs of 1, 2 and 13 yards. And Drew Hill added another from 11 yards out. Final score: Georgia 42, Tech 26.

Georgia would go on to lose to Arkansas in the '76 Cotton Bowl.

UGA All-American in 1975:
Randy Johnson (OG).
UGA All-SEC in 1975:
Kevin McLee (RB), Glynn Harrison (RB), Bill King (FS), Ben Zambiasi (LB), Mike Wilson (T).
Tech All-American in 1975:
Leo Tierney (C).
Tech All-SI in 1975:
Hunter (OG), Steve Raible (TE), Rick Gibney (DT), Lucius Sanford (LB).

Bucky Dilts gets off a good punt as Georgia beat Vandy by a score of 47-3.

Gene Washington, Georgia's All-SEC flanker.

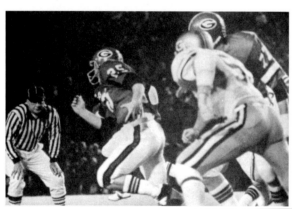

Glynn Harrison gets a block then takes off 78 yards for a touchdown to stretch Georgia's lead to 14-0 over Tech.

Rusty Russell corners this Richmond runner in a game won by Georgia 28-24.

Excited Bulldog players and fans just prior to kickoff in the '76 Cotton Bowl. Arkansas took this one 31-10.

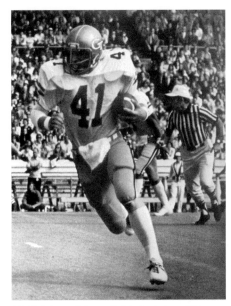

All-SI tight end Steve Raible had three TD receptions in Tech's 30-0 win over Florida State.

Bucky Shamburger accepts the hand-off as Tech fell to Auburn 31-27.

Lucius Sanford, an All-American linebacker and a member of the All-Time Tech Football Team.

Danny Myers takes the pass in for a TD as Tech beat Miami 38-23.

Elliott Price took this Danny Myers pass for a first down as Tech lost to Georgia 42-26.

1976: 10-2 Bulldogs Play For All the Marbles

It was November 27, 1976, and Vince Dooley's Junkyard Dogs were 9-1 at this point, with wins over California, Clemson, South Carolina, Alabama, Vanderbilt, Kentucky, Cincinnati, Florida and Auburn. Indeed, their only loss to date came at the hands of Ole Miss, a 21-17 upset.

This was certainly one of the finest teams in the history of Georgia football. They were ranked number four nationally, were winners of the SEC, and had accepted a bid to play Pittsburgh, the number one team in America, in the '77 Sugar Bowl.

Things were not going as well for Pepper Rodgers and his Yellow Jackets. They were suffering through a mediocre season at this point, with a 4-5-1 record. They had defeated Virginia, Auburn, Tulane and Notre Dame (number eight in the country), while losing to South Carolina, Pitt, Tennessee, Duke and Navy, and tying Clemson.

Harper Brown averaged 41.1 yards per punt during his career, still an all-time Tech record.

Some 60,000 fans turned out at Sanford Stadium to watch Georgia easily smash the outclassed Yellow Jackets.

But Tech played tough, and the first quarter ended a 0-0 tie.

To begin the second quarter Tech quarterback Gary Lanier led the Jackets on a 53-yard drive down to the Georgia 14. But then Eddie Lee Ivery took a hard hit and bobbled the ball. It was quickly covered by Georgia's Lawrence Craft, and that was the end of Tech's big threat.

After an exchange punts, Tech moved to the Georgia 21, but a field goal try from there was no good and again Georgia had dodged a bullet.

The Bulldogs took the ball at their own 20. Ray Goff completed three straight passes, two to Gene Washington and one to Ulysses Norris, good for 32 yards, to the Tech 48. Then came runs by Kevin McLee and Al Pollard, and suddenly the Bulldogs were at the Tech 3. Ray Goff sneaked it in from there, Alan Leavitt kicked the PAT and Georgia was finally in the lead 7-0.

To open the third period Georgia moved to the Tech 13, and from there Leavitt kicked a field goal and Georgia led by a score of 10-0.

Now, with the rain coming down in torrents, Tech moved 50 yards, down to the Georgia 2. Facing a fourth down at that point, Danny Smith came in and booted a field goal, cutting Georgia's lead to 10-3.

On the next series Georgia was forced to punt and Tech took the ball at their 46. Lanier ran to his right for 14 yards, then lateralled back to Sims who ran it down to the 26. On the next play Eddie Lee Ivery ran all the way for a TD,

Georgia concluded the '76 season with a big 13-10 win over Tech, giving them a 10-1 record, the SEC championship, and a trip to the Sugar Bowl. Here Tech's Bob Bowen puts the stop on Ray Goff.

Danny Smith kicked the PAT and the underdogs tied it up 10-10. There was 6:30 showing on the clock and the Sugar Bowl folks were beginning to look a little uncomfortable.

Georgia then drove to the Tech 31, but a fumble ended that threat. Tech took the ball at their 34 with 3:04 showing on the clock, and the Tech fans were going wild.

But then Tech fumbled the ball right back. Georgia then drove to the Tech 15 with nine seconds remaining. At that point Leavitt came in, kicked the field goal, and Georgia excaped with a 13-10 win.

The Bulldogs then went on to New Orleans to play Pitt in the Sugar Bowl for the national championship. But led by the great Tony Dorsett, the Panthers beat Georgia 27-3.

Tech's great All-American Eddie Lee Ivery follows Adrian Rucker's block for a first down as Tech lost to Pitt 42-14.

Eddie Lee Ivery broke the all-time NCAA record in '78 when he rushed for 356 yards in Tech's 42-21 win over Air Force.

David Sims averaged 6.0 yards per carry during his career, still number one in the Tech record book. He averaged 8.2 yards per carry in '75, an all-time Tech single-season record. Here Sims takes a handoff from Gary Lanier in Tech's 27-17 loss to USC.

Lanier dives in for a TD as Tech beat Auburn 28-10.

Ray Goff pursued by a Golden Bear as Georgia beat California 36-24 to kick off a great '76 season.

Allan Leavitt, Georgia's great All-American place kicker, nails one as the Bulldogs beat Vandy 45-0.

Kevin McLee powers for yardage as Georgia beat Alabama 21-0.

Team captain and quarterback Ray Goff took a spill on this play as he ran for a first down in Georgia's 31-7 win over Kentucky.

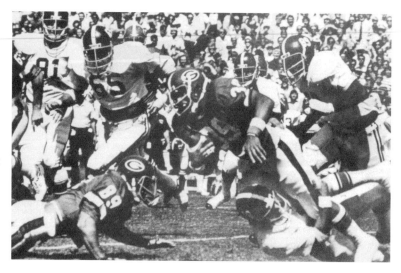

1977: Tech Dominates Bulldogs

It was November 26, 1977, and the defending SEC champions from Athens were limping along with a 5-5 won-loss record. To date they'd beaten Oregon, South Carolina, Ole Miss, Vanderbilt and Richmond, and lost to Clemson, Alabama, Kentucky, Florida and Auburn. This was not, in other words, the usual wrecking crew that Georgia fans had come to know and love.

In Atlanta, meanwhile, the Yellow Jackets were also suffering through their own 5-5 season, with wins over Miami, Air Force, Tennessee, Auburn and Tulane, and losses to South Carolina, Duke, Navy and Notre Dame. Tech lost to Notre Dame 69-14, their worst loss since their 77-0 loss to Florida in 1904.

For the first time in fourteen years neither Georgia nor Tech would be expecting a big bowl bid following this game.

But it was still Georgia vs. Georgia Tech, and over 60,000 fans turned out on a sunny but windy day at Grant Field for this encounter.

The Bulldogs couldn't move following the opening kickoff and punted to the Georgia 48 where the Yellow Jackets took over. Ten plays later, facing a fourth down at the Bulldog 18, Danny Smith came in and booted a perfect field goal, and Tech was on top 3-0.

Later, with only three minutes left in the quarter, Tech's Reggie Wilkes intercepted a Randy Cook pass at the Tech 41. Freshman quarterback Gary Hardie started moving the Jackets at that point by running for 8 yards on a bootleg. Then came Bucky Shamburger with a 17-yard dash, down to the Georgia 34. Then, with Rodney Lee, Eddie Lee Ivery and Hardie alternating runs, Tech was looking at a first down at the Bulldog 18. Ivery rammed down to the 3, then on the next play Hardie sneaked in for the touchdown. Johnny Henderson blocked the PAT, but Tech was out front, 9-0.

Georgia again took the ball, but again their offense sputtered and they were again forced to punt, this time down to the Tech 20. The Jackets then moved 80 yards in 12 plays, the big gainers being Ivery's 15-yard run, Hardie's 26 yarder, and Ivery's 13-yard touchdown run. Smith kicked the PAT and Tech stretched their lead to 16-0.

Indeed, as the two teams went in at halftime there was no doubt that Georgia Tech had completely controlled this game, not only the score but the statistics as well.

Early in the third period Georgia's Mark Farriba recovered Ivery's fumble at the Tech 24. Over the next

Eddie Lee Ivery, an All-American tailback and a member of the Tech All-Time Football Team, rushed for 1,562 yards in '78, still an all-time Tech single season record. The old single-season rushing record had been set by Red Barron in 1921.

Eddie Lee Ivery struggles into the end zone as Georgia Tech defeated Georgia 16-7 on a chilly afternoon at Grant Field.

three plays, however, Georgia lost 28 yards, back to their own 48. At that point Tech's Lawrence Lowe recovered a Cook fumble and again the Bulldogs were forced into bankruptcy.

Tech finally punted out on the Georgia 8, and at that point Georgia's sixth string quarterback, Davey Sawyer, came into the game.

It was Sawyer who led Georgia to their only score of the day. Following Bobby Thompson's block of a Jacket punt at the Tech 17-yard line, Sawyer came in and directed the Bulldogs to a touchdown, James Womack ploughing in from the 1. Rex Robinson converted, but Tech won 16-7.

Georgia still led the series 36-31-5.

All-SEC tailback Willie McClendon blocks a Rebel as Jeff Pyburn looks downfield for Jesse Murry.

Kevin McLee slams into the Ole Miss defense as Georgia won a close one 14-13.

Willie McClendon slams into the line as Georgia beat Vandy by a score of 24-13.

Randy Cook looks downfield for a receiver as the Bulldogs struggled to overcome Tech's big lead. The Yellow Jackets would take this one by a score of 16-7.

Drew Hill averaged 25.4 yards per KO return during his career, still number one in the Tech record book. He returned a kickoff 101 yards for a TD vs. Georgia in '78, the second longest KO return in the Tech record book.

The Yellow Jackets stack up this Georgia runner as Tech went on to a big win.

Gary Lanier is still remembered as one of the finest quarterbacks in the history of Georgia Tech football.

Rodney Lee is smothered by Blue Devils after a 5-yard gain, as Tech lost to Duke 25-24.

1978: One of the Wildest Shootouts Ever

It was December 2, 1978. To date the 7-3 Yellow Jackets had beaten Tulane, The Citadel, South Carolina, Miami, Auburn, Florida and Air Force, and lost to California, Duke and Notre Dame. Indeed, they'd lost to both Duke and California to kick off the '78 season, then reeled off seven consecutive wins before losing to Notre Dame, the number ten team in America, the week before the Georgia shootout. Following this day's game Tech would go on to lose to Purdue in the Peach Bowl.

As for the 8-1-1 Bulldogs, they were enjoying a banner year in '78, with wins over Baylor, Clemson, Ole Miss, LSU, Vanderbilt, Kentucky, VMI and Florida, and a tie with Auburn. Their only loss of the season had come at the hands of South Carolina in an upset. They were ranked number eight nationally. Following this day's game Georgia would go on to lose to Stanford in the Bluebonnet Bowl.

Lindsay Scott returned a kickoff 99 yards for a TD vs. LSU, an all-time UGA record.

Some 60,000 fans turned out at Sanford Stadium to watch the 73rd meeting between these two ancient rivals. Georgia took the opening kickoff and moved to their own 46 where Willie McClendon fumbled and Al Richardson recovered for Tech. Four plays later freshman quarterback Mike Kelley completed a 14-yard pass to Drew Hill, and Tech had a first down at the Georgia 4. Eddie Lee Ivery scored on the next play, Johnny Smith kicked the point, and Tech went up 7-0.

Coach Rodgers then fooled everyone in the stadium when Tech pulled an on-side kick. Jeff Shank covered the ball at the Georgia 47 and the Jackets were back in business. Nine plays later Georgia was called for interference in the end zone and Tech had a first down at the 1. Rodney Lee scored from there, the PAT was good and Tech led 14-0. The first quarter was only half over.

Lindsay Scott fumbled the ensuing kickoff and Tech's Sheldon Fox recovered at the Georgia 16. Four plays later Smith kicked a field goal and Tech led the Dogs 17-0. Fans were stunned.

Early in the second quarter, Georgia fumbled at the Tech 17 and the Jackets recovered. Nine plays later they had moved 78 yards, down to the Georgia 5. From there Johnson kicked another field goal and Tech now led 20-0.

With five minutes remaining in the half Coach Dooley put freshman quarterback Buck Belue in the game. Starting from his own 45, Belue led the Bulldogs on a 55-yard scoring drive that ended

Captain Willie McClendon, Georgia's All-SEC tailback, breaks into the Tech secondary on his way to a touchdown as the Bulldogs took a close one 29-28 at Sanford Stadium to complete a great 9-1-1 season and a trip to the Bluebonnet Bowl.

with McClendon going in for the TD. Rex Robinson kicked the point and Tech's lead was cut to 20-7.

Early in the second half Scott Woerner intercepted a Kelley pass and returned it to the Tech 39. Nine plays later McClendon took it in from the 2, Robinson kicked the point, and Georgia now trailed 20-14.

On the next series Woerner took a Tech punt at his own 28 and didn't pause until he'd crossed the Jackets' goal some 72 yards downfield. The PAT was good, and Georgia took the lead at 21-20. Georgia fans were going wild, but their ecstasy was short-lived. For Drew Hill took the ensuing kickoff and raced it back upfield 101 yards for another Georgia Tech touchdown. This remains the second longest KO return in the Tech record book. Then Kelley threw complete to George Moore for the 2-point conversion, and Tech reclaimed the lead at 28-21.

With five minutes remaining, Georgia took the ball at their own 16. Six plays later Belue threw a 43-yard completion to Amp Arnold for another Bulldog touchdown. Arnold then ran the ball in for the 2-point conversion and Georgia took the lead (and the game) 29-28.

"Durn! Never a fire hydrant around when you need one!"

Willie McClendon turns the corner for a nice gain as Georgia beat Vanderbilt 31-10.

Big Matt Simon skirts end for a 14-yard gain as Georgia blanked Clemson 12-0.

All-American Rex Robinson kicked two field goals in Georgia's 12-0 win over Clemson.

All-American Eddie Lee Ivery confronts Duke defenders as Tech lost to the Blue Devils 28-10.

Drew Hill takes a Mike Kelley pass for a first down vs. Georgia.

Ivery crunches over for a TD as Tech lost to Georgia 29-28.

Tech made a great goal line stand early in the game, but in the end Purdue would take the '78 Peach Bowl by a score of 41-21.

1979: Six Turnovers Spell Doom For Jackets

It was November 24, and folks all over Georgia were still talking about that wild gridiron affair of '78 as they drove to Atlanta to see what would happen in '79. Tech at this point was 4-5-1 on the season, with wins over William & Mary, Duke, Air Force and Navy, and losses to Alabama, Notre Dame, Tennessee, Auburn and Tulane, and a tie with Florida. In fact, Coach Pepper Rodgers would resign at the end of the season and in his place would come Bill Curry.

Mike Kelley had an 80-yard punt vs. Alabama, still number two in the Tech record book.

As for Georgia, the Bulldogs were doing better with a 5-5 record going into the Tech game. To date they'd beaten Ole Miss, LSU, Vanderbilt, Kentucky and Florida, and lost to Wake Forest, Clemson, South Carolina, Virginia and Auburn.

Oddly enough, only Auburn was an SEC foe, while Georgia's other four losses were to ACC members.

Scott Woerner returned an interception 98 yards for a TD vs. Clemson, still number two in the UGA record book.

A cold rain was coming down in torrents as the two teams lined up for the kickoff. Now it was learned that Buck Belue, who had been injured the week before, would not be starting at quarterback for the Bulldogs. That job would go to senior Jeff Pyburn.

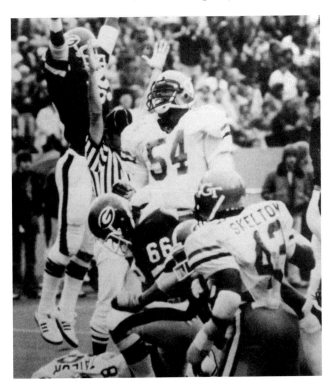

Matt Simon goes in for a TD to put Georgia up 7-3 over Tech.

Midway through the first quarter Tech fans stood and cheered when Lawrence Lowe intercepted Pyburn at the Jackets' 10-yard line, ending an early scoring drive. Tech then began a drive of their own which ended with Johnny Smith kicking a 43-yard field goal, and the Jackets took the lead 3-0.

That score stood until midway through the second quarter when Pyburn led the Bulldogs on a 51-yard scoring drive of their own. After only four plays Matt Simon ran for 5 yards and a touchdown. Rex Robinson kicked his 70th consecutive PAT and Georgia led 7-3. Tech fans quieted down just a bit.

Tech threatened again just before halftime when Mike Kelley hit George Moore with a 27-yard strike at the Georgia 34. But Jeff Hipp forced a fumble and Pat McShea recovered for Georgia.

Pyburn again moved the Bulldogs into Tech territory, and when the drive stalled at the 18, Robinson came in and kicked another field goal, and the score went to 10-3.

That was all the scoring until the fourth quarter when Robinson again kicked a field goal, this one of 38 yards, to give Georgia a 13-3 lead.

Then with only three minutes remaining, Bob

Kelly took a pitchout and raced 52 yards, down to the Tech 7. But Tech held, and Robinson came in and booted his third field goal of the afternoon, extending Georgia's lead to 16-3, which was the final score.

Georgia intercepted Mike Kelley four times this afternoon (Jeff Hipp took down three of those) to go with the two fumbles lost by Tech. As a result of these six turnovers Tech ran only 20 offensive plays during this game while the Bulldogs took 51 snaps. And therefore a Georgia victory.

UGA All-American in 1979:
Rex Robinson (PK).
UGA All-SEC in 1979:
Ray Donaldson (C), Scott Woerner (CB), Matt Brasswell (OT).

Rex Robinson, All-American placekicker, booted three field goals vs. Tech in '79.

Mike Fisher congratulates All-American safety Scott Woerner who had just run back an interception 50 yards for a TD as Georgia lost to Wake Forest 22-21.

Matt Braswell, All-SEC guard.

Jeff Hipp, All-SEC safety, whose three interceptions sank Tech in '79.

Buck Belue, All-SEC quarterback, and Scott Woerner, All-American cornerback, heroes of Georgia's wild win over Tech in '78.

Coach Bill Curry took over from Coach Pepper Rodgers at the end of the '79 season. Seven years later, in '86, he would resign with a 31-43-4 record.

Joel Peeples scrambles as Tech beat William & Mary 33-7. Peeples completed a 90-yard TD pass to Drew Hill vs. Duke, still number two in the Tech record book.

Jeff Hipp had three interceptions vs. Tech in '79. Here he takes one away from Matt Rank.

Bo Thomas dashes through a gaping hole in the Georgia defense, but in the end the Bulldogs would take this one 16-3.

1980: 12-0 Georgia Wins Another National Championship

1980 turned into quite a season for the Georgia Bulldogs. With the emergence of the great Herschel Walker at tailback, plus the presence of Buck Belue at quarterback and excellent offensive and defensive lines, the Bulldogs simply could not be beat. Indeed, as the Tech game rolled around on November 29, 10-0 Georgia had already rolled over Clemson, Texas A&M, Tennessee, TCU, Ole Miss, Vanderbilt, Kentucky, Florida, South Carolina and Auburn. This was their first undefeated team since 1946.

As SEC champs, they would go on to defeat Notre Dame in the Sugar Bowl and win the national championship.

Buck Belue threw a 93-yard touchdown pass to Lindsay Scott vs. Florida, still an all-time UGA record.

Rex Robinson kicked a 57-yard field goal vs. Georgia Tech, then an all-time UGA record.

Things were not going quite so well at Georgia Tech. Under new head coach Bill Curry, they had won only one game all season (Memphis State), while losing to Alabama, Florida, UNC, Tennessee, Auburn, Tulane, Duke and Navy. In an incredible upset, they had also tied (3-3) the number one team in the nation, Notre Dame, the team Georgia would play in the '81 Sugar Bowl.

Georgia's great Heisman Trophy winner Herschel Walker goes in for Georgia's first TD of the day as the Bulldogs beat the Jackets 38-20 in 1980. Georgia would go on to defeat Notre Dame in the Sugar Bowl and be declared national champions.

Over 62,000 fans were on hand at Sanford Stadium as Georgia ran the opening kickoff back to their own 28. On first down Buck Belue threw 31 yards to Herschel Walker at the Tech 41.

Four plays later Rex Robinson booted a 57-yard field goal and the Bulldogs went up 3-0.

Following a Tech punt Georgia again went in for a score after nine plays when Walker bolted in from the 1. Robinson kicked the point and Georgia led 10-0.

Then, with 4:16 remaining in the half, Belue moved the Bulldogs 50 yards in seven plays for a score. From the five Belue threw to Ronnie Stewart for the touchdown, the PAT was good and Georgia led 17-0.

But Tech was far from beaten. They took the second half kickoff and moved 55 yards for a score. First, David Allen burst around end for 46 yards, down to the 5. Then Mike Kelley threw complete in the end zone to Leon Chadwick, Johnny Smith kicked the point, and Georgia led 17-7.

Scott Woerner then returned the ensuing kickoff 71 yards, down to the Tech 24. On the next play Walker dashed around end for his second TD of the day. The PAT was good, and Georgia led 24-7.

Tech then took possession at their own 45. Nine plays later they scored again when David Allen went over from the 4. The PAT was good, and Tech trailed 24-14.

But Georgia came right back. They moved 58 yards in eight plays, with Belue going in from the 1. The PAT was good and Georgia led 31-14.

Then it was Tech's turn, moving 86 yards in 13 plays, with Kelley tossing 5 yards to Steve Henderson for the touchdown. The kick was no good and Georgia led 31-20.

Now, with Tech back in contention, Belue pitched out to Walker who put the game away with a 65-yard run for his third TD of the afternoon

Final score: Georgia 38, Tech 20.

The Bulldogs would go on to defeat Notre Dame 17-10 in the Sugar Bowl and be declared national champions.

David Allen took this Mike Kelley handoff to go into the Georgia end zone standing up for a TD.

In '80 junior quarterback Mike Kelley held all career passing and total offense records at Georgia Tech.

End Ken Whisenhunt is the only Tech player in history to earn five letters in football (1980-1984).

Georgia's All-SEC Eddie Weaver in pursuit of Tech's Mike Kelley.

Future Heisman Trophy winner Herschel Walker in action as Georgia beat Florida 26-21.

Amp Arnold powers his way for a first down as Georgia beat Vanderbilt 41-0.

Marty Ballard, a hardnosed offensive linemen on Georgia's national championship team of '80.

The national champion Bulldogs of '80 walked away with enough awards to fill several trophy cases.

And this about says it all! Georgia had just demolished Notre Dame 17-10 in the '81 Sugar Bowl and fans were jubilant.

1981: Walker Scores Four TDs As Georgia Blasts Tech

It was December 5, the latest date that Georgia and Tech had ever met for a football contest. But the day was sunny and bright as some 58,000 fans converged on Grant Field to watch the 9-1 Bulldogs battle the 1-9 Yellow Jackets.

Indeed, Tech fans were hoping for a big upset today, for their team should certainly be relaxed for this game. After all, what did they have to lose? To date, they'd beaten only Alabama, the number two team in the nation, in a tremendous upset in their season opener. Since then they'd reeled off nine consecutive defeats, losing to Florida, Memphis State, UNC, Tennessee, Auburn, Tulane, Duke, Notre Dame and Navy. To put it bluntly, Coach Bill Curry's second year with the Yellow Jackets was not going well. Indeed, 1981 was their worst season since they'd gone 0-6-2 in 1902.

Georgia fans, on the other hand, were urging their Bulldogs, who were ranked number two nationally, not to take this game lightly. Any team, they pointed out, that could go out and beat Alabama the way Tech did was deserving of respect. But they really had little to fear. At this point Georgia had handily beaten Tennessee, California, South Carolina, Ole Miss, Vanderbilt, Kentucky, Temple, Florida and Auburn. Their only loss had come at the hands of a great Clemson team who went on to win the '81 national championship.

Georgia Tech wore their navy blue jerseys for the first time since 1947, but that would not be enough to save them today.

Mike Kelley completed 391 passes for 5,249 yards during his career at Tech, still number two in the Tech record book. Here he throws to John Kearney as the Yellow Jackets lost to Georgia by a whopping 44-7 score at Grant Field in '81.

Georgia took the opening kickoff back to their own 20, and on first down Buck Belue took the snap from center, faked a handoff to Herschel Walker, then calmly tossed an 80-yard scoring strike to his favorite target Lindsay Scott. Kevin Butler kicked the point, and Georgia was on the board, 7-0. That opening play set the tone for this whole game.

Then it became Herschel Walker's story as he scored Georgia's next three touchdowns on runs of 3, 1, and 2 yards.

And if it wasn't Walker, it was Kevin Butler kicking field goals of 52 and 46 yards.

Indeed, Georgia scored on their first five possessions, and the halftime score was Georgia 34, Tech 0.

The second half was similar to the first, only not quite as bad. Herschel Walker scored another touchdown, giving him four on the afternoon, while Kevin Butler added another field goal. On the Tech side, freshman sensation Robert Lavette scored on a 7-yard scamper in the third quarter, and that was about it.

Final score: Georgia 44, Tech 7.

Walker's four touchdowns this afternoon would tie the record for this series set by Tech's George Maloof in 1951.

Georgia would go on to lose 24-20 to Pitt in the '82 Sugar Bowl.

The Georgia Bulldogs of 1981 enjoyed a great 10-1 season, won the SEC championship, and played Pitt in the 1982 Sugar Bowl.

Herschel Walker goes head on with the Auburn Tigers after taking this Buck Belue hand off. Georgia won 24-13.

Herschel Walker scored twice on the day as Georgia beat USC 24-0.

The 10-1 Bulldogs met Pitt in the 1981 Sugar Bowl. Here Walker bulls his way into the end zone for a TD, but Pitt won 24-20.

Ron Rice boots a 24-yard field goal to upset Alabama 24-21 in '81.

The Yellow Jackets stop Herschel Walker for no gain on this play.

Stu Rogers pitches to All-ACC tailback Robert Lavette as Tech fell to Auburn 31-7.

Greg Snell nails this Notre Dame runner as Tech lost to the Irish 35-3.

Historic Grant Field and the Atlanta skyline as they appeared in '81. The Varsity Grill, though not visible in this photo, is to the upper right.

1982: Georgia Wins SEC and Fifth Straight from Tech

It was November 27, 1982, and a great Bulldog team picked up right where they'd left off in '81, beating everything that wore football britches. At this point the 10-0 Bulldogs were the nation's number one team, and had already won the SEC championship. To date they'd beaten Clemson, Ole Miss, Brigham Young, South Carolina, Mississippi State, Vanderbilt, Kentucky, Memphis State, Florida and Auburn. And now they were looking forward to demolishing Georgia Tech on their way to a big Sugar Bowl showdown with number two Penn State.

At Georgia Tech, meanwhile, the Jackets had won exactly two games during the '80 and '81 campaigns but were doing somewhat better in '82 with a 6-4 record coming into the Georgia game. At this point they had beaten The Citadel, Memphis State, Tulane, Tennessee, Virginia and Wake Forest, while losing to Alabama, UNC, Auburn and Duke. The experts gave them little chance this day.

Ron Rice kicked five field goals vs. The Citadel, still an all-time Tech record.

It was a beautiful day at Sanford Stadium as a record crowd of some 82,000 fans came out for this annual slugfest.

They had hardly gotten seated when Herschel Walker took a hand-off at the Georgia 41, and powered his way 59 yards for a touchdown. Kevin Butler kicked the point and Georgia took a quick lead, 7-0.

But that was it for the Bulldogs in the first half. The Yellow Jackets furnished the rest of the fireworks. Following Walker's score, they took the ball at their own 20, and quickly moved to the Georgia 8. But then Tony Flack intercepted Tech's Jim Bob Taylor, and that was the end of that threat.

Indeed, Tech's super soph tailback Robert Lavette ran the ball from one end of the field to the other, outgaining even the great Herschel Walker, but he could not find his way into the Georgia end zone.

In the second quarter Tech moved to the Georgia 6, but Taylor was rushed out of the pocket and retreated to the 26 where he fumbled the ball. Will Forts recovered for Georgia.

Tech's six points in the first half came on two Ron Rice field goals from 47 and 30 yards. So Georgia went in at halftime holding a slim 7-6 lead.

But it was in the third quarter that the Bulldogs exploded.

First came a 39-yard Kevin Butler field goal, which ran the score up to 10-6.

Tech couldn't move and again punted to Georgia. Then, in a span of only 4:15, the Bulldogs exploded for 21 points. First, John Lastinger threw a 63-yard TD pass to Herman Archie, then came a 1-yard plunge

Georgia's Herschel Walker was named All-American for three consecutive years, then was awarded the Heisman Trophy in '82. His is one of only four jerseys ever retired by the University of Georgia.

Among the numerous offensive records he set during his career with the Bulldogs, note the following:
- He rushed for 5,259 yards.
- He averaged rushing for 159.4 yards per game.
- He averaged 5.3 yards per carry.
- He scored 52 touchdowns.

from Walker for another score, and finally Tron Jackson ran 36 yards for another. At that point Georgia led 31-6.

In the fourth quarter, once the game was out of reach, Tech scored twice, Robert Lavette going in on both occasions, to bring the score to 31-18. But then Jackson scored again for Georgia and that was it, a 38-18 win for the Bulldogs.

Georgia would go on to lose 27-23 to Penn State in the '83 Sugar Bowl.

Ted Roof nails Herschel Walker.

UGA All-American in 1982: Herschel Walker (TB), Terry Hoage (ROV), Jimmy Payne (DT). **UGA All-SEC in 1982:** Wayne Radloff (C), Jimmy Harper (OT), Tommy Thurson (LB), Fred Gilbert (DE), Jeff Sanchez (SAF). **Tech All-ACC in 1982:** Robert Lavette (TB).

Cleve Pounds goes in for a TD as Tech lost to Alabama 45-7.

Jim Bob Taylor, Tech quarterback in '82.

Jack Westbrook ran this punt back 72 yards for a TD as Tech upset the Tennessee Vols 31-21.

Mitch Frix and All-American end Freddie Gilbert go out for the coin toss.

SEC champions with an 11-0 record, Georgia met Penn State in the '83 Sugar Bowl.

The amazing Herschel Walker vaults Vandy's line as Georgia took a 27-13 win.

Jeff Sanchez looks on as Terry Hoage intercepts a Tech pass. Hoage led the nation in interceptions in '82. Both he and Sanchez were named to the All-American team.

1983: Great Georgia Team Dodges the Bullet

Georgia had won 33 games over the past three years and they'd add another 10 wins to that total in 1983 for a combined record of 43-4-1. If the early fifties are remembered as the Golden Age of Georgia Tech football, then the early eighties must be remembered as the Golden Age of Georgia football.

As November 26 rolled around Georgia was 8-1-1 on the season with wins over UCLA, South Carolina, Ole Miss, Mississippi State, Vanderbilt, Kentucky, Temple and Florida. Their only loss had come at the hands of Auburn (13-7) in the tenth game of the season. Plus they had that 16-16 tie with pesky Clemson. Still they were ranked seventh in the nation.

As for Bill Curry's Yellow Jackets, they were struggling along now with a poor 3-7 record. To date they'd beaten NC State, Virginia and Wake Forest, while losing to Alabama, Furman, Clemson, UNC, Auburn, Tennessee and Duke.

Certainly they were not given much of a chance today to stop that runaway train known as the Georgia Bulldogs.

It was a warm sunny day at Grant Field and the 59,000 fans on hand had hardly taken their seats when, on the third play of the game, Tech's Robert Lavette took a pitchout at his own 28-yard line, then outraced everyone 72 yards for a touchdown. Ron Rice kicked the point and Tech led 7-0.

Tron Jackson bolts over for a first down as the Bulldogs went on to defeat Tech by a score of 27-24, giving them a 9-1-1 record and a trip to face Texas in the Cotton Bowl.

Georgia finally got on the board when John Lastinger went in from 6 yards out on a keeper. Kevin Butler kicked the point and the game was tied 7-7.

With ten minutes remaining in the second quarter Tech again scored when John Dewberry, a transfer from Georgia, scrambled out of the pocket and dashed 25 yards for another Jacket touchdown. The PAT was good and Tech led 14-7.

But Georgia came right back. Todd Williams, now in at quarterback for the ailing Lastinger, threw a 48-yard completion to Herman Archie at the Tech 4. Barry Young scored from there and the PAT made it a 14-14 tie game.

Later, with only a minute remaining in the half, Gary Cantrell blocked a Ron Rice punt at the Tech 4. But Tech held, and Butler came in with 17 seconds remaining and booted a field goal.

Early in the third period Tech struck again when Rice kicked a 37-yard field goal, tying the score at 17-17.

But minutes later, the Bulldogs had a 91-yard drive which ended when Latstinger hit Kevin Harris with a 4-yard TD pass. The PAT was good and Georgia led 24-17.

Early in the fourth quarter, after Georgia stalled at the Tech 19, Butler came in and booted another field goal, and Georgia's lead went to 27-17.

But Tech came right back. To cap a 65-yard drive, John Dewberry hit Lavette with a 30-yard TD pass, Rice kicked the PAT and Georgia's lead was cut to 27-24.

And then came the real fireworks. With only minutes remaining and Georgia fans wringing their hands in anguish, Tech began a last determined march. Suddenly, from midfield, Dewberry spotted Daryl Wise open down the right sideline and let fly with a long one. But at the last moment Georgia's Tony Flack made an impossible leaping interception. And that was the old ball game. Georgia had escaped with a close 27-24 win.

They would go on then to defeat Texas in the Cotton Bowl 10-9 to complete a great 10-1-1 season.

UGA All-American in 1983:
Terry Hoage (ROV), Freddie Gilbert (DE), Kevin Butler (PK).
UGA All-SEC in 1983:
Guy McIntyre (OT), Tommy Thurson (LB), Clarence Kay (TE), Winford Hood (OT), Knox Culpepper (LB).

Georgia's defense was superb as the Bulldogs beat Texas 10-9 in the '84 Cotton Bowl.

John Lastinger scores on a draw late in the game to defeat Vandy 20-13.

Barry Young goes in for Georgia's only TD of the day as they beat Florida, 10-9.

With only three minutes remaining in the game and the Bulldogs trailing Texas 9-3, John Lastinger dashed 17 yards for this Georgia TD. It was all the Bulldogs needed to win 10-9.

Tech's John Dewberry, a transfer from Georgia, played a great game against the Bulldogs.

Robert Lavette outran everyone 61 yards for a TD, though Tech lost to UNC 31-28.

Jack Westbrook runs back a timely interception as Tech lost to Alabama 20-7.

Richard Salem makes a great catch for a TD as Tech defeated NC State 20-10 in Raleigh.

1984: Pay Back Time Is _____ (Fill in the Blank)

After Georgia's past four super seasons, 1984 came as something of a letdown. As of December 1, they had beaten Southern Mississippi, Clemson, Alabama, Ole Miss, Vanderbilt, Kentucky and Memphis State, while losing to South Carolina, Florida and Auburn. Still they were ranked number eighteen in the country and had already accepted a bid to play Florida State in the '84 Citrus Bowl.

Kevin Butler kicked 77 field goals during his career, still an all-time UGA record.

As for Georgia Tech, Jacket fans were hoping Bill Curry's rebuilding program would soon be completed. To date they'd beaten Alabama, The Citadel, Clemson, Duke and Wake Forest, while losing to NC State, Auburn, Tennessee, and UNC, and tying Virginia. Still, if they could put it all together, they'd be hard to handle. On December 1 they did just that.

Some 82,000 fans turned out on a beautiful day at Sanford Stadium to watch this 79th meeting.

Following several punt exchanges, Georgia got on the board midway through the first quarter when, after their drive stalled at the Tech 37-yard line, Kevin Butler came in and booted a 53-yard field goal.

It was in the second quarter that Tech began to assert themselves. First came freshman Malcolm King, dashing 58 yards, down to the Georgia 3. Then it was Robert Lavette going over on the next play for a touchdown. David Bell kicked the point and Tech led 7-3.

Just two minutes later, with 12:14 showing on the clock, John Dewberry scored again for Tech on a 30-yard quarterback draw. Again the point was good, and Tech led 14-3.

Then it was Georgia's turn. When their next drive again stalled, Butler returned to the field and kicked a 34-yard field goal, and Tech's lead was cut to 14-6.

Then, with less than a minute remaining in the half, Tech's Dewberry capped a 62-yard drive with a 10-yard touchdown pass to Gary Lee. The PAT was good and Tech led 21-6.

Tech erupted for another 14 points in the third. First came Malcolm King on a 31-yard scamper into the end zone, then it was Dewberry hitting Gary Lee with a 9-yard pass for another Tech score. Both PATs were good and Tech now led 35-6.

A minute later, with 4:00 remaining in the third quarter, a long Georgia drive again stalled, and again it was Butler coming in to kick a 50-yard field goal. Now Tech led 35-9 as the third quarter came to a close.

Five minutes into the fourth period Georgia closed

All-American Robert Lavette, Tech's all-time scoring and rushing leader with 46 TDs and 4,066 yards to his credit.

All-ACC linebacker Ted Roof and Don Chisholm nail David McCluskey as Tech won in a big upset 35-18 at Sanford Stadium.

the gap when Fred "Fast" Lane returned a punt 72 yards for a score. The PAT was good, and now Tech's lead was cut to 35-16. There were still 10 minutes remaining, and Georgia fans and Citrus Bowl representives were beginning to hope.

But with only seconds remaining in the game, Tech punter Mike Snow gave up a 2-point safety and that was all the scoring for the day. Tech took it, 35-18.

But Tech would stay at home on Bowl Day, while Georgia went on to tie Florida State 17-17 in the 1984 Citrus Bowl.

Keith Glanton, led by Tony Kepano and Pete Blazek, sweeps past this Deacon defender. Tech won 24-7.

All-ACC tight end Ken Whisenhunt takes a Dewberry pass for a first down as Tech fell to Auburn 48-34.

All-ACC quarterback John Dewberry barks out signals as Tech goes up against the bowl-bound Bulldogs.

Robert Lavette, John Dewberry and Gary Lee celebrate their win over Georgia in '84 by eating a branch of their host's famous hedge.

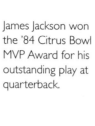

James Jackson won the '84 Citrus Bowl MVP Award for his outstanding play at quarterback.

All-American placekicker Kevin Butler breaks the all-time SEC scoring record.

Freshman sensation Lars Tate goes over for his second TD of the day as Georgia and Florida State tied 17-17 in the '84 Citrus Bowl.

All-American safety Terry Hoage was an Academic All-American and became a starter with the Washington Redskins.

Scott Williams adds to Vandy's woes with this catch of a David Dukes pass for another Bulldog TD.

1985: Tech Makes It Two In a Row

It was November 30, 1985, and the Bulldogs were 7-2-1 coming into their big game with Tech. To date they'd beaten Baylor, Clemson, South Carolina, Ole Miss, Kentucky, Tulane and Florida, while losing to Alabama and Auburn, and tying Vanderbilt. They were ranked number twenty in the nation and had accepted a bid to meet Arizona in the Hall of Fame Bowl on December 23.

Tim Worley ran 89 yards for a TD vs. Florida, still number two in the UGA record book.

As for the Yellow Jackets, they too were having a great year. They had an identical 7-2-1 record coming into the Georgia game, with wins over NC State, Clemson, UNC, Western Carolina, Duke, Chattanooga and Wake Forest, losses to Auburn and Virginia, and a tie with Tennessee. They were unranked but had accepted a bid to play Michigan State in the All-American Bowl on December 31.

Some 45,000 fans gathered at Grant Field on a moonlit Saturday evening for this nationally broadcast game.

As had happened so often in the past, the first quarter consisted mainly of both teams feeling the other out, then punting on fourth down. But then, late in the quarter, Tech drove 51 yards, down to the Georgia 5. There they stalled and David Bell came in and kicked a field goal to put the Jackets up 3-0.

Two minutes into the second quarter Georgia tied it up when Steve Crumley booted a 21-yarder.

Minutes later the Bulldogs had the ball again. Lars Tate took a pitchout at the Georgia 31 and raced 39 yards, down to the Tech 29. But he fumbled when hit and Mark White recovered for the Jackets. They then drove 71 yards for another score when freshman Nate Kelsey went over from the 1. Bell's PAT made the score 10-3, Tech's favor.

With only moments remaining in the half, Georgia drove to the Tech 1-yard line. At that point freshman Jacobs came in and kicked a FG, cutting Tech's lead to 10-6.

Things got off with a bang in the third period. Georgia scored first on a one-yard plunge from Kelsey to make the score 13-10, and for the first time that night the Bulldogs took the lead. Then five minutes later, after Georgia stalled at the Tech 13, they padded their lead with a 23-yard field goal to make the score Georgia 16, Tech 10.

But the Yellow Jackets weren't through. Gary Lee took the ensuing kickoff at his 5 and raced it back 95 yards for a TD. It was a sensational run and put Tech up for good, 17-16.

In the fourth period Georgia crossed midfield only

Aaron Chubb sacks Tech's John Dewberry as John Holcomb and Mike Brown stand by. But Tech went on to win this game 20-16 and accept a bid to play Michigan State in the All-American Bowl.

once, and that drive went nowhere. Tech managed one more score when Bell booted a 46-yard field goal with seven minutes remaining, to make the final score Tech 20, Georgia 16. For the first time since 1970 Tech had now beaten Georgia two years in a row. They would go on now to defeat Michigan State (17-14) in the '85 All-American Bowl to complete a great 9-2-1 season, their best since 1966.

Georgia would tie Arizona (13-13) in the '85 Sun Bowl.

David McCluskey runs for a first down as Georgia lost to Tech 20-16.

All-American Tim Worley breaks out for a TD as Georgia smashed Tulane 58-3.

Cris Carpenter lofts a high punt as Georgia beat Clemson 20-13.

Keith Henderson runs into heavy traffic as Georgia tied Arizona 13-13 in the '85 Sun Bowl.

Mike Snow gets off a punt in the Georgia game.

Ted Roof, now a Tech assistant coach, had 25 tackles vs. Tennessee in '85, number two in the Tech record book.

Todd Rampley throws for Robert Massey in Tech's great 17-14 win over Michigan State in the '85 All-American Bowl.

John Dewberry completed 310 passes for 4,193 yards during his career, still number three in the Tech record book.

Georgia's Retired Jerseys

On September 2, 1985, the jersey of Herschel Walker was retired during halftime ceremonies at the Georgia-Alabama game. Walker was joined by the three other great Bulldog players who've also had their jerseys retired over the years: Theron Sapp, Charley Trippi and Frankie Sinkwich.

Herschel Walker, 1980–82   Theron Sapp, 1956–58   Charley Trippi, 1945–46   Frankie Sinkwich, 1940–42

1986: Georgia Wins a Real Nail-Biter

It was November 29, 1986, a chilly afternoon with dark storm clouds hanging low in the sky as some 82,000 fans made their way to Sanford Stadium to watch this contest between a 7-3 Georgia team and a 5-4-1 Tech team.

To date the Bulldogs had beaten Duke, South Carolina, Ole Miss, Vanderbilt, Kentucky, Richmond and Auburn, while losing to Clemson, LSU and Florida. They were ranked number eighteen nationally and had accepted a bid to play Boston College in the '86 Hall of Fame Bowl.

Gary Moss returned an interception 81 yards for a TD vs. Boston College, number four in the UGA record book.

Georgia's defense rose to the occasion on this play to stop Nate Kelsey as the Bulldogs went on to win 31-24, concluding an 8-3 season. They would later lose to Boston College in the Hall of Fame Bowl.

As for Georgia Tech, they had suffered a relapse following their great 9-2-1 season of '85, and to date had beaten VMI, Virginia, NC State, Tennessee and Duke, while losing to Clemson, UNC, Auburn and Wake Forest and tying Furman. They would be going nowhere on Bowl Day.

Gary Lee returned a kickoff 99 yards for a TD vs. NC State, number three in the Tech record book.

Still, despite the experts predicting that Georgia would run the Jackets out of the stadium, Tech led 7-0 at the end of the first quarter after quarterback Rick Strom hit Gary Lee with a 45-yarder down to the Georgia 1. Malcolm King, Tech's "Mighty Might," went in on the next play, Dave Bell kicked the point and the Underdogs were suddenly looking like Big Dogs.

But then in the second quarter the Bulldogs marched 51 yards, down to the Tech 4. On first down Lars Tate blasted off a tackle for the touchdown. Steve Crumley kicked the point and the game was all tied up.

Fifty seconds later the Jackets marched 71 yards in just three plays, the big gainer a Strom pass to Lee for 55 yards down to the Georgia 5. Jerry Mays took it in on the next play and Tech went back in the lead 14-7.

As though that were not enough excitement, Georgia took the ensuing kickoff and marched 60 yards in eight plays before James Jackson hit Nathaniel Lewis with a 20-yard completion for a touchdown. The PAT was good and the two teams went in at halftime tied 14-14.

But midway the third quarter the Bulldogs began to assert themselves. Starting at their own 30 they drove 70 yards in 10 plays with Tate finally scoring from the 8. The

PAT was good, and Georgia led 21-14.

Two minutes later Tech came back with a march of their own. This one stalled at the Georgia 45, but from there Bell kicked a 55-yard field goal, cutting Georgia's lead to 21-17. This remains the longest field goal on record for Tech.

With less than a minute left in the quarter Tech would again assert themselves when Strom hit Lee with a 14-yard pass in the end zone. The PAT was good, and Tech bolted back into the lead, 24-21.

But the fourth quarter belonged to Georgia. Following a drive of 41 yards, Crumley came in and booted a 39-yard field goal to tie the score at 24-24. Then, with 4:38 remaining, the Bulldogs capped an 86-yard drive when Lars Tate scored from the 5. The PAT was good, and Georgia took this one, 31-24.

The Bulldogs, now 8-3 on the season, would go on to lose 27-24 to Boston College in the '86 Hall of Fame Bowl.

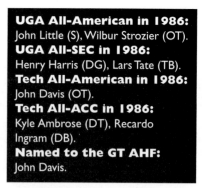

UGA All-American in 1986:
John Little (S), Wilbur Strozier (OT).
UGA All-SEC in 1986:
Henry Harris (DG), Lars Tate (TB).
Tech All-American in 1986:
John Davis (OT).
Tech All-ACC in 1986:
Kyle Ambrose (DT), Recardo Ingram (DB).
Named to the GT AHF:
John Davis.

Cornerback Reggie Rutland is a member of the All-Time Tech Football Team.

Bobby Ross would replace Bill Curry as head coach of the Yellow Jackets at the end of the '86 season. Ross, a VMI graduate, would remain at Tech for the next five years and compile a 31-26-1 record.

Rick Strom hands off to Jerry Mays as Tech lost to Clemson 27-3.

Jerry Mays runs for a touchdown to give the Yellow Jackets a 14-7 lead over Georgia.

Lars Tate, Georgia's All-SEC tailback, scored 37 TDs during his career, still number two in the UGA record book.

Lars Tate runs for a TD as Georgia beat Kentucky 31-9.

James Jackson looks for a receiver as Georgia beat Richmond 28-13.

The Junkyard Dogs put the stop on an ambitious Tiger as Georgia upended Auburn 20-16.

1987: Tate and Hampton Lead Georgia to Big Win

It was November 28, 1987, a cold soggy night in Atlanta as some 45,000 fans made their way into Grant Field to watch the 7-3 Bulldogs grapple in the mud with the 2-8 Georgia Tech Yellow Jackets before a national TV audience.

To date Georgia had beaten Virginia, Oregon State, South Carolina, Ole Miss, Vanderbilt, Kentucky and Florida, while losing very close games to Clemson, LSU and Auburn. They were ranked number fourteen nationally and had already accepted a bid to play Arkansas in the '87 Liberty Bowl.

As for Tech, under new head coach Bobby Ross they had beaten only The Citadel and Indiana State, while losing to all the Division One schools on their schedule: UNC, Clemson, NC State, Auburn, Tennessee, Virginia, Wake Forest and Duke. Truly, it was not a good year for the Jackets, and few gave them any chance at all of upsetting a good Georgia team. Still, the Jackets gave a good account of themselves.

It was a miserable night for football, and as usual the two teams spent much of the first quarter feeling each other out.

But then with 2:47 remaining, Tech struck paydirt after their 59-yard drive stalled at the Georgia 15. In came Thomas Palmer who booted a 25-yard field goal and lowly Tech was up 3-0.

Georgia took the kickoff and then moved from their own 35 to the Tech 4. Lars Tate scored on the next play, John Kasay kicked the PAT and Georgia gained the lead, 7-3.

But Tech came right back. After driving 65 yards, quarterback Darrell Gast hit Steve Davenport in the end zone with a 14-yard completion for a touchdown. The PAT missed, but Tech was back on top, 9-7. There was 13:15 remaining in the second quarter.

Tech was then penalized on the kickoff and Georgia took the ball at their own 49. Seven plays later James Jackson threw 7 yards to Troy Sadowski in the end zone for another Bulldog touchdown. Jackson then went in for the 2-point conversion, and Georgia led 15-9, which was the halftime score.

Early in the third quarter Lars Tate took a swing pass for 20 yards and he ran for 11. Then he took a pitchout and ran down the sideline 34 yards for a touchdown. Jackson threw to Amp Ellis for the 2-pointer, and Georgia led 23-9.

Five minutes later Tech's Rod Stephens intercepted a Jackson pass at the Tech 41. After seven plays, facing a

Malcolm King, who stood 5-8 and weighed 165, managed to get into the corner of the end zone for a TD but it was too little too late as Georgia went on to win 30-16 at Grant Field and accept a bid to play Arkansas in the Liberty Bowl.

third-and-ten at the Georgia 11, Malcolm King shook off tacklers and raced on into the end zone. Thomas Palmer kicked the PAT and Georgia's lead was cut to 23-16. It was still anybody's ball game.

Then, with seven minutes remaining in the contest, the Bulldogs moved 60 yards for another score. On first down Rodney Hampton ran 24 yards, then on the next play he dashed 36 yards for the touchdown. The PAT was good, and Georgia took this game 30-16.

The Bulldogs would go on to defeat Arkansas 20-17 in the '87 Liberty Bowl to conclude a good 9-3 season.

Steve Crumley kicks a 42-yard field goal vs. LSU, but the Bulldogs still fell a few points shy.

The '87 Bulldogs await the kickoff with Auburn, a game they lost 27-11.

James Jackson took a swing pass good for 14 yards and a first down as Georgia lost a 21-20 squeaker to Clemson, one of only three games the Bulldogs would lose in '87.

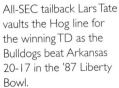

All-SEC tailback Lars Tate vaults the Hog line for the winning TD as the Bulldogs beat Arkansas 20-17 in the '87 Liberty Bowl.

The Yellow Jackets of 1987.

Richard Hills zooms past these Tiger defenders on his way for a big pickup as Tech lost to Auburn 20-10.

Sean McDevitt gets off a punt as Tech kicked off the '87 season with a 51-12 win over The Citadel.

Darrell Gast had 416 yards in total offense vs. Duke in '87, still number two in the Tech record book.

1988: Dooley Bows Out On a Winning Note

It was November 26, 1988, a cool but sunny afternoon in Athens as some 82,000 excited fans made their way to Sanford Stadium to watch this 83rd meeting between the 3-7 Yellow Jackets and the 7-3 Bulldogs.

Bobby Ross was in his second year as head coach at Tech, but to date things had not gone well. At this point they had beaten Chattanooga, South Carolina and VMI, and lost to Virginia, Clemson, NC State, Maryland, UNC, Duke and Wake Forest. Indeed, South Carolina was the only Division One team Tech had beaten over the past two years.

As for Georgia, this would be Vince Dooley's final year with the Bulldogs. Over the past 25 years he had compiled an amazing 201-77-10 record, won six SEC titles, a national championship, and gone to 20 bowl games. Not even the great Wally Butts could approach this record.

In '88 they'd beaten Tennessee, TCU, Mississippi State, Ole Miss, Vanderbilt, William & Mary and Florida, and lost to South Carolina, Kentucky and Auburn. They were ranked twentieth in the nation and had accepted a bid to play in the '89 Gator Bowl.

Georgia All-American Tim Worley is stopped on this play by a determined Tech defense. The 8-3 Bulldogs would win this game, then go on to defeat Michigan State 34-27 in the '89 Gator Bowl.

Tech kicked off, and Georgia came out throwing. Starting at their own 30, quarterback Wayne Johnson completed four passes, down to the Tech 36. From there, John Kasay kicked a field goal and the Bulldogs were up 3-0. And that was the score at the end of the first quarter.

With five minutes elapsed in the second, Tech's Sean McDevitt got off a wobbly 3-yard punt and the Bulldogs took over at their own 37. Nine plays later Tim Worley burst off the left side 3 yards for Georgia's first touchdown of the afternoon. Kasay kicked the PAT and Georgia led 10-0.

With eleven seconds remaining in the quarter, Tech got on the board following a 30-yard run by Jerry Mays, down to the Georgia 34. From there Thomas Palmer hit a field goal, and Georgia's lead was cut to 10-3 at halftime.

But with five minutes elapsed in the third, with the Jackets facing a first-and-ten at their own 34, Georgia lineman Wycliffe Lovelace intercepted a Todd Rampley swing pass. He didn't pause until he'd crossed the goal line for another Georgia touchdown. The PAT was good and Georgia led 17-3.

Essentially, from outmanned Tech's standpoint, that was the ball game. But Georgia came back to score again in the fourth quarter when, after driving 60 yards, Johnson hit Keith Henderson in the end zone with a 5-yard pass. The PAT was good, and Georgia won this one 24-3.

The Bulldogs would then go on to defeat Michigan State 34-27 in the '89 Gator Bowl.

In December, after 25 years at the helm, Vince Dooley retired as head coach of the Bulldogs.

All-SEC tailback Rodney Hampton barges in for a TD as Georgia beat Tennessee 28-17.

All-American tailback Tim Worley bolts off tackle for a first down as Georgia beat Tech 24-3.

Rodney Hampton scored three TDs on the day as Georgia finished the season with a great Gator Bowl win.

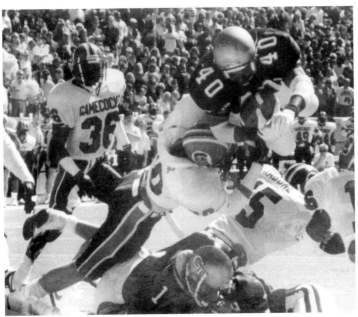

The great Jerry Mays proves what a slippery guy he really is.

Malcolm King bursts into the end zone as Tech beat South Carolina 34-0 at Grant Field.

Tech celebrates their 34-7 romp over VMI in '88.

Todd Rampley completed 28 passes for 282 yards as Tech lost to Wake Forest 28-24.

1989: Tech Ruins Georgia's Peach Bowl Appearance

I t was Ray Goff's first year as head coach of the Georgia Bulldogs and Georgia wasn't doing badly as they prepared to meet Tech on December 2. To date they were 6-4 on the season with wins over Baylor, Mississippi State, Vanderbilt, Kentucky, Temple and Florida, and losses to South Carolina, Tennessee, Ole Miss and Auburn. Though not ranked, they had accepted a bid to meet Syracuse in the '89 Peach Bowl.

Greg Talley's 93-yard TD pass to Kevin Maxwell vs. Vanderbilt remains tied for number one in the UGA record book.

Meanwhile, Georgia Tech's Bobby Ross was finally getting things cranked up. After losing their first three games of the season, Tech had gone 6-1 over the next seven weeks and were now 6-4 overall, with wins over Maryland, Wake Forest, UNC, Western Carolina, Clemson and Boston College, and losses to Virginia, NC State, South Carolina and Duke. Still, despite their identical records, Georgia had a big bowl bid waiting in the wings while Tech did not.

Some 46,000 fans showed up on a cold but clear afternoon at Grant Field for this 84th meeting.

With seven minutes gone in the first quarter, Tech made their move. Starting at their own 22, they drove down to the Georgia 15. At this point Scott Sisson came in and booted a 25-yard field goal and Tech was ahead 3-0. Then, six minutes later, following a pass interception, the Jackets began an 80-yard drive. Three plays later Stefen Scotton bulled his way over from the 1, Sisson kicked the PAT and Tech led 10-0.

All-time Tech great Shawn Jones struggles for a first down as Tech beat Georgia 33-22 at Grant Field in '89.

But early in the second quarter Georgia closed the gap. After a drive of 70 yards, Rodney Hampton swept right for 4 yards and a Georgia touchdown. Kasay kicked the point and Tech's lead was cut to 10-7. Three minutes later Georgia again scored after driving from their own 22 to the Tech 1. At that point Hampton went in for his second TD of the day, Kasay kicked the PAT and the Bulldogs took the lead 14-10. Two minutes later, however, Tech came back with a 39-yard Sisson field goal to cut the lead to 14-13.

In the third quarter Tech again took the lead after driving 69 yards, down to the Georgia 7. At that point Jerry Mays went over for the TD, Sisson kicked the PAT and Tech's lead went to 20-14.

On the first play of the fourth period, after recovering a fumble at the Georgia 1, Scotton went in for another Tech score. The PAT failed, and Tech led 26-14.

Ten minutes later Tech put the game (and the Peach Bowl Committee) on ice when Mays took a 22-yard pass from Shawn Jones and danced into the end zone.

Former Georgia quarterback Ray Goff became head coach of the Bulldogs in '89.

Georgia would score again with only a minute remaining when Preston Jones hit Sean Hummings with a 15-yard TD pass. Jones then threw to Arthur Marshall for the 2-pointer, but Tech took this one, 33-22.

Georgia would lose to Syracuse 19-18 in the Peach Bowl.

Tech All-ACC quarterback Shawn Jones held the ACC record in total offense in '90, and set new Tech records in passing yardage and TD passes.

Jerry Mays rushed for 3,699 yards and scored 28 TDs during his career, both still number two in the Tech record book.

Buzz, Tech's famous mascot, flits about with a rubber chicken just prior to the South Carolina game.

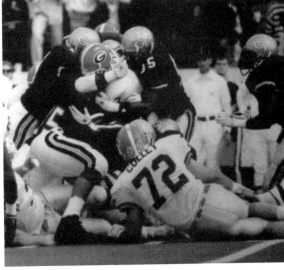

Tech's defensive line made this Bulldog runner earn his scholarship money.

Preston Jones rolls out on this play as Georgia beat Florida.

Coach Ray Goff at Grant Field.

Defensive tackle Bill Goldberg gives the victory sign as Georgia stopped a late Syracuse drive in the '89 Peach Bowl, but Georgia dropped this one 19-18.

The Dawgs hold the line though they finally lost to Auburn 20-3.

1990: 11-0-1 Georgia Tech Wins National Championship

It was December 1, 1990, and the Jackets were having a great year. To date they were 9-0-1 on the season, with very convincing wins over NC State, Chattanooga, Duke, VPI, South Carolina, Maryland, Clemson, Virginia and Wake Forest. Indeed, the only blemish on their record was a 13-13 tie with UNC. They were ranked number two in the nation coming into the Georgia game and had already accepted a bid to play number three Nebraska in the '91 Citrus Bowl.

Georgia, on the other hand, was having problems. They were 4-6 at this point, with wins over Southern Mississippi, Alabama, East Carolina and Vanderbilt, and losses to LSU, Clemson, Ole Miss, Kentucky, Florida and Auburn. This was their first losing season since '77, and for the first time since '79 they would not be going to a bowl game come New Year's Day.

Some 82,000 fans jammed Sanford Stadium to see if Tech, a 13-point favorite, could really pull it off.

And to begin with it looked as though they wouldn't. Only three minutes into the game Georgia moved 44 yards before Garrison Hearst burst over left tackle 5 yards for a touchdown. John Kasay's PAT was blocked, but Georgia was up 6-0.

Two minutes later Georgia recovered a Shawn Jones fumble at the Tech 41. Then came a personal foul penalty and the Bulldogs were back in business at the Tech 27. Four plays later Kasay kicked a 42-yard field goal and Georgia led 9-0.

Georgia's Chris Wilson and Willie Jennings meet Tech's Stefen Scotton. The Yellow Jackets would take this one 40-23, defeat Nebraska in the Citrus Bowl and be crowned national champions.

In the second quarter a Tech drive of 49 yards ended with William Bell going in from the 3. Scott Sisson kicked the PAT and Tech closed the gap to 9-7.

Five minutes later, moving 79 yards in only two plays, Shawn Jones hit Bobby Rodriquez with a 49-yard TD pass, then he threw to Greg Lester for the 2-point conversion, and Tech took the lead at 15-9. As though that were not enough, on their next possession Tech moved 38 yards in six plays before Jones hit Emmett Merchant with a 21-yard pass for another Jacket touchdown. Jones then ran for the 2-point conversion, and Tech increased its lead to 23-9.

With three seconds left in the half, Georgia moved to the Tech 20. From there Kasay kicked a field goal and Tech led 23-12.

In the third quarter Tech moved 41 yards before Jones hit James MacKendree with a 7-yard TD pass. The PAT was good and Tech now led 30-12. As though that were not enough, five minutes later Tech scored again when Jones hit Rodriquez with a 25-yard pass in the end zone. The PAT was good and the score became 37-12.

Georgia closed the gap then when Greg Talley completed a 31-yard pass to Andre Hastings for a TD. Mack Strong ran for the 2-point conversion, and now Tech led 37-20.

In the fourth quarter, after a drive of 60 yards, Kasay kicked a 48-yard field goal to cut Tech's lead to 37-23. But then Tech came right back with a field goal of their own when Sisson kicked a 22-yarder.

Final score: Tech 40, Georgia 23.

Tech went on to defeat Nebraska in the '91 Citrus Bowl and were declared national champions.

All-SEC linebacker Morris Lewis and the Bulldog defense celebrate their successful goal line stand as Georgia beat Vandy 39-28.

Willie Jennings nails this Tech runner.

Greg Talley hands off to Mack Strong in Georgia's loss to Georgia Tech.

Greg Talley sprints down the sideline for a first down in Georgia's 40-23 loss to Tech.

Keith Holmes goes high in the air to block this VPI field goal as Tech won 6-3.

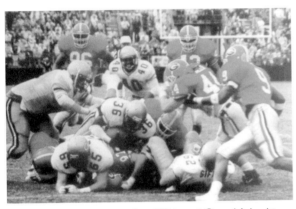

William Bell squeezes over for a TD to cut Georgia's lead to 9-7 early in the second quarter. There were eleven scores made in this contest, five by Georgia, six by Georgia Tech. Shawn Jones threw four TD passes in this contest, still number two in the Tech record book.

All-ACC receiver Emmett Merchant took this Shawn Jones pass in for a TD and a big 7-0 lead over undefeated Nebraska in the '90 Citrus Bowl.

William Bell blasts in for another TD as Georgia Tech wolloped mighty Nebraska 45-21 in the Citrus Bowl to complete a great 11-0-1 season and be crowned national champions. They had last been declared national champions in '52. This was their first season to win eleven games since '51.

1991: Georgia's Defense Stymies Jackets

I t was November 30, 1991, and under Coach Ray Goff the 7-3 Bulldogs were enjoying their best record since '88, with wins over Western Carolina, LSU, Cal State-Fullerton, Clemson, Ole Miss, Kentucky and Auburn, and losses to Alabama, Vanderbilt and Florida. And they had already accepted a bid to play Arkansas in the '91 Independence Bowl.

As for Georgia Tech, the defending national champions, things were also going well. They were 7-4 at this point, with wins over Boston College, Virginia, Maryland, UNC, Duke, Furman and Wake Forest, and losses to Penn State, Clemson, NC State and South Carolina. Thanks to their Kickoff Classic Game vs. Penn State to open the season, Tech played a 12-game schedule in '91. And they had already accepted a bid to play Stanford in the '91 Aloha Bowl.

Willie Clay had 16 career interceptions, still an all-time Tech record.

Over 46,000 fans attended this game at Grant Field on a cool overcast afternoon. They had hardly taken their seats when Georgia's Stuart Saussy attempted to punt from his own 5. But Tech's Mike Williams blocked the kick, the ball rolled out of the end zone, and suddenly Tech had a big 2-0 lead over the Bulldogs.

Ten minutes later Tech again got on the board. Following a 50-yard drive Scott Sisson booted a 24-yard field goal and Tech stretched their lead to 5-0.

But just before the end of the quarter Georgia took the ball at their own 32. On first down Garrison Hearst took a handoff and then raced 68 yards for a touchdown. Todd Peterson kicked the PAT, and Georgia took the lead at 7-5.

With five minutes elapsed in the second quarter Tech began a march at their own 28. Eight plays later Sisson kicked a 51-yard field goal and Tech reclaimed the lead at 8-7.

Five minutes later, following a drive of 68 yards, Georgia seesawed back into the lead when Frank Harvey took it over from the 1. Eric Zeier threw complete to Arthur Marshall for the 2-point conversion, and Georgia led 15-8.

In the third quarter Tech got a break when Ken Swilling intercepted a Zeier pass at the Georgia 19. Six plays later Shawn Jones went in on a keeper from the 4 for Tech's only TD of the evening. Sisson kicked the PAT, and the score was tied 15-15.

With less than two minutes remaining in the quarter, the Bulldogs took the ball at the Tech 39 following a short Jason Bender punt. Six plays later, facing a fourth down, Kanon Parkman came in and kicked a 34-yard field goal, and the Bulldogs were back up 18-15, the final score.

1991 would be the final year for Coach Bobby Ross. He would resign with a 31-26-1 record and a national championship to his credit.

Georgia linebacker John Allen nabs fullback Dave Hendrix as Georgia took this one 18-15 at Grant Field.

Georgia would go on to complete a 9-3 season with a 24-15 win over Arkansas in the Independence Bowl.

Tech would complete a good 8-5 season, a number seventeen national ranking and an 18-17 win over Stanford in the Aloha Bowl.

Tech faced Stanford in the Aloha Bowl on Christmas Day. Woodie Milam celebrates Jimmy Lincoln's TD that put Tech up 9-7.

All-American Scott Sisson (middle) scored 299 points during his career, still an all-time Tech record. Here he is congratulated by his teammates following his big field goal that beat Virginia 24-21.

Marlon Williams, Erick Fry and Kevin Peoples make life rough for this Stanford receiver. Tech finally took this one 18-17 to conclude a good 8-5 season.

Coach Bobby Ross accepts the Winner's Trophy following the Jackets good win over Stanford in the '91 Aloha Bowl.

Georgia tailback Garrison Hearst was named All-American in '92.

Hearst runs for yardage vs. Tech.

Eric Zeier celebrates Georgia's win in the Independence Bowl.

Georgia defeated Arkansas 24-15 in the '91 Independence Bowl and finished the season with a great 9-3 record.

Bernard Williams goes high in the air in hopes of blocking this field goal as Georgia beat Auburn 37-27.

1992: Hearst Leads Georgia To a Tough Win

Georgia's Garrison Hearst was named SEC Player of the Year and to the All-American team in 1992. He is shown here holding the Doak Walker Award, presented annually to the nation's outstanding running back.

In 1992 Shawn Jones held the all-time ACC record for total offense and most Tech records for passing yardage, completions and touchdowns. These records would later be broken by Joe Hamilton in 1999.

It was November 28, 1992, and Bill Lewis was the new head coach of the Georgia Tech Yellow Jackets. To date, Tech was experiencing a 5-5 season, with wins over Western Carolina, Maryland, Clemson, NC State and Duke, and losses to Virginia, Florida State, UNC, Wake Forest and Baylor.

As for Ray Goff's 8-2 Bulldogs, they were having a great year, with wins over South Carolina, Cal State-Fullerton, Ole Miss, Arkansas, Georgia Southern, Vanderbilt, Kentucky and Auburn, and losses to Tennessee and Florida. They were ranked tenth nationally and had already accepted a bid to play Ohio State in the Citrus Bowl.

A record crowd of 85,434 fans showed up at Sanford Stadium on a beautiful afternoon for this latest showdown.

Things got off with a bang when Georgia kicked off and the Jackets' receiver inadvertently stepped out of bounds at his own 1. As though that were not bad enough, on the next play Georgia's Tom Wallace recovered a Tech fumble at the 1, and on the next play Mack Strong bolted through the line for a touchdown. Todd Peterson kicked the PAT and Georgia led 7-0.

Then, with five minutes remaining in the second quarter, Georgia scored again. After driving from their own 35, Peterson booted a 32-yard field goal, and Georgia led 10-0.

But with only seconds left in the half, Tech stalled after a 42-yard drive and Scott Sisson came in and kicked a 37-yarder to cut Georgia's lead to 10-3.

But the third period belonged to Georgia. Just two minutes into the quarter they scored after an 11-play, 80-yard drive when Garrison Hearst bulled in from 3 yards out. The PAT was good and Georgia increased their lead to 17-3.

Ten minutes later Georgia again got on the board. After a 48-yard drive, Hearst went over from the 3 for his second touchdown of the afternoon. Peterson's PAT was good, and the Bulldogs now led 24-3.

But in the fourth quarter Tech made a comeback. After driving from their own 33, Shawn Jones hit Bobby Rodriquez with a 3-yard pass in the end zone for a touchdown. Sisson's kick was good, and the Georgia lead was cut to 24-10 with 14:30 remaining on the clock.

Twelve minutes later, after driving 33 yards, Jones hit Dorsey Levens with a 32-yard pass for another Tech touchdown. The PAT was good, and now the Jackets trailed 24-17.

But that was as close as Tech could get. They tried an on-side kick with two minutes remaining, but in a disputed call the Bulldogs were awarded possession at the Tech 41. Seven plays later

Hearst scored his third touchdown of the day when he went in from the 4. The PAT was good, and the Bulldogs took the game 31-17.

Georgia would then go on to defeat Ohio State 21-14 in the '93 Citrus Bowl to complete a great 10-2 season.

All-American quarterback Eric Zeier.

Tailback Frank Harvey.

With a 9-2 record, Georgia defeated a strong Ohio State team in the '93 Citrus bowl.

All-SEC flanker Andre Hastings.

Flanker Keenan Walker took this reception for a first down as Tech beat Duke 20-17 at Grant Field.

Bobby Rodriquez had 115 receptions during his career, a Tech record that would later be broken by Harvey Middleton.

Mike Smith returned this Blue Devil punt 72 yards for a TD in Tech's win over Duke.

Bill Lewis would become head coach at Georgia Tech in '92, and compile a 11-19 record over the next three years.

Tech's All-ACC quarterback Shawn Jones quickly back peddles in the Jackets 16-13 win over NC State.

1993: Five Tech Turnovers Spell Doom

I t was November 25, 1993, a sunny Thanksgiving Day as 46,000 fans gathered at Grant Field to watch this 88th meeting between the Yellow Jackets and the Bulldogs. Georgia now held a commanding lead in the series, 47-35-5, and would help themselves considerably this day.

Bill Lewis was in his second year as head coach of the Jackets and they had a so-so 5-5 record, with wins over Furman, Maryland, Duke, Baylor and Wake Forest, and losses to Virginia, Clemson, Florida State, UNC and NC State.

As for Georgia, their record was even worse. They were 4-6 at this point, with wins over Texas Tech, Kentucky, Southern Mississippi and Vanderbilt, and losses to Tennessee, Ole Miss, South Carolina, Arkansas, Florida and Auburn.

These two old rivals were playing simply for bragging rights in '93. Both teams would be at home watching the bowl games on TV this year.

Midway through the first quarter Georgia finally got on the board after Charlie Clemons intercepted a Donnie Davis pass at the Tech 47. Seven plays later Kanon Parkman kicked a 38-yard field goal and Georgia was up 3-0.

In the second, after Tech's 63-yard drive stalled at the Georgia 30, Tyler Jarrett booted a 41-yard field goal to tie the score.

But two minutes later Georgia drove 78 yards in 12 plays. Terrell Davis then went over from the 2. The PAT was good and the Bulldogs led 10-3.

With a minute left in the quarter, after an 80-yard Tech drive, Donnie Davis threw 3 yards to Todd Vance in the end zone. Jarrett kicked the PAT, and the score was tied 10-10.

Now, with only seconds remaining, Eric Zeier drove the Bulldogs 34 yards in three plays and in came Parkman. He kicked a 38-yard field goal as time expired to give Georgia the lead at 13-10.

The only fireworks in the third quarter came when Georgia drove 77 yards, down to the Tech 28. Again Parkman came in and kicked a 27-yard field goal and Georgia's lead went to 16-10. It was still anybody's ball game.

But the fourth quarter belonged to the Bulldogs. Carlos Yancy intercepted a Davis pass at the Tech 36. Nine plays later Bill Montgomery went over from the 1, Parkman's kick was good, and Georgia increased their lead to 23-10.

Six minutes later Tech went for it on fourth down from their own 23, but they failed in their attempt, and Georgia took the ball. Three

Bill Montgomery fights his way into Tech territory as Georgia breezed to a 43-10 win on Thanksgiving Day at Grant Field. Both teams finished with 5-6 records in '93.

All-American quarterback Eric Zeier would break every passing record in the Georgia record book.

plays later Frank Harvey broke off the left side 14 yards for a score. The PAT failed, and Georgia led 29-10.

Following the kickoff, Greg Tremble intercepted Davis at the Tech 20 and ran the ball back all the way for a Bulldog TD. The PAT was good, and Georgia led 36-10.

Then, with only a minute remaining, Georgia's Mitch Davis recovered a fumble at the Tech 23. Six minutes later Zeier hit James Warner with a 4-yard pass in the end zone. The PAT was good, and Georgia walked away with a 43-10 win.

Donnie Davis hands off to Chris Haney in Tech's 47-14 win over Duke.

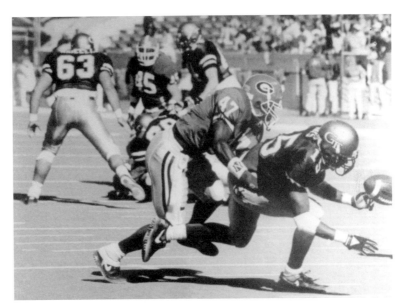

A Bulldog goes after the Yellow Jacket fumble.

Derrick Steagall averaged 24.5 per kickoff return during his career, still number three in the Tech record book. Here Steagall picks up yardage as Tech suffered a big 51-0 loss to Florida State.

In '93 All-ACC tailback Dorsey Levens averaged 7.2 yards per carry, an all-time Tech record.

Terrell Davis goes in for a Bulldog TD as Georgia fell to South Carolina 23-21.

All-SEC receiver Brice Hunter is in mud up to his knees as he takes this Zeier pass for a first down. Florida took it 33-26 in a game played in Jacksonville.

Georgia gives this Tiger running back a rude greeting, but Auburn took the game 42-28.

Sanford Stadium has a seating capacity of 86,117. The University of Georgia has consistently finished among the nation's top six colleges in home attendance since 1980.

1994: Georgia Mauls Tech, Discovers Mike Bobo

It was November 25, 1994, and Georgia and Tech were playing on a frigid Friday evening to a national TV audience, while another 84,000 crowded into Sanford Stadium.

Georgia at this point was bumping along with a 5-4-1 record, with wins over South Carolina, NE Louisiana, Ole Miss, Clemson and Kentucky, and losses to Tennessee, Alabama, Vanderbilt and Florida, and a tie with Auburn. It was rumored that the only thing that would save Coach Goff's job would be a big win against Tech.

Aside from the numerous records he set at Georgia, Eric Zeier remains one of only three college quarterbacks in the history of the game to throw for over 11,000 yards during his career (11,153).

Among his other records:
- He threw for 544 yards vs. Southern Mississippi in '93, a single-game passing record.
- On two occasions he completed 36 passes in a single game (vs. Florida in '93 and Kentucky in '94).
- On four occasions he completed four touchdown passes in a single game.
- He completed 838 passes during his career, a 59.7% completion rate.
- He completed 67 touchdown passes during his career.

At Tech, meanwhile, Coach Bill Lewis had now departed the scene as of November 5 and in his place as interim coach came George O'Leary. Indeed, at this point the 1-9 Jackets had lost handily to Arizona, Duke, NC State, UNC, Virginia, Maryland, Florida State, Clemson and Wake Forest. Their only win of the season came on September 10 against Western Carolina.

Jason Bender averaged 45.5 yards per punt in '94, still number two in the Tech record book.

As in '93, neither team had a big post-season bowl game lined up. They were playing strictly for pride.

Tech took the opening kickoff, and on first down Georgia's Will Muschamp intercepted a Tommy Luginbill pass at midfield. Four plays later Kanon Parkman booted a 46-yard field goal and the Bulldogs led 3-0.

Ten minutes later Tech drove 54 yards before Chris Leone came in and tied the score with a 28-yard field goal.

Following an exchange of punts Georgia's Robert Edwards picked off a Tech fumble and ran it back to the Tech 28. Five plays later Eric Zeier hit Brice Hunter with a 7-yard pass for the touchdown. The PAT was good and Georgia led 10-3.

From this point on, the game was all Georgia. To open the second quarter Georgia's Carlos Yancy intercepted Luginbill at the Tech 33. Four plays later Zeier hit Juan Daniels with a 19-yard pass in the end zone, the PAT was good and Georgia led 17-3.

But Tech came back when second-string quarterback Graham Stroman hit Michael Smith with a 41-yard pass, down to the Georgia 10. Smith ran the ball in on the next play, Chris Leone kicked the PAT and Georgia led 17-10.

Five minutes later Georgia drove 37 yards, down to the Tech 27. From there Parkman kicked another field goal, and Georgia increased its lead to 20-10.

On Georgia's first possession of the second half Mike Bobo replaced the injured Zeier at quarterback and immediately hit Juan Daniels with a 30-yard scoring pass. The PAT was good and Georgia led 27-10.

On Georgia's next series, they drove 97 yards for a score after Bobo completed two passes good for 81 yards. Davis went in from the 1, the PAT was good, and Georgia led 34-10.

On Tech's next series Greg Bright intercepted Stroman at the Tech 29. Five plays later Davis went in from the one. Parkman kicked the PAT and Georgia led 41-10.

Finally, with time running out in the fourth period, after an 80-yard march Bobo hit Hines Ward with a 5-yard pass in the end zone, giving Georgia a 48-10 win.

Randall Godfrey snags a loose Tiger fumble as Georgia whopped Clemson 40-14.

Eric Zeier played his final game vs. Tech in '94. It was a good one as he led the Bulldogs to a 48-10 win over the Jackets at Sanford Stadium.

The University of Georgia's hallowed Arches. At one time freshman were not even allowed to enter the campus through these Arches, but apparently things have changed somewhat. Still, these Arches have stood the test of time since 1864 and it isn't likely that they're going to buckle any time soon.

Georgia wouldn't go out of business with Zeier's graduation. There was a young man named Mike Bobo just waiting for a chance.

Tommy Luginbill threw four TD passes vs. Western Carolina in '94, still number two in the Tech record book.

Derrick Steagall took this Tommy Luginbill pass for a TD as Tech lost to Arizona 19-14.

Fullback Michael Smith is stacked up at the line of scrimmage as Tech lost to Duke 27-12.

Tech receiver Harvey Middleton caught 165 passes during his career, still an all-time Tech record. Here Luginbill completes a pass to Middleton for a first down in Tech's 27-12 loss to Duke.

1995: Georgia Wins In a Great Comeback

I t was November 23, 1995, Ray Goff's seventh year as head coach of the Bulldogs, and at this point Georgia was plodding along with a 5-4-1 record, showing wins over South Carolina, New Mexico State, Clemson, Vanderbilt and Kentucky; losses to Tennessee, Ole Miss, Alabama, and Florida; and a tie with Auburn. Still, it was rumored that should Georgia beat Tech today, a Peach Bowl bid would be theirs for the taking.

As for Tech, this was George O'Leary's first full year as head coach and to date the Yellow Jackets with a 6-4 record were one game better off than Georgia. They had beaten Furman, Virginia, Maryland, Duke, NC State and Wake Forest, and lost to Arizona (20-19), Clemson, Florida State (the number one team in America) and UNC. They were unranked but would go to the Carquest Bowl should they beat Georgia.

Brandon Shaw threw 96 yards to Charlie Rogers for a TD vs. Central Florida, still an all-time Tech record.

It was Thanksgiving Day as some 46,000 fans made their way to Bobby Dodd Stadium. They knew there was much on the line for both teams.

The first quarter was scoreless, but five minutes into the second, Tech struck for a score. Starting at their own 23, they marched down to the Georgia 47. From there Donnie Davis hit Harvey Middleton with a 53-yard TD pass, David Frakes kicked the PAT and Tech was up 7-0.

Five minutes later Tech fans got another boost when the Jackets struck for another score. Following a 56-yard punt return by Nathan Perryman, down to the Georgia 36-yard line, the Jackets drove to the 6. From there Davis hit Cedric Zachery with a pass in the end zone for a TD. The PAT was good and Tech led 14-0, which was the half-time score.

But in the third quarter Georgia made a comeback. After driving 76 yards following the opening kickoff, Hines Ward handed off to Torin Kirtsey who dashed 7 yards for a score. Kanon Parkman kicked the PAT, and Tech led 14-7.

To conclude the third quarter and open the fourth, Tech took the ball at their own 20. They then used 18 plays and 8:26 off the clock to drive down to the Georgia 20. From there Frakes came in and kicked a 30-yard field goal, stretching Tech's lead to 17-7.

But Georgia made an incredible comeback. With less than nine minutes remaining, they drove from their own 22 to the Tech 6 in 10 plays. From there

Torin Kirtsey dashes in for a TD to bring Georgia to within two points of Tech on Thanksgiving Day, 1995, at Bobby Dodd Stadium

Kirtsey ran it in for a TD, Ward hit Brice Hunter with a pass for the 2-point conversion, and Georgia trailed 17-15

Following a Tech punt, Geogia began a drive from their own 26-yard line with 6:36 showing on the clock. Sixteen plays later, with only :47 remaining, Parkman came in and kicked a 34-yard field goal, and Georgia took the lead, and the game, 18-17. It was a great win for Georgia, and a tough loss for Tech.

Georgia would go on to lose to Virginia 34-27 in the Peach Bowl to conclude a 6-6 season.

Vernon Strickland and Nick Ferguson force Wake Forest to turn the ball over as Tech beat Wake 24-23.

Tech's leading receiver in '95, All-ACC end Harvey Middleton, zooms for a TD as Tech beat Furman 51-7.

Mike Cheever celebrates C. J. Williams' TD catch as Tech beat UNC 37-35.

All-ACC center Michael Cheever and Don Davis.

Mike Bobo and the Bulldogs kicked off the '95 season with a solid 42-23 win over South Carolina.

All-SEC receiver Hines Ward scrambles for a first down as Georgia beat New Mexico State 40-13.

Selma Calloway put Georgia in field goal position with this run as Georgia beat Kentucky 12-3.

Kanon Parkman kicked a record five field goals as Georgia fell 34-27 to Virginia in the Peach Bowl. He also kicked 10 PATs vs. NE Louisiana, tying the all-time Georgia record. He kicked 61 field goals during his career, still number two in the UGA record book.

1996: Bobo Leads Dogs To Victory

It was November 30, 1996, and gone from the Georgia scene was Ray Goff. In his place came Jim Donnan and a struggling Bulldog team. At this point they were sporting a mediocre 4-6 record, with wins over Texas Tech, Mississippi State, Vanderbilt and Auburn, and losses to Southern Mississippi, South Carolina, Tennessee, Kentucky, Florida and Ole Miss.

At Tech, things were not going quite as well in '96 as they had in '95. At this point they were 5-5 on the season with wins over NC State, Wake Forest, Duke, Virginia and Central Florida, and losses to UNC, Clemson, Florida State, Maryland and Navy. Five weeks into the season Tech had a 4-1 record and were ranked eleventh nationally. But then the bottom fell out and they lost four of their next five games.

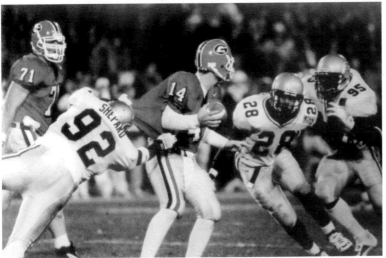

Tech's defensive unit closes in on Mike Bobo as Georgia went on to win 19-10 at Sanford Stadium in '96. Both teams ended the season with mediocre 5-6 records.

Brandon Shaw completed a 96-yard TD pass to Charlie Rogers vs. Central Florida, an all-time Tech record.

It was a cold overcast day as some 78,000 fans crowded into Sanford Stadium to watch this 91st meeting between the Bulldogs and the Yellow Jackets.

They had hardly gotten seated when Georgia punted to Tech. Nathan Perryman was waiting at his own 28-yard line. He caught the punt then dashed 72 yards for a touchdown. Brad Chambers kicked the point and Tech took a 7-0 lead.

On the next series Georgia drove to the Tech 26 but could go no further. On fourth down Hap Hines came in and booted a 43-yard field goal, and Tech led, 7-3.

Early in the second quarter Georgia again went on a long drive, this one 82 yards in 12 plays, which ended with Odell Collins running in from the 10 for a touchdown. The PAT was good and the Bulldogs took the lead 10-7.

But three minutes later Tech came back. Following a drive of 51 yards, Brad Chambers kicked a 27-yard field goal and the score was all tied up, 10-10.

Five minutes later Georgia bounced back. After a drive of 47 yards, Hap Hines trotted onto the field and kicked his second field goal of the afternoon, this one a 41-yarder and the Bulldogs led 13-10 at halftime.

Later, with only two minutes remaining in the third quarter, Georgia's Champ Bailey made his second interception of the day at the Tech 48. Two plays later Mike Bobo hit Juan

Daniels with a long pass and Daniels ran it on into the end zone. The PAT failed, but Georgia took the lead and the game, 19-10.

There would be no post-season play this year for either team.

Future All-SEC running back Robert Edwards scored five TDs vs. USC in '95, still an all-time UGA record. Here he follows Hines Ward for a first down as Georgia beat Tech 19-10.

Patrick Pass gained 33 yards on this play, down to the Tech 25.

Uga, Georgia's twelfth man, warns a careless Auburn runner to stay out of his backyard.

Quarterback Brandon Shaw, who holds the Tech record for the longest TD pass ever thrown, scrambles as the Bulldogs close in.

Charlie Rogers runs for a TD as Tech lost to Navy 36-26.

Tech cornerback Jason Bostic gives this Clemson receiver something to think about.

Nate Perryman breaks out for a TD but Clemson took it 28-25.

Future All-American Joe Hamilton hands off as Tech lost to Clemson 28-25.

1997: Georgia Wins In Miracle Finish

It was November 29, 1997, and new head coach Jim Donnan finally had the Bulldogs back on track. They were 8-2 with wins over Arkansas State, South Carolina, Northeast Louisiana, Mississippi State, Vanderbilt, Kentucky, Florida and Ole Miss, and losses to Tennessee and Auburn. As they prepared to meet Tech this afternoon they were ranked number fourteen nationally and had accepted a bid to play Wisconsin in the '98 Outback Bowl.

Mike Bobo completed 445 passes for 6,334 yards and 38 touchdowns during his career, still number two in the UGA record book.

Over at Tech, meanwhile, Coach George O'Leary and his Yellow Jackets were also having a good year. They were 6-4 with wins over Wake Forest, Clemson, Boston College, NC State, Duke and Maryland, and losses to Notre Dame, Florida State, UNC and Virginia. They were unranked but they were champions of the ACC and had accepted a bid to play West Virginia in the '97 Carquest Bowl.

In '97 Rodney Williams averaged 45.6 yards per punt, an all-time Tech record.

Tech had last beaten Georgia in '90, and 46,000 fans streamed into Bobby Dodd Stadium now to see if this would be the year that Tech would end the drought.

Apparently not.

Georgia took the opening kickoff on their own 20 and gained 26 yards on two running plays before Mike Bobo hit Hines Ward with a 54-yard pass for a Bulldog touchdown. Dax Langly kicked the PAT and the Bulldogs were up 7-0.

On their first possession, Tech drove all the way to the Georgia 1 before fumbling the ball. But then on first down, Jesse Tarplin intercepted Bobo at the 6, and Tech was right back in business. On first down Joe Hamilton ran it in on a keeper, David Frakes kicked the PAT and the score was tied at 7-7.

To open the second quarter Georgia took the ball at their own 28. On first down Bobo completed a 13-yard pass to Corey Allen. On the next play Bobo hit Allen with a 59-yard TD completion. The PAT was good and Georgia led 14-7.

Tech then marched 61 yards on five straight Hamilton pass completions, down to the Georgia 4. Four plays later Frakes came in and kicked a 21-yard field goal, and Georgia led 14-10.

Midway through the third quarter Georgia drove 74 yards, down to the Tech 1. Four plays later Bobo hit Hines Ward with a short pass in the end zone for a TD. The PAT was good and Georgia stretched its lead to 21-10.

Late in the third period Tech got on the board again after a 68-yard drive stalled at the Georgia 10. From there Frakes kicked another field goal, cutting Georgia's lead to 21-13.

To open the fourth period Frakes kicked his third field goal of the day, a 46-yarder, cutting Georgia's lead to 21-16.

Mike Bobo who threw for 6,334 yards during his career with the Bulldogs. His 65.03 completion percentage in '97 is still the best in the UGA record book. He is second only to Eric Zeier in most other catagories.

Then, with only a minute remaining, it appeared that Tech had pulled off a great win when, capping a 65-yard drive, Charles Wiley went in for a touchdown from the 3. Hamilton passed to Mike Sheridan for the 2-pointer and Tech took the lead at 24-21. It would have been a miracle finish.

However there were still 40 seconds on the clock, and in that time, thanks to Bobo's arm and a big interference call, the Bulldogs moved 65 yards to score again when Corey Allen took an 8-yard Bobo pass into the end zone. Georgia took another one, 27-24.

Georgia would go on to defeat Wisconsin 33-6 in the '98 Outback Bowl to complete a great 10-2 season.

Tech would defeat West Virginia 35-30 in the '97 Carquest Bowl to complete a solid 7-5 season.

Kofi Smith joins the fans in celebrating Tech's 37-18 win over Maryland in the '97 ACC Championship.

Dan Witherspoon (#94), Ron Rogers (#50) and Jesse Tarplin (#41) celebrate Tech's great 23-20 win over Clemson in '97.

Flanker Conrad Daniels holds onto this Joe Hamilton TD pass as Tech beat West Virginia 35-30 in the '97 Carquest Bowl.

Tech's all-time great quarterback Joe Hamilton struggles forward for a first down as the Bulldogs close in.

Coach George O'Leary, assisted by Buzz, proudly holds the Carquest Bowl trophy following the Yellow Jackets' great win over West Virginia.

Corey Allen catches the game winner vs. Tech.

Michael Greer races through the Auburn defense.

Tech's defense doesn't move quickly enough to stop Olandis Gary before he can pick up a first down.

It's that tough Bulldog defense to the rescue once again as they stop this Tech runner for no gain.

Mike Bobo and the tough Georgia offense met Wisconsin in the '98 Outback Bowl. Robert Edwards scored three TDs in this contest as the Bulldogs roared to a 33-6 win over their Big Ten opponents.

1998: Tech Proves Miracles Work Both Ways

It was November 28, 1998, and the 8-2 Bulldogs were enjoying another banner season under Coach Jim Donnan. At this point they had defeated Kent State, South Carolina, Wyoming, LSU, Vanderbilt, Kentucky, Auburn and Ole Miss, and suffered losses to only Tennessee and Florida. They were ranked number fifteen in the nation and had already accepted a bid to play Virginia in the '98 Peach Bowl.

As for the Yellow Jackets, George O'Leary was now in his fifth year as head coach and his program was going better than anyone had expected at this point. The Jackets, like the Bulldogs, were sporting an 8-2 record, with wins over New Mexico State, UNC, Duke, NC State, Virginia, Clemson, Maryland and Wake Forest, and losses to Boston College and Florida State. Led by Heisman candidate Joe Hamilton, Tech was averaging 37 points per contest and Georgia fans knew they'd have to score some points to defeat the Yellow Jackets.

Many of the 86,000 fans on hand for this contest were still streaming into Sanford Stadium when Georgia scored their first TD of the afternoon on a trick play. On their first possession, from their own 32, Quincy Carter tossed a lateral to flanker Michael Greer, who spotted a wide open Larry Brown streaking down the left sideline. Brown caught the pass and rambled on into the end zone. Hap Hines kicked the point and Georgia was up 7-0.

Early in the second quarter Tech answered that score when Charlie Rogers returned a punt 65 yards for what appeared to be a touchdown, but the refs ruled that Rogers had signaled a fair catch and the ball was brought back. But on first down Joe Hamilton threw a 65-yard bomb to Kelly Campbell who took the ball into the end zone for a Tech TD. Brad Chambers kicked the point and the score was tied 7-7.

Then, with only two minutes remaining in the half, Georgia's Orantes Grant recovered a fumble at his own 35. In six plays the Bulldogs moved to the Tech 20, but could go no further. Hap Hines kicked a field goal at that point, and Georgia went in at halftime leading 10-7.

To open the second half Georgia's Larry Mann intercepted a Hamilton pass at the Tech 47. Orlandis Gary took the ball down to the Tech 5 on four straight carries, but the drive stalled at that point and Hines came in and kicked a 24-yard field goal to make the score 13-7.

On the next series Tech was again forced to punt and Georgia took the

Quincy Carter, Georgia's All-SEC quarterback, stretches for a big first down, but in the end a missed 2-point conversion would spell doom for the Bulldogs.

ball at their 35. Eight plays later Gary went over from the 2. The two-point conversion failed and Georgia led 19-7.

Georgia's failure on this conversion would later prove a disaster. For Tech was already marching when the fourth period opened. They moved 62 yards in 12 plays before Joe Burns went in from 10 yards for the touchdown. Hamilton scored the 2-point conversion, and Tech now trailed 19-15.

Later, with five minutes remaining, Tech concluded a short drive when Chambers kicked a 49-yard field goal to narrow the score to 19-18.

Then, with two seconds showing on the clock, Chambers kicked his second field goal of the afternoon, this one a 35-yarder, and Tech had a miraculous come-from-behind 21-19 win. It was their first win over the Bulldogs since '90.

The Yellow Jackets would go on to defeat a tough Notre Dame team 35-28 in the '99 Gator Bowl to complete a fine 10-2 season.

Georgia, playing in the '98 Peach Bowl, would take a great come-from-behind win over Virginia to complete a 9-3 season.

UGA All-American in 1998:
Matt Stinchcomb (OT), Champ Bailey (WR).
UGA All-SEC in 1998:
Kirby Smart (SS), Chris Terry (OT), Larry Brown (TE), Orantes Grant (LB), Quincy Carter (QB).
Tech All-American in 1998:
Craig Page (C).
Tech All-ACC in 1998:
Joe Hamilton (QB), Rodney Williams (P), Jason Burks (G), Charlie Rogers (SP), Jesse Tarplin (DE), Travares Tillman (FS), Dez White (SE).

All-American center Craig Page joins a long list of great Tech centers.

Dez White, an All-American candidate at split end.

All-American Joe Hamilton is closing in on every Tech passing record.

Phillip Rogers, Tech's leading ball carrier in '98 had 67 yards vs. Georgia.

Linebacker Mat Uremovich, returns a Duke fumble 54 yards for a TD.

Delaunta Cameron returns a New Mexico State fumble 25 yards for a TD.

Big Jon Carman was twice named ACC Lineman of the Week in '98.

Kofi Smith returns a fumble 90 yards for a TD vs. Wake Forest, an all-time Tech record.

Hap Hines, one of the finest place kickers in the SEC and winner of the Hartman Football Scholarship.

Matt Stinchcomb, an All-American tackle and one of the finest all-around athletes ever to wear the red and black.

Greg Bright and Brandon Tolbert, two of the finest linebackers in the SEC.

Kirby Smart, All-SEC free safety and winner of the Wallace Butts Football Scholarship.

Flanker Michael Greer is congratulated after taking a TD pass vs. Vandy.

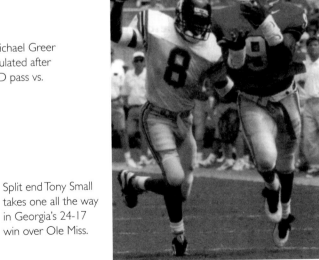

Split end Tony Small takes one all the way in Georgia's 24-17 win over Ole Miss.

1999: Tech Wins Wildest Scoring Spree Ever

It was November 27, 1999, a date that will live long in the memories of Bulldog and Yellow Jacket fans throughout the world, for this was the day that these two old adversaries played what must go down as their wildest, most exciting and probably their most bizarre game ever. Truly, it was a game at historic Grant Field that had just a little bit of everything, including controversy.

As for the Bulldogs, led by quarterback Quincy Carter, they were enjoying a good 7-3 season coming into this day's game, with wins over Utah State, USC, Central Florida, LSU, Vanderbilt, Kentucky and Ole Miss, and losses to Tennessee, Florida and Auburn. Indeed, a win today would give them an 8-3 record and a chance to play in the Outback Bowl come New Year's Day.

As for the Yellow Jackets, they were led by quarterback Joe Hamilton, a top Heisman Trophy candidate, who could do it all. Like Georgia, they were enjoying a good 7-3 season at this point, with wins over Navy, Central Florida, Maryland, UNC, Duke, NC State and Clemson, and losses to Florida State, Virginia and Wake Forest. And, again like Georgia, a win should send them on their way to an engagement in the Gator Bowl on New Year's Day.

Joe Hamilton tied the all-time Tech record when he threw five TD passes vs. Clemson.

The odds makers rated this contest a tossup, and for once they knew what they were talking about.

Tech kicked off to open this 94th meeting of the series and for the next eight minutes the teams exchanged punts as they had done so often, and fans settled back to watch a typical defensive struggle.

To date Tech had scored a total of 397 points against ten opponents, an average of 39.7 points per game, while Georgia had scored a total of 261 points against ten opponents, an average of 26.1 points per game. It was more than likely that the offensive fireworks would soon break loose.

With 8:00 remaining in the first quarter Georgia's Wynn Kopp got off a 28-yard punt which was taken by Tech at their own 45. Several plays later, from the Georgia 27, Luke Manget came in and booted a 44-yard field goal and Tech took a 3-0 lead.

At last Tech fans could relax. If they could just hold Georgia scoreless now, they already had enough to win.

But then with four minutes remaining in the quarter, the Bulldogs began a sustained drive. Eight plays later, facing a fourth-and-two from the Tech 26, Quincy Carter scrambled for 9 yards, down to the Tech 17, but they stalled at the 11. With :56 showing on the clock, Hap Hines tied the game with a 30-yard field goal.

Fifteen seconds later Tech had the ball at the Georgia 47. From

All-American quarterback Joe Hamilton who broke every quarterback record in the GT record book and came in runnerup for the Heisman Trophy, an award he truly deserved.

Georgia's team captains for 1999

TOP:
Steve Herndon (OG)

MIDDLE:
Orantes Grant (WLB)

BOTTOM:
Richard Seymour (DT).

there Joe Hamilton spotted Kelly Campbell dashing down the left sideline and threw a long one. Campbell took it on the fly and trotted into the end zone. Manget kicked the PAT and Tech took a 10-3 lead into the second quarter. Then, some four minutes into the second, Tech increased their lead to 17-3 when, after a short drive, Hamilton hit Kerry Watkins with a 28-yard pass, down to the Georgia 1. Sean Gregory blasted in on the next play and Tech had another TD.

A minute later, from the Tech 29, Georgia came back when Carter faked to Patrick Pass, then spotted Randy McMichael flying all alone towards the Tech end zone. Carter threw the ball right on the money, McMichael made the catch and the Bulldogs had another six points. Hines kicked the PAT and Tech's lead was cut to 17-10.

Some five minutes later Georgia tied the score on Robert Arnaud's 19-yard scamper into the Tech end zone. Hines' kick was good, and the Georgia folks breathed a sigh of relief.

But then, with only 1:16 remaining in the half, Georgia was called for pass interference and Tech had a first down at the Bulldog 8. Three plays later Gregory went in for his second TD of the day on a 1-yard plunge, and Tech went to the sidelines holding a 24-17 lead.

To start the third quarter Tech began a drive from their own 20. Eleven plays later they had covered 68 yards and were facing a fourth down at the Georgia 12. Manget then came in and booted another field goal and Tech increased their lead to 27-17.

On the next series Tech's Travares Tillman intercepted Carter at the Georgia 17. On first down Hamilton hit White with a zinger in the end zone, Manget's kick was good and Tech went up 34-17.

Just three minutes later Georgia closed the gap. Starting from their own 31, they scored when Arnaud went over from the 2. Hines kicked the PAT and Tech now led 34-24.

But Tech wasn't finished. With 3:20 remaining in the third, Tech ripped off 72 yards in just seven plays. They scored when Conrad Andzjewski took a 5-yard pass from Hamilton in the end zone. Manget's kick was good and Ted led 41-24.

With just 1:34 left in the third, Tech fumbled at their own 10. Georgia recovered, and on first down Carter scrambled in for the touchdown. Hines kicked the PAT and Georgia closed the gap to 41-31.

Then came the fourth quarter. Georgia got the scoring rolling after a 69-yard drive when Jasper Sanks darted 15 yards for the score. Hines' kick was good and Tech's lead was cut to 41-38.

Three minutes later it was again Georgia getting on the board when Hines came in on fourth down and booted a 23-yard field goal, tying up the game at 41-41.

Then, with 6:48 showing on the clock, Georgia drove 16 yards in four plays before Carter hit Jervais Johnson with a 30-yard scoring strike. Again Hines was good with the PAT and the Bulldogs were up for the first time, 48-41.

It had been a tremendous comeback for the Bulldogs, and Georgia fans were already making plans for a big bowl game come January 1.

But wait! Hold on!

With 5:12 showing on the clock, Tech drove 68 yards in just seven plays, down to the Georgia 6. Hamilton zinged a pass to Will Glover in the end zone,

Manget's kick was good and the Yellow Jackets had staged a terrific comeback of their own, tying the game at 48-48.

Georgia had one last shot and drove 63 yards in ten plays before Tech's Chris Young recovered a Bulldog fumble at the Tech 2, thus ending the regulation game. (This fumble immediately became a highly controversial call!)

And that's when they went into overtime.

Georgia had the ball first and almost scored, but then Carter was intercepted and suddenly Tech was back in business.

From the Georgia 29, Tech ran two plays, down to the 25, then on third down Coach O'Leary decided to play it safe and go for a field goal. but Manget's attempt was blocked.

However, it was only third down, and Tech's holder George Godsey caught the ball in the air to retain possession.

The teams lined up again. The ball was snapped. Manget's kick split the uprights and Grant Field exploded.

Tech had finally won this record-smashing game in overtime by a score of 51-48.

Tech scored 51 points in this contest, the most points ever scored by either team since 1893. Georgia tied the old record with 48 points. Georgia and Tech each had 1,102 combined total yards in this contest, the most ever. They also combined for a total of 62 first downs. From an offensive standpoint, this truly was a phenomenal performance.

Tech's Joe Hamilton rushed for 94 yards and passed for another 341 yards and four touchdowns.

Georgia's Quincy Carter rushed for 18 yards and threw for another 345 yards and two touchdowns.

Jevaris Johnson had just taken a 30-yard TD pass into the end zone to give Georgia the lead at 48-41 with only six minutes remaining in the fourth quarter.

Postscript

Unquestionably, Georgia holds the lead in this series but, true to the intense nature of the rivalry, even the final stats are bitterly contested. While Tech claims a win-loss-tie record of 52-37-5 in UGA's favor, Georgia does not count two of the games played during World War II (1943 and 1944) and figures the record as 52-35-5 in its favor. Georgia Tech had a Navy flight school during the war years which, quite by accident, had many fine players among its enlistees. On the other hand, UGA, like most schools during that time, had a small student base and thus a dramatically less selective team.

As for overall records, Georgia has now played a total of 1,045 games since 1892, with a standing record of 633-358-54, a .631 winning percentage.

Georgia Tech, on the other hand, has played a total of 1,036 games since 1892, with a standing record of 592-401-43, a .592 winning percentage.

Tech's Jamara Clark was a presence on defense throughout this record-breaking afternoon.

Tech's All-American quarterback Joe Hamilton is surrounded by veteran teammates Jon Carman, Chris Edwards, Felipe Claybrooks, Matt Miller, Ed Wilder, Phillip Rogers, Noah King, Travares Tillman and Dez White. Behind them is a print of Coach John Heisman and his 1917 national championship team.

Kelly Campbell, the fastest man on the Tech squad, ambles back to the huddle after Joe Hamilton took a hard lick on this play. Georgia's Terreall Bierria very innocently looks on.

Chris Young and Jamara Clark come up fast to lend support as Jeremy Muyres goes high to bat away this pass from Carter to Phillips.

Quincy Carter, Georgia's All-SEC quarterback, goes in for a late third quarter TD. The score at this point was 41-31, Tech's favor.

Tech cornerback Shannon Ashmon returns a crucial interception for yardage late in the game. That's quarterback Cory Phillips making the stop.

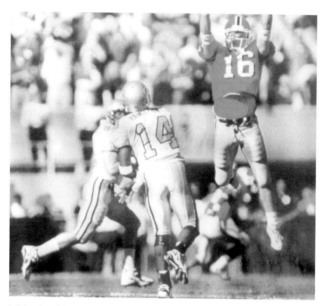

Jolting Joe Hamilton threw for 341 yards and four touchdowns in this contest, the wildest shootout ever between Tech and Georgia.

Runningback Patrick Pass zoomed into the end zone to help Georgia to a great comeback win over Purdue in the Outback Bowl.

The Folks Who Make It All Happen

The University of Georgia Athletic Board of Directors (Front row, L-R): Jane Reid, Gary Couvillon, Athletic Director Vince Dooley, Mary Frasier, Anne Sweaney, President Michael Adams, Jack Turner; (Second row, L-R): Billy Payne, Jim Trieschmann, Allan Barber, Ryan Schwartz, Don Leebern III; (Third row, L-R): Trey Sipe, Gary Hill, Bob Bishop, Happy Dicks, Scott Shamp, Tom Nash.

The Georgia Sports Information staff: (Back row, L-R): Claude Felton (Sports Communications Director), Tim Hix, Mike Mobley, Chris Lakos, Steve Colquitt, Steve Rodriguez; (Front row, L-R): Leigh Dillard, Karlene Lawrence and Karen Huff.

Tech Athletic Director Dave Braine and wife Carole. Braine assumed his duties with the Yellow Jackets on June 3, 1997, only the sixth athletic director in the illustrious sports history of Georgia Tech.

The voice of Georgia football, Larry Munson. He arrived in Athens in 1966, the year that Kirby Moore led the Bulldogs to a 10-1 season, an SEC championship and a 24-9 win over SMU in the '66 Cotton Bowl. He has, in other words, seen a lot of Georgia football!

The Voices of the Yellow Jackets: former quarterback great Kim King (left), color analyst since 1974, and Wes Durham the play-by-play man since 1995.

Mike Finn, Tech's very personable Director of Communications.

Tech Lettermen

(c) = captain
(m) = manager
(t) = trainer

A

Adams, Albert (m) 1930
Adams, B.R. 1918
Adams, H.H. 1937
Adams, J.Q. 1932
Adams, John D. 1966-67-68
Aderhold, Robert ...1938-39-40
Akins, Marion 1950
Albright, J.G. 1923
Aldredge, Steven Scott 1989-90
Alexander, J.C. .1913-14-15-16
Alexander, William A..1911-12
Allen, David B. 1979-80-81
Allen, Ermal K. 1964-65
Allen, H.T. 1918
Allen, John (m) 1990
Allen, Kikie (m) 1950
Allen, Proctor M. 1971-72
Allen, Rudolph C. 1974-75
Allen, T.R. 1938
Allen, Ty (m) 1990-91-92-93
Allen, William C. 1990
Allison, Robert B.........1979-81
Allvine, Douglas W...........1989
Almond, Stephen E.....1965-67
Ambrose, Kyle 1984-85-86
Amis, T.B. 1919-20-21
Anderson, Edwin B., Jr....1968
Anderson, J.C. 1947-48-49
Anderson, Jim ..1982-83-84-85
Anderson, L.F.............1937-38
Anderson, Mark H. 1974
Anderson, Ormand G. 1954-
    55-56
Anderson, R.E. 1938
Anderson, T.G. 1940-41-42
Anderson, T.L., Jr. .1957-59-60
    (c)
Anderson, Warren (t).1978-79-
    83
Andrews, Robert Boyd 1991-
    92-93-94
Andrzejewski, Alan Conrad......
    1998-99
Angley, Tom 1925-26
Appleby, H.H.........1935-36-37
Armentrout 1922
Arnall, H.C. (m)..............1918
Arnett, James E. 1972
Arno, Teddy (m) 1947-48
Arrington, Art (m)1981-82-83-
    84
Arthur, H.B. 1939-40
Asbury, F.L. (m)..............1920
Ashley, Mitch 1980
Ashmon, Shannon............1999
Ashmore, Frederick M. ...1965-
    66-67
Askew, Leon C.......1955-56-57
Asti, Erica (m)............1989-90
Atkinson, J.E. 1943
Atkinson, Michael (t) 1993
Aton, B.B.........................1945
Auer, Joseph 1961-62-63
Austin, David F. 1963-64
Austin, Michael B.............1952
Avers, Elaine R. (m)...1975-76-
    77-78
Avery (m) 1935
Ayres, Asher 1908

B

Bagwell, Gary D. 1955
Bahin, Jim (m) 1990
Bailes, Elbert L. (m) 1954
Baker, Jeffrey L. 1971
Baldwin, J.S. (m)..............1908
Balkcom, Thomas T. ..1988-89-
    90
Ballard, Thomas R. 1962-63-64
Balogun, Kamal...........1995-96
Banks, William O........1951-52
Barber, David C. 1965-66-67
    (c)
Barber, Henry J. 1962-63
Barber, Stephen (m)...1987-88-
    89-90-91
Barkley, Bobbie L..............1978
Barksdale, Michele (m) ...1995-
    96-97-98-99
Barnes, Karl W..................1972
Barnwell...........................1915
Barr, Robert H.............1970-71
Barron, Carter........1924-25-26
Barron, D.I..1918-19-20-21-22
    (c)
Barron, G.W. 1945
Barron, L.F. 1930-31-32
Barron, Scott 1988-89
Barron, Tommy K.1979-80-81-
    82
Bartlett, J.S.................1938-39
Basquin, Brett C..........1998-99
Bates, C.R.......................1940
Battle, John M. .1963-64-65 (c)
Battle, Erron Kevin 1989-90-
91-92 (c)
Baughan, Maxie1957-58-59 (c)
Baum, Phillip 1955,58
Baumgartner, Chris (m) ..1996-
    97-98-99
Baxter, Bryan K.1990-91-92-93
Baynham, Grant A. 1993-94-
    95-96
Baynham, Gordon C..1964-65-
    66
Bazemore, Curtis W. ...1974-75
Bazemore, Preston (t).......1986
Beall, F.R. 1942-43-46
Beard, P.E...............1913-14-15
Beard, R.A..................1934-36
Beard, W.R. 1939
Bearden, Charles E. ...1985-86-
    87-88 (c)
Beasley, James E. 1958-59
Beavers, David S. ...1969-70-71
Beavers, Scott T. ...1986-87-88-
    89
Beavin, Thomas D. 1969-70-71
Beck, Ray M. 1949-50-51
Beck, Thomas M. 1971-72
Beers, R.E. 1938-39-40
Belflower, Bradley (m) 1990-
    91-92-93
Bell, David.............1984-85-86
Bell, J.R. 1943
Bell, Jeb (m) 1974
Bell, John L. 1966
Bell, R.S. 1915-16-17
Bell, William 1989-90-92-93
Bellamy, Eric J. 1989-90
Bender, Greg (m)..1986-87-88-
    89
Bender, Jason B. ...1991-92-93-
    94 (c)
Bennett, Benjamin (m)1957-58
Bennett, Milford H. 1951-52
Bennett, Richard D. 1978
Benson, James E. 1957
Bentley, Clarence F...........1961
Bercegeay, Julie (m) ...1981-82-
    83-84
Bessillieu, Donald A...1975-76-
    77-78
Bethea, L.A. 1947-48-49-50
Bettress, Fred D...............1973
Betts, Charles H. (m) ..1964-65
Bevier, Scott H. 1972-73-74
Biddle, William M.......1960-61
Billingslea, Eric E. 1991-92-93-
94
Bills, J.T. 1946-47
Black, D.C. 1911
Blackwell, Ceylon B. 1965
Blake, J.A. 1945
Blane, Watkins J. ...1964-65-66
Blanton, Michael J. 1975-76-
    77-78
Blasetti, Tony....................1982
Blazek, Peter J.........1981-83-84
Bleick, Thomas W..1963-64-65
Bloodworth, Charles H.....1974
Bogue, Doug 1980
Boldin, Carl 1976-77
Bonifay, Cameron H...1971-72-
    73
Bonifay, Kenneth B.1964-66-67
Bonnewell, Sheldon E. 1971
Booker, Donte M. .1996-97-98-
    99
Boone, Harry A......1959-60-61
Boozer, David R...............1960
Bormolini, John 1975
Borum, Vernon L..............1922
Bosch, J.W. 1939-40-41
Bossons, R.R.....1947-48-49-50
Bostic, Jason D. 1995-96-97-98
Boulware, H.B. 1934
Boulware, Raleigh J....1992-93-
    94
Bounds, Kenneth E. 1968-69
Bourne, W.B. 1943
Bourne, William B. 1970-71-72
    (c)
Bourne, Matthew M...1993-94-
    95
Bowen, Allen....1944-46-47-48
Bowen, J.L........1944-45-46-47
Bowen, Robert C. ..1974-75-76
Bowen, Sheppard A..........1976
Bowen, Tami (m) 1980-81
Bowley, Paul R. 1971-72-73
Bowman, Paul D. 1990
Boyd, A.M........................1934
Boyd, Mark 1991
Bracken, Samuel R.1981-84-85
Bradach, D.D.........1946-47-48
Bradford, Jack C..............1943
Bradford, Patrick ..1994-95-96-
    97
Bradford, Robert R. 1972-73
Bradley, Mark S. ...1978-79-80-
    81 (c)
Bradley, Michael O.1967-68-69
Brady, C.C. 1932
Bramlett, Jocelyn (m).1995-96-

97-98

Brannon, Charles N...1951-52-53

Brantley, James R. 1957

Braselton, Freddie G..1957-58-59

Braswell, Jeff (t) 1982-84

Bravy, Brian R...1991-92-93-94

Breece, Donald C. 1975-76

Breland, James E....1965-66 (c)

Brenner, Dale F. (m) 1966

Brewer, John M. 1925-26

Brewster, J.D. 1921-22

Bridge, Robert S. 1972-73

Briggs, Herbert A. (m).....1963-64-65-66

Brigman, William H...1952-53-54

Brittain, J.F. 1934-35

Broach, R.A. (m).........1942-43

Brodnax, G.H...1945-46-47-48 (c)

Brooke, J.O............1928-29-30

Brooking, Keith H. ....1994-95-96-97 (c)

Brooks, Christopher P. 1990-91

Brooks, Franklin D. ...1952-53-54-55

Brooks, J.L. 1937-38

Broome, Timothy C. ...1969-70

Brown, Adam (t) 1998

Brown, Charles H. 1949-50

Brown, Christopher D.....1997-98-99

Brown, Gary L. 1992-93

Brown, Harper L. 1975-76

Brown, J.C. 1907

Brown, J.E. 1943-46-47-48

Brown, James A. 1965-66-67

Brown, Mandy (t).............1986

Brown, Michael D. 1992

Brown, Neil N. (m).....1959-60

Brown, Samuel .1979-80-81-82

Brown, Samuel 1950-51-52

Brown, Timothy L. 1999

Brownlee, Kevin..........1982-83

Broyles, J.F. 1943-44-46

Bruce, Stephen B.........1972-73

Bruenderman, Robert J. ..1974-75-76

Brumberg, Sara (t) 1997-98

Brumby, C.R...................1929

Bryan, William A. 1974-75

Bryant, C.Matthew.1979-80-81

Bryant, W.G. 1914-15

Buchanon, C..............1907-08

Buchner, Marc E. (m)..1974-75

Buckley, Grant (t) ..1981-82-83

Bullard, R.G. 1926

Burch, Gerald T. ....1958-59-60 (c)

Burdell, George P. ..1928-29-30

Burke, Al (t) 1987

Burke, Damian .1982-83-84-85

Burke, Greg (t)............1986-87

Burke, Sam F. ("Bo") (t) ...1965-66-67-68

Burke, Samuel W. ..1964-65-66 (c)

Burkholder, Gary L. 1963-64-65

Burks, Jason L. 1997-98-99

Burks, Willie L. 1986-87-88-89

Burns, Joe F. 1998-99

Burns, Justin R. 1975-76-77

Burroughs, C.E. 1940-41

Burt, A.M. 1909-10

Burton, Richard E. (t) 1968-69-70

Busbin, W.E. 1945-46-47

Bussell, Gerald W...1962-63-64

Bynum, H.W. 1938

C

Cabrel, Francis G...1978-79-80

Cain, J.T. 1930-31-32

Caldwell, Jerry R. .1995-96-97-98 (c)

Caldwell, Robert S.1960-61-62

Callan, John P. 1969-70-71

Cameron, Delaunta L.1995-96-97-98

Cammack, Clayton L........1958

Camp, Larry B...................1963

Campagna, Richard C. 1975

Campbell, Antoine (t) 1999

Campbell, Dean W. 1973

Campbell, Douglas A. .1972-73

Campbell, L. Kelly 1998-99

Campbell, Randall W........1971

Carden, Gary M.....1970-71-72

Carey, Tony 1984-85

Carithers, Edward E. .1951-52-53

Carlen, James A. 1953-54

Carlisle, Thomas I. 1965-66-67

Carlson, Paul (t)..............1981

Carmack, Charles M........1961

Carmack, J.E. 1935-37

Carman, Jonathan D..1997-98-99

Carmichael, Thomas A....1965-66-67

Carney, Kenneth S., Jr.1981 (c)

Carolina, Marvin ..1982-83-84-85

Carpenter, S.M............1923-25

Carpenter, T.G. 1943-44-46

Carpenter, W.G.1914-15-16-17

Carson, R.E. 1926

Carson, Stanley, L............1955

Carter, Belfield H. ..1958-59-60

Carter, David B................1976

Carter, E.V. (m) 1940

Carter, H.M. 1923

Carter, Joel T.........1983-84-85

Carter, Stewart (m) 1989-90-91-92

Cassidy, Omar A. ...1993-94-95

Castleberry, Clinton D......1942

Castleberry, Don..............1980

Castleberry, J.W. ...1944-46-47-48 (c)

Castro, Timothy P............1996

Caudle, Chris..............1986-87

Cavan, Harry J. 1964

Caviness, Bryan (t) 1988

Caviness, George (t) ..1986-87-88-89

Cavette, N.M. ...1938-39-40 (c)

Cawthon, Wally H. 1979-80-81-82

Celaj, Kujtim ("Ken").1994-95-96-97 (c)

Chadwick, Leon..........1979-80

Chambers, John Bradley .1996-97-98

Chambers, W.J. 1943-44

Chamblin, Gerald ..1986-87-88

Chance, P.M. 1935-36

Chancey, James E...1960-61-62

Chapman, J.G. 1908

Chapman, Joseph R. ..1961-62-63

Chapman, Thomas A. 1967-68-69

Cheever, Michael J. ....1992-93-94-95 (c)

Cheney, Charles E. 1969-70

Cherry, B.T. 1930-31-32

Chisholm, Donalthan 1981-82-83-84

Chivington, J.L. 1936-37-38 (c)

Christensen, Scott (t).1986-87-88

Christy, Frank J. ...1953-54-55-56

Chubbs, William ...1989-90-91

Churchill, D.N. 1914

Clare, Ben (m) 1998-99

Clark, Jack L. 1964

Clark, Jamara..............1998-99

Clarkson, Massey (m)1947-48-49

Clay, J.P. 1939

Clay, R.A. 1914

Clay, Willie J.....1988-89-90-91 (c)

Claybrooks, Felipe A. 1997-98-99

Clements, Jimmy..1993-94-95-96

Clifford, Harold C. 1966

Clingan, L.H. 1931

Clingan, Larry E. 1959

Cobb, F.R. 1918-19

Cobb, Joe E. 1948-49-50

Cochran, William S..........1955

Coger, Frederick L. 1992-93-94

Coker, Donald R. 1960

Colbert, Freeman D...1975-76-77 (c)

Colbert, W.D. 1944

Colcord............................1917

Cole, David (m).....1954-55-56

Cole, Robert T. 1963

Coleman, J.T. ...1946-47-48-49 (c)

Coleman, James P. .1973-74-75

Coleman, Marco D.1989-90-91

Coleman, Marcus J. ...1990-91-92-93

Coleman, W.C. 1909-10-11

Coley, Mike (t) 1983-84

Coley, Pam (t) 1986

Colley, C.S......................1912

Collier, Cory.....1983-84-85-86

Collins, Cory....................1999

Collins, E.R. 1935-36-37

Collins, John P. 1966-67-68

Colquitt, Carey D........1980-81

Colvin, Joseph T. .1963-64-65

Colvin, S.C. 1929-30

Comer, Dave (t) 1984-85-86

Conard, Chris 1986

Cone, Ronny L. 1979-80-81-83

Connally, Vaughn........1924-25

Connell 1922

Conniff, Jack (m) 1931

Cook, H.1909-10-11-12-13 (c)

Cooksey, Douglas A...........1974

Cooksey, Robert T. 1978-79

Cooper, G.F. 1925

Cooper, Douglas A.1961-62-63

Copeland, Charles W........1972

Copeland, Steve E. 1962-64-65

Cord, Robert T. 1973

Cordrey, Peter D. ...1969-70-71

Corhen, Bryan N. ..1997-98-99

Corker, Newman (m).......1930

Costello, Glenn S...1970-71-72

Covington, Thomas P.1988-89-90-91

Cox, Jack T......................1975

Cox, Jamal K. ..1991-92-93-94 (c)

Cox, Orion V. 1988-89-90

Crawford, Elbert D. ...1949-50-51

Crawford, Steven G. ..1973-74-75

Crockett, L.D. 1938

Crockett, Willis R. 1985-86-87-88

Crowe, David (t) 1990-94

Crowley, E.J......1925-26-27 (c)

Crowley, Thomas L. 1974-75

Crum, Richard M. 1962

Culton, John B.......1966-67-68

Cummings, R.H. 1943

Cundy, Christine (t) 1998

Cunningham, Douglas Brent 1969-70-71

Corley, Robert E.....1974-75-76

Curry, Shane 1986

Curry, Terence W.........1986-88

Curry, William A. ..1962-63-64
(c)
Cushing, Glenn 1936-37-38
Cushman, H.W. 1913-14
Cutting, Michael D. 1975-77

D

Daffer, Terrell E......1971-72-73
Dale, Thomas D.....1966-67-68
Daniel, J.E...................1943-44
Daniel, Stephen E. 1973-74
Daniel, Thomas D..1977-78-79
(c)
Daniels, Condrad M....1996-98
Darby, Bobby (m).............1983
Darby, Mike.....................1982
Daugherty, Ben T. ..1952-53-54
Davenport, Steven D..1985-86-
87-88
Davis, A. 1923
Davis, Darish...................1978
Davis, David H. 1951-52-53
Davis, Donald L., Jr. ..1993-94-
95 (c)
Davis, Ellis B. (m) 1941
Davis, Forrest D. 1969
Davis, John H...1983-84-85-86
Davis, J.R. 1907-08
Davis, John J. 1962-64
Davis, Marcus A. 1959
Davis, Michael E. 1992
Davis, O.G. ..1918-19-20-21-22
Davis, R.T....1944-45-46-47 (c)
Davis, Richard K....1961-62-63
Davis, V.L. 1918-19
Davis, Wingfield A. 1960-61
Davis, W.A. 1931-32-33
Day, A.M. 1918
Day, Curley R. ..1989-90-91-92
Daykin, Anthony A....1974-75-
76 (c)
Daykin, Richard.....1976-77-78
Dean, Allen N. (m) 1961-62
Dean, David 1984
Dean, Doug.....................1987
Dean, Norris C. 1932-33-34
DeBardelaben, Stephen L. ....
1968-69
Dee, Michael E. 1993-94-95-96
Deeds, Derrick 1981
Deese, Marion D....1957-58-59
de la Guardia, Mario 1980
Delany, Joe H.........1956-57-58
Denney, Walter C...1965-66-67
Denning, Donald L...........1957
DeVaughn, M.S. 1927
Dewberry, John......1983-84-85
Dickey, Allison (m) 1996-97-98
Dickinson, Jon (m) 1983-84-
85-86
Dobyns, Robert B. 1961
Dodd, R.O............1940-41-42
Dodd, Walter O. 1956
Dollar, Charles R. 1990

Dombach, R.D. 1944
Dorough, J.H. 1943-44
Douglas, Carl E. 1969
Douglas, John F. 1966
Douglas, Tracy (m)......1998-99
Dover, Robert L. 1956-57
Dowling, J.H. 1917-19
Doyal, R.L...................1919-20
Doyal, R.L., Jr...1945-47-48-49
Drennon, R.E...........1926-27-28
Dripps, Charles S. 1974
DuBard, W.H. 1910
Duckworth, Randy A. 1969-70-
71
Dudish, Andrew C. 1969
Dudley, Derrick M............1999
Duke, P.A..............1944-45-46
Dukes, Jimmy Jason ..1992-93-
94-95
Duncan 1915
Duncan, Curtis D. 1992
Duncan, Johnny W......1968-69
Dunlap, E.O. ....1928-29-30 (c)
Dunn, Duncan F. 1965
Dunwoody, H.R...............1916
Durant, R.J...................1927-28
Durden, Wanda (t)...........1989
Durham, James L...1952-53-54
Dyett, Marvin B....1978-80-81-
82
Dyke, Daniel 1999
Dyke, H.E..............1939-40-41

E

Eastburn, Reid P. 1992
Eastman, William P. ...1965-66-
67
Easley, Chuck 1983-84-85
Eaves, S.P. 1940
Echols, Berwin C..............1999
Ecker, Harry A.......1954-55-56
Eckford, Erroll (m)...........1923
Ector, W.H. 1937-38-39
Edge, Arthur B. 1952
Edwards, Christopher B..1996-
97-98-99
Edwards, Darrell 1987
Edwards, G.L. 1936-37
Edwards, J.E. 1941
Edwards, Kenneth M........1965
Edwards, Howard T.J.1988-89-
90
Edwards, W.H........1928-29-30
Elders, William E. 1961
Eldredge, D.C. 1941-42
Ellerbee, Terry E. ...1972-73-74
Elliott...................1925
Elliott, Bruce E. 1971-72-74
Elliott, Thomas......1965-66-67
Ellis, Carl S. 1976-77
Ellis, Marion D. 1954-55-56
Ellis, William C. 1965

Elmer, E.E. 1909-10-11
Elrod, Ronald H. 1965
Emerson, C.L. 1908
Emerson, Richard L. ...1963-64
Engel, Curtis S.......1970-71-72
Enzweiler, Ronald J.....1970-71
Ericksen, Harold J. 1959-60-61
Erickson, Kristen (t) ..1993-94-
95-96
Escoe, Kenneth D. 1981-83
Etheridge, Robert G...1979-80-
81-82
Eubank, Kim (m)...1987-88-89
Eubanks, Bobby Joe 1955
Eubanks, R.W...1933-34-35 (c)
Eubanks, Timothy E. ..1967-68
Evans, Larry (m) 1999
Evatt, Richard I......1968-69-70
Everett, Charles B.............1960
Everhart, Clayton W....1971-72
Ewing, Tim 1988-89
Ezell, C.S. 1929-30-31

F

Fair 1925
Faisst, H.A. 1928-29
Faith, Joseph W. 1967-68-69
Farmer, I.L. 1930
Farnsworth, W.B....1921-23-24
Farr, Clay (t) 1992-93-94-95
Farrer, Danny F. (m).........1968
Farrington, William E. 1961-
62-63
Faucette, Floyd S...1957-58-59
(c)
Faulk, Waymon D.......1963-64
Faulkinberry, David L. 1975-76
Faulkner, A.J...............1942-43
Faulkner, Gary A. 1971-72
Faulkner, Mike (t) .1980-81-82
Ferguson, Edwin L. 1996
Ferguson, Nicholas A. 1995
Ferris, Henry A......1949-50-51
Ferst, F.W. 1918-19-20-21
Fiebelkorn, Thomas M. 1965
Fielder, K.J..1912-13-14-15 (c)
Fields, Mark B. 1971-72-73
Fincher, J.T......................1921
Fincher, S.W. 1929-30-31
Fincher, W.E. ..1916-17-18-19-
20 (c)
Finley, Arley D. 1957
Fischer, Bruce A..........1963-64
Fitzgerald, C.W.....1927-28-29
Fitzsimons, A.F................1907
Fitzsimons, J.M. 1934-35-36
(c)
Flanagan, D. 1947-48-50
Flatau, Arthur 1975
Fleetwood, C.G...........1922-23
Fleming, Louis S. 1974
Flowers, A.R.....1918-19-20-21
(c)
Flowers, Kim (m) .1983-85-86-

87-88
Flowers, Lethon, III ...1991-92-
93-94
Flowers, M.J. 1930-31
Flowers, Stanley M. ...1955-56-
57
Flowers, William C....1968-69-
70
Floyd, Charles R. 1976-77
Fonts, Eladio L. 1957
Ford, Doug (m) 1983-85-86-87
Ford, Gregory N. 1981-82
Ford, Jeffrey S........1969-70-71
Foret, Russell A. 1959-60-61
Forrester, Wallace 1924-25
Fortier, Edmund A.1979-81-82
Fortier, Michael E..1964-65-66
Fortune, Elliott D. .1992-93-94
Foscue, C. (m) 1944
Foster, Dave (m)...1979-80-81-
82-83
Foster, John D.............1965-66
Foster, Stephen F....1968-69-70
Fox, Gary (t)..........1973-74-75
Fox, Sheldon J. 1978-79-80
Foy, William S. 1973
Foyle, R.A. (m)................1945
Frakes, David H. ..1994-95-96-
97
Frederick, Kyle W. 1990-91
Freeman, Russell W. ..1989-90-
91
Frey, Roger A. 1952-53
Friday, Raymond J........1978-79
Friscia, Joe (m)................1953
Frizzell, Everett E........1949-50
Fry, Erick J. 1989-90-91-92
Fry, F.E. 1933
Frye, C.A. 1921-22-23
Frye, C.A. 1921-22-23
Fulcher, Sim B. 1957-59
Fulcher, William M....1953-54-
55
Furchgott, M.H. 1943-44
Furlow, T.M. 1937-38

G

Gaines, H.D. 1944-45-46
Gaiver, W.E. 1919-20
Gallagher, James J...1988-89-90-
91
Galloway, C.M. 1931-32-33
Gathers, Gregory A. 1999
Gann, Stanley, V. 1960-61-62
Gardner, Ellis P. 1979-80-81-82
Gardner, G.C. ..1922-23-24 (c)
Gardner, Richard W. ..1968-69-
70
Garrett, James W. 1975-76
Gariety, Tony L. 1990
Garner, Robert D. ..1993-94-95
Gast, Darrell 1983-86-87
Gaston, Joe L. 1971-72
Gaston, R.W. 1943
Gebhart, Smylie L..1969-70-71

Geertgens, Paul (m)...1989-90-91-92
Geiger, Josh (m) 1999
George, Anthony (m).1984-85-86-87
George, Vincent B.1979-80-81-82
Georgeton, Gus (m)...1978-79-80-81-82-83-84-85
Geren, Preston, M. 1972
Gerhardt, Alfonso W. .1965-66-67
Germany, Charles (m) 1972
Gibbs, Wesley W. 1956-57
Gibney, Richard B.1972-73-74-75 (c)
Gibson, E.H...........1933-34-35
Gibson, James L. 1966
Gibson, W.C. ....1937-38-39 (c)
Giddens, Scott.................1991
Gilbreath, George C. ...1949-50
Gilchrist, Jerry M. 1989-90
Gilliland, Robert F. 1952
Gilmer, C.L. 1938
Givens, Benjamin F. ...1951-52-53
Glad, Maurice L. 1966-68
Glanton, T. Keith..1981-82-83-84
Glazier, Weyman A. 1955-56
Gleason, W.H. (m) 1946
Glendenning, L.B. 1935
Glenn, Jack 1931
Glenn, John.....................1924
Glenn, L.E........1944-45-47-48
Glenn, W. (m) 1927
Glisson, Alan A. 1965-66
Glover, R.G. 1915-16
Glover, William................1999
Godsey, George R. 1999
Godwin, Walter 1924-25
Godwin, Jason 1994
Gold, Scott H..............1990-91
Golden, R.F. (m) 1909-10
Goldsmith, J.W. 1930-31-32
Good, Larry V. 1966-67-68
Goodier, L.E. (m) 1907
Gooding, H.T. 1932
Goodroe, Robert S............1958
Gookin, Richard B. 1954-55-56
Goolsby, Brent S. ..1989-90-91-92
Goree, A.W. 1914-15
Goree, C.P. 1939-40
Goree, C.P.............1909-10-11
Goshay, Derek B. ..1989-90-91-92
Goss, Harry.....................1952
Gossage, Tommy L.1953-54-55
Gossage, Walker E. 1951-52-53 (c)
Gossett, A.H....................1945
Gould, Janet (t)...........1987-88
Grace, Mike 1976

Graham, Reggie S. 1992
Graham, Zollie S. 1970
Granade, Kasey 1999
Granger, H.G...................1921
Graning, Charles H....1959-60-61 (c)
Grant, Lawton E. 1951
Grant, Walter B......1953-54-55
Grantham, John M. 1998
Gravely, Adria (t)..............1999
Graydon, E.D. 1929
Green, Jerome A. ...1956-57-58
Greer, David L...................1974
Greer, Henry C. (m)....1965-66
Gregory, Sean A. 1998-99
Gresham, Thomas S. 1965-66
Gresham, William J. ..1962-63-64 (c)
Griffin, Edward D. 1961-62
Griffin, J.S. 1946-47-48-49
Griffin, Jesse (m) 1999
Griggs, Steve (m) 1971-72
Grimes, Bill R. 1960
Grosz, Esmond A. 1987-88
Grubbs, Ronald L. 1961
Gubba, Matthew S. 1995-96-97-98
Guill, M.F...............1916-17-19
Gunter, George S. ..1968-69-70
Guthrie, Dallis R....1960-61-62
Guyon, J.N. 1917-18
Gwinn, Derek...1980-81-82-83
Gwynn, Robert S. 1968

H

Hackett, R.W. 1935
Haddock, Terry Edmond 1963-64-65
Hair, Henry R. 1951-53-54
Haley, William T. 1978-79
Hall, H.E. 1923
Hall, Joseph A. 1951-52-53
Hallman, Jay (t)...............1989
Hamilton, Joseph F. ...1996-97-98-99 (c)
Hamilton, Keena (t) 1993-97
Hamilton, Tim (m)...........1990
Hancock, J.K. 1940-41
Hand, Wesley R................1963
Haney, Christopher M......1993-94-96
Hardeman, Windle L. 1951-52-53
Harden, Patrick (t) 1999
Harden, Wesley C. 1975
Hardie, Gary E.......1976-77-78
Hardin, Allen 1950-51
Hardison, C. Hugh...........1951
Hardwick, Joseph W. .1968-69-70
Hardy, H.B. 1941-42
Harkey, Stephen D. 1968-69-70
Harlan, J.W.......1917-19-20-21
Harper, W.Z. 1943

Harrington, Mike 1982-84
Harris, Ali G. 1991-92
Harris, Bobby G. 1959
Harris, Ed (m) 1927-28
Harris, Fred L. (m)..........1960
Harris, F.G. 1923
Harris, Joseph A. ...1972-73-74 (c)
Harris, Leslie.........(tr) 1996-97
Harris, Mackel J. ..1976-77-78-79
Harris, William J. (m) 1964-65-66-67
Harrison, Anthony.....1983-84-85-86
Harrison, C.G. 1943
Harrison, Danny K.1987-88-89
Harrison, M.E........1947-48-49
Harrison, N.C. (m)...........1937
Hart, J.W.............1930-31-32
Harvin, Charles R..1948-49-50
Harvin, Harry T. 1965-66-67
Harwood, James G. 1962
Hauck, A.E......................1929
Hauenstein, Rudolph (m).........1952-53-54
Hawkins, James D. 1964
Haycock, Michael S...........1962
Hayes, J.A. 1914
Haygood, Jimmy 1968
Hays, L.C. 1934-35-36
Head, Anthony L. ..1974-75-77
Healy, Robertson L.1970-71-72
Healy, W.R. .1942-46-47 (c), 48
Heard, Ralph L. (m)...1957-58-59
Hearn, Andy 1984-85
Hearn, W.W. 1926
Heflin, Malcolm D. 1978-79
Heggs, Marlon 1979-80
Helinger, Kerry S..............1970
Heller, Louis J. 1966
Helm, Michael G. ..1977-78-79
Helmase, Mike (t) 1975-76
Helms, Jeannae (m) 1983-84
Helmer, Percy C..........1967-69
Helms, J.A. 1941-42-45
Helzer, C.W. 1944
Henderson, Keith (m)1970-71-72
Henderson, Kevin 1984-85
Henderson, Steven M......1978-79-80-81
Henderson, Warren (t) 1979
Hendley, Daniel R............1965
Hendricks, Thomas E. (m) 1961-62-63
Hendrix, David T..1991-92-93-94
Henefield, George P. 1972
Hennessey, Alan W. 1971-72
Henry, Georgia W...1964-65-66
Henry, Urban A...........1956-57
Hensley, Sam P. 1951-52-53

Henson, Douglas C. 1978-79
Herrington, Tommy (t) ...1978-79-80-81
Herron, E.D. 1928-30
Hertenstein, James M. 1969
Hester, Marvious D. 1999
Hicks, David L. 1986-87-88-89
Hicks, John H. 1951
Hickson, Donald N....1991-92-93-94
Higgins 1917
Hightower, J.T. 1919
Hightower, W.H. 1918
Hill, A.B. 1915-16-17
Hill, Andrew 1975-76-77-78
Hill, D. 1907-08-11
Hill, Dennis (m) 1969-70-71
Hill, Harold C. 1965-66
Hill, Kent A. 1976-77-78
Hill, M.E. 1943
Hill, R.G. (m) 1944
Hill, Richard 1973-74
Hillmeyer, Greg...............1984
Hills, G.B. 1943-44-45
Hills, Richard 1985-86-87
Hinson, Wayne D. 1974
Hoats, John R. 1969-70
Hodgdon, Greg (t).1982-83-84
Hodge, Bobby G. ...1981-82-83
Hoffman, Marvin D. 1969
Hoffman, Stacey (m)..1989-90-91-92
Hogan, Mark 1983-84-85
Holland, R.F...........1925-27-28
Hollander, Robert E. 1966
Hollomon, Curtis J. ...1996-97-98
Holloway, F.A.L. (m).........1934
Holmes, Keith F. ...1987-88-89-90
Holt, Clifford R. 1960
Holt, F.L. 1929-30
Holtsinger, E.M...........1944-45
Hood, E.J..............1925-26-27
Hood, R.E. 1935
Hook, L.W. 1946-47-48
Hoover, C.M. 1943
Horn 1926
Hornbuckle, Robert E. 1969
Horne, Gregory K..1971-72-73
Horton, Robert.1980-81-82-83
Horton, Tommy 1967
Houck, J.F. 1945
Howard, Jeffrey A. .1990-91-92
Howard, Walter E..1958-59-60
Howell, Kenneth R. ...1979-80-81-82
Howington, Dan 1980-81
Huddleston, Gregory D...1972-73
Huff, Charles F. 1954-55
Huffines, R.D. ..1918-19-23-24
Hughes, Eddie L....1969-70-71
Hughes, Ralph J. ..1994-95-96-

97
Hughley, Kelvin K. 1999
Humphreys, George W....1952-53-54
Humphreys, Henry C., Jr. 1948-49-50
Hunsinger, John S.......1953-54
Hunt, A.T. 1921-22-23
Hunt, Alex.............1950-51-52
Hunt, Alexander Trotter, IV......1998
Hunter, Mark........1973-74-75
Huntley, Sammy L.......1981-83
Hutchinson, H.G.............1938
Hutko, Albert J. 1969-70
Hutto, David M...........1989-90
Hutton, W.B. 1912
Hydrick, Lawton A. ...1974-75-76-77
Hyland, Tim....................1976

I

Inglett, Forest W. 1965-66
Ingram, Riccardo..1984-85-86-87
Inman, Richard E. .1951-52-53
Irby, C.P. (m) 1935
Irwin, B. King 1979
Irwin, F.L. 1925-26
Isaacs, R.C. 1929-30-31
Isom, Roosevelt 1984-85-86-87
Ison, R.L...............1938-39-40
Ivemeyer, John .1982-83-84-85
Ivery, Eddie Lee 1975-76-77-78 (c)

J

Jackson, Albert J...............1995
Jackson, Gary C. (m) .1970-71-72
Jackson, C. Huntington....1992
Jackson, Reginald P...........1976
Jackson, Stephen H. (m) ..1973
Jackson, Steven A. .1994-95-96
Jackson, Terry C. (m) 1973
Jackson, Thomas E. ...1962-63-64
Jackson, Vernon E. 1971-72-73
James, Calvin E. 1957-58-59
James, Dennis H. ...1967-68-69
James, John E...................1948
James, Lois (m) 1986-87-88-89-90
James, Patrick M. .1985-86-87-88
Jamison............................1926
Jane, Jay.....................1986-87
Jaracz, Robert 1980-81-82
Jarrett, Roy E. 1964-66
Jarrett, Robert Tyler1991-92-93
Jarvis, Matt (m) 1994-95-96-97-98
Jenkins, Herbert R. 1974-75-76
Jenkins, W.K. 1909-10

Jenkins, Darryl G. 1987-88-89-90 (c)
Jerkins, Walter T. 1949
Jobson, Robert W., Jr. 1971
Johnson, C.E. 1917-20-21
Johnson, Charles M..........1974
Johnson, Cleo C..........1972-73
Johnson, Gary L. 1999
Johnson, G.L.............1909-19
Johnson, Henry W., III 1976-77-78-79
Johnson, James H.............1975
Johnson, James L. (m).1953-54
Johnson, James M. 1974
Johnson, James R...1952-55-56
Johnson, Tim L. 1991
Johnson, Thomas B. ..1990-91-92-93 (c)
Johnson, Virgil L...1996-97-98
Johnston, J.T. ...1913-14-15-16 (c)
Jolly, Michael R. 1976
Jones, A.E. 1935-36-37
Jones, Andrew Shawn 1989-90-91-92 (c)
Jones, Bart 1983-84-85-86
Jones, C.D. 1908
Jones, J.T. 1930-31-32
Jones, James A., Jr.1952-53-54
Jones, James D. 1965
Jones, J. Dante..1981-82-83-84
Jones, T.G. 1928-29-30
Jones, Thomas F., Jr. ..1971-72-73
Jordan, Dewey E. 1963
Jordan, Hugh Mitchell 1991-92
Jordan, J.A........1946-47-48-49
Jordan, J.P......................1942
Jordan, R.J. 1946-47
Jordan, W.H..........1935-36-37
Jordan, W.W...............1940-41
Joseph, Gary V. 1994-95-96
Josephson, Andrew D. 1998-99
Jurgensen, Paul......1985-86-87

K

Kalasky, Richard (t)1994-95-96
Karlo, Daniel M...............1971
Katz, Morris 1934
Kaylor, J. Leroy, Jr..1979-81-82
Keener, L. 1927-28
Keisler, Jeffrey ..1980-81-82-83
Kelley, John L. ..1975-76-77-78
Kelley, Michael (m) 1970-71
Kelley, Michael D..1978-79-80-81
Kelly, L.W. (m) 1940
Kelly, Sam 1980-81
Kelly, W.J..........................1945
Kelsey, Nathaniel..1985-86-87-88
Kentera, Larry K. ...1979-80-82
Kepano, Anthony H...1981-82-83-84

Kercher, Jim.................1996-97
Kercher, Mark E. 1976
Ketzner, Joe (t) 1996
Key, Donald Brent..1997-98-99
Kicklighter, Haven L., Jr..1964-65-66
Kidd, Charles W. ...1966-67-68
Kidd, John Paul 1920-21
Kiltie, James H. 1966
Kilzer, J.W...........1943-45-46
Kimsey, Richard A...1990-91-92-93
Kinard, William D. 1966-67-68 (c)
King, Chris (m) 1991-92-93-94
King, Cliff 1924
King, Donald K......1965-66-67
King, Malcolm..1984-85-86-87 (c)
King, Noah H. 1998-99
Kingrey, Carlo 1946
Kirkpatrick, Robert G. (m).......1967-68
Klare, John..................1984-85
Knapp, Kevin R. 1998-99
Knox, Lambert J..........1951-52
Konemann, M.J. 1935-36-37
Kramer, Stephen A.1968-70-71
Kroll, E. James.......1973-74-75
Kroner, F.R. 1931
Kryszon, Guenter........1998-99
Kryszon, Kim (m) 1998
Kuhn, James 1941-42
Kupper, Robert G........1974-75
Kushon, James E. ..1990-91-92
Kyker, D.C. 1945
Kyle, George G., Jr. 1974-75-76
Kyle, Ronald K. (m) 1954-55

L

Lackey, D.E............1937-38-39
Lackey, J.D.............1931-32-33
Ladner, Larry 1950
Lafkowitz, Larry M. ...1959-60-62
Lagana, John E. 1965-66-67
Laircey, Jim L. 1969-70-71
Lam, Herman..............1969-71
Lamar, L.H. 1918
Lamb, H.W. 1941
Lambert, Carole (m)........1978
Lamprey, Ruth (t) 1988
Lang, R.M. 1913-14-15-16
Lang, Thomas D. ...1971-72-74
Langstaff, Witt 1948-49
Lanier, Gary A. .1976-77-78-79
Lansing, A.R. 1945-48
Lantz, Richard W., Jr..1970-71-72 (c)
Lantz, Toby................1982-83
Lasch, John A. 1956-57-58
Lassiter, Issac H., III 1965
Lavallee, Charles R. (m)..1964-65-66-67

Lavette, Robert L. .1981-82-83-84
Lavin, James W. 1988-89-90
Law, H.G. 1929-30
Lawrence, Allen (m)....1978-79
Laws, E.E. ....1931-32-33 (c)
Lawson, Carl A. 1989-90
Lawson, Clyde W. 1959
Lawson, John W. 1961
Laxson, Victor V. 1961
Leach, John (m) 1928
Lear, Donald J.............1987-88
LeBey, C.D. 1920-21
Lederle, Albert J. 1961
Ledford, Parvin E., Jr........1963
Lee, C.L. 1940
Lee, Garrett P. 1962-63-64
Lee, Gary..........1983-84-85-86
Lee, Ivery ....1983-84-85-87 (c)
Lee, Rodney J. 1977-78-79
Leidy, Dale W. 1979
Leone, Christopher M. 1994
Lester, Gregory J...1987-88-90-91
Leuhrman, H. 1909-10-11
Levens, Herbert Dorsey...1992-93 (c)
Lewis, Charles M..............1958
Lewis, Clifford S...............1976
Lewis, F.C. 1909-10
Lewis, John D. 1990-91
Lewis, Richard O. ...1969-70-71
Lewis, Ronald W..............1958
Lillard, J.B....................1926-27
Lillie, Michael J. 1997
Lilly, Sammy.....1983-84-85-87
Lincoln, James M. 1991-92-93-94
Lincoln, Robert W. 1961
Lindsey, J.B. 1934-35-36
Lindsey, Steven L..............1987
Lindsley, Charles S. 1969-70
Linginfelter, William S......1955
Littleton, Harry J. 1961
Liu, Arnold (t)..................1998
Lloyd, Steve (m) 1978-79-80
Loeb, A.L...............1911-12-13
Logan, M.J. ....1943-44 (c)
Logan, Reginald B. 1958
Logan, W.W.....................1942
Long, Joshua W. 1998
Long, Stanley M...........1972-73
Loome, Brian (m) ..1989-90-91
Lothridge, Billy L...1961-62-63 (c)
Lowe, Lawrence D. 1977-78-79-80
Lowrey, R.O. 1942
Lubischer, Anthony J.1973-74-75
Lucas, J., Jr..................1913-14
Luck, C.F.........................1907
Luck, J. 1910
Luck, J.K. 1942

Luck, James K., III 1970
Luginbill, Thomas C. 1994
Lukkar, Steven B. 1975-76
Lumpkin, Roy 1928
Luna, R.C. 1929
Lupton, Dale B. 1948-49
Lusk, Bob 1950
Lutz, David G. ...1979-80-81-82
(c)
Lyman, W.P. 1921-22
Lyons, Matthew A. .1950-51-52
Lyons, R.M. 1934

M

Mabra, Ronald 1998-99
MacIntyre, George Michael.......
1987-88
Mack, Charles 1985-86
MacKendree, James A. 1989-
90-92
Mackley, Roy L. 1958
Macy, Richard T. 1970-71-72
Madigan, William V. 1999
Maiello, Peter P. 1994-95
Maggiore, Joe (t) 1994-95
Maier, Frank H., Jr. (m) ..1958-
59
Maker, David 1995
Malone, George R. 1985-86-87-
88
Malone, K.G. (m) 1914
Malone, Ralph ..1982-83-84-85
Maloney, William H., Jr. ...1981
Maloof, George B. ...1949-50-51
Maloof, Jeffrey R. 1987-88
Malta, Joseph W. 1974-75
Mancaruso, James M. 1988
Mancil, Steven Wade 1993
Maness, Devon 1978-79
Manget, Thomas Luke......1999
Manion, Tim 1982-83-85-86
Mann, Devon 1978-79
Mann, Danny J. 1978
Manning, George ...1941-42-43
(c)
Manning, Mark 1980
Manzoor, Ashley (t)..........1999
Marble, James A. 1977-78
Marion, Jessie D. ..1986-87-88-
89
Marium, Adele (m)...........1982
Maree, G.L. 1928-29-30
Marshall, J.A. ....1940-42 (c)
Marshall, John 1924-25-26
Marston, Sean (m)1994-95-96-
97-98
Martimucci, Lisa (m)........1980
Martin, Buck 1950-51-52
Martin, Christie (m) 1987
Martin, Stephen (m).........1999
Martin, Jake W.1961-62-63 (c)
Martin, Jake W., Jr. 1986-87-
89-90
Martin, Jon S. 1961-62-63

Martin, L.J. 1925-26-27
Martin, Michael D. 1980-81-
82-83
Martin, Ryan (m)..1991-92-93-
94
Martin, W.S. 1933-34
Mason, Kent L. 1974
Mason, Rausey W., Jr. ...1957-58
Massa, Alison (m)..1995-96-97
Massey, Irving M. (m).......1939
Massey, Robert..1984-85-86-87
Mathews, George..1944-45-46-
47
Mathias, Clark 1915-17-18
Mathis, Jeffrey D...1986-87-88-
89
Matlock, John R.....1961-62-63
Matthews, W. Clay.1947-48-49
Mattison, Richard C...1954-55-
56
Matvay, Russell...........1998-99
Mauck, H.M. 1914-15-16
Mauldin, Tim 1984-85
Maynard, Charles N....1956-57
Mays, Jerry D. ..1985-86-88-89
(c)
Mays, Reggie 1983
Mayton, John A...........1969-71
McAden, Rufus Y., III 1962
McArthur, J.R. 1930-31-32
McAshan, Eddie, III...1970-71-
72
McCaskill, Robert M. 1974-75
McCauley, George R. 1955
McClary, Jerimiah.1987-88-89-
90 (c)
McCloskey, Frank.1968-69-70-
71
McCommons, Stephen R.1976-
77
McConnell, F. 1922-23
McCord, D.E. 1913-14
McCoy, Delma S. ...1964-65-66
McCoy, Robert H..1947-48-49-
50
McDaniel, William D., III..1974-
75
McDevitt, Sean L. ..1986-87-88
McDonald, Alf 1912-13
McDonough, J.J....1919-20-21-
22
McDowell, M.C. 1908
McElroy, Joshua 1999
McEwen, Jeni (t).........1991-92
McFadden, Robert (t) 1989-90-
93
McGaughey, William C. ..1959-
60-61 (c)
McGee, Curtis L. ..1993-94-95-
96 (c)
McGill, Jason 1990-91-92
McHugh, W.P. 1941-42-46
McIntosh, J.C. ..1944-45-46 (c)
McIntyre, D.I., III (m) 1939

McIntyre, J.F. ....1921-22-23 (c)
McKay, Antonio................1983
McKee, J.W. 1929-30-31
McKenzie, Michael A. 1971-72-
73
McKinley, J.E. 1934-35
McKinney, R.H. 1945-46-47-48
McKinney, William S...1958-59
McKinnon, Bobby 1968
McLaughlin, Mark P. ...1972-73
McLean, O.C. (m) 1937
McLeod, William L. 1972-73-
74
McMath, H. (m) 1919
McNabb, Dale (m).1985-86-87
McNamara, Kevin M..1970-71-
72
McNamara, Sean (t)...1988-89-
90-91
McNames, Patrick M. 1960-61-
62
McNeill, Charles A. (m) ..1963-
64
McPhaul, L.G. 1908
McRae, D.F. 1925-26
McRee, C.A. 1921
Means, C.P. 1908
Means, E.B. 1911-12-13
Medintz, Jeff (m).........1975-76
Meier, Julie (t) 1992
Melvin, Lamar C. 1966-67
Melvin, Michael.....1985-86-87
Mendheim, James R...1961-62-
63
Menegazzi, Paul D. 1981-83-84
Menger, Johnny V. 1953-54-55-
56
Mercer, Michael K. 1972-74
Merchant, Emmett A. 1988-89-
90-91
Meridieth, Lonnie L., III....1978
Merkle, Gus 1924-25
Merritt, James 1990
Middlebrooks, Jack S. 1965
Middleton, Harvey.....1994-95-
96-97 (c)
Milam, Woodrow M. .1989-90-
91-92
Miles, Jermaine L. 1995-96
Miller, Birl B., Jr. 1972-73
Miller, Don E. 1954-55-56
Miller, Hal 1950-51-52
Miller, Matthew L. 1997-98
Miller, Veryl E. 1989-90
Milligan, Harry.................1931
Mills, H.F. 1943
Milo, Michael W. 1971
Minter, Michael M. 1995-96
Mitchell, Christopher M...1969
Mitchell, LaShon D. 1994
Mitchell, Ross 1998-99
Mitchell, R.M. 1945
Mitchell, W.M. 1921-22
Mitchell, Wade T. .1953-54-55-

56 (c)
Mizell, L.W. 1927-28-29
Modrak, Frank M.............1976
Molina, Yoel 1993-96
Momon, Clinton....1977-78-79
Montague, A.F.......1912-13-14
Montgomery, Joe 1982
Moody, Travis..............1986-87
Mooney, Michael P. 1988-89-
90-91 (c)
Mooney, Stephen W. ..1979-80-
82
Moore, Daniel (m)1994-95-96-
97-98
Moore, F.B. 1923-24
Moore, Gary M. (m) 1971
Moore, George E. 1978-79
Moore, H. 1908
Moore, Jack G. 1969-70
Moore, Justin (m).............1999
Moore, J.S. 1934
Moore, Mike (m).........1970-72
Moore, W.A. 1912
Moorer, W. Daniel..1964-65-66
(c)
Moorhead, Robert, Jr. 1950-51-
52
Morelock, Delmar C.........1976
Morgan, J.P................1935-37
Morgan, Mark 1980
Moriarty, Patrick J.1973-74-75-
77
Morris, George 1950-51-52
Morris, George W........1962-64
Morris, Greg A.......1992-93-94
Morris, James L...........1952-54
Morris, Jimmy M. ..1953-54-55
(c)
Morris, Larry C.1951-52-53-54
(c)
Morris, Peyton (t).1989-90-91-
92
Morris, W.H. 1932
Morrison, D.E. .1914-15-16 (c)
Morrison, Mot J. 1954
Morrow, H.K. 1943
Morton, Joel T. (m) 1962
Moss, Jack S................1959-61
Mote, Wayne G. ...1985-86-87-
88
Muerth, A.M. 1939-40
Mugg, Kenneth E. 1966
Mulherin, Matthew W. 1949
Mullen, William S......1986-87-
88-89
Mumford, Galin E.......1968-69
Mundorff, Roy M., Jr. (m) ....
1950-51-52
Murchison, Jef.................1993
Murdock, C.H. 1944-46
Murphy, Fred J............1958-59
Murphy, R.W. ...1937-38-39 (c)
Murphy, T.M. 1922
Murphy, Thomas J............1964

Murray, J.A. 1931
Murray, James G. 1974
Murray, John A. 1925
Murray, Matthew T. 1978
Murray, Sam D. 1924-25-26
Muyres, Jeremy J. 1999
Muyres, Jon R. 1996-97-99
Myddleton, W. Smith.1964-65-66
Myers, Charles D., Jr..1973-74-75
Myers, Christopher T. 1995-96-97
Myers, Don 1950

N

Nabelle, E.G. 1921-23-24
Nabors, Jerry H. 1955-56-57
Nail, Jimmy A. 1959-60-61
Nance, A.S. 1913
Naples, Andrew P. 1974
Negus, Dale.....................1983
Neblett, H.C. .....1930-31-32 (c)
Neese, Darrell 1991
Nelson, Richard R..1965-66-67
Nephew, David S., Jr. 1975
Nesbitt, M.M. 1918-19
Nettles, J.E. 1940
Neuss, William J...1991-92-93-94
Newmenner, Mike (m)....1968-69-70
New, Wayne C..................1969
Newman, Robert B. ...1977-78-79
Newmarker, Michael W. (m) 1968-70
Nicholl, Michael O. ...1959-60-61
Nichols, Scott (m) .1980-82-83
Nicholson, Erick M. 1970
Niebanck, Michael E..1979-81-82
Nilson, Rodney C.............1992
Nix, Frank H., Jr. 1958
Nix, John P. 1963
Nixon, J.U. 1935-36-37
Noe, James M...................1955
Nolan, James S. 1946-47-48
Norris, Steven H. 1969-70
North, Don (m)................1978
North, Robert E. 1948-49-50
Norton, Darrell D. 1981-82-83-84
Novak, George A..............1971
Nuener, Donald F. (m) 1970-71-72-73
Nutting, John E., Jr. 1959-60

O

Oenbrink, Robert M.........1969
O'Kelley, C.S. 1945
O'Leary, Timothy..............1991
Olive, Sammy R. 1979-80

Olson, J.W. 1945
Oltz, H.F. 1927
O'Neal, John F. 1978
O'Neill, John C., III ...1969-70-71
O'Neill, John H., Jr. 1948-49
O'Neill, Michael O. 1961
Ormsby, W.J. (m) 1945
Orr, Jeffrey E. 1977
Osborne, Terrell H. 1977-78
Oven, John M. 1970-71-72
Owen, Charles L....1987-88-89
Owen, Kenneth S. .1954-55-56
Owens, Phillip A. 1979
Owings, James B., Jr. .1971-72-73

P

Padgett, Travis (m).....1983-84-85-86-87
Page, J.A. 1937-38
Page, P.F. 1942
Page, Warren Craig 1996-97-98
Pair, R.H. 1939
Pallman, Charles M. ("Chip") ...1968-69-70
Palmer, Brian (m) ..1986-87-88
Palmer, Thomas M. ...1985-86-87-88
Papushak, Jeffrey A. 1991-92-93-94
Parham, R.S. 1926-28
Parker, Ken 1982-83-84-85
Parker, Stacy J. .1989-90-91-92
Parise, Ron 1972
Pasanella, Dave 1983-84
Paschal, William A. 1942
Paschal, William A.1962-63-64
Paschel, R.S. (m) 1946
Pass, James R....1975-76-77 (c)
Patman, Todd (m) 1992
Patterson, Donald R...1976-77-78 (c)
Patterson, H.W. 1908-09-10-11
Patterson, Jack D. 1951-52
Patton, George Lee, Jr. 1994-95
Patton, J.S. 1913-14
Patton, James W. ..1947-48-49-50
Paul, Jerry L. 1968
Pauline, James V. 1965
Paynem, Robert G. 1975
Pearce, Edmund F. (m)1958-59
Pearson, Toby...1984-85-86-87
Pedrick, L.E. (m)..............1945
Peek, J.W. 1945
Peeler, T.B. 1931
Peeler, Patrick 1993
Peeples, Frank (m) 1946-47-48
Peeples, Joel T. .1977-78-79-80
Penley, James W., Jr....1965-66-67
Peoples, Kevin L...1989-90-91-92

Perdoni, Renso G. 1969-70
Perdue, Dan (m) 1999
Perkerson, J.G.............1933-34
Perkerson, L.N. 1939
Perkins, Thomas B., Jr.1978-79
Perry, Elton P. 1954
Perryman, Nathan 1993-94-95-96 (c)
Person, James W., III...1968-69
Petersen, W.B.........1931-32-33
Petit, J.W. 1946-47-48
Pettis, Terry L. ..1987-88-89-90
Pharr, Stephen B....1989-90-91 (c), 92 (c)
Phenix, H. Rees, Jr. 1952-54
Phillips ....1919 (c)
Phillips, D.J. ......1932-33-34 (c)
Phillips, G.M. 1915-16-17
Phillips, J.R. 1943-44-46-47
Phillips, Michael D. ...1981-82-83
Phillips, Otis D., III (m)..1958-59-60
Pickering, Deidre (t) ...1994-97
Pierce, Jeffrey A. ...1978-79-80-81
Pike, Mark........1982-83-84-85
Pilgrim, Raymond W..1957-58-59
Piller, Zachery P. 1994
Pippin, John (m) ...1975-76-77
Pitts, Fred (t) 1975-76
Pizzati, H.E. (m)..............1933
Plaster, R.A. ....1940-41-42 (c)
Polk, Charles D...........1968-69
Poole, George 1950-51-52
Poole, J.M. 1932-33
Poole, W. Owen1924-25-26 (c)
Pope, E.G. 1946-47-48-49
Porter, C.E. 1912
Porter, Joel E. ...1973-74-75-76
Porter, John K........1983-84-85
Porter, John T.............1986-87
Potts, William (m)1989-90-91-92
Pounds, Cleve ..1982-83-84-85
Powell, David C. 1998
Powell, James R. 1959-60
Prather, Robert S. 1963
Preas, J.H. 1913-14-15-16
Preston, C.B. 1934-35-36
Pretz, Dick............1950-51-52
Price, Elbert L. 1966
Price, Elliot A. 1974-75-76
Price, Mitchell 1993
Priestley, Jerry M....1963-64-65
Prokop, E.S. 1942-43
Pund, H.R. ....1926-27-28 (c)
Purvis, James A. (m) ...1970-71
Putnal, Stephen S. .1971-72-73

Q

Queen, William L. .1947-48-49
Quigg, B.G..................1939-40

Quinn, Martin.................1993
Quinton, Billy D., Jr. 1977

R

Ragains, Stephen (m)..1988-89
Raible, Steven C. ...1973-74-75
Raine, J.M. 1935
Rainey, H.W. 1913
Rampley, C. Todd ..1985-87-88
Randolph, R.L. 1926-27-28
Rank, Matthew B. ..1978-79-80
Rassau, Thomas J. 1974
Rathbun, Ira....................1950
Ratterman, G.A. 1920
Rawlins, Ricky A. 1973
Razayeski, Jerome (t) .1989-90-91-92-93
Read, R.C. 1927
Redford, David E. 1951-54
Reed, John N. 1957-58-59
Reed, Lamont S. 1993
Reese, Boyd T. (m).1964-65-66
Reese, James C. 1990
Reese, Larry C. 1976-77-78
Reeves, Charles E. (m) 1956-57-58
Reeves, H.L. 1923
Reeves, Robert.................1924
Register, Gerry G..............1974
Reid, Lee R. 1959-60-61
Reid, R.C.........................1926
Rhino, Chappell 1950-51-52
Rhino, Daniel V......1974-75-76
Rhino, Kelley W. 1999
Rhino, Randall P. ...1972-73-74
Rhodes, Robert M. 1988
Rice, Anthony L. ..1990-91-92-93
Rice, Ronald 1980-81-82-83
Richards, C.P. 1939
Richards, Charles James ...1994
Richardson, Alpette ...1975-78-79
Richie, Robert W. (m) 1962-63-64
Riddle, Dave....................1982
Riede, Brian (t) 1982-83
Riggle, John O. 1969-70
Rimmer, Walter...........1937-38
Ritter, W.O. 1943-44
Robert, L.W. 1907
Roberts, C.H. 1933-34
Roberts, Linwood............1954
Roberts, Roderick D. 1996-97-98
Roberts, S.A. 1935-37
Roberts, Tommy (t)1978-79-80
Robertson, Greg..............1985
Robertson, Justin E....1995-96-97-98
Robinson, C.B.............1909-10
Robinson, Donald R. .1971-72-73
Robinson, James P..1972-73-74

Robinson, Robie 1950
Robinson, Tony 1997-98-99
Robison, David M., Jr..1956-58
Rochester, Denny A. ..1979-81-82
Rodgers, Franklin C. .1951-52-53
Rodriguez, Robert E. .1989-90-91-92
Rogers, Bill 1980
Rogers, Charles B. IV........1965
Rogers, J.R. 1917-18
Rogers, John E. ("Charlie")....... 1995-96-97-98 (c)
Rogers, Nicholas Q. 1999
Rogers, Phillip F....1995-97-98-99
Rogers, Ronald W. 1994-95-96-97 (c)
Rogers, Stuart...1980-81-82-83
Rollow, T.A. (m) 1944
Roof, Terence E. ...1982-83-84-85 (c)
Roper, Bradley R. 1977-78
Rosamilia, Mike 1983-84-85-86
Rosamond, W.I.................1935
Rose, John L. 1975-76
Rose, Shane (t) 1990-91-92
Rose, Thomas E. 1955-56-58
Rosinski, Michael D. 1970
Ross, Arthur E. 1950-51
Rotenberry, Paul D.1954-55-56
Rountree, A.J...................1914
Roush, Elena (m) 1988
Roush, Mike (t) 1986-87-88-89
Rowlett, Mark 1977
Rucker, Charles A.1974-75-76-77
Rudolph, Coleman H.1989-90-91-92 (c)
Rudolph, Jake........1950-51-52
Rudolph, John L....1957-58-59
Rudolph, Russ (m) 1986-87-88-89
Ruffin, Larry W. 1951-52-53
Rush, Angelo 1989-90
Rusk, W...........1927-28-29 (c)
Rutherford, Bruce F. 1969-71
Rutland, Reginald.1983-84-85-86
Ryckeley, A.E. 1941-42

S

Sackett, G.W...................1934
Sale, Oliver H. 1954-55
Salem, Richard 1981-82-83
Salisbury, Kevin M. 1986-87-88-89
Salome, Joe M. 1950
Sammons, David 1994
Sams, Russell (m)............1991
Sanders, C.R.....1939-40-41 (c)
Sanders, Hugh A. 1964
Sanders, Leavitt F. 1972-73

Sanders, R.J. (m) 1941
Sandlin, Elizabeth (t) 1992
Sanford, Lucius M., Jr. ....1975-75-76-77 (c)
Santospago, Louis F. 1968
Sargent, John A......1972-73-74
Satterfield, James (m)..1966-67
Saussy, Hugh....................1924
Scales, Herbert K., III 1974-75-76
Scarboro, D.D. .1918-19-20-21
Scharfschwerdt, E. 1943
Scharfschwerdt, William R. 1949
Schmidt, Robert K. 1978-79
Schnitzer, Ray L. ..1974-75-76-77 (c)
Schroeder, Charles (m) ...1968-69-70
Schroer, John W. ....1964-65-66 (c)
Schultz, Mark H. ...1980-81-82
Schwetje, Craig 1993
Scott, Franklin R. ...1990-91-92
Scotton, Stefen D..1987-88-89-90
Scully, Dennis W. 1972-73
Seamon, Robert B. .1966-67-68
Sellinger, Frank L. 1965
Sendobry, Doug 1985-87
Sennett, Bill 1953-54
Senules, Edward A. 1975
Senter, J.C. 1914-15-16
Sernulka, Leonard S. 1975
Sessions, Lee 1924
Seward, James P., Jr....1962-63-64
Sewell, Charles D.........1963-64
Sewell, Donald R. ..1976-77-78
Sexton, Frank M....1961-62-63
Sexton, Thomas K.......1976-77
Shamburger, Ellis L. 1954
Shamburger, Ellis L., III ..1975-76-77-78
Shank, Donald P. ...1973-74-75
Shank, Jeffrey E. ....1977-78 (c)
Sharp, Anthony Scott 1994
Sharpe, John F. 1963
Shaver, T.W. 1917
Shaw, C.F. 1933-34
Shaw, C. Brandon ..1995-96-97
Shaw, Gene...........1938-39-40
Shaw, Jamie (m) 1996-97
Shaw, William L.....1958-59-60
Sheffer, Powell P., Jr. ..1949-50-51
Sheffield, Mark J...1979-80-81-82
Sheldon, R.W. 1941-42
Shell, John W., Jr. 1963
Shelley, Robert S. (t)....1968-69
Shepard, Derrick L. .1994-95-96-97
Sheppard, Steve V. .1975-76-77

Sheridan, Michael A. .1995-96-97-98
Sheridan, Robert E. 1961
Sherman, Robert G. ...1951-52-53
Sherrill, Jeff 1986
Shershin, Mike (m)....1979-80-81-82
Shields, William D.1972-73-74
Shiver, David N. 1968-69-70
Shoemaker, Jacob W., Jr. .1952-53
Shook, Claude E....1965-66-67
Showman, Mark A. 1975-76
Shuberg, David A. 1992
Shuler, Theodore R. 1951-52
Shulman, I. 1927-28
Shuman, Jimmy H. 1960
Sias, John R. 1966-67-68
Sides, James V. 1959-60
Siffri, Joseph C. 1987-88-89-90
Silvers, Chris (t) 1986-87-88
Simerville, Lester T. 1957-58
Simmons, Charlie..1991-93-94
Simmons, Christopher 1987-88-89-90
Simmons, David A.1962-63-64
Simmons, DeShaan Z.1995-96-97
Simmons, Reid W. (m)....1967-68-69-70
Simmons, Roy F...1975-76-77-78
Simons, James S. ...1977-78-79
Sims, David B. 1974-75-76
Sims, Jack 1986
Sims, T.F. ....1935-36-37 (c)
Sims, W.E. 1937
Sinclair, B.W..............1909-10
Singleton, Timothy M. 1957
Sircy, Walter Z. 1960-61-62
Sisson, Scott O. 1989-90-91-92
Skalko, John J.............1972-73
Skelton, Lancen S. 1978-79-80-81 (c)
Slaten, R.L. 1942-46-47
Slater, Alicia (m) 1988-89
Sloan, B.H. 1929
Slocum, J.R...........1931-32-33
Smales, Bill......................1985
Smith, A. Nelson (m) 1953
Smith, B.D. (m)................1945
Smith, Ben S. 1959-60
Smith, Brad 1985
Smith, C.B........................1907
Smith, C.S. 1926-27-28
Smith, Carlos L. 1994-95
Smith, Daniel J., Jr. 1957-58-59
Smith, David (t) ...1975-76-77-78
Smith, Forrest 1945
Smith, Fred 1950
Smith, George B. ...1936-37-38
Smith, Giles R........1964-65-66

Smith, H.R. 1947-48
Smith, Hester (m) 1985-86
Smith, James R. 1972
Smith, Jeff (m) 1980-81-82
Smith, Jeffrey L. 1973
Smith, Jessica (t) 1988-89
Smith, Johnny S. ..1977-78-79-80
Smith, Kenneth L. (m) 1973-74-75-76
Smith, Kamau Kofi ....1995-96-97-98 (c)
Smith, Michael C..1991-92-93-94
Smith, Murry D. 1974-75-76
Smith, O.D......................1934
Smith, Sean W. .1986-87-88-89
Smith, Ted N. 1955-56-57
Smith, W.D. 1918
Smith, W.N. 1943
Smoots, Jonathan 1983
Smrekar, Jacob 1997
Sneed, P.C. 1914
Snell, Gary 1981
Snow, Leonard N. ..1965-66-67
Snow, Mike 1984-85
Snyder, Adam (t) ...1997-98-99
Snyder, Kenneth D. ...1949-50-51
Snyder, W.R. 1907
Solomon, Robert S. 1960-61
Sorrells, Tyrone 1985-86
Southall, Bruce C...1970-72-73
Southard, J.W. ..1946-47-48-49
Southerland, Ken 1983-84
Spalding, J.J...........1908-09-10
Sparks, R. Stan 1981
Spears, Leon B., Jr. 1951-52
Speer, F. 1927-28-30
Spence, T.L. 1914-15-16
Spencer, Glenn.1982-83-84-85
Spiotta, Eugene J., Jr. ..1968-69
Sprading, T.L. 1932-33
Spratlin, H. Dean (m).......1938
Spratte, Gerald E.............1954
Sprayberry, Bryan (m)1994-95-96-97-98
Sprayberry, J.P. 1939-40
Spriggs, David E..............1949
St. Hilaire, Chris (m)........1994
Stacy, G.T. 1934
Stallings, Larry.......1960-61-62
Stallworth, Cedric T...1985-86-87-88 (c)
Stallworth, Dexter .1994-95-96
Stamps, Charles W., Jr. 1972
Stanfill, Tom 1980-81-83
Stanley, Jimmy 1980-81
Stansbury, M. Todd 1981
Staton, A.H. 1919-20-21-22
Staton, J.C. 1920-21-22-23
Steadman, David A...........1961
Steagall, Derrick L. 1993-94-95-97

Steber, John W. ....1943 (c)
Steele, John A. 1974-76-77
Stegall, C.R. 1912
Stegall, William David. ...1988-89-90-91
Stein, Wilbur 1941-42-43
Stephens, Rodrequis L. ...1984-86-87-88
Stephenson, Donald P. ....1955-56-57 (c)
Stevens, James A. 1972-73
Stevenson, Joel C...1966-67-68 (c)
Stevenson, Robert O..1971-72-73
Stewart, Ryan E. ...1992-93-94-95 (c)
Stickel, Andy (m) 1993
Still, J.E......................1946-47
Stimson, Nathan K......1996-98
Stokes, Ivey J. 1978-79-80
Stokes, Kip (m) 1989
Stone, Robert M..........1957-58
Stoner, Ed (m) 1984-85-86-87-88
Story, Lyles W.........1966-67-68
Stover, Clarence B. 1980
Stover, R.W. (m) 1945
Stradley, Jim 1986
Strain, Lee O., Jr. 1959
Street, W.O. 1934-35
Strickland, David L. 1976-77
Strickland, R.E. 1929-30
Strickland, Vernon 1994-95
Strohmeier, Richard F. 1989
Strom, Rick 1983-84-86-87
Strom, Robert B...............1969
Stroman, Graham L. ...1993-94
Strupper, George E. ...1915-16-17
Studdard, Larry G..1969-70-71
Sudderth, James T. 1963
Sulhoff, David (m) 1998
Summer, James L...1953-54-55
Sumpter, Levon................1978
Sutton, S.B. 1939-40-41
Swaim, James C. 1968
Swank, Richard (t)1987-88-89-90
Swanson, Courtney (t) 1996
Swanson, David H............1981
Swanson, George P.1959-60-61
Sweeney, Ryan (m).1992-93-94
Swilling, Darrell G. ...1988-89-90-91
Swilling, Jerry Kenneth ...1988-89-90-91
Swilling, Pat 1982-83-84-85
Sykes, Lewis W. 1949-50
Sykora, James J. 1974

T

Tarplin, Jesse A.1995-96-97-98
Tattich, Robert B. 1974

Taylor, James S. 1967
Taylor, Jim B. 1981-82
Taylor, John H., Jr. 1963-64
Taylor, Kenneth T. .1978-79-80
Taylor, Michael H. .1976-78 (c)
Taylor, Rumsey B. 1948-49
Taylor, Steven H. (m).1969-70-71
Taylor, Tom.................1982-83
Teas, William T., Jr. 1952-53
Tedder, David K. 1976
Templeton, Peden 1950
Terry, James L. 1975
Tetterton, Alex G. 1999
Thaden, Bill...........1950-51-52
Tharpe, E.S. 1935-36
Tharpe, Mack 1924-25-26
Tharpe, R.H. ....1931-32-33 (c)
Theodocion, Charles D. ..1952-56-57
Thomas, Landers A. 1987-88
Thigpen, Robert F., Jr. .1971-72
Thomas, Andre A. 1985-86-87-88
Thomas, Andy..................1983
Thomas, Dana (m).1985-86-87
Thomas, Darrell 1979-80
Thomas, Eric F.1986-87-88-89 (c)
Thomas, John J......1983-84-85
Thomas, Michael (t) ..1990-92-93-94
Thomas, Robert D............1962
Thomas, Robert P...1975-77-79
Thomas, Ted...........1956-57-58
Thomason, E.K......1911-12-13
Thomason, J.G. 1927-28-29
Thomason, John M. 1956
Thompson, Alex..............1998
Thompson, Charles K. 1959
Thompson, Jimmy E..1954-55-56
Thompson, Kenny 1981
Thompson, Larry 1945
Thompson, E.O. 1934-35
Thompson, Roy L., Jr. 1949
Thrash, K.M. 1926-27-28
Thrash, Kenneth M., Jr....1955-56
Thrash, W.G. 1938
Thurson, Theodore N. 1979-80-81-82
Thurson, Timothy H...1978-79
Thweatt............................1917
Tibbetts, Marvin O., Jr. ...1958-59-60
Tidwell, Robert H.............1957
Tierney, Clarence L. ...1974-75-76
Tiggle, Calvin B...........1989-90
Tillman, Travares A....1996-97-98-99 (c)
Timmons, Stephen G. 1971
Tinsley, P.R............1943-44 (c)

Tisdel, Kevin A. 1990-91-92
Tolbert, Troy T. 1997-98
Toner, Donald W. 1961-62
Tortorici, Anthony J. 1989
Trainer, Cecil E., Jr.1951-52-53
Trapnell, James H........1964-66
Travis, Mike 1982-83-84-85
Travis, Scott E........1990-91-92
Trawick, C.B. 1913
Traylor, Robert 1955-56
Tsoukalas, Tessa (t)1997-98-99
Tucci, John A. 1972-73
Turner, Dewitt T., III..1965-66-67
Turner, Glenn O. ...1951-52-53
Turrentine, Thomas L..1971-72
Tye, Leonidas W. 1958

U

Ulrich.............................1917
Urczyk, Jeffrey L. ...1973-74-75
Uremovich, Matthew........1999
Usry, Joe 1922-23-24
Utt, Benjamin M. ...1978-79-80

V

Vance, John Todd .1991-92-93-94
Van Dora, Tash J. 1968-69
Van Houten, John (m).....1956-57-58
Vann, Ronald 1956-57
Varner, Edwin S. 1964-65
Vatney, Tim (m) 1995-96-97
Veazey, Norman D.......1957-58
Vereen, Carl H..1953-54-55-56
Vereen, Orville P. ...1951-52-53 (c)
Vernau, Charles A..1993-94-95
Vezey, Stanley A., Jr.....1969-70
Vickers, Paul A. 1955-56-57
Viereck, G.W..............1931-32
Vines, John E. 1950-51
Vinson, Mike (m)............1989
Vitunic, Joseph A. 1967-69
Volkert, George A. 1953-54-55-56 (c)
Volley, Lynwood, Jr. ...1978-79-80
VonWeller, P.J. 1928

W

Waddey, F.O................1927-28
Wakefield, M.L.................1943
Walker, Keenan E. .1991-92-93
Walker, Steve C...........1978-79
Walker, Warren L. 1970
Wallace, Donald W......1966-68
Walters, Grady (m) 1976-79
Warner, R.J......................1934
Warren, Harry C. 1966
Warren, James A. (m).......1973
Waskey, Carlton B.......1960-61
Waters, J. Alan .1988-89-90-91

Waters, Dean B.1979-81-82-83
Waters, Mitch 1985-86
Watkins, G.C. 1927-28-29
Watkins, Hugh R. .1962-63-64
Watkins, James F...1956-57-58 (c)
Watkins, Kerry J...............1999
Watson, Alonzo1985-86-87-88
Watson, Carl D......1960-61-62
Watson, Merrix W. 1998-99
Watterworth, Bradley A....1975
Weaver, Dean ...1984-85-86-87
Weaver, John B. 1966-67-68
Weaver, Keith B...............1995
Weaver, William H. ...1989-90-91-92
Webb, B.P. 1918-19-20
Webb, G.I. 1939-40-41
Webster, Grady F. 1954
Weigle, John.....................1950
Weiman, Edward A..1961-62-63
Weinstein, Scott (t) 1982
Weintraub, Glenn (m).....1975-76-78
Welch, John J...............1959-60
Welchel, Dan....................1917
Wellington, Ralph W. 1962
Wells, Thomas E....1958-59-60
Werner, S.A. 1923
West, G.R. 1916
West, Charles G. 1952
West, Edward P., Jr. (t) 1969-70-71
West, W.P. 1941-42
Westbrook, J.J........1927-28-29
Westbrook, Jack, Jr. ...1980-81-82-83
Westmoreland, Marc 1996
Whatley, Melvin 1998
Whealler, Edward O. .1972-73-74-75
Wheat, Johnny L. ..1949-50-51
Wheby, E.M. 1938-39
Whisenhunt, Kenneth.....1980-81-82-83-84
White, Edward Dezmon .1997-98-99
White, Mark J. .1985-86-87-88
Whitehead, Hugh P. (m) .1955-56
Wilcox, A.L. 1936-37-38
Wilcox, E.D. 1932-33-34
Wilcox, Eric D. 1966-67-68
Wilcox, J.R. 1933-34-35
Wilcox, Reggie D. ..1997-98-99
Wilder, Edwin 1997-98-99
Wiley, Charles A. ..1995-96-97-98
Wiley, Floyd M. 1955-56
Wilhoit, Billy....................1943
Wilkerson, Rodney K.1991-92-93-94
Wilkes, Gregory C. 1967-69

Wilkes, Reginald W....1974-75-76-77

Wilkins, Brian E. ...1995-96-97-98

Wilkins, G.C. 1940

Wilkins, Gary C. ..1981-82-83-84

Wilkins, Scott 1998

Williams, A.S. 1929-31-32

Williams, B.W. 1944-45-47

Williams, C.W. 1932-33-34

Williams, Calvin L., Jr. 1994-95-96

Williams, Gary T....1963-64-65

Williams, I.A. 1923-24-25

Williams, John B. 1975

Williams, John W. ...1968-69-70

Williams, Jerrelle L. ...1988-89-90-91

Williams, Marlon C. ..1990-91-92-93

Williams, Michael A. .1990-91-92-93

Williams, Michael G. (m)1965-66-67

Williams, Larry E. 1969

Williams, Rodney C...1995-96-97-98

Williams, Sidney E.1949-50-51

Williams, Wes (m)1983-84-85-86-87

Williamson, Grady Lee..1988-89

Williamson, William M...1959-60-61 (c)

Willoch, Raymond 1953-54

Wills, John T. 1952

Wilson, Don.....1984-85-86-87

Wilson, Eddie (m)............1989

Wilson, J.I. 1943-44

Wilson, Kenneth J. 1987-88-89

Wilson, Lauri (m) 1993-94

Wilson, William C. 1961-62

Wimbush, Recardo L........1999

Windham, William (m)...1990-91-92-93

Winegar, James M. 1978

Wingo, Gary L. 1971

Winingder, Thomas K.....1960-61-62 (c)

Wise, Daryl D. 1983-84

Wiseman, Dale (t).......1990-92

Wisman, Witt B. 1971-72-73

Witherspoon, Dan, III..1994-96-97

Wofford, David (m).........1996

Wolfe, Richard C..............1969

Wolfe, Robert V. 1984

Wolkoff, Paul (t)...1989-90-91-92

Wood, C.R.............1937-38-39

Wood, Dan L. 1979-80

Wood, Duane R....1979-80-81-82

Woodall, Timothy M. 1968

Woodhull, Maury T. 1968

Woodruff, Brent (t) 1983-84-85-86

Woodruff, Jimmie (m).....1959-60-61-62

Woodruff, Paul (m) 1942

Woods, James W. 1975-76

Woodward, Douglas L. (m) 1958

Woolley, Rand (m)1991-92-93-94

Woolf, John R...................1955

Wright..............................1925

Wright, Harry 1950-51-52

Wright, J.E. ......1939-40-41 (c)

Wright, James L. 1964-65-66

Wright, Jeffrey M..1990-91-92-93

Wright, John W. 1961-62

Wycoff, S.D. 1923-24-25

Wysong, Michael J.1968-69-70

Y

Yates, Brian J. 1979

Yates, George B. 1962-63

Yeager, Bruce D. ...1974-75-76-77

Young, Christopher L..1998-99

Young, Clyde A. 1951-52

Z

Zachery, Cedric T. 1992-93-94-95

Zawoysky, Ronald J. 1969

Ziegler, F.R. 1946-47-48

Ziegler, John A. 1960

Zimmerman, Jeff.........1986-87

Tech Scores

★ = championship team
◆ = bowl team

1892: 0-3
Coach and Captain: E.E. West

Date	Result		Opponent	Record
N. 5	aL	6-12	Mercer (Central Park)	0-1
N. 19	hL	0-20	Vanderbilt (Piedmont Park)	0-2
N. 25	hL	0-26	Auburn (Brisbine Park)	0-3

1893: 2-1-1
Coaches: Frank O. Spain, Lt. Leonard Wood; Captain: W.W. Hunter

Date	Result		Opponent	Record
N. 4	aW	28-6	Georgia	1-0
N. 11	hW	10-6	Mercer	2-0
N. 30	hL	0-6	St. Albans (Piedmont, Thanksgiving)	2-1
D. 7	hT	0-0	Auburn	2-1-1

1894: 0-3
Coaches: Frank O. Spain, Lt. Leonard Wood; Captain: Thomas Rauol

Date	Result		Opponent	Record
O. 27	hL	0-8	Savannah A.A.	0-1
N. 17	hL	0-94	Auburn (Athletic Park)	0-2
N. 29	hL	0-34	Ft. McPherson (Athletic Park)	0-3

1896: 1-1-1
No Captain

Date	Result		Opponent	Record
O. 31	aW	6-4	Mercer (Central Park)	1-0
N. 7	aL	0-45	Auburn	1-1
N. 21	hT	12-12	Mercer (Brisbine Park)	1-1-1

1897: 0-1
No Captain

Date	Result		Opponent	Record
O. 23	aL	0-28	Georgia	0-1

1898: 0-3
Coach: R.B. "Cow" Nalley; No Captain

Date	Result		Opponent	Record
N. 5	aL	6-29	Auburn	0-1
N. 24	nL	0-23	Clemson (@ Augusta)	0-2
O. 22	aL	0-15	Georgia	0-3

1899: 0-5
Coach: Mr. Collier; Captain: Pete Wooley
Home games at Piedmont Park

Date	Result		Opponent	Record
O. 14	aL	0-63	Auburn	0-1
O. 23	hL	0-30	Sewanee	0-2
O. 28	aL	0-20	Georgia	0-3
N. 11	hL	0-15	Nashville	0-4
N. 30	aL	5-41	Clemson (@ Greenville, Thanksgiving)	0-5

1900: 0-4
Captain: W.J. Holman
Home games at Piedmont Park

Date	Result		Opponent	Record
O. 13	hL	0-12	Georgia	0-1
O. 20	hL	0-23	Nashville	0-2
O. 29	hL	0-34	Sewanee	0-3
D. 7	hL	6-38	Davidson	0-4

1901: 4-0-1
Coach: Dr. Cyrus W. Strickler; Captain: A.B. Hoilson
Home games at Piedmont Park

Date	Result		Opponent	Record
O. 12	hW	29-0	Gordon	1-0
O. 15	hW	17-0	Furman	2-0
O. 18	nW	33-0	Wofford (@ Augusta)	3-0
O. 26	aT	5-5	Furman	3-0-1
N. 9	hW	13-0	South Carolina	4-0-1

1902: 0-6-2
Coach: John McKee; Captain: Bully Young
Home games at Brisbine Park

Date	Result		Opponent	Record
O. 11	hL	6-18	Auburn	0-1
O. 18	hL	5-44	Clemson	0-2
O. 25	hT	0-0	Georgia	0-2-1
N. 1	aT	0-0	Furman	0-2-2
N. 8	hL	0-17	St. Albans (Va.)	0-3-2
N. 13	hL	6-7	Davidson	0-4-2
N. 22	hL	6-10	Tennessee	0-5-2
N. 27	aL	0-26	Alabama (@ Birmingham, Thanksgiving)	0-6-2

1903: 2-5
Captain: Jesse Thrash
Home games at Piedmont Park

Date	Result		Opponent	Record
O. 17	hL	0-73	Clemson	0-1
O. 24	hL	0-38	Georgia	0-2
O. 31	aW	37-0	Howard College (Ala.)	1-2
N. 7	hW	17-0	Florida State College	2-2
N. 14	hL	5-10	Auburn	2-3
N. 21	aL	0-11	Tennessee	2-4
N. 26	hL	0-16	South Carolina (Thanksgiving)	2-5

1904 (8-1-1)
Captain: Barien Moore
Home games at Piedmont Park

Date	Result	Opponent	Record
O. 1	hW 11-5	Ft. McPherson	1-0
O. 8	hW 35-0	Florida State College	2-0
O. 15	hW 51-0	Mooney School (Tenn.)	3-0
O. 17	hW 77-0	Florida	4-0
O. 22	hW 2-0	Tennessee	5-0
O. 29	aL 0-12	Auburn	5-1
N. 5	hT 11-11	Clemson	5-1-1
N. 12	hW 23-6	Georgia	6-1-1
N. 16	hW 59-0	Tennessee Meds	7-1-1
N. 24	hW 18-0	Cumberland (Thanksgiving)	8-1-1

1905: 6-0-1
Captain: Louie Clark
Home games on campus at The Flats, future site of Grant Field

Date	Result	Opponent	Record
O. 7	hW 54-0	Dahlonega	1-0
O. 21	hW 12-5	Alabama	2-0
O. 28	hW 18-0	Cumberland	3-0
N. 4	hW 45-0	Tennessee	4-0
N. 11	hT 18-18	Sewanee	4-0-1
N. 18	hW 46-0	Georgia	5-0-1
N. 30	hW 17-12	Clemson (Thanksgiving)	6-0-1

1906: 5-3-1
Captain: E.C. Davies
Home games at The Flats

Date	Result	Opponent	Record
S. 29	hT 6-6	Maryville	0-0-1
O. 6	hW 11-0	Dahlonega	1-0-1
O. 13	hW 18-0	Grant University (Tenn.)	2-0-1
O. 20	hL 0-16	Sewanee	2-1-1
O. 27	hW 4-0	Davidson	3-1-1
N. 3	hW 11-0	Auburn	4-1-1
N. 10	aW 17-0	Georgia	5-1-1
N. 17	hL 6-37	Vanderbilt	5-2-1
N. 29	hL 0-10	Clemson (Thanksgiving)	5-3-1

1907: 4-4
Captain: C.A. Sweet

Date	Result	Opponent	Record
O. 5	hW 51-0	Gordon (The Flats)	1-0
O. 12	hW 70-0	Dahlonega (The Flats)	2-0
O. 19	hW 6-4	Tennessee (Ponce de Leon Park)	3-0
O. 26	hL 6-12	Auburn (Ponce de Leon Park)	3-1
N. 2	hW 10-6	Georgia (Ponce de Leon Park)	4-1
N. 9	hL 0-18	Sewanee (Ponce de Leon Park)	4-2
N. 16	aL 0-54	Vanderbilt	4-3
N. 28	hL 5-6	Clemson (Thanksgiving, Ponce de Leon Park)	4-4

Note: Home games from 1908-1912 were played at Ponce de Leon Park

1908: 6-3
Captain: L.W. Robert

Date	Result	Opponent	Record
O. 3	hW 32-0	Gordon	1-0
O. 10	hW 30-0	Mooney School (Tenn.)	2-0
O. 17	hW 23-0	Mississippi A&M	3-0
O. 24	hW 11-6	Alabama	4-0
O. 31	hL 5-6	Tennessee	4-1
N. 7	hL 0-44	Auburn	4-2
N. 14	hL 0-6	Sewanee	4-3
N. 19	aW 16-6	Mercer	5-3
N. 26	hW 30-6	Clemson (Thanksgiving)	6-3

1909: 7-2
Captain: John Davis

Date	Result	Opponent	Record
O. 2	hW 18-6	Gordon	1-0
O. 9	hW 35-6	Mooney School (Tenn.)	2-0
O. 16	hW 59-0	South Carolina	3-0
O. 23	hL 0-15	Sewanee	3-1
O. 30	aW 29-0	Tennessee	4-1
N. 6	hL 0-8	Auburn	4-2
N. 13	aW 35-0	Mercer	5-2
N. 20	hW 12-6	Georgia	6-2
N. 25	hW 29-3	Clemson (Thanksgiving)	7-2

1910: 5-3
Captain: Dean Hill

Date	Result	Opponent	Record
O. 1	hW 57-0	Gordon	1-0
O. 8	hW 18-0	Chattanooga	2-0
O. 15	hW 46-0	Mercer	3-0
O. 22	aW 36-0	Alabama	4-0
N. 5	hL 0-16	Auburn	4-1
N. 12	hL 0-23	Vanderbilt	4-2
N. 19	hL 6-11	Georgia	4-3
N. 24	hW 34-0	Clemson (Thanksgiving)	5-3

1911: 6-2-1
Captain: H.W. Patterson

Date	Result	Opponent	Record
S. 30	hW 22-5	11th Cavalry	1-0
O. 7	aW 28-0	Howard College (Ala.)	2-0
O. 14	hW 24-0	Tennessee	3-0
O. 29	hT 0-0	Alabama	4-0-1
N. 4	hL 6-11	Auburn	4-1-1
N. 11	hW 23-0	Sewanee	5-1-1
N. 18	hL 0-5	Georgia	5-2-1
N. 30	hW 31-0	Clemson (Thanksgiving)	6-2-1

1912: 5-3-1

Captain: Hugh Leuhrman

Home games at The Flats

Date	Result		Opponent	Record
S. 28	hT	0-0	11th Cavalry	0-0-1
O. 5	aW	20-16	The Citadel	1-0-1
O. 12	hW	20-3	Alabama	2-0-1
O. 19	aW	14-7	Florida (@ Jacksonville)	3-0-1
O. 26	aW	16-6	Mercer	4-0-1
N. 2	hL	7-27	Auburn	4-1-1
N. 9	hL	0-7	Sewanee	4-2-1
N. 16	hL	0-20	Georgia	4-3-1
N. 28	hW	23-0	Clemson (Thanksgiving)	5-3-1

Note: Grant Field, with its first permanent seating, was built prior to the 1913 season. From that point on, all home games were played at Grant Field unless otherwise noted.

1913: 7-2

Captain: Homer Cook

Date	Result		Opponent	Record
S. 27	hW	19-0	Ft. McPherson	1-0
O. 4	aW	47-0	The Citadel	2-0
O. 11	aW	71-6	Chattanooga	3-0
O. 18	hW	33-0	Mercer	4-0
O. 25	aW	13-3	Florida (@ Jacksonville)	5-0
N. 1	hW	33-0	Sewanee	6-0
N. 8	hL	0-20	Auburn	6-1
N. 15	hL	0-14	Georgia	6-2
N. 27	hW	34-0	Clemson (Thanksgiving)	7-2

1914: 6-2

Captain: K.J. Fielder

Date	Result		Opponent	Record
O. 3	hW	20-0	South Carolina	1-0
O. 10	hW	105-0	Mercer	2-0
O. 17	aL	0-13	Alabama (@ Birmingham)	2-1
O. 24	hW	28-7	VMI	3-1
O. 31	hW	20-0	Sewanee	4-1
N. 7	hL	0-14	Auburn	4-2
N. 14	hW	7-0	Georgia	5-2
N. 26	hW	26-6	Clemson (Thanksgiving)	6-2

1915: 7-0-1

Captain: D.E. Morrison

Date	Result		Opponent	Record
O. 2	hW	52-0	Mercer	1-0
O. 9	hW	27-7	Davidson	2-0
O. 16	hW	67-0	Transylvania	3-0
O. 23	aW	36-7	LSU (@ New Orleans)	4-0
O. 30	hW	23-3	North Carolina	5-0
N. 6	hW	21-7	Alabama	6-0
N. 13	hT	0-0	Georgia	6-0-1
N. 25	hW	7-0	Auburn (Thanksgiving)	7-0-1

1916: 8-0-1 ★

SIAA Champions

Captain: J.T. Johnson

Date	Result		Opponent	Record
S. 30	hW	61-0	Mercer	1-0
O. 7	hW	222-0	Cumberland	2-0
O. 14	hW	9-0	Davidson	3-0
O. 21	hW	10-6	North Carolina	4-0
O. 28	hT	7-7	Washington & Lee	4-0-1
N. 4	hW	45-0	Tulane	5-0-1
N. 11	hW	13-0	Alabama	6-0-1
N. 18	aW	21-0	Georgia	7-0-1
N. 30	hW	33-7	Auburn (Thanksgiving)	8-0-1

1917: 9-0 ★

Co-National Champions (INS)

SIAA Champions

Captain: W.G. Carpenter

Date	Result		Opponent	Record
S. 29	hW	25-0	Furman (DH)	1-0
S. 29	hW	33-0	Wake Forest (DH)	2-0
O. 6	hW	41-0	Pennsylvania	3-0
O. 13	hW	32-10	Davidson	4-0
O. 20	hW	63-0	Washington & Lee	5-0
N. 3	hW	83-0	Vanderbilt	6-0
N. 10	aW	48-0	Tulane	7-0
N. 17	hW	98-0	Carlisle	8-0
N. 29	hW	68-7	Auburn (Thanksgiving)	9-0

1918: 6-1 ★

SIAA Co-Champions

Captain: W.R. Fincher

Date	Result		Opponent	Record
O. 5	hW	28-0	Clemson	1-0
O. 12	hW	118-0	Furman	2-0
O. 19	hW	123-0	11th Cavalry	3-0
O. 26	hW	28-0	Camp Gordon	4-0
N. 10	hW	128-0	NC State	5-0
N. 23	aL	0-32	Pittsburgh	5-1
N. 28	hW	41-0	Auburn (Thanksgiving)	6-1

1919: 7-3

Captain: G.M. Phillips

Date	Result		Opponent	Record
S. 20	hW	48-0	5th Division	1-0
S. 27	hW	74-0	Furman	2-0
O. 4	hW	14-0	Wake Forest	3-0
O. 11	hW	28-0	Clemson	4-0
O. 18	hW	20-0	Vanderbilt	5-0
O. 25	aL	6-16	Pittsburgh	5-1
N. 1	hW	33-0	Davidson	6-1
N. 8	hL	0-3	Washington & Lee	6-2
N. 15	hW	27-0	Georgetown	7-2
N. 27	hL	7-14	Auburn (Thanksgiving)	7-3

1920: 8-1 ★

SIAA Co-Champions

Captain: A.R. Flowers

Date	Result		Opponent	Record
S. 25	hW	44-0	Wake Forest	1-0
O. 2	hW	55-0	Oglethorpe	2-0
O. 9	hW	66-0	Davidson	3-0
O. 16	aW	44-0	Vanderbilt	4-0
O. 23	aL	3-10	Pittsburgh	4-1
O. 30	hW	24-0	Centre	5-1
N. 6	hW	7-0	Clemson	6-1
N. 13	hW	35-6	Georgetown	7-1
N. 25	hW	34-0	Auburn (Thanksgiving)	8-1

1921: 8-1 ★

SIAA Co-Champions

Captain: J.W. Harlan

Date	Result		Opponent	Record
S. 24	hW	42-0	Wake Forest	1-0
O. 1	hW	41-0	Oglethorpe	2-0
O. 8	hW	70-0	Davidson	3-0
O. 15	hW	69-0	Furman	4-0
O. 22	hW	48-14	Rutgers	5-0
O. 29	nL	7-28	Penn State (Polo Grounds, N.Y.)	5-1
N. 5	hW	48-7	Clemson	6-1
N. 12	hW	21-7	Georgetown	7-1
N. 24	hW	14-0	Auburn (Thanksgiving)	8-1

1922: 7-2, 4-0 SC ★

Southern Conference Co-Champions

Captain: Red Barron

Date	Result		Opponent	Record
S. 30	hW	31-6	Oglethorpe	1-0
O. 7	hW	19-0	Davidson	2-0
O. 14	hW	33-7	Alabama	3-0
O. 21	aL	0-13	Navy	3-1
O. 28	hL	3-13	Notre Dame	3-2
N. 4	hW	21-7	Clemson	4-2
N. 11	hW	19-7	Georgetown	5-2
N. 18	hW	17-0	NC State	6-2
N. 30	hW	14-6	Auburn (Thanksgiving)	7-2

1923: 3-2-4, 1-0-4 SC

Captain: J.F. McIntyre

Date	Result		Opponent	Record
S. 23	hW	28-13	Oglethorpe	1-0
O. 6	hW	10-7	VMI	2-0
O. 13	hT	7-7	Florida	2-0-1
O. 20	hW	20-10	Georgetown	3-0-1
O. 27	aL	7-35	Notre Dame	3-1-1
N. 3	hT	0-0	Alabama	3-1-2
N. 10	aL	0-7	Penn State	3-2-2
N. 17	nT	3-3	Kentucky	3-2-3
N. 29	hT	0-0	Auburn (Thanksgiving)	3-2-4

1924: 5-3-1, 3-2-1 SC

Captain: George Gardner

Date	Result		Opponent	Record
S. 27	hW	19-0	Oglethorpe	1-0
O. 4	hW	3-0	VMI	2-0
O. 11	hT	7-7	Florida	2-0-1
O. 18	hW	15-13	Penn State	3-0-1
O. 25	hL	0-14	Alabama	3-1-1
N. 1	aL	3-34	Notre Dame	3-2-1
N. 8	hW	28-7	LSU	4-2-1
N. 15	hL	0-3	Vanderbilt	4-3-1
N. 27	hW	7-0	Auburn (Thanksgiving)	5-3-1

1925: 6-2-1, 4-1-1 SC

Captain: S.D. Wycoff

Date	Result		Opponent	Record
S. 28	hW	13-7	Oglethorpe	1-0
O. 3	hW	33-0	VMI	2-0
O. 10	nW	16-7	Penn State (Yankee Stadium, N.Y.)	3-0
O. 17	hW	23-7	Florida	4-0
O. 24	hL	0-7	Alabama	4-1
O. 31	hW	0-13	Notre Dame	4-2
N. 7	aW	7-0	Vanderbilt	5-2
N. 14	hW	3-0	Georgia	6-2
N. 26	hT	7-7	Auburn (Thanksgiving)	6-2-1

1926: 4-5, 4-3 SC

Captain: Owen Pool

Date	Result		Opponent	Record
S. 25	hL	6-7	Oglethorpe	0-1
O. 2	hW	13-0	VMI	1-1
O. 9	hW	9-6	Tulane	2-1
O. 16	hL	0-21	Alabama	2-2
O. 23	hW	19-7	Washington & Lee	3-2
O. 30	aL	0-12	Notre Dame	3-3
N. 6	hL	7-13	Vanderbilt	3-4
N. 13	hW	13-14	Georgia	3-5
N. 25	hW	20-7	Auburn (Thanksgiving)	4-5

1927: 8-1-1, 7-0-1 SC ★

Southern Conference Champions

Captain: E.J. Crowley

Date	Result		Opponent	Record
O. 1	hW	7-0	VMI	1-0
O. 8	hW	13-6	Tulane	2-0
O. 15	hW	13-0	Alabama	3-0
O. 22	hW	13-0	North Carolina	4-0
O. 29	aL	7-26	Notre Dame	4-1
N. 6	aT	0-0	Vanderbilt	4-1-1
N. 12	hW	23-0	LSU	5-1-1
N. 19	hW	19-7	Oglethorpe	6-1-1
N. 24	hW	18-0	Auburn (Thanksgiving)	7-1-1
D. 3	hW	12-0	Georgia	8-1-1

1928: 10-0, 7-0 SC ★ ◆
Co-National Champions (INS)
Southern Conference Champions
Captain: H.R. Pund

Date	Result		Opponent	Record
O. 6	hW	13-0	VMI	1-0
O. 13	aW	12-0	Tulane	2-0
O. 20	hW	13-0	Notre Dame	3-0
O. 27	aW	20-7	North Carolina	4-0
N. 3	hW	32-7	Oglethorpe	5-0
N. 10	hW	19-7	Vanderbilt	6-0
N. 17	hW	33-13	Alabama	7-0
N. 29	hW	51-0	Auburn (Thanksgiving)	8-0
D. 8	hW	20-6	Georgia	9-0
J. 1	nW	8-7	California (Rose Bowl)	10-0

1929: 3-6, 3-5 SC
Captain: Harold Rusk

Date	Result		Opponent	Record
O. 5	hW	27-13	Mississippi A&M	1-0
O. 12	hL	7-18	North Carolina	1-1
O. 19	hW	19-6	Florida	2-1
O. 26	aL	14-20	Tulane	2-2
N. 2	hL	6-26	Notre Dame	2-3
N. 9	aL	7-23	Vanderbilt	2-4
N. 16	hL	0-14	Alabama	2-5
N. 28	hW	19-6	Auburn (Thanksgiving)	3-5
D. 7	aL	6-12	Georgia	3-6

1930: 2-6-1, 2-4-1 SC
Captain: Earl Dunlap

Date	Result		Opponent	Record
O. 4	hW	45-0	South Carolina	1-0
O. 11	aL	0-31	Carnegie Tech	1-1
O. 18	hW	14-12	Auburn	2-1
O. 25	hL	0-28	Tulane	2-2
N. 1	aT	6-6	North Carolina	2-2-1
N. 8	hL	0-6	Vanderbilt	2-3-1
N. 15	aL	7-34	Pennsylvania	2-4-1
N. 27	hL	7-55	Florida (Thanksgiving)	2-5-1
D. 6	hL	0-13	Georgia	2-6-1

1931: 2-7-1, 2-4-1 SC
Captain: H.C. Neblett

Date	Result		Opponent	Record
O. 3	hW	25-13	South Carolina	1-0
O. 10	hL	0-13	Carnegie Tech	1-1
O. 17	hL	0-13	Auburn	1-2
O. 24	aL	0-33	Tulane	1-3
O. 31	hL	7-49	Vanderbilt	1-4
N. 7	aT	19-19	North Carolina	1-4-1
N. 14	aL	12-13	Pennsylvania	1-5-1
N. 21	hW	23-0	Florida	2-5-1
N. 28	aL	6-35	Georgia	2-6-1
D. 26	hL	6-21	California	2-7-1

1932: 4-5-1, 4-4-1 SC
Captain: H.C. Neblett

Date	Result		Opponent	Record
O. 1	hW	32-14	Clemson	1-0
O. 8	hW	6-12	Kentucky	1-1
O. 15	hL	0-6	Auburn	1-2
O. 22	aW	43-14	North Carolina	2-2
O. 29	aL	0-12	Vanderbilt	2-3
N. 5	hL	14-20	Tulane	2-4
N. 12	hW	6-0	Alabama	3-4
N. 19	aW	6-0	Florida	4-4
N. 26	hT	0-0	Georgia	4-4-1
D. 17	aL	7-27	California	4-5-1

1933: 5-5, 2-5 SEC
Captains: E.E. Laws, R.H. Tharpe

Date	Result		Opponent	Record
S. 30	hW	39-2	Clemson	1-0
O. 7	aL	6-7	Kentucky	1-1
O. 14	hW	16-6	Auburn	2-1
O. 21	hL	0-7	Tulane	2-2
O. 28	aW	10-6	North Carolina	3-2
N. 4	hL	6-9	Vanderbilt	3-3
N. 11	hW	19-7	Florida	4-3
N. 18	hL	9-12	Alabama	4-4
N. 25	hL	6-7	Georgia	4-5
D. 2	hW	6-0	Duke	5-5

1934: 1-9, 0-6 SEC
Captain: Jack Phillips

Date	Result		Opponent	Record
S. 29	hW	12-7	Clemson	1-0
O. 6	hL	12-27	Vanderbilt	1-1
O. 13	aL	0-20	Duke	1-2
O. 20	aL	2-9	Michigan	1-3
O. 27	aL	12-20	Tulane	1-4
N. 3	hL	0-26	North Carolina	1-5
N. 10	hL	6-18	Auburn	1-6
N. 17	hL	0-40	Alabama	1-7
N. 24	aL	12-13	Florida	1-8
D. 1	aL	0-7	Georgia	1-9

1935: 5-5, 3-4 SEC
Captain: R.W. Eubanks

Date	Result		Opponent	Record
S. 28	hW	33-0	Presbyterian	1-0
O. 5	hW	32-0	Sewanee	2-0
O. 12	aL	6-25	Kentucky	2-1
O. 19	hW	6-0	Duke	3-1
O. 26	aL	0-19	North Carolina	3-2
N. 2	hL	13-14	Vanderbilt	3-3
N. 9	hL	7-33	Auburn	3-4
N. 16	aL	7-38	Alabama (@ Birmingham)	3-5
N. 23	hW	39-6	Florida	4-5
N. 30	hW	19-7	Georgia	5-5

1936: 5-5-1, 3-3-1 SEC
Captain: J.W. FitzSimmons

Date	Result		Opponent	GT	Opp	Record
S. 26	hW	55-0	Presbyterian (First night game)			1-0
O. 3	hW	58-0	Sewanee			2-0
O. 10	hW	34-0	Kentucky			3-0
O. 17	aL	6-19	Duke			3-1
O. 24	aT	0-0	Vanderbilt			3-1-1
O. 31	hL	13-14	Clemson			3-2-1
N. 7	hL	12-13	Auburn		20	3-3-1
N. 14	hL	16-20	Alabama		4	3-4-1
N. 21	hW	38-14	Florida			4-4-1
N. 28	aL	6-16	Georgia			4-5-1
D. 26	hW	13-7	California			5-5-1

1937: 6-3-1, 3-2-1 SEC
Captain: Fletcher Sims

Date	Result		Opponent	GT	Opp	Record
S. 24	hW	59-0	Presbyterian			1-0
O. 2	hW	28-0	Mercer			2-0
O. 9	aW	32-0	Kentucky			3-0
O. 16	hL	19-20	Duke		*10	3-1
O. 23	hL	0-21	Auburn		20	3-2
O. 30	hW	14-0	Vanderbilt			4-2
N. 6	hW	7-0	Clemson			5-2
N. 13	aL	0-7	Alabama (@ Birmingham)		3	5-3
N. 20	aW	12-0	Florida			6-3
N. 27	hT	6-6	Georgia			6-3-1

* Ranking in first poll released Oct. 18

1938: 3-4-3, 2-1-3 SEC
Captain: Jack Chivington

Date	Result		Opponent	GT	Opp	Record
O. 1	hW	19-0	Mercer			1-0
O. 8	hL	6-14	Notre Dame		*5	1-1
O. 15	aL	0-6	Duke		*9	1-2
O. 22	hW	7-6	Auburn			2-2
O. 29	aL	7-13	Vanderbilt			2-3
N. 5	hW	19-18	Kentucky			3-3
N. 12	hT	14-14	Alabama		16	3-3-1
N. 19	hT	0-0	Florida			3-3-2
N. 26	aT	0-0	Georgia			3-3-3
D. 26	aL	0-13	California			3-4-3

* Ranking in first poll released Oct. 17

1939: 8-2, 6-0 SEC ★ ◆
SEC Co-Champions
Captain: R.W. Murphy

Date	Result		Opponent	GT	Opp	Record
O. 7	aL	14-17	Notre Dame		*2	0-1
O. 14	hW	35-0	Howard (Ala.)			1-1
O. 21	hW	14-6	Vanderbilt			2-1
O. 28	hW	7-6	Auburn			3-1
N. 4	hL	6-7	Duke		12	3-2
N. 11	hW	13-6	Kentucky		18	4-2
N. 18	aW	6-0	Alabama (@ Birmingham)			5-2
N. 25	aW	21-7	Florida		19	6-2
D. 2	hW	13-0	Georgia			7-2
J. 1	nW	21-7	Missouri (Orange Bowl)	16	6	8-2

* Ranking in first poll released Oct. 16

1940: 3-7, 1-5 SEC
Captain: N.W. Cavette

Date	Result		Opponent	GT	Opp	Record
O. 5	hW	27-0	Howard (Ala.)			1-0
O. 12	aL	20-26	Notre Dame		*6	1-1
O. 19	hW	19-0	Vanderbilt			2-1
O. 26	hL	7-16	Auburn			2-2
N. 2	aL	7-41	Duke		18	2-3
N. 9	aL	7-26	Kentucky (@ Louisville)			2-4
N. 16	hL	13-14	Alabama		14	2-5
N. 23	hL	7-16	Florida			2-6
N. 30	aL	19-21	Georgia			2-7
D. 28	hW	13-0	California			3-7

* Ranking in first poll released Oct. 14

1941: 3-6, 2-4 SEC
Captain: C.R. Sanders

Date	Result		Opponent	GT	Opp	Record
O. 4	hW	20-0	Chattanooga			1-0
O. 11	hL	0-20	Notre Dame		*8	1-1
O. 18	aL	7-14	Vanderbilt	St.	18	1-2
O. 25	hW	28-14	Auburn	St.		2-2
N. 1	hL	0-14	Duke		4	2-3
N. 8	hW	20-13	Kentucky			3-3
N. 15	aL	0-20	Alabama (@ Birmingham)		9	3-4
N. 22	aL	7-14	Florida			3-5
N. 29	hL	0-21	Georgia		20	3-5

* Ranking in first poll released Oct. 13

1942: 9-2, 4-1 SEC ◆
Captain: Jack Marshall

Date	Result		Opponent	GT	Opp	Record
S. 26	hW	15-0	Auburn	*6	4	1-0
O. 3	aW	13-6	Notre Dame	*6		2-0
O. 10	hW	30-6	Chattanooga	*6		3-0
O. 17	hW	33-0	Davidson	6		4-0
O. 24	aW	21-0	Navy	6		5-0
O. 31	aW	26-7	Duke	5		6-0
N. 7	hW	47-7	Kentucky	3		7-0
N. 14	hW	7-0	Alabama	2	5	8-0
N. 21	hW	20-7	Florida	2		9-0
N. 28	aL	0-34	Georgia	2	5	9-1
J. 1	nL	7-14	Texas (Cotton Bowl)	5	11	9-2

* Ranking in first poll released Oct. 12

1943: 8-3, 3-0 SEC ★ ◆
SEC Champions
Captains: George Manning, John Steber

Date	Result		Opponent	GT	Opp	Record
S. 25	hW	20-7	North Carolina			1-0
O. 2	aL	13-55	Notre Dame		*1	1-1
O. 9	hW	35-7	Ga. Navy Pre-Flight			2-1
O. 16	hW	27-0	Ft. Benning			3-1
O. 23	nL	14-28	Navy (@ Baltimore, Md.)		3	3-2
O. 30	hL	7-14	Duke		8	3-3
N. 6	hW	42-7	LSU		20	4-3
N. 13	aW	33-0	Tulane		19	5-3
N. 20	hW	41-6	Clemson		15	6-3
N. 27	hW	48-0	Georgia		14	7-3
J. 1	nW	20-18	Tulsa (Sugar Bowl)	13	15	8-3

* Ranking in first poll released Oct. 4

1944: 8-3, 4-0 SEC ★ ◆
SEC Champions
Captain: Phillip Tinsley

Date	Result		Opponent	GT	Opp	Record
S. 30	hW	51-0	Clemson	*10		1-0
O. 7	hW	28-0	North Carolina	*10		2-0
O. 14	hW	27-0	Auburn	10		3-0
O. 21	hW	17-15	Navy	8	9	4-0
O. 27	hW	13-7	Ga. Navy Pre-Flight	5		5-0
N. 4	aL	13-19	Duke	5		5-1
N. 11	hW	34-7	Tulane	13		6-1
N. 18	aW	14-6	LSU	9		7-1
N. 25	hL	0-21	Notre Dame	10	18	7-2
D. 2	hW	44-0	Georgia			8-2
J. 1	nL	12-26	Tulsa (Orange Bowl)	13		8-3

Ranking in first poll released Oct. 9

1945: 4-6, 2-2 SEC
Captain: Paul Duke

Date	Result		Opponent	GT	Opp	Record
S. 29	aW	20-14	North Carolina			1-0
O. 6	hL	7-40	Notre Dame	*3		1-1
O. 13	hW	43-0	Howard (Ala.)			2-1
O. 20	nL	6-20	Navy (@ Baltimore, Md.)	2		2-2
O. 27	hW	20-7	Auburn			3-2
N. 3	hL	6-14	Duke	18		3-3
N. 10	aW	41-7	Tulane			4-3
N. 17	hL	7-9	LSU			4-4
N. 24	hL	7-21	Clemson			4-5
D. 1	hL	0-33	Georgia			4-6

Ranking in first poll released Oct. 8

1946: 9-2, 4-2 SEC ◆
Captain: R.T. Davis

Date	Result		Opponent	GT	Opp	Record
S. 28	aL	9-13	Tennessee	*8		0-1
O. 5	hW	32-6	VMI			1-1
O. 12	hW	24-7	Mississippi			2-1
O. 19	aW	26-7	LSU	12		3-1
O. 26	hW	27-6	Auburn	15		4-1
N. 2	aW	14-0	Duke	16	19	5-1
N. 9	hW	28-20	Navy	8		6-1
N. 16	hW	35-7	Tulane	7		7-1
N. 23	hW	41-7	Furman	6		8-1
N. 30	aL	7-35	Georgia	7	3	8-2
J. 1	nW	41-19	St. Mary_s (Oil Bowl)	11		9-2

Ranking in first poll released Oct. 7

1947: 10-1, 4-1 SEC ◆
Captain: Bill Healy, Rollo Phillips

Date	Result		Opponent	GT	Opp	Record
S. 27	hW	27-0	Tennessee	*4		1-0
O. 4	aW	20-6	Tulane	*4		2-0
O. 11	hW	20-0	VMI	4		3-0
O. 18	hW	27-7	Auburn	5		4-0
O. 25	hW	38-0	The Citadel	7		5-0
N. 1	hW	7-0	Duke	6	9	6-0
N. 8	nW	16-14	Navy (@ Baltimore, Md.)	6		7-0
N. 15	aL	7-14	Alabama (@ Birmingham)	6	14	7-1
N. 22	hW	51-0	Furman	10		8-1
N. 29	hW	7-0	Georgia	9		9-1
J. 1	nW	20-14	Kansas (Orange Bowl)	10	12	10-1

Ranking in first poll released Oct. 6

1948: 7-3, 4-3 SEC
Captains: George Brodnax, Jim Castleberry

Date	Result		Opponent	GT	Opp	Record
S. 25	aW	13-0	Vanderbilt	*6		1-0
O. 2	hW	13-7	Tulane	*6		2-0
O. 9	hW	27-0	Washington & Lee	*6		3-0
O. 16	hW	27-0	Auburn	7		4-0
O. 23	hW	42-7	Florida	6		5-0
O. 30	aW	19-7	Duke	6		6-0
N. 6	hL	6-13	Tennessee	6		6-1
N. 13	hL	12-14	Alabama	11		6-2
N. 20	hW	54-0	The Citadel	20		7-2
N. 27	aL	13-21	Georgia	12		7-3

Ranking in first poll released Oct. 4

1949: 7-3, 5-2 SEC
Captain: Tom Coleman

Date	Result		Opponent	GT	Opp	Rec	Att
S. 24	hW	12-7	Vanderbilt			1-0	39,000
O. 1	aL	0-18	Tulane	*4		1-1	55,000
O. 8	hW	36-0	Washington & Lee			2-1	25,000
O. 15	hW	35-21	Auburn			3-1	33,000
O. 22	aW	43-14	Florida			4-1	27,000
O. 29	hL	14-27	Duke			4-2	38,000
N. 5	hW	30-13	Tennessee	14		5-2	NA
N. 12	aL	7-20	Alabama (@ Birmingham)			5-3	43,000
N. 19	hW	13-3	South Carolina			6-3	20,000
N. 26	hW	7-6	Georgia			7-3	40,000

Ranking in first poll released Oct. 3

1950: 5-6, 4-2 SEC
Captain: Bob Bossons

Date	Result		Opponent	GT	Opp	Rec	Att
S. 23	aL	13-33	SMU	10*		0-1	NA
S. 30	hL	0-7	South Carolina			0-2	25,000
O. 7	hW	16-13	Florida			1-2	25,000
O. 14	aW	13-0	LSU			2-2	42,000
O. 21	hW	20-0	Auburn			3-2	30,000
O. 28	hL	14-28	Kentucky		4	3-3	35,000
N. 4	aL	21-30	Duke			3-4	30,000
N. 11	hL	13-14	VMI			3-5	22,000
N. 18	hL	19-54	Alabama			3-6	38,000
N. 25	hW	46-14	Davidson			4-6	20,000
D. 2	aW	7-0	Georgia			5-6	50,000

Preseason poll

1951: 11-0-1, 7-0 SEC ★ ◆
SEC Champions
Captain: Lamar Wheat

Date	Result		Opponent	GT	Opp	Rec	Att
S. 22	hW	21-7	SMU			1-0	33,000
S. 29	aW	27-0	Florida			2-0	39,000
O. 6	aW	13-7	Kentucky	11	17	3-0	35,000
O. 13	hW	25-7	LSU	8		4-0	30,000
O. 20	hW	27-7	Auburn	5		5-0	31,000
O. 27	aW	8-7	Vanderbilt	3		6-0	26,000
N. 3	hT	14-14	Duke	5		6-0-1	36,000
N. 10	hW	34-7	VMI	8		7-0-1	21,000
N. 17	aW	27-7	Alabama (@ Birmingham)	7		8-0-1	35,000
N. 24	hW	34-7	Davidson	7		9-0-1	18,000
D. 1	hW	48-6	Georgia	6		10-0-1	40,000
J. 1	nW	17-14	#Baylor (Orange Bowl)	5	9	11-0-1	65,837

1952: 12-0, 6-0 SEC ★ ◆
Co-National Champions (INS)
SEC Champions
Captains: George Morris, Hal Miller

Date	Result	Opponent	GT	Opp	Rec	Att
S. 20	hW 54-6	The Citadel	*3		1-0	22,000
S. 27	hW 17-14	Florida	*3		2-0	30,939
O. 4	aW 20-7	SMU	6		3-0	41,000
O. 11	hW 14-0	Tulane	5		4-0	27,913
O. 18	hW 33-0	Auburn	4		5-0	34,689
O. 25	hW 30-0	Vanderbilt	5		6-0	35,373
N. 1	aW 28-7	Duke	4	6	7-0	40,000
N. 8	hW 45-6	Army	3		8-0	40,000
N. 15	hW 7-3	#Alabama	2	12	9-0	38,063
N. 22	hW 30-0	Florida State	2		10-0	25,000
N. 29	aW 23-9	Georgia	3		11-0	50,000
J. 1	nW 24-7	#Mississippi (Sugar Bowl)	2	7	12-0	80,187

Preseason poll
= televised game

1953: 9-2-1, 4-1-1 SEC ◆
Captains: Sam Hensley, Ed Gossage, Orville Vereen

Date	Result	Opponent	GT	Opp	Rec	Att
S. 19	hW 53-0	Davidson	*3		1-0	22,000
S. 26	aT 0-0	Florida	*3	15	1-0-1	41,000
O. 3	hW 6-4	SMU	9		2-0-1	37,000
O. 10	aW 27-13	Tulane	10		3-0-1	30,000
O. 17	hW 36-6	Auburn	6	19	4-0-1	39,500
O. 24	aL 14-27	Notre Dame	4	1	4-1-1	58,254
O. 31	aW 43-0	Vanderbilt	8		5-1-1	24,000
N. 7	hW 20-7	Clemson	6		6-1-1	35,000
N. 14	aL 6-13	Alabama (@ Birmingham)	5		6-2-1	42,500
N. 21	hW 13-10	Duke	12	15	7-2-1	40,000
N. 28	hW 28-12	Georgia	10		8-2-1	41,000
J. 1	nW 42-19	#West Virginia (Sugar Bowl)	8	10	9-2-1	70,500

Preseason poll

1954: 8-3, 6-2 SEC ◆
Captain: Larry Morris

Date	Result	Opponent	GT	Opp	Rec	Att
S. 18	hW 28-0	Tulane	*7		1-0	28,000
S. 25	hL 12-13	Florida	5		1-1	30,000
O. 2	aW 10-7	SMU			2-1	34,000
O. 9	hW 30-20	LSU			3-1	28,000
O. 16	hW 14-7	Auburn		19	4-1	40,000
O. 23	hL 6-13	Kentucky		15	4-2	34,000
O. 30	aL 20-21	Duke		16	4-3	33,000
N. 6	hW 28-7	Tennessee			5-3	40,000
N. 13	hW 20-0	#Alabama			6-3	40,000
N. 27	aW 7-3	Georgia			7-3	50,000
J. 1	nW 14-6	#Arkansas (Cotton Bowl)		10	8-3	75,500

Preseason poll

1955: 9-1-1, 4-1-1 SEC ◆
Captain: Jimmy Morris

Date	Result	Opponent	GT	Opp	Rec	Att
S. 17	hW 14-6	#Miami (Fla.)	*10		1-0	39,500
S. 24	aW 14-7	Florida	2	19	2-0	40,000
O. 1	hW 20-7	SMU	3		3-0	34,000
O. 8	aW 7-0	LSU	4		4-0	60,000
O. 15	hL 12-14	Auburn	5	17	4-1	40,000
O. 22	hW 34-0	Florida State	13		5-1	30,000
O. 29	hW 27-0	Duke	12	17	6-1	40,000
N. 5	aT 7-7	Tennessee	8		6-1-1	50,000
N. 12	aW 26-2	Alabama (@ Birmingham)	11		7-1-1	38,000
N. 26	hW 21-3	Georgia	9		8-1-1	40,000
J. 2	nW 7-0	#Pittsburgh (Sugar Bowl)	7	11	9-1-1	80,174

Preseason poll

1956: 10-1, 7-1 SEC ◆
Captains: Wade Mitchell, George Volkert

Date	Result	Opponent	GT	Opp	Rec	Att
S. 22	aW 14-6	#Kentucky	*4		1-0	30,000
S. 29	aW 9-7	SMU	2	5	2-0	46,000
O. 13	hW 39-7	LSU	3		3-0	39,500
O. 20	hW 28-7	Auburn	3		4-0	40,000
O. 27	hW 40-0	Tulane	3	15	5-0	40,000
N. 3	aW 7-0	Duke	2		6-0	38,000
N. 10	hL 0-6	Tennessee	2	3	6-1	40,000
N. 17	hW 27-0	Alabama	4		7-1	38,500
N. 24	aW 28-0	Florida	5	13	8-1	37,000
D. 1	aW 35-0	Georgia	4		9-1	50,000
D. 29	nW 21-14	#Pittsburgh (Gator Bowl)	4	13	10-1	37,683

Preseason poll

1957: 4-4-2, 3-4-1 SEC
Captain: Don Stephenson

Date	Result	Opponent	GT	Opp	Rec	Att
S. 21	hW 13-0	Kentucky	*11	20	1-0	40,000
S. 28	hT 0-0	SMU	3	15	1-0-1	39,000
O. 12	aL 13-20	LSU		17	1-1-1	62,500
O. 19	hL 0-3	Auburn		9	1-2-1	40,000
O. 26	aW 20-13	Tulane			2-2-1	25,000
N. 2	hW 13-0	Duke		7	3-2-1	40,000
N. 9	aL 6-21	Tennessee	18	9	3-3-1	45,500
N. 16	aW 10-7	Alabama (@ Birmingham)			4-3-1	30,000
N. 23	hT 0-0	Florida			4-3-2	40,000
N. 30	hL 0-7	Georgia			4-4-2	40,000

Preseason poll

1958: 5-4-1, 2-3-1 SEC
Captain: Foster Watkins

Date	Result	Opponent	GT	Opp	Rec	Att
S. 20	aL 0-13	Kentucky			0-1	30,000
S. 26	hW 17-3	Florida State			1-1	40,391
O. 4	hW 14-0	Tulane			2-1	38,000
O. 11	hW 21-7	Tennessee			3-1	44,726
O. 18	hT 7-7	Auburn		2	3-1-1	44,726
O. 25	aL 0-20	SMU		17	3-2-1	27,000
N. 1	aW 10-8	Duke			4-2-1	30,000
N. 8	hW 13-0	Clemson		17	5-2-1	44,726
N. 15	hL 8-17	Alabama		20	5-3-1	44,726
N. 29	aL 3-16	Georgia			5-4-1	50,000

1959: 6-5, 3-3 SEC ◆
Captain: Maxie Baughan

Date	Result		Opponent	GT	Opp	Rec	Att
S. 19	aW	14-12	Kentucky			1-0	35,000
S. 26	hW	16-12	SMU	16	6	2-0	43,000
O. 3	hW	16-6	Clemson	7	6	3-0	44,174
O. 10	aW	14-7	Tennessee	3	8	4-0	45,021
O. 17	hL	6-7	Auburn	4	11	4-1	44,174
O. 24	aW	21-13	Tulane	9		5-1	30,000
O. 31	hL	7-10	Duke	9		5-2	44,174
N. 7	aW	14-10	Notre Dame	19		6-2	58,575
N. 14	aL	7-9	Alabama (@ Birmingham)	15		6-3	43,500
N. 28	hL	14-21	Georgia		6	6-4	44,174
J. 2	nL	7-14	#Arkansas (Gator Bowl)	9		6-5	45,104

1960: 5-5, 4-4 SEC
Captain: Gerald Burch

Date	Result		Opponent	GT	Opp	Rec	Att
S. 17	hW	23-13	Kentucky			1-0	40,594
S. 24	aW	16-13	Rice	13		2-0	35,000
O. 1	aL	17-18	Florida	10		2-1	39,000
O. 8	hW	6-2	LSU			3-1	44,176
O. 15	nL	7-9	Auburn (@ Birmingham)	19		3-2	44,000
O. 22	hW	14-6	Tulane			4-2	43,608
O. 29	aL	0-6	Duke		15	4-3	40,000
N. 5	hW	14-7	Tennessee	8		5-3	45,072
N. 12	hL	15-16	Alabama			5-4	44,006
N. 26	aL	6-7	Georgia			5-5	55,000

Note: From 1961 - 1967, the AP poll ranked only 10 teams

1961: 7-4, 4-3 SEC ◆
Captains: Chick Graning, Willie McGaughey, Billy Williamson

Date	Result		Opponent	GT	Opp	Rec	Att
S. 22	aW	27-7	Southern Cal	9	10		39,590
S. 30	hW	24-0	Rice			2-0	43,501
O. 7	aL	0-10	LSU	3		2-1	66,000
O. 14	hW	21-0	Duke			3-1	44,015
O. 21	hW	7-6	Auburn	8		4-1	45,376
O. 28	aW	35-0	Tulane	9		5-1	18,000
N. 4	hW	20-0	Florida	7		6-1	44,940
N. 11	aL	6-10	Tennessee	9		6-2	46,000
N. 18	aL	0-10	Alabama (@ Birmingham)	2		6-3	53,000
D. 2	hW	22-7	Georgia	2		7-3	47,098
D. 30	nL	15-30	#Penn State (Gator Bowl)	13	17	7-4	50,202

1962: 7-3-1, 5-2 SEC ◆
Captain: Tom Winingder

Date	Result		Opponent	GT	Opp	Rec	Att
S. 22	hW	26-9	Clemson			1-0	51,140
S. 29	aW	17-0	Florida	8		2-0	44,500
O. 6	hL	7-10	#LSU	5		2-1	49,744
O. 13	hW	17-0	Tennessee	11		3-1	52,223
O. 20	aL	14-17	Auburn (@ Birmingham)			3-2	56,319
O. 27	hW	42-12	Tulane			4-2	46,370
N. 3	aW	20-9	Duke			5-2	44,000
N. 10	hT	14-14	Florida State			5-2-1	43,802
N. 17	hW	7-6	Alabama	1		6-2-1	52,971
D. 1	aW	37-6	Georgia			7-2-1	55,000
D. 22	nL	10-14	#Missouri (Bluebonnet Bowl)			7-3-1	55,000

1963: 7-3, 4-3 SEC
Captain: Billy Lothridge

Date	Result		Opponent	GT	Opp	Rec	Att
S. 14	hW	9-0	#Florida			1-0	43,000
S. 28	hW	27-0	Clemson	9		2-0	33,916
O. 5	aL	6-7	LSU	7		2-1	68,000
O. 12	aW	23-7	Tennessee			3-1	51,527
O. 19	hL	21-29	Auburn	8		3-2	53,091
O. 26	aW	17-3	Tulane			4-2	15,000
N. 2	hW	30-6	Duke			5-2	52,266
N. 9	hW	15-7	Florida State			6-2	49,804
N. 16	aL	11-27	Alabama (@ Birmingham)	7		6-3	54,000
N. 30	hW	14-3	Georgia			7-3	53,052

1964: 7-3
Captains: Bill Curry, Johnny Gresham

Date	Result		Opponent	GT	Opp	Rec	Att
S. 19	hW	14-2	Vanderbilt			1-0	44,288
S. 26	hW	20-0	Miami (Fla.)			2-0	44,115
O. 3	hW	14-7	Clemson			3-0	46,571
O. 9	nW	17-0	Navy (@ Jacksonville, Fla.)			4-0	40,000
O. 17	nW	7-3	Auburn (@ Birmingham)			5-0	57,000
O. 24	hW	7-6	Tulane			6-0	45,129
O. 31	aW	21-8	Duke	8		7-0	45,000
N. 7	hL	14-22	Tennessee	7		7-1	50,763
N. 14	hL	7-24	Alabama	10	2	7-2	53,505
N. 28	aL	0-7	Georgia			7-3	52,000

1965: 7-3-1 ◆
Captains: John Battle, Tommy Bleick

Date	Result		Opponent	GT	Opp	Rec	Att
S. 18	aT	10-10	Vanderbilt			0-0-1	22,275
S. 25	hL	10-14	Texas A&M			0-1-1	45,843
O. 2	hW	38-6	Clemson			1-1-1	46,736
O. 9	aW	13-10	Tulane			2-1-1	35,000
O. 16	hW	23-14	Auburn			3-1-1	50,164
O. 23	hW	37-16	Navy			4-1-1	49,793
O. 30	hW	35-23	Duke			5-1-1	46,981
N. 6	aL	7-21	Tennessee			5-2-1	52,174
N. 13	hW	42-19	Virginia			6-2-1	40,094
N. 27	hL	7-17	Georgia			6-3-1	52,013
J. 1	nW	31-21	#Texas Tech (Gator Bowl)	10		7-3-1	60,127

1966: 9-2 ◆
Captains: Jim Breland, Bill Moorer, Billy Schroer, Sammy Burke

Date	Result		Opponent	GT	Opp	Rec	Att
S. 17	hW	38-3	Texas A&M			1-0	36,215
S. 24	hW	42-0	Vanderbilt			2-0	42,260
O. 1	hW	13-12	Clemson	9		3-0	44,735
O. 8	hW	6-3	#Tennessee	9	8	4-0	52,180
O. 15	aW	17-3	Auburn (@ Birmingham)	7		5-0	54,000
O. 22	hW	35-17	Tulane	6		6-0	44,355
O. 29	aW	48-7	Duke	6		7-0	42,000
N. 5	hW	14-13	Virginia	5		8-0	42,126
N. 12	hW	21-0	Penn State	5		9-0	50,172
N. 26	aL	14-23	Georgia	5	7	9-1	48,782
J. 2	nL	12-27	#Florida (Orange Bowl)	8		9-2	72,426

1967: 4-6

Captains: Kim King, David Barber, Randall Edmunds

Date	Result	Opponent	GT Opp	Rec	Att
S. 23	aW 17-10	Vanderbilt		1-0	24,000
S. 30	hW 24-7	Texas Christian		2-0	55,299
O. 7	hW 10-0	Clemson		3-0	59,588
O. 14	aL 13-24	#Tennessee		3-1	55,119
O. 21	hL 10-28	Auburn		3-2	59,603
O. 28	aL 12-23	Tulane		3-3	29,643
N. 4	hW 19-7	Duke		4-3	50,103
N. 10	aL 7-49	Miami (Fla.)		4-4	48,267
N. 18	hL 3-36	Notre Dame	9	4-5	60,024
N. 25	hL 14-21	#Georgia		4-6	53,699

1968: 4-6

Captains: Bill Kinard, Joel Stevenson

Date	Result	Opponent	GT Opp	Rec	Att
S. 21	hW 17-7	Texas Christian		1-0	43,273
S. 28	hL 7-10	Miami (Fla.)	15	1-1	44,774
O. 5	hW 24-21	Clemson		2-1	56,116
O. 12	hL 7-24	Tennessee	10	2-2	60,011
O. 19	aW 21-20	Auburn (@ Birmingham)		3-2	50,000
O. 26	hW 23-19	Tulane		4-2	47,481
N. 2	aL 30-46	Duke		4-3	25,000
N. 9	hL 15-35	Navy		4-4	31,624
N. 16	aL 6-34	Notre Dame	9	4-5	50,075
N. 30	aL 8-47	Georgia	4	4-6	59,537

1969: 4-6

Captains: Gene Spiotta, Renso Perdoni

Date	Result	Opponent	GT Opp	Rec	Att
S. 20	hW 24-21	SMU		1-0	46,624
S. 27	hW 17-10	Baylor		2-0	37,776
O. 4	hL 10-21	Clemson		2-1	50,224
O. 11	aL 8-26	Tennessee	10	2-2	63,171
O. 18	hL 14-17	Auburn	15	2-3	59,464
O. 25	aL 18-29	Southern Cal	7	2-4	53,341
N. 1	hW 20-7	Duke		3-4	41,113
N. 8	aL 7-14	Tulane		3-5	19,450
N. 15	hL 20-38	#Notre Dame	9	3-6	41,104
N. 29	hW 6-0	Georgia		4-6	60,106

1970: 9-3 ◆

Captains: Jack Williams, Renso Perdoni

Date	Result	Opponent	GT Opp	Rec	Att
S. 12	hW 23-20	South Carolina	17	1-0	51,206
S. 19	hW 23-13	Florida State		2-0	50,324
S. 26	hW 31-21	Miami	19	3-0	44,246
O. 3	hW 28-7	Clemson	15	4-0	50,113
O. 10	hL 6-17	Tennessee	13	20	4-1	59,624
O. 17	aL 7-31	Auburn	16	8	4-2	62,391
O. 24	hW 20-6	Tulane		5-2	32,129
O. 31	aW 24-16	Duke		6-2	32,650
N. 7	hW 30-8	Navy		7-2	50,105
N. 14	aL 7-10	Notre Dame	1	7-3	59,075
N. 28	aW 17-7	Georgia	16	8-3	59,803
D. 19	nW 17-9	#Texas Tech (Sun Bowl)	13	19	9-3	30,512

1971: 6-6 ◆

Captains: Brent Cunningham, Jeff Ford

Date	Result	Opponent	GT Opp	Rec	Att
S. 11	aL 7-24	South Carolina	17	0-1	54,842
S. 18	hW 10-0	Michigan State	18	1-1	50,646
S. 25	hL 13-16	Army		1-2	40,123
O. 2	hW 24-14	Clemson		2-2	50,239
O. 9	aL 6-10	Tennessee	13	2-3	63,671
O. 16	hL 14-31	Auburn	5	2-4	60,204
O. 23	aW 24-16	Tulane		3-4	50,248
O. 30	hW 21-0	Duke		4-4	49,886
N. 6	hW 34-21	Navy		5-4	44,821
N. 13	hW 12-6	Florida State		6-4	44,261
N. 25	hL 24-28	#Georgia (Thanksgiving)	7	6-5	60,124
D. 30	nL 18-41	#Mississippi (Peach Bowl)	17	6-6	36,771

1972: 7-4-1 ◆

Captains: Brad Bourne, Rick Lantz

Date	Result	Opponent	GT Opp	Rec	Att
S. 9	hL 3-34	#Tennessee	15	0-1	52,112
S. 16	hW 34-6	South Carolina		1-1	48,224
S. 23	aW 21-16	Michigan State	18	2-1	44,141
S. 30	hT 36-36	Rice		2-1-1	41,179
O. 7	hW 31-9	Clemson		3-1-1	50,239
O. 21	aL 14-24	Auburn	14	3-2-1	60,261
O. 28	hW 21-7	Tulane		4-2-1	48,096
N. 4	aL 14-20	Duke		4-3-1	37,300
N. 11	hW 42-10	Boston College		5-3-1	36,114
N. 18	hW 30-7	Navy		6-3-1	39,233
D. 2	aL 7-27	Georgia		6-4-1	60,241
D. 18	nW 31-30	#Iowa State (Liberty Bowl)		7-4-1	50,021

1973: 5-6

Captains: Bill Owings, Steve Putnal

Date	Result	Opponent	GT Opp	Rec	Att
S. 15	aL 28-41	South Carolina		0-1	51,584
S. 22	hL 6-23	Southern Cal	1	0-2	58,228
S. 29	hW 29-21	Clemson		1-2	48,062
O. 6	hW 14-10	Army		2-2	50,111
O. 13	aL 14-20	Tennessee	8	2-3	70,616
O. 20	hL 10-24	Auburn		2-4	59,123
O. 27	aL 14-23	Tulane		2-5	66,826
N. 3	hW 12-10	Duke		3-5	47,129
N. 10	hW 36-7	VMI		4-5	38,112
N. 17	nW 26-22	Navy (@ Jacksonville)		5-5	26,235
D. 1	hL 3-10	Georgia		5-6	60,316

1974: 6-5

Captains: Billy Shields, Joe Harris, Randy Rhino

Date	Result	Opponent	GT Opp	Rec	Att
S. 9	hL 7-31	#Notre Dame (Monday)	2	0-1	44,228
S. 14	hW 35-20	South Carolina		1-1	47,171
S. 21	hL 17-27	Pittsburgh	15	1-2	37,361
S. 28	aL 17-21	Clemson		1-3	42,000
O. 5	hW 28-24	Virginia		2-3	26,371
O. 12	hW 29-28	North Carolina		3-3	38,413
O. 19	aL 22-31	Auburn	5	3-4	62,907
O. 26	hW 27-7	#Tulane	18	4-4	48,623
N. 2	aL 0-9	Duke		4-5	34,500
N. 16	hW 22-0	Navy		5-5	41,132
N. 30	aW 34-14	Georgia		6-5	47,500

1975: 7-4

Captains: Mark Hunter, Rick Gibney, Steve Crawford

Date	Result	Opponent	GT	Opp	Rec	Att
S. 13	aL 17-23	South Carolina			0-1	51,428
S. 20	hW 38-23	Miami (Fla.)			1-1	32,334
S. 27	hW 33-28	Clemson			2-1	46,212
O. 4	hW 30-0	Florida State			3-1	35,261
O. 11	hW 38-10	VMI			4-1	40,194
O. 18	hL 27-31	Auburn			4-2	58,316
O. 25	aW 23-0	Tulane			5-2	63,333
N. 1	hW 21-6	Duke			6-2	44,116
N. 8	aL 3-24	Notre Dame		12	6-3	59,075
N. 15	hW 14-13	Navy			7-3	36,231
N. 27	hL 26-42	#Georgia (Thanksgiving)		15	7-4	55,135

1976: 4-6-1

Captains: Lucius Sanford, Leo Tierney, Tony Daykin

Date	Result	Opponent	GT	Opp	Rec	Att
S. 11	hL 17-27	#South Carolina			0-1	38,923
S. 18	hL 14-42	Pittsburgh		3	0-2	43,424
S. 25	hT 24-24	Clemson			0-2-1	43,937
O. 2	hW 35-14	Virginia			1-2-1	38,119
O. 9	hL 7-42	Tennessee			1-3-1	55,631
O. 16	aW 28-10	Auburn			2-3-1	63,876
O. 23	hW 28-16	Tulane			3-3-1	31,214
O. 30	aL 7-31	Duke			3-4-1	30,300
N. 6	hW 23-14	Notre Dame		11	4-4-1	50,079
N. 13	aL 28-34	Navy			4-5-1	20,010
N. 27	aL 10-13	Georgia		4	4-6-1	60,500

1977: 6-5

Captains: Lucius Sanford, Randy Pass, Freeman Colbert, Lawton Hydrick

Date	Result	Opponent	GT	Opp	Rec	Att
S. 10	aL 0-17	South Carolina			0-1	55,934
S. 17	hW 10-6	Miami (Fla.)			1-1	31,916
S. 24	aL 14-31	Clemson			1-2	50,116
O. 1	hW 30-3	Air Force			2-2	30,067
O. 8	aW 24-8	Tennessee			3-2	82,631
O. 15	hW 38-21	Auburn			4-2	54,961
O. 22	aW 38-14	Tulane			5-2	28,345
O. 29	hL 24-25	Duke			5-3	47,131
N. 5	aL 14-69	Notre Dame		5	5-4	59,075
N. 12	aL 16-20	Navy			5-5	18,590
N. 26	hW 16-7	Georgia			6-5	60,104

1978: 7-5 ◆

Captains: Eddie Lee Ivery, Donald Patterson, Jeff Shank, Mike Taylor

Date	Result	Opponent	GT	Opp	Rec	Att
S. 8	aL 10-28	Duke			0-1	27,865
S. 19	hL 22-34	California			0-2	26,577
S. 23	hW 27-17	Tulane			1-2	25,805
S. 30	hW 28-0	The Citadel			2-2	21,802
O. 7	hW 6-3	South Carolina			3-2	36,128
O. 14	hW 24-19	Miami (Fla.)			4-2	29,695
O. 21	aW 24-10	#Auburn			5-2	59,111
O. 28	hW 17-13	#Florida			6-2	44,866
N. 11	aW 42-21	Air Force			7-2	19,564
N. 18	hL 21-38	Notre Dame	20	10	7-3	54,526
D. 2	aL 28-29	#Georgia		11	7-4	59,700
D. 25	nL 21-41	Purdue (Peach Bowl)		7	7-5	20,277

1979: 4-6-1

Captain: Tom Daniel

Date	Result	Opponent	GT	Opp	Rec	Att
S. 8	hL 6-30	Alabama		2	0-1	57,621
S. 22	aT 7-7	Florida			0-1-1	60,313
S. 29	hW 33-7	William & Mary			1-1-1	28,511
O. 6	aL 13-21	Notre Dame		10	1-2-1	59,075
O. 13	aL 0-31	Tennessee			1-3-1	85,524
O. 20	hL 14-38	Auburn		14	1-4-1	54,236
O. 27	aL 7-12	Tulane			1-5-1	51,963
N. 3	hW 24-14	Duke			2-5-1	23,445
N. 10	hW 21-0	Air Force			3-5-1	30,113
N. 17	hW 24-14	Navy			4-5-1	24,318
D. 1	aL 3-16	#Georgia			4-6-1	48,781

1980: 1-9-1

Captains: Ben Utt, Duane Wood, Ken Taylor, Darrell Thomas

Date	Result	Opponent	GT	Opp	Rec	Att
S. 6	aL 3-26	Alabama (@ Birmingham)		2	0-1	78,410
S. 20	hL 12-45	Florida			0-2	35,165
S. 27	hW 17-8	Memphis State			1-2	28,062
O. 4	aL 0-33	North Carolina		10	1-3	49,750
O. 11	hL 10-23	Tennessee			1-4	50,127
O. 18	aL 14-17	Auburn			1-5	57,950
O. 25	hL 14-31	Tulane			1-6	35,119
N. 1	aL 12-17	Duke			1-7	18,200
N. 8	hT 3-3	Notre Dame		1	1-7-1	41,226
N. 15	hL 8-19	Navy			1-8-1	17,631
N. 29	aL 20-38	Georgia		1	1-9-1	62,800

1981: 1-10

Captains: David Lutz, Lance Skelton, Mark Bradley, Ken Carney

Date	Result	Opponent	GT	Opp	Rec	Att
S. 12	aW 24-21	#Alabama (@ Birmingham)		4	1-0	78,865
S. 19	aL 6-27	Florida			1-1	63,876
S. 26	hL 15-28	Memphis State			1-2	32,463
O. 3	hL 7-28	North Carolina		6	1-3	39,263
O. 10	aL 7-10	Tennessee			1-4	94,478
O. 17	hL 7-31	Auburn			1-5	50,263
O. 24	aL 10-27	Tulane			1-6	37,431
O. 31	hL 24-38	Duke			1-7	30,232
N. 7	aL 3-35	Notre Dame			1-8	59,075
N. 14	hL 14-20	Navy			1-9	20,129
N. 28	hL 7-44	#Georgia		3	1-10	58,623

1982: 6-5

Captains: David Lutz, Sammy Brown, Kevin Brownlee

Date	Result	Opponent	GT	Opp	Rec	Att
S. 11	hL 7-45	Alabama		4	0-1	57,126
S. 18	hW 36-7	The Citadel			1-1	24,463
S. 25	aW 24-20	Memphis State			2-1	15,061
O. 2	aL 0-41	North Carolina		12	2-2	49,500
O. 9	aW 19-13	Tulane			3-2	34,321
O. 16	aL 0-24	Auburn			3-3	57,000
O. 23	hW 31-21	#Tennessee			4-3	43,182
O. 30	hL 21-38	Duke			4-4	36,562
N. 6	hW 38-32	Virginia			5-4	22,103
N. 13	aW 45-7	Wake Forest			6-4	19,257
N. 27	aL 18-38	Georgia		1	6-5	82,122

1983: 3-8, 3-2 ACC (3rd)

Captains: Rob Horton, Dean Waters, Ron Rice

Date	Result		Opponent	GT	Opp	Rec	Att
S. 10	aL	7-20	Alabama (@ Birmingham)	14		0-1	77,143
S. 17	hL	14-17	Furman			0-2	24,311
S. 24	aL	14-41	#Clemson			0-3	73,000
O. 1	hL	21-38	North Carolina	5		0-4	34,000
O. 8	aW	20-10	NC State			1-4	40,800
O. 15	hL	13-31	Auburn	5		1-5	55,112
O. 22	aL	3-37	Tennessee			1-6	94,768
O. 29	aL	26-32	Duke			1-7	17,650
N. 3	hW	31-27	#Virginia (Thursday)			2-7	22,032
N. 12	hW	49-33	Wake Forest			3-7	26,330
N. 26	hL	24-27	Georgia	7		3-8	59,113

1984: 6-4-1, 2-2-1 (5th) ACC

Captains: David Bell, Donnie Chisholm, Robert Lavette

Date	Result		Opponent	GT	Opp	Rec	Att
S. 15	hW	16-6	#Alabama	19		1-0	56,107
S. 22	hW	48-3	The Citadel			2-0	31,684
S. 29	hW	28-21	#Clemson	18	13	3-0	57,704
O. 6	hL	22-27	#NC State	12		3-1	32,627
O. 13	aT	20-20	Virginia	20		3-1-1	40,067
O. 20	aL	34-48	Auburn		13	3-2-1	75,216
O. 27	hL	21-24	Tennessee			3-3-1	45,167
N. 3	hW	31-3	Duke			4-3-1	36,393
N. 10	aL	17-24	North Carolina			4-4-1	47,000
N. 17	aW	24-7	Wake Forest			5-4-1	22,700
D. 1	aW	35-18	#Georgia	18		6-4-1	82,122

1985: 9-2-1, 5-1 ACC (2nd) ◆

Captains: John Ivemeyer, Ted Roof, Mike Snow

Date	Result		Opponent	GT	Opp	Rec	Att
S. 14	aW	28-18	#NC State			1-0	32,100
S. 21	hL	13-24	Virginia			1-1	38,291
S. 28	aW	14-3	Clemson			2-1	78,000
O. 5	hW	31-0	#North Carolina			3-1	35,625
O. 12	hW	24-17	Western Carolina			4-1	36,111
O. 19	hL	14-17	#Auburn		8	4-2	57,501
O. 26	aT	6-6	#Tennessee		16	4-2-1	94,575
N. 2	aW	9-0	Duke			5-2-1	14,400
N. 9	hW	35-7	UT-Chattanooga			6-2-1	25,763
N. 16	hW	41-10	#Wake Forest			7-2-1	28,575
N. 30	hW	20-16	#Georgia	20		8-2-1	59,602
D. 31	nW	17-14	#Michigan St. (All-American Bowl)			9-2-1	45,000

1986: 5-5-1, 3-3 ACC (4th)

Captains: Cory Collier, Kyle Ambrose, Bart Jones

Date	Result		Opponent	GT	Opp	Rec	Att
S. 13	hT	17-17	Furman			0-0-1	33,352
S. 20	aW	28-14	Virginia			1-0-1	34,800
S. 27	hL	3-27	#Clemson			1-1-1	46,062
O. 4	aL	20-21	North Carolina			1-2-1	50,000
O. 11	hW	59-21	#NC State			2-2-1	24,110
O. 18	aL	10-31	Auburn	7		2-3-1	72,500
O. 25	hW	14-13	#Tennessee			3-3-1	28,432
N. 1	hW	34-6	Duke			4-3-1	37,102
N. 8	hW	52-6	VMI			5-3-1	23,542
N. 22	aL	21-24	#Wake Forest			5-4-1	17,300
N. 29	aL	24-31	#Georgia	18		5-5-1	82,122

1987: 2-9, 0-6 ACC (8th)

Captains: Ivery Lee, Malcolm King

Date	Result		Opponent	GT	Opp	Rec	Att
S. 12	hW	51-12	The Citadel			1-0	31,211
S. 19	hL	23-30	North Carolina			1-1	33,151
S. 26	aL	12-33	#Clemson		9	1-2	80,000
O. 3	aL	0-17	#NC State			1-3	36,300
O. 10	hW	38-0	Indiana State			2-3	30,039
O. 17	hL	10-20	Auburn		5	2-4	45,559
O. 24	aL	15-29	Tennessee		13	2-5	93,011
O. 31	aL	14-48	Duke			2-6	30,800
N. 7	hL	14-23	#Virginia			2-7	38,111
N. 21	hL	6-33	Wake Forest			2-8	21,114
N. 28	hL	16-30	#Georgia		14	2-9	45,103

1988: 3-8, 0-7 ACC (8th)

Captains: Eric Bearden, Cedric Stallworth

Date	Result		Opponent	GT	Opp	Rec	Att
S. 10	hW	24-10	UT-Chattanooga			1-0	22,720
S. 17	aL	16-17	#Virginia			1-1	24,800
S. 24	hL	13-30	Clemson		12	1-2	45,106
O. 1	hL	6-14	#NC State			1-3	36,892
O. 8	aL	8-13	#Maryland			1-4	36,969
O. 15	hW	34-0	South Carolina		8	2-4	45,103
O. 22	aL	17-20	North Carolina			2-5	42,000
O. 29	hL	21-31	Duke			2-6	40,393
N. 5	hW	34-7	VMI			3-6	26,923
N. 12	aL	24-28	Wake Forest			3-7	21,500
N. 26	aL	3-24	#Georgia		20	3-8	82,011

1989: 7-4, 4-3 ACC (T-4th)

Captains: Jerry Mays, Eric Thomas

Date	Result		Opponent	GT	Opp	Rec	Att
S. 9	aL	28-38	#NC State		25	0-1	40,800
S. 16	hL	10-17	#Virginia			0-2	38,062
S. 23	aL	10-21	South Carolina			0-3	70,018
O. 7	hW	28-24	Maryland			1-3	32,062
O. 14	aW	30-14	Clemson		14	2-3	82,500
O. 21	hW	17-14	North Carolina			3-3	41,114
O. 28	aL	19-30	Duke			3-4	38,621
N. 4	hW	34-7	Western Carolina			4-4	28,821
N. 18	hW	43-14	#Wake Forest			5-4	26,114
N. 25	hW	13-12	Boston College			6-4	28,221
D. 2	hW	33-22	Georgia			7-4	46,064

1990: 11-0-1, 6-0-1 ACC (1st) ★ ◆

National Champions (UPI)
Atlantic Coast Conference Champions

Captains: Darryl Jenkins, Jerimiah McClary

Date	Result		Opponent	GT	Opp	Rec	Att
S. 8	hW	21-13	#NC State			1-0	40,021
S. 22	hW	44-9	UT-Chattanooga			2-0	32,911
S. 29	hW	27-6	#South Carolina	25/NR		3-0	46,011
O. 6	aW	31-3	#Maryland	23/18		4-0	31,941
O. 13	hW	21-19	#Clemson	18/15	15/14	5-0	46,066
O. 20	aT	13-13	North Carolina	11/11		5-0-1	48,000
O. 27	hW	48-31	#Duke	16/12		6-0-1	44,061
N. 3	aW	41-38	#Virginia	16/14	1/1	7-0-1	49,700
N. 10	hW	6-3	Virginia Tech	7/7		8-0-1	43,011
N. 17	aW	42-7	Wake Forest	4/5		9-0-1	13,493
D. 1	aW	40-23	#Georgia	2/3		10-0-1	82,122
J. 1	nW	45-21	#Nebraska (FL Citrus Bowl)	2/2.19/13		11-0-1	73,328

Note: For 1990, rankings listed are AP / UPI. Beginning with 1991, rankings listed are AP / USA Today.

1991: 8-5, 5-2 ACC (T-2nd) ◆

Captains: Mike Mooney, Willie Clay, Steve Pharr

Date	Result	Opponent	GT Opp	Rec	Att
A. 31	nL 22-34	#Penn State (Kickoff Classic, E. Rutherford, N.J.)	*8/6 ...7/8	0-1	77,409
S. 14	aW 30-14	Boston College	17/18	1-1	26,108
S. 19	hW 24-21	#Virginia (Thursday)	17/19	2-1	42,192
S. 28	aL 7-9	#Clemson	19/18 ...7/5	2-2	83,500
O. 5	aL 21-28	#NC State	21/23 ..19/18	2-3	44,105
O. 12	hW 34-10	#Maryland		3-3	42,011
O. 19	aL 14-23	South Carolina		3-4	67,220
O. 26	hW 35-14	#North Carolina		4-4	45,542
N. 2	aW 17-6	Duke		5-4	38,732
N. 9	hW 19-17	Furman		6-4	40,039
N. 16	hW 27-3	#Wake Forest		7-4	38,124
N. 30	hL 15-18	#Georgia	25/NR	7-5	46,053
D. 25	nW 18-17	#Stanford (Aloha Bowl)	17/17	8-5	34,433

Preseason poll

1992: 5-6, 4-4 ACC (T-4th)

Captains: Shawn Jones, Coleman Rudolph, Kevin Battle, Steve Pharr

Date	Result	Opponent	GT Opp	Rec	Att
S. 12	hW 37-19	Western Carolina	24/24	1-0	41,911
S. 19	aL 24-55	Virginia	22/20 ..20/19	1-1	42,100
S. 26	hW 20-16	#Clemson	16/14	2-1	46,033
O. 3	hW 16-13	#NC State	23/23 ..21/18	3-1	40,761
O. 10	aW 28-26	Maryland	17/17	4-1	26,250
O. 17	hL 29-24	#Florida State	16/17 ....6/6	4-2	46,226
O. 24	aL 14-26	#North Carolina	19/19	4-3	52,800
O. 31	hW 20-17	#Duke		5-3	44,129
N. 7	aL 27-31	Baylor		5-4	38,213
N. 14	hL 23-10	Wake Forest		5-5	40,066
N. 28	aL 17-31	#Georgia	9/10	5-6	85,434

1993: 5-6, 3-5 ACC (6th)

Captains: Tom Johnson, Dorsey Levens

Date	Result	Opponent	GT Opp	Rec	Att
S. 11	hW 37-3	Furman		1-0	43,200
S. 16	hL 14-35	#Virginia (Thursday)	25/23	1-1	41,300
S. 25	aL 13-16	Clemson		1-2	75,000
O. 2	aL 0-51	#Florida State	1/1	1-3	74,611
O. 9	hW 38-0	Maryland		2-3	36,218
O. 16	hL 3-41	#North Carolina	14/13	2-4	39,216
O. 23	aL 23-28	#NC State		2-5	40,123
O. 30	aW 47-14	#Duke		3-5	30,470
N. 6	hW 37-27	Baylor		4-5	42,175
N. 13	aW 38-28	#Wake Forest		5-5	21,113
N. 25	hL 10-43	#Georgia (Thanksgiving)		5-6	46,018

1994: 1-10, 0-8 ACC (9th)

Captains: Jason Bender, Jamal Cox

Date	Result	Opponent	GT Opp	Rec	Att
S. 1	hL 14-19	#Arizona (Thursday)	*7/8	0-1	45,112
S. 10	hW 45-26	Western Carolina		1-1	40,012
S. 24	hL 12-27	Duke		1-2	40,107
O. 1	aL 13-21	#NC State	22/20	1-3	43,216
O. 8	aL 24-31	#North Carolina	14/14	1-4	52,200
O. 15	hL 7-24	Virginia		1-5	38,365
O. 22	aL 27-42	Maryland		1-6	30,429
N. 5	hL 10-41	#Florida State	8/6	1-7	45,206
N. 12	aL 10-20	#Clemson		1-8	71,000
N. 19	hL 13-20	Wake Forest		1-9	35,706
N. 25	aL 10-48	#Georgia (Friday)		1-10	84,113

Note: Arizona was the preseason No. 1 by Sports Illustrated.

Note: George O'Leary was named interim head coach on Nov. 7, 1994, with three games remaining in the season. He was named permanently on Nov. 28, 1994.

1995: 6-5, 5-3 ACC (4th)

Captains: Michael Cheever, Donnie Davis, Ryan Stewart

Date	Result	Opponent	GT Opp	Rec	Att
S. 2	hW 51-7	#Furman		1-0	38,511
S. 7	aL 19-20	#Arizona (Thursday)	17/15	1-1	46,786
S. 16	aL 41-14	Virginia	16/17	1-2	36,500
S. 28	hW 31-3	#Maryland (Thursday)	16/17	2-2	44,137
O. 7	aW 37-21	Duke		3-2	20,110
O. 14	hW 27-25	#North Carolina		4-2	40,201
O. 21	aL 10-42	#Florida State	1/1	4-3	76,400
O. 28	hL 3-24	#Clemson		4-4	45,245
N. 4	aW 24-23	Wake Forest		5-4	23,114
N. 11	hW 27-19	NC State		6-4	33,121
N. 23	hL 17-18	#Georgia (Thanksgiving)		6-5	46,205

1996: 5-6, 4-4 ACC (5th)

Captains: Curtis McGee, Nathan Perryman

Date	Result	Opponent	GT Opp	Rec	Att
S. 7	aW 28-16	#NC State		1-0	41,500
S. 14	hW 30-10	Wake Forest		2-0	45,750
S. 21	aL 0-16	#North Carolina	11/13	2-1	50,000
S. 26	hW 48-22	#Duke (Thursday)		3-1	44,145
O. 5	hW 13-7	#Virginia	12/11	4-1	44,900
O. 19	aL 25-28	#Clemson	22/24	4-2	70,000
O. 26	hW 27-20	#Central Florida		5-2	43,610
N. 2	hL 3-49	#Florida State	3/2	5-3	46,311
N. 14	aL 10-13	#Maryland (Thursday)		5-4	22,510
N. 23	hL 26-36	Navy		5-5	44,415
N. 30	aL 10-19	#Georgia		5-6	78,062

1997: 7-5, 5-3 ACC (T-3rd) ◆

Captains: Keith Brooking, Ken Celaj, Harvey Middleton, Ron Rogers

Date	Result		Opponent	GT	Opp	Rec	Att
S. 6	aL	13-17	#Notre Dame	11/13		0-1	80,225
S. 20	aW	28-26	Wake Forest			1-1	22,832
S. 27	hW	23-20	#Clemson	17/21		2-1	45,275
O. 4	aW	42-14	#Boston College			3-1	38,462
O. 11	hW	27-17	#NC State	25/NR		4-1	44,915
O. 18	aL	0-38	#Florida State	21/25	3/3	4-2	78,157
O. 30	hL	13-16	#North Carolina (Thursday)	5/5		4-3	45,126
N. 8	aL	31-35	#Virginia			4-4	41,000
N. 15	aW	41-38	Duke			5-4	22,638
N. 22	hW	37-18	#Maryland			6-4	35,267
N. 29	hL	24-27	#Georgia	14/14		6-5	46,015
D. 29	nW	35-30	#West Virginia (Carquest Bowl)			7-5	28,262

1998: 10-2, 7-1 ACC (T-1st) ★ ◆

Atlantic Coast Conference Co-Champions

Captains: Jerry Caldwell, Charlie Rogers, Kofi Smith

Date	Result		Opponent	GT	Opp	Rec	Att
S. 5	hL	31-41	#Boston College			0-1	38,229
S. 12	hW	42-7	New Mexico State			1-1	36,382
S. 26	aW	43-21	#North Carolina			2-1	59,500
O. 3	aW	41-13	#Duke			3-1	35,724
O. 10	aW	47-24	#NC State	23/23		4-1	48,600
O. 17	hW	41-38	#Virginia	25/25	7/6	5-1	46,018
O. 24	hL	7-34	#Florida State	20/19	6/6	5-2	46,362
O. 31	aW	31-14	#Maryland*	23/24		6-2	25,183
N. 12	aW	24-21	#Clemson (Thursday)	22/23		7-2	62,000
N. 21	hW	63-35	Wake Forest	21/21		8-2	40,110
N. 28	aW	21-19	#Georgia	17/18	12/12	9-2	86,117
J. 1	nW	35-28	#Notre Dame (Toyota Gator Bowl)	12/12	17/18	10-2	70,791

Ravens Stadium at Camden Yards, Baltimore, Md.

1999: 8-4, 5-3 ACC (T-2nd) ◆

Captains: Joe Hamilton, Travares Tillman

Date	Result		Opponent	GT	Opp	Rec	Att
S. 4	aW	49-14	#Navy	10/11		1-0	30,311
S. 11	aL	35-41	#Florida State	10/10	1/1	1-1	80,187
S. 18	hW	41-10	Central Florida	12/13		2-1	45,355
S. 30	hW	49-31	#Maryland (Thursday)	10/12		3-1	44,612
O. 9	hW	31-24	#North Carolina (OT)	7/8		4-1	46,110
O. 16	aW	38-31	#Duke	8/9		5-1	16,648
O. 30	hW	48-21	#NC State	7/7		6-1	46,012
N. 6	aL	38-45	#Virginia	7/7		6-2	44,500
N. 13	hW	45-42	#Clemson	13/14		7-2	46,085
N. 20	aL	23-26	Wake Forest	14/12		7-3	25,230
N. 27	hW	51-48	#Georgia (OT)	20/16	16/21	8-3	46,450
J. 1	nL	13-28	#Miami (Toyota Gator Bowl)	17/15	23/23	8-4	43,416

Georgia Lettermen

(a) = alternate captain
(at) = assistant trainer
(c) = captain
(h) = honorary
(m) = manager
(t) = trainer
(v) = video

A

Aaron, Phil 1978
Abram, John Desmond ...1985-86-87
Adams, Donald (t)............1957
Adams, Gary..........1965-66-67
Adams, Scott Alexander ..1985-86-87-88
Adrine, Bruce Earl 1998-99
Ainslie, William (m).........1942
Akacki, John 1979
Albright, Zach (m) 1997
Alexander, Brantley (m) ...1958
Alexander, Eugene .1944-45-46
Alford, Neal (t).................1946
Allen, Corey Demond 1994-95-96-97
Allen, Donnie 1970-71-72
Allen, Ed....................1968-69
Allen, Heyward (c) 1939-40-41
Allen, John Reed 1988-91
Allen, Robert 1960-61-62
Allen, V............................1902
Allsion, Robert 1979
Almond, Kevin (t) .1975-76-78
Amtower, Frederick 1960-61
Anderson, Alfred ...1934-35-36
Anderson, Charles............1953
Anderson, Michael.1956-57-58
Anderson, Paul Kemper ..1920-22
Anderson, Peter Richard (c) 1983-84-85
Anderson, Sheldon Claus1987-88
Andrews, E.E.(m)............1919
Andrews, Melvin ("Chip") 1983-84
Andrews, William Edwin 1989-90
Andros, Chris H. 1986
Anglin, Bobby........1950-51-52
Ansley, Abb (c) 1972-73-74
Ansley, Brad 1982-83
Anthony, Thurston Lafayette 1919-20-21-23
Appleby, Richard ...1973-74-75

B

Babb, Michael........1961-62-63
Babcock, Harry......1950-51-52
Baccus, Pat (m) 1955
Badgett, Willis 1936-37-38
Bailey, Derrick Terrell 1991
Bailey, Sam M..............1944-45
Bailey, Robert, Jr. 1960
Bailey, Robert Henry.........1985
Bailey, Rodney A. ("Boss") 1998-99
Bailey, Roland, ("Champ")(c)....1996-97-98
Bailey, Ronald Marcus 1995-96-97
Baker, Buck......................1968
Baker, Jim..............1973-74-75
Baker, Mike (t) .1988-89-90-91
Baker, Sam ("Buck")....1972-73
Baker, Ted 1992
Baker, Theodore Stuart (m) 1992
Ballard, Marty 1979-80
Barbas, Constino John......1944
Barber, Fred, Jr. 1962-63-64
Barbre, Ned C. 1937-38
Barchan, Joe 1919
Barnum, Casey Eugene....1989, 91-92

Barrett, Pearce, Jr.............1942
Barrow, Craig 1893-95
Barrow, Thomas A. 1902
Barrow, Craig, Jr.(m) 1928
Bartenfeld, Charles (m) ...1955-56
Bartenfeld, Richard (m)....1957
Bass, Wesley E..................1925
Bassett, Troy Christopher .1992
Batchelor, Graham (c)1931-32-33
Battey, George McGruder .1906
Baxter, Julian F. 1900-01-02
Beadles, Resty Alan 1994-95-96
Beall, Jeremiah 1997
Beasley, Donald Griffith(m) 1985-86-87
Beasley, Russell Brian .1985-86-87-88
Beasley, Tom R..1915-16-17-18
Beaver, Sandy..............1901-02
Beckwith, Charles 1950-51
Bedingfield, Walter 1959-60
Belflower, Charles Scott (m) 1985
Belk, Robert 1943
Bell, Greg 1977-78-79-80
Bell, Herman..............1993-94
Bell, John...............1953-54-55
Bell, Kendrell A. 1999
Bell, Robert Lionel 1988-89
Belson, Marty (m) 1986
Belue, Benjamin F.(c) .1978-79-80-81
Bennett, Brad (m) 1983-84
Bennett, Daniel Paige ...1920-21
Bennett, Joseph 1929
Bennett, Roger 1977-78
Bennett, Jasper Carl, Jr. 1930-31
Bennett, Joe J., Jr.(c) ..1920-21-22-23
Benton, Gene 1943
Benton, Phillip Todd ...1994-95
Berry, Illya Hiawatha..1986-87-88-89
Betsill, Roy..................1959-60
Bierria, Terreal M.............1999
Bilyeu, Fred 1950-51-52
Biser, Mark (t)............1971-72
Bishop, Alan....................1956
Bissell, Hal 1971-72
Black, Charles H. 1898
Black, Dameron...............1904

Black, J.C. 1892-93
Blackburn, Donald (a) 1960-61-62
Blackburn, Donnie (m) 1989
Blackman, Lew..................1994
Blackmon, Joe W.........1919-20
Blakewood, James C. ..1979-80-81
Blalock, Stanley 1984-85
Blanch, Wright B. 1896
Blanchard, Elmer 1961
Blank, John Fletcher (m) ...1985
Blanton, Brooker, Jr. 1940
Bobo, Timothy Owens 1980-81-82
Bobo, Robert Michael (c) 1994-95-96-97
Bodine, Alvin (a) ...1947-48-49
Boersig, Dave.........1976-77-78
Bohannon, Brian Lloyd ...1990-91-92-93
Boland, Joseph H.(c) .1927-28-29
Boland, Frank Kels, Jr. 1924-25-26
Boler, Sylvester............1973-74
Bond, Claude (t) 1948
Bond, Ed V. 1897
Bond, John (c) 1933-34-35

Boney, Sam M. 1921-22
Born, Wade H. 1895
Boshears, Buster (at)........1964, 1966
Bostwick, Henry G......1908-09
Bostwick, Hugh (c) 1908-09
Boswell, Steve (c) .1983-84-85-86
Bouchillon, Keith........1979-80
Bouley, Laurent 1944-45
Bowden, Timon D. 1910-11-12
Bowen, Marcus..................1966
Bowen, Michael...............1987
Bower, John D. 1902-03
Bowers, Brian Ward..........1990
Bowers, Nelson (t,m)...1966-67
Bowie, Larry Darnell, Jr...1994-95
Bowles, Jessie G. 1944
Box, Aaron 1957-58-59
Box, Gary ("Butch") ...1973-74-75-76
Boyd, Benny 1962-63
Boyd, Mike (m)...........1968-69
Boyd, Sterling 1993

Boyd, Willard...................1942
Boykin, Richard.....1961-62-63
Boynton, Rooks...............1961
Bracco, Nicholas.........1957-58
Brackett, Neal..............1984 (t)
Bradberry, George.1944-46-47-48
Bradley, Richard 1959
Bradley, Rolando Tangier.1997-98
Bradshaw, William..1947-48-49-50
Bramlett, Randy 1975
Brandon, Collin Vincent-Roy ...1991
Brannen, Jim (t).....1976-77-79
Brannen, Millard 1968
Brannon, Mike (t) 1992-93
Brantley, John P.(c)..1984-85-86-87
Brantley, Wayne 1963-64-65
Brasher, Larry 1968-69-70
Braswell, Kim 1970-71-72
Braswell, Matt ..1976-77-78-79
Braswell, Stewart (m) 1991
Bratkowski, Edmund ("Zeke") (c)...................1951-52-53
Bratton, Edgar 1943
Bray, Mell....................1941-46
Bray, Ralph.......................1965
Breedlove, Kevin J. 1999
Brewer, George Bernard....1989
Brice, Billy 1968-70-71
Brice, Frank 1972-73
Bridges, Stacy Kyle (t) 1985
Bright, Timothy Gregory.1994-95-96-97
Brinson, Michael D. 1983-84
Britt, Charles William 1957-58-59
Broadnax, John E. 1926-27
Broadnax, O. Sam (m)......1931
Broadway, James M....1980-81-82
Brookins, Tate (m) 1992-93
Brookins, Tripp (m)..........1989
Brooks, Steve....................1977
Broom, Christopher Hase1988-89-90
Brown, David 1960
Brown, Frederick...1958-59-60
Brown, Henry C...........1892-93
Brown, James.........1954-55-56
Brown, James A. ...1979-81-82-83
Brown, John C...... 1932-33-34
Brown, John A. 1903-04-06
Brown, Johnny S. 1999
Brown, Johnny Louis ..1945-46
Brown, Kevin Dewitt .1986-87-88-89
Brown, Larry 1984-85-86
Brown, Larry Lovett...1995-96-97-98

Brown, Lloyd D.(m) 1911
Brown, Michael Stuart 1985-86-87
Brown, Norris W. .1979-80-81-82
Brown, Sam 1932-33
Brown, Steve.............1968-69
Brown, William Wedford..1906
Brown, Woodrow........1939-40
Brownholtz, Scott K. 1993-94
Broyles, Edwin N. 1912-13
Broyles, N.A. 1919
Bruce, Milton.........1971-72-73
Brunson, Lewis.1947-48-49-50
Bryan, Kenneth M. 1984
Bryan, William, Jr............1944
Bryant, Stephen H.(t).1979-80-81
Bryant, Vernon H. 1928
Buckler, Alonzo M. 1980-81
Bulloch, Cyprian 1965
Burgamy, Jeff, Jr. 1950-51
Burke, Fred 1943
Burkhalter, Edward 1956
Burnett, Cap 1999
Burnett, Doug.............1971-72
Burns, Bob (c) 1971-72-73
Burns, Sam (c) 1970
Burroughs, G. Mack ..1984-85-86-87
Burroughs, Steve 1983
Burson, Joseph 1962-64-65
Burt, Will...................1940-41
Burt, William 1953
Bush, Jackson 1946-47-48
Bush, Marion 1956
Butler, Carlo Durane 1990, 1992-93
Butler, Curry (m) 1977-78
Butler, George P.(c) 1892-93-94
Butler, Jacob J...1922-23-24-25
Butler, Kevin G.(c)1981-82-83-84
Buttolph, Lyman, Jr.(m) ...1943
Byars, Charles 1956
Byrd, Derrick M....1993, 1996-97
Byrd, Gregg (h) 1970
Byrd, Henry 1943
Byrd, Wayne..........1967-68-69
Byus, Harry (t) .1988-89-90-91

C

Cagle, Jim..............1971-72-73
Caldwell, John 1967-68
Calhoun, Andrew............1901
Callaway, Nick 1998-99
Callaway, Tim 1967-68-69
Calloway, Selma W. 1994-95-96-97
Camp, Drew.....................1998
Camp, John (m) 1978
Camp, Preston (m)..........1971
Campagna, James ..1952-53-54

Campbell, John 1952
Campbell, Johnny.......1969-70
Campbell, Kevin B.(t).......1995
Campbell, Marion (a) 1949-50-51
Campbell, Robert L.(m) ...1990
Campbell, Scott...............1983
Campbell, William Harold, Jr. ..1919-20
Cancel, Jason (m).............1994
Candler, Asa 1934-35-36
Cantrell, Gary 1983-84
Caprara, Anthony 1951-52
Carden, Joel 1963
Carpenter, Cris Howell ...1985-86
Carrollton, William 1954-55
Carson, Johnny.......1950-52-53
Carswell, Charles Edward (c) ...1988-90-91
Carter, Ed V. 1909
Carter, Millard Filmore.....1939
Carter, Quincy L. (c)...1998-99
Carter, Rusty 1971-72
Carver, Dale K.(c).1979-80-81-82
Case, Ronald Lee ("Pete") (c)....1959-60-61
Case, Timothy, R....1980-81-82
Case, Jr., Clifford 1960
Casey, J. V. ("Sonny")........1957
Castronis, Mike J.(c,a).....1943-44-45
Cate, Vassa (c) 1937-38-39
Causey, Paul L. 1936
Cavan, Mike 1968-69-70
Cavan, James, Jr............1936-37
Cawthon, Mike 1971
Cescutti, Brad 1974-75-76
Chadwick, Andrew Simon..1992
Chafin, Charles Steve 1982
Chamberlin, Steve 1969-71
Chambers, Douglas A.(t).1982-83-84
Chambers, Earl Lamont ..1996-97-98-99
Chambers, Jeffery (t) 1990
Chandler, Bob 1969
Chandler, Charles 1952
Chandler, Edgar 1965-66-67
Chandler, Spurgeon ...1929-30-31
Chandler, Eugene, Jr..1946-47-48-49
Chandley, David I.(t)...1982-83
Chapman, Andy (m)...1981-82
Chapman, George..1932-33-34
Chapman, Tim (m,t)...1980-81
Charping, Stanmore G. 1982
Chavious, Charles 1972
Cheek, George 1961
Chesna, Joe L. 1945
Cheves, James P...........1919-20
Childers, Clyde...........1960-61

Childs, R.R. 1911
Chonko, Bill 1943-44-45
Chosewood, Chadwick ...1992-93-94-95
Christian, Charles D. .1939-40-41
Christian, Robert (m) 1947
Christianson, David 1972-74
Christie, Robert (m) 1959
Chubb, Aaron Nathaniel .1985-86-87-88
Chumley, Donald W.(c)...1982-83-84
Clamon, Joe 1967-68
Clanton, Michael D.(t) 1986-87-88
Clark, Cleve..........1953-54-55
Clark, David Michael 1985
Clark, Dicky (c).....1974-75-76
Clark, Greg (m) 1983-84-85
Clark, Matthew J. 1982
Clark, Ralph....................1973
Clark, Raymond (c)...1960-61-62
Clark, Stan (t)........1974-75-76
Clarke, Arthur.................1897
Clarke, Lee A. 1995
Clarke, T. Burton..............1897
Clarke, W.W. 1894-95
Clay, Frank.....................1905
Clay, Herbert 1901
Cleckley, Hervey 1922-23
Clemens, Robert (a)...1952-53-54
Clemons, Charlie F (c)1992-93
Cleveland, Brian Keith (c) 1988-89-90
Cleveland, Robert.............1957
Clincy, Anthony 1984-85
Cloer, Billy 1965
Coates, Jesse 1892
Cobb, Johnny..................1971
Cocke, Jr., Erle (m) 1941
Cochran, Antonio 1997-98
Cochran, JoAnna (t) 1994
Colby, Glenn 1907
Cole, Bill 1978
Cole, Bobby Virgil.......1988-89
Cole, Jimps Wooster ...1987-89
Cole, Mike 1963
Coleman, John S. .1914-15-16-17-18
Colley, William Richard ..1988-89
Collier, Barry 1972-73-74
Collier, Steve 1975-76-77
Collings, Jr., David A. 1919-20-21-22
Collins, Bobby (m) 1977-79-80
Collins, Donnie Ray 1989-90
Collins, George (c).1975-76-77
Collins, James Brent....1986-87
Collins, Odell 1995-96
Collins, Pat 1977-78-79

Comfort, Joseph 1955-56-57
Cone, James................1960-61
Coney, Eric Eugene 1990-91
Conger, Melvin................1941
Conklin, Hughbert William......
  1910-11-12-13
Conn, Dick............1971-72-73
Connally, Joe 1948
Connally, Joe Brown..1895-1948
Connan, Mandy (t) 1994
Conyers, James Bennett ..1911-
  12-13-14-15
Cook, Buster 1928
Cook, Fred Hills, Jr. 1989
Cook, Harold Dean.....1953-56
Cook, Johnny 1943-46
Cook, Malcolm......1949-50-51
Cook, Randy 1977-78-79
Cooley, James 1964-65-66
Cooley, Michael..1944-45-46-47
Cooper, Clenton 1955-56-57
Cooper, David 1966
Cooper, Lawson 1995
Cooper, Rahmon Debray ..1996
Cooper, William A. ("Bull") ......
  1931-32-33
Cooper, William Anthony
  ("Bill") (t) 1958
Coram, Jay (t) 1978
Coram, John (t)...............1977
Cordell, Lew 1934
Costa, Leonard, Jr. ...1940-41-
  42
Cothran, Walter S. 1895-96
Couch, Tommy......1969-70-71
Covington, Dean (m) 1936
Covington, Leon H. 1910-12
Cowan, Zach (m) 1912
Cowins, Norman Louis ...1988-
  89
Cox, Bryant 1943
Cox, Charles..........1903-04-06
Cox, Harmon 1898
Cox, John B. 1909-10
Cox, Marvin 1930
Craft, Lawrence 1974-75-76
Crane, George S. 1893
Crawford, Stanley ..1964-65-66
Crawford, James Ray, Jr. ..1962-
  63-64
Creamons, Joseph K. ..1979-80-
  81
Creech, Glenn.............1964-65
Creech, Glenn Eldon........1986
Crenshaw, McCarthy...1930-31
Crisp, Dan 1976
Cronick, Andrew 1996-97
Crook, Melvin.............1962-63
Crouch, Joe 1932
Crowe, Timothy F.(c) .1979-80-
  81-82
Crumley, Jonathon Steven ....
  1985-86-87-88
Crump, Stephen A.1911-12-13

Culpepper, Knox (c)..1954-55-
  56
Culpepper, W. Knox (c) ..1981-
  82-83-84
Cumming, D.R. 1909
Cummings, David 1959
Cunard, Vernon 1958
Curington, Jim 1971-72-73
Curran, Jack 1924-25-26
Curtis, Roy 1981
Cushenberry, Anthony 1954-
  55-56

D

Daniel, Lee (c) 1967-68-69
Daniels, Juan D. ...1993-94-95-
  96
Daniels, Phillip (c)1992-93-94-
  95
Dantzler, Danny 1971-72-73
Darby, Billy (c).......1968-69-70
Darden, Joel 1962-63-64
Daugherty, Jim S. 1895
David, Drew Daniel (c) ...1991-
  92-93-94
David, William............1932-33
Davidson, John 1929-30
Davis, B 1908-1909
Davis, Brent 1996
Davis, Dan 1960
Davis, Doug 1998-99
Davis, Edward H. 1930
Davis, Glenn 1968-69
Davis, Hal 1955-58
Davis, Hinton 1959-60
Davis, J.B.(c)..........1955-56-57
Davis, John 1936-37
Davis, Ken 1963-64-65
Davis, Lamar 1940-41-42
Davis, Louis Seaborn........1915
Davis, Mitchell Lestron (c) ....
  1990-91-92-93
Davis, Paul Jack 1965-66
Davis, Quentin A..1996-97-98-
  99
Davis, R. Cooper 1909
Davis, Steve 1974-75-76
Davis, Terrell Lamar...1992-93-
  94
Davis, Van 1940-41-42
Davis, Wallace R...............1999
Davis, William M.(m).......1900
Day, A.M. (c) 1919-20-21
Day, T. Roosevelt 1923-24
Dean, Charlie 1981-82-83
Dean, Sidney 1901
Deavers, Clayton ...1944-46-47
Decarlo, Arthur, Jr. ...1950-51-
  52
Decharleroy, Abert............1938
DeFoor, Russell Baxter 1988-
  89-90-91
Delaperriere, Arthur L......1911-
  12-13

Delaperriere, Herman P. (c) ......
  1905-06-07-08
Deleski, Gerald 1945-46
Dellinger, Robert 1952
Demersseman, Paul..........1975
Demos, George.................1970
Dennard, Anthony.1964-65-66
Denney, Jimmy 1964-65
Dennis, Steve (c) ...1976-77-78
Denyer, Richard 1977
Derrick, Claude................1908
Dewitt, Ashley (t)........1989-90
Dezendorf, E.H. 1915-1916
Dicharry, Ray...................1970
Dickens, Marion 1929-30-31
Dickens, Pete 1963-64-65
Dickinson, Marvin D. 1900-01-
  02
Dicks, Robert ("Happy") .1966-
  67-68
Dickson, Matt R. 1995-96
Dilts, Douglas ("Bucky") .1974-
  75-76
Dipietro, Francis 1951
Dixon, Timothy Micahel ..1985
Dobbs, George 1950-51
Donaldson, John ..1945-46-47-
  48
Donaldson, Ray 1977-78-79
Donnelly, William P....1916-17-
  18
Dooley, Stan............1981-82-83
Dooley, Vincent Daniel (m) ......
  1985
Dooley, Vincent J. (h) 1988
Dorsey, Cam D.......1900-01-02
Dorsey, Ed H. 1913
Dorsey, W. 1904
Dotson, Richard Andrew.1986-
  87
Doubek, Richard F.(t) 1983
Douglas, Curtis Michael..1988-
  89-91
Douglas, Demetrius ...1986-87-
  88-89
Downes, Austin, Jr. (c)....1929-
  30-31
Drayton, Keith Dewayne ..1995
Driskell, Kenneth D. 1984
Dubignon, Charles...........1898
Dudish, Andrew 1940-41-42
Dudley, Frank C..........1927-28
Duke, John 1948-49-50
Dukes, David W. ..1984-85-86-
  87
Dukes, Leroy 1962-63-64
Dukes, Jr., Henry ...1955-56-57
Dumbleton, Ken 1970
Dupree, Joseph, Jr. 1990
Dupriest, Bob.............1967-68
Durand, Robert...........1949-50
Dye, Nat (a)...........1956-57-58
Dye, Patrick (a)......1958-59-60
Dye, Wayne, Jr.......1954-55-56

E

Eades, Mark S.(t)..............1988
Earnest, Charles 1951-52-53
Eaves, Charles (c) ..1943-44-45
Eberhart, Robert (m)........1984
Echols, W.R. 1920
Edwards, Dan (c) .1944-45-46-
  47
Edwards, Robert L.(c)1993-94-
  96-97
Edwards, Terrence J. 1999
Egins, Paul (t) 1986
Ehrhardt, Clyde 1941-42
Eldredge, Knox......1937-38-39
Elkins, Sylvester...............1979
Ellenson, Eugene ...1940-41-42
Ellis, Alphonso.1987-88-89-90
Ellspermann, Lenny 1971-72
Elrod, Craig...........1966-68-69
Elsberry, Kent (t).........1989-90
Engel, Wayne 1965-66-67
England, Jon 1997-98
Epperson, Rusty..........1967-68
Eskew, Sammy 1970-71
Estes, A.B. 1910
Estes, Roy E...........1925-26-27
Etheridge, Paul William-1989-
  90-91-92
Etter, Robert 1964-65-66
Eubank, Nathan B.......1925-26
Eubanks, Preston (m) .1971-72
Evans, Damon M..1989-90-91-
  92
Evans, Demetric U. 1998-99
Evans, Robert P................1966
Evans, Torrey Foster ..1989-90-
  91-92
Evans, Vance..........1963-64-65
Everett, Thomas Bailey.....1996
Ewings, Landy 1981
Exley, James W. 1994
Ezelle, Percy P..................1893

F

Faircloth, MacArthur .1961-63-
  64
Fales, Charlie.........1976-77-78
Farah, Freddy 1960
Farish, James 1951-52
Farmer, Steven (m)...........1998
Farnsworth, Rick 1972-73
Farnsworth, Steve..1967-68-69
Farriba, Mark 1977
Farris, E. 1906
Faulkner, Darrell 1975
Feagin, Robert Douglas, Jr. (m)
  1929
Feher, Nick 1947-48-49-50
Fellows, Michael Scott 1989-
  90, 1992-93
Fender, W.B......................1893
Ferguson, Jason O.(c) .1995-96
Ferguson, J.P. 1916-17-18
Ferguson, Robert Drew (m)......

1973

Fernandez, Vince 1988
Ferrell, Fortune Chisolm..1895
Ferson, Paul 1970-71-72
Ferst, Frank W. 1916
Fesperman, George T.(m.)1923
Field, Patrick 1948-49-50
Filipkowski, Chris 1951-52
Filipovits, Edward .1949-50-51
Finch, Jesse F., Jr. 1989
Fincher, Robert Lee 1989
Finnegan, B.E...................1899
Fisher, Mike 1978-79-80
Fitts, Sheldon 1920
Fitzgerald, Hugh 1904
Fitzpatrick, Henry (m) 1920
Fitzpatrick, Littleton Hill (m)...
    1908-09
Flack, Anthony, T. 1982-83-84-
    85
Fleming, Antonio M. .1994-95-
    96-97
Fleming, Claude A. 1893
Fleming, Paul L.(m)....1893-94
Fleming, Ryan M. 1998-99
Fleming, Thomas Farrar...1907
Fletcher, John...................1973
Fletcher, John H. (c)..1921-22-
    23-24
Florence, Michael (m).1983-84
Flournoy, Walker R. 1913
Floyd, Jay.........................1983
Foran, Pat (t)....1988-89-90-91
Forbes, Walter T., Jr. 1925-26
Ford, Craig Davis 1996
Ford, Glenn Thomas.1994, 96-
    97-98
Ford, George...............1949-50
Fordham, James 1937-38-39
Forehand, Bill 1972
Forts, William B. ..1979-80-81-
    82
Foster, Clayton.................1984
Foster, George A...............1999
Fouch, Larry Earl, Jr. .1990-91-
    92-93
Fowler, William 1954-55
Fox, Glenn (m)...........1953-54
Fox, Lawrence J......1916-17-18
Francis, Albert 1957
Franklin, Allen (v)............1997
Franklin, Neal 1978
Franklin, Omer W.(c)..1909-10
Frate, Paul........................1983
Fredenburg, Michael Lewis ......
    1992
Freedman, Louis....1976-77-78
Freeman, David (m)....1966-67
Fricks, L.D. 1892
Frier, W.R., Jr...................1923
Frisbie, Theodore ..1927-28-29
Frix, James M. 1981-82
Fromm, Richard Friedrich........
    1985-86

Fruehauf, Ben 1953-54
Furchgott, Charles M..1944-45

G

Gaines, Turner P. 1966
Galbreath, Robert.............1958
Gammon, Von Albade
    (Richard)...............1896-97
Gantt, Bryant Keith.....1989-90
Garasic, George 1943
Gardiner, James, Jr. 1931
Garmany, W.W..1914-15-17-18
Garrard, Robert (c) 1952-53-
    54-55
Garrard, William T......1914-15
Garrett, Danny (at)...........1964
Garrett, Mike 1977-78-79
Garrett, Thomas (t) 1960
Gary, Cleveland 1984
Gary, Orlandis (c) 1997-98
Gaston, Marion, Jr.......1932-33
Gatchell, Roy 1935-36
Gates, Steven Donald 1992
Gatewood, James 1947
Gearreld, William P. 1894
George, Carl 1947-48
Geri, Joseph...........1946-47-48
Germany Howard (m).1976-77
Gerson, Joe (m)................1938
Ghedine, Scott J. 1993
Gibbs, Bobby 1973-74
Gibson, Demetrius (m) 1994
Gibson, Quinton Lamar (m).....
    1944
Gilbert Antonio C. 1999
Gilbert Brad (m) 1997-98-99
Gilbert, Freddie G.(c) 1980-81-
    82-83
Gilbert, Paul 1967-69-70
Gilbert, William 1958
Giles, Johnny Paul ..1985-86-87-
    88
Gillespie, Billy (t) 1973-74
Gillespie, B. Russell 1984
Gillespie, Marvin (a)..1936-37-
    38
Gilliam, Rosey...................1977
Gillis, Neal L. (m) 1915
Gilmore, Lloyd............1930-31
Glass, John 1964-65
Glover, Gary.....................1960
Goddard, Charles Odell ...1987
Godfrey, David Aaron 1959-60-
    61
Godfrey, Randall E. 1992-93-
    94-95
Godwin, William 1941-42
Goff, Ray (c) 1974-75-76
Goldberg, William Scott (c)......
    1986-87-88-89
Golden, Don..........1971-72-73
Golf, S.B..........................1899
Gooding, T.H. 1899

Goodman, Winfred..1939-40-41
Goodman, Adrian Paul ...1995-
    96-97-98
Goodwin, Robert ...1977-78-79
Goolsby, Barry (t) 1986
Gordon, Alan Clyde 1989
Gordon, Hugh 1969-70
Gordon, Hugh H..............1900
Gordon, James 1945
Gordy, Leigh Ann (t) 1998
Gouse, Ilyse Lauren..........1996
Grace, David Dawayne1989-90
Graff, Joseph 1953-54
Graham, Don 1968-69
Graham, Hason Arron (c)1992-
    93-94
Grant, Charles G. 1999
Grant, Joseph Arston .1932-33-
    34
Grant, Orantes Laquay (c)........
    1996-97-98-99
Grant, William 1950-51
Grate, Carl 1940
Graves, Richard A. 1906
Gray, Phillip N. 1981
Gray, Daniel Warren 1959
Gray, Warren D.1980-81-82-83
Grayson, Spencer M.........1923
Green, Bobby.........1959-60-61
Green, DeJuan J. 1999
Green, Floyd 1944
Green, Philip 1962
Greene, Daniel T. 1982
Greene, Maurice 1934-35-36
Greene, Mike 1969-70-71
Greene, Robert E. 1993
Greene, Thomas 1939-40-41
Greenway, Brett (m)...1997-98-
    99
Greenway, Edward.1949-50-51
Greer, Michael William ...1997-
    98-99
Greer, Robert 1948-49-50
Greer, Steve (c) 1967-68-69
Griffin, John 1967-69
Griffin, Tuck.....................1903
Griffin, Gerald D., Jr. .1952-53-
    54-55
Griffith, Donald C. 1973
Griffith, Jim 1975-76-77
Griffith, John....................1946
Griffith, Roy...............1908-10
Griffith, Byron, Jr...1932-33-34
Griffith, Vernon 1951-52
Griffith, William A. 1973
Grubbs, Clayton...............1955
Guest, Judson (m) .1979-81-82
Guest, Mack (c) 1976-77-78
Guest, C.B., Jr...........1939-40
Guisler, George 1957-58-59
Gulick, John (m)........1947-48
Gunby, Cooper.................1974
Gunn, Earl.................1951-52
Gunnels, Riley 1956-57-58

Gunnels, Sandy Crawford ....
    1933-34
Gurley, John...............1973-74
Guthrie, Carlton 1961-62-63
Guthrie, David Michael (c).......
    1986-87-88
Guthrie, Ed................1979-80
Guthrie, Gary (m).......1980-81
Guthrie, Vincent Leon 1985-
    86-87-88

H

Hague, Bobby 1943
Haley, Bill.......................1944
Haley, Eugene S. 1927-28
Hall, Burl F. 1915
Hall, James (c) 1934-35-36
Hall, M. Pliny (m) 1895
Hall, Michael Keith 1981
Hall, Orville Duane1915-17-18
Halliburton, Julian (m).....1939
Halsey, A.O. 1892
Halsey, Lindsley (c).1893-1894
Hamilton, Tom 1964
Hamilton, W.....................1899
Hammond, Chris...1971-72-73
Hampton, Donnie..1967-68-69
Hampton, Rodney Craig (c) .....
    1987-88-89
Hamrick, Jim 1930-31
Handmacher, Paul 1966-67
Hansen, Brett 1999
Hansen, George 1957-58
Happe, Joseph H., III.1980-81
Harber, William 1965-66
Hardin, Nat......................1936
Hardwick, Omari L. 1995
Hardy, Wilson M. 1901
Hargett, David Jerome.....1987-
    88-89-91
Hargrove, Lauren...1950-51-52
Harmon, W. 1902
Harmon, Harry, III(c) 1934-35-
    36
Harmon, Harry E., Jr..1906-07
Harmon, Stephen Michael........
    1986-87-88-89
Harper, James Keller ...1919-20
Harper, Jeff 1978-79-80
Harper, Jimmy.......1971-72-73
Harper, Jimmy L...1980-81-82-
    83
Harper, James, Jr. .1952-53-54-
    55
Harrell, James S....1981-82-83-
    84
Harrell, Ronnie Maurice..1991-
    92-93-94
Harris, Benjamin C...........1995
Harris, Charles............1954-55
Harris, Derrick Dewayne..1988
Harris, Henderson............1943
Harris, Henry ...1983-84-85-86
Harris, Jeffrey Terris...1996-97-

98-99

Harris, Keith (c).....1972-73-74

Harris, Kevin G. 1982-83-84

Harris, Robert ("Chuck") 1975-76

Harris, Ronnie W. 1981-82

Harrison, Clyde...............1951

Harrison, Glynn (c) ...1973-74-75

Harrison, Norman............1942

Hartley, Hugh Vinson.......1920

Hartley, Richard 1921

Hartman, Kevin................1973

Hartman, William, Jr. (c) 1935-36-37

Hartridge, Julian 1905

Harvey, Willie Frank..1990-91-92-93

Hastings, Andre Orlando 1990-91-92

Hatcher, Herbert Clifford 1907-08-09-10

Hatcher, Samuel B............1906

Hatcher, William J. 1925-26

Hauss, Leonard......1961-62-63

Hay, Hafford....................1910

Hayes, Donald 1965-66-67

Hayes, James T.(m) 1929

Hayes, Zach C.(m) 1923

Haygood, Thomas .1935-36-37

Haynes, Benjamin (m)......1998

Haynes, Verron U. 1999

Hazelhurst, William 1932

Head, James C.(m)...........1924

Heard, Chuck........1969-70-71

Hearin, Gerald 1960

Hearn, William, Jr.......1956-57

Hearst, Gerard Garrison..1990-91-92

Hebbard, Billy (m) 1971

Heidt, Jule......................1898

Helms, Ken...........1974-75-76

Henderson, Jamie.............1999

Henderson, John G.(c)....1912-13-14-15

Henderson, Johnny.....1976-77

Henderson, Keith Pernell ..1985-86-88

Henderson, Rudolph Melvin 1988

Henderson, Terry 1968

Henderson, William ..1946-47-48-49

Hendrix, Hugh 1974-75-76

Hene, Doug......................1998

Herlong, Grig...................1967

Herman, Ronald W...........1984

Herndon, Steven Marshall (c)... 1996-97-98-99

Herron, William..........1958-59

Hertwig, Craig (c)..1972-73-74

Hester, Dennis.......1971-72-73

Hester, Joseph M. .1986-87-88-89

Hewatt, Carlyle 1981-82-83-84

Hewlett, Samuel D..1899-1900

Heyward, George (m).......1902

Hickey, James William 1986-87

Hiers, William Lee, Jr..1944-45

Highsmith, E. Way......1919-20

Hill, B. Harvey 1928

Hill, Cliff (m) 1945

Hill, J.M.(m) 1904

Hill, Jack 1950-51-52

Hillyer, George (m) 1892

Hines, James Harris ...1996-97-98-99

Hipp, Jeff (c)..........1978-79-80

Hipps, Claude (c).1944-49-50-51

Hirsch, D. 1893

Hirsch, Harold, Sr. 1900-01

Hirsch, Harold, Jr............1934

Hise, Earl 1938

Hitchcock, William Edgar 1912-13-14

Hlebovy, Gus 1949-50

Hoage, Terrell L....1980-81-82-83

Hobbs, Homer.......1946-47-48

Hockaday, James E.....1982-83-84-85

Hodge, Mark (c) 1976-77-78

Hodges, Billy 1944-46-47

Hodgson, Hutch 1933

Hodgson, Morton Strahan 1906

Hodgson, Pat.........1963-64-65

Hodgson, Winston 1938

Hogan, Hank 1973

Hoke, Eugene 1903-04

Holland, Randy 1977

Holland, Ward 1937

Holleman, Chad 1998-99

Hollingshed, Adrian L.1997-98

Hollingsworth, Joe 1943

Hollis, Howell T.....1924-25-26

Holmes, Andre.................1983

Holmes, Mark 1966-67

Holmes, John Paul, Jr.1960-61-62

Holt, Tom 1972-73

Holton, Jimmy Bryant.1983-84

Honeycutt, Robert (c)1970-71-72

Hood, Winford D. .1981-82-83

Hooks, Robert G...........1926-28

Hope, Robert 1976-77-78

Hopp, Clifford..................1948

Horne, Everett 1940-41

Horne, John B., Jr............1934

Horton, Chuck.................1975

Horton, Dwight, Jr. 1957

Howell, Cindy (t) 1997

Howell, William Walker (m) 1928

Hubbard, Douglas Wayne 1990

Hubert, Harold D.(t) 1995

Hudgins, Mark (t) 1985

Hudson, Harry.................1966

Hudson, Nat (c) 1978-79-80

Huff, Douglas...................1996

Huff, E. Olin..........1925-26-28

Huff, James Blanchard......1898

Huggins, Ronnie....1967-68-69

Hughes, Dennis 1967-68-69

Hughes, Preston, IV 1994

Hughes, Steve........1939-40-41

Hughes, Turner Lynn .1964-65-66

Hughes, Woody (m).........1999

Hull, Augustus Longstreet 1900

Hummings, Sean ...1988-89-90

Hunnicutt, Lynn (c)...1970-71-72

Hunnicutt, Oliver..1937-38-39

Hunnicutt, William O. ("Pat") .. 1962-64

Hunter, Brice H....1992-93-94-95

Hunter, Homer.................1910

Hunter, Marcus A. .1995-96-97

Hurst, Marvin........1963-64-65

Hurt, Jason Bryant 1992-93

Hutchinson, A.G....1917-1918

Huzzie, Tracy Lamar 1990

Hyde, Glenn 1950-52

I

Ingalsbe, Thomas Richard 1989

Ingle, Wayne 1965-66-67

Ingram, Johnny 1967

Ingram, Kenley William ..1996-97

Inman, Frank (h) 1978

Ivester, Kelly J.(m)............1995

Ivey, William 1960-61-62

J

Jackson, Alex Stillman......1999

Jackson, Alfonza...1989-90-91-92

Jackson, Bertrand F. ("Tron") 1982-83-84-85

Jackson, Gregory (c)..1989-90-91-92

Jackson, James O..1984-85-86-87

Jackson, Jerone 1971-72-73

Jackson, Kevin R....1980-81-82

Jackson, Randy M. 1984-88

Jackson, William 1960

Jackson, Willie Kevin..1985-86

Jackura, Joseph 1944-47-48-49

Jacobs, David L. 1999

Jacobson, Roy H.(c) 1927-28

James, Randy 1979

James, Skip (t) 1980-81

Jamison, Joe 1940

Janko, Morris 1943

Jeffrey, Al..........................1945

Jenkins, David L...............1999

Jenkins, Donald 1946

Jenkins, Ronald 1965-66-67

Jennings, John 1968-70-71

Jennings, Jonas 1997-98-99

Jennings, Willie E., Jr..1990-91

Jerman, Jerry Robert ...1993-94

Jernigan, George T. 1943-44-45-46

Johnson, Andy........1971-72-73

Johnson, Arthur (m)..1988-89-90-91

Johnson, Brad (c)...1966-67-68

Johnson, Chandler V..1994-95-96-97

Johnson, Corey A. (c) 1993-94-95-96

Johnson, E.F. 1926

Johnson, Frank W..1933-34-35

Johnson, Glenn 1934-35-36

Johnson, Howard ..1937-38-39

Johnson, Howard ("Moose")(a) 1946-47

Johnson, Jervaris Tobbar .1997-98-99

Johnson, Keith .1982-83-84-86

Johnson, Mark Brescia......1997

Johnson, Michael 1978

Johnson, Randy (c) 1973-74-75

Johnson, Rodney ...1974-75-76

Johnson, Roy....................1926

Johnson, Sandy...........1966-67

Johnson, Travis Barry 1996

Johnson, Wayne (c) ...1985-86-87-88

Johnson, William Franklin 1965

Johnson, H.F., Jr..........1927-28

Jones, A.C. 1897

Jones, Alvin......................1962

Jones, Bryan T. .1993-94-95-96

Jones, Danny 1971-72-73

Jones, Daryll K. 1981-82-83

Jones, E. William, Jr...1984-85-86-87

Jones, Jarod (m).....1997-98-99

Jones, Jake (m).................1999

Jones, John 1934-35-36

Jones, Lanice ("Chuck") ..1980-81-82

Jones, Michael 1990-91-92

Jones, Michael D. .1980-81-82-83

Jones, Patrick (m) 1992

Jones, Preston Wayne 1989-90-91-92

Jones, Raymond 1971

Jones, Robert (m, t).....1967-68

Jones, Robert P. 1898

Jones, Spike...........1967-68-69

Jones, Travis Orlando (c) 1990-91-92,94

Jones, Hurley, Jr. 1951-52

Jordan, Blanford Eugene ..1987

Joselove, Ike 1922-23-24

Judson, Ronald (m)..........1958

Junior, Charles S....1980-81-82

K

Kain, Thomas G. ...1924-25-26

Kaiser, James Jeffrey 1992, 1994

Kardian, Andrew Layne....1997

Kasay, John 1965-66

Kasay, John David (c).1987-88-89-90

Kavouklis, Mike 1975-76

Kay, Clarence H....1980-81-82-83

Keith, Kendall (c) ..1969-70-71

Kelley, Gorden Bond..1957-58-59

Kelley, Weddington1929-30-31

Kelly, Bob 1978-79-80

Kelly, Howard 1953-54

Kelly, Phil (t)..........1978-79-80

Kelly, Richard.............1960-62

Kelly, Steven E. (c)1978-79-80-81

Keltner, Greene, Jr.......1939-41

Kemp, Bruce (c) 1967-68-69

Kennedy, Bob 1977

Kent, William B. (c)...1894-95-96-97

Kersey, Ben, Jr. 1938

Kesler, George T. 1979-81

Ketron, Grover C.............1906

Ketron, Harold (c) 1901-02-03-06

Keuper, Kenneth....1940-41-42

Key, Homer............1931-32-33

Kight, Tony 1976

Kilgo, Jonathan Paul.........1999

Killorin, Joseph Ignatius (c) 1894-95,1903-04

Kilpatrick, Martin E...1923-24-25

Kimsey, Bucky 1969

Kimsey, Cliff (a) 1939-40-41

King, Hardy 1966-67

King, Horace 1972-73-74

King, Lafayette 1942

King, Norman 1958

Kinnebrew, Chuck .1972-73-74

Kirouac, Brett Eric............1999

Kirtsey, Torin Niangelo 1996

Kitchens, Steve 1969-70-71

Kluk, Paul 1940

Knowles, William, Jr..1961-62-63

Kohn, Larry 1965-66-67

Kopp, David G............1998-99

Kotes, Harry.....................1954

Krug, Bill 1975-76-77

Kuniansky, Harry 1941-42

L

Lake, Ricky............1970-71-72

Lamar, Henry J.........1899-1901

Lambe, Earnest (m)..........1951

Lammert, Steve (t) 1983-84

Lancaster, Robert Larry ...1958-59

Landry, John, Jr..........1960-61

Lane, Ben Lee...................1989

Lane, Fred 1983-84-85-86

Lanford, Leroy C. 1928

Langley, Derwent, Jr. (a)-1950-52-53

Langley, Dwight Daxon ...1994-95-96-97

Lankewicz, Frank ..1962-63-64

Larkin, Clint 1998

Lastinger, Brad (m) 1986-87-88

Lastinger, John A...1981-82-83

Latimer, John P. 1943

Laurent, Andy 1964

Lautzenhiser, Glenn (c)...1926-27-28

Law, Robert 1934-35-36

Lawhorne, Tommy 1965-66-67

Lawrence, Frederick ..1958-59-60

Lawrence, Kelley Kent (t) .1997

Lawrence, N. Kent.1966-67-68

Layfield, Jimmy...........1967-68

Leath, Dennis 1970

Leathers, Milton 1929-30-31

Leavitt, Allan....1973-74-75-76

Ledbetter, Danny Wayne .1992-93

Ledsinger, Lewis, Jr. (m)...1945

Lee, James...................1941-42

Lee, Richard Morgan 1945

Lee, Ryals 1942-45

Leebern, Donald 1936

Leebern, Donald M., Jr....1957-58-59

Leffler, Lee R. 1925-26

Legg, Will 1973-74-76

Lenderman, Lee 1970

Leroy, Emarlos 1997-98

Leusenring, Dan...............1980

Leverett, Jason (m) 1988

Levie, Marshall C...1923-24-25

Lewis, Jeff (c).........1975-76-77

Lewis, Jeremy...................1998

Lewis, Jim 1941

Lewis, Jimmy (t)..............1986

Lewis, Jody (m) 1976-77

Lewis, Keith (m) 1927

Lewis, Mark 1987-88

Lewis, Morris C. (c)...1987-88-89-90

Lewis, Nathaniel 1986-87

Lewis, Thomas H. 1983

Lewis, Thomas, Jr. 1957-59

Lindsey, Jack R. 1980-81-82

Lindsey, Kiefer 1898-99

Lister, Jennifer Lynn 1996

Little, John Steven (c) 1983-84-85-86

Little, Lisa (t)...................1979

Littleton, Eugene ...1956-57-58

Lloyd, David 1957-58

Lloyd, Mayfield 1942

Locke, James 1952

Lofton, Wilbur, Jr. .1955-56-57

Logan, Harry B.................1913

Lokey, Tom (t)............1968-67

Long, Cary 1977

Lonon, Anthony Lovell ...1996-97

Lopatka, Mike.............1969-70

Lorendo, Eugene ...1947-48-49

Lott, Jeffrey S. 1981

Lott, Stanley (t)

Love, Armin Robert..........1995

Love, Henry 1948-49

Lovejoy, R. Hatton..........1896

Lovelace, Wycliff C. (c)...1984-85-86-88

Lowenthal, Pat (m)...........1965

Lowery, Bradley E.(t) .1982-83-84

Lowndes, J. Dozier (c) 1905-06

Loy, Andy J.......1981-83-84-85

Lucas, Cicero.........1956-57-58

Lucas, James E.......1907-08-09

Lucas, W.M. 1909-10-11-12

Luck, John, Jr. 1954-55-56

Luckey, J. Curtis 1924-25-26

Luckie, Dustin Anderson 1996-97-98-99

Luckie, Michael Elijah.....1996-97-98

Luckie, Miles Jon...1997-98-99

Ludwig, Paul..............1932-33

Luke, John Robert 1973

Lumpkin, Quinton (c) 1936-37-38

Lumpkin, Frank G., Jr.1929-30

Lyndon, Ed 1898

Lyons, Tommy (c)..1968-69-70

M

MacDonald, Alexander.....1956

MacDonald, James Jeffrey (t)....1973

MacKenna, William (m)..1943-46

Maddox, Arthur K. 1908-09-10-11

Maddox, Ralph 1930-31

Maddox, Raymond 1961-62-63

Maddox, W.A. (m)............1935

Madison, Charles...1952-53-54

Madray, Ashley 1977-78-79

Madray, Clint, Jr..........1950-51

Maffett, Herbert S. .1928-29-30

Maffett, Otis 1935-36-37

Maginnis, Davis (m).........1994

Magoni, Charles........1950-51

Maguire, Walter 1942

Maib, Donald Eugene, Jr. ..1990-91-92

Makowski, Henry 1951-52

Mallard, Joshua B........1998-99

Malinowski, Francis ..1951-52-53

Malkiewicz, Mark............1980

Malone, Kirby S....1911-12-13

Malone, Tom..............1939-40

Mangram, Tony..........1984-85

Manisera, Conrad 1951-55

Mann, Larry LaFronce.....1996-97-98-99

Manning, Carl Edward....1956-57-58

Manning, Elbert 1983

Mapp, Armand................1924

Maricich, Eli, Jr. ...1946-47-48-49

Marlow, Dan....................1980

Marshall, Arthur James ...1988-89-91

Marshall, Cledious 1996

Marshall, Earl..................1941

Marshall, T. Whitfield (c)1992-93-94-95

Marshburn, Walter O.(m) 1906

Martin, Frank...................1904

Martin, Joe B. 1928

Martin, Tim.....................1978

Mashburn, Mike (m) .1988-90-91

Massey, Charles William .1938-39

Massey, Jim (t) 1968-69-70

Mathews, Dooley...1937-38-39

Mathis, Buddy..................1952

Matthews, Jack.................1940

Maughon, Chris (t)1979-81-82

Maxwell, Kevin J. .1988-89-90-91

Maxwell, Richard, Jr. 1932

McAlister, Jay R...........1982-83

McArthur, James 1971-72

McBride, Ricky (c)1975-76-77-78

McBride, Walt (t) 1979

McCall, Kenneth ..1944-47-48-49

McCalla, James H. 1900

McCarley, Hugh, Jr......1948-49

McCarthy, Christopher A..........1979-80-81-82

McCaskill, Alex...........1938-39

McCay, E.T. 1905

McClelland, James Franklin 1956

McClelland, Jim 1956

McClelland, W.F. 1910

McClendon, J. Tyrone .1986-87

McClendon, Willie (c) 1976-77-78

McClung, Jerry 1950-51

McClure, Ardie 1942

McCluskey, David.1983-84-85-86

McConnell, Bright 1915-16

McCormick, Matthew Locke ....

1988-89

McCoy, Mike 1971

McCoy, Rodney Alfonzo..1989-90- 91-92

McCrainie, Christopher J. 1993-94-95-96

McCranie, Ken 1979

McCrary, Herdis W.1926-27-28

McCrary, Josea Mark ...1986-88

McCullough, David ...1932-33-34

McCullough, Jim ...1967-68-69

McCullough, William .1962-63

McCutcheon, C. D. 1893

McCutchen, Fran Kelly (c) 1899-00

McDonald, Alexander 1954-55-56

McDonald, David........1976-77

McDonald, John N. 1905

McDonald, Lillard 1954

McEachern, Brandon (m).1997

McEachern, John 1960-62

McEwen, Brent (v) 1997

McFalls, Douglas (c)..1963-64-65

McFerrin, Rob (m) 1992-93

McGill, Curtis........1967-68-69

McGill, Curtis J., Jr...........1999

McGinty, Wadsworth (m).1937

McHugh, Jack 1949

McIntire, Frank P.............1902

McIntosh, John Houston.1898-99

McIntyre, Guy (c).1979-81-82-83

McKenny, Charles J., III ...1961

McKenny, William .1959-60-61

McKever, S. Deshay ...1992-93-94-95

McKinney, Lee 1939

McKinnon, D.T. 1913

McKnight, David R. 1966-68-69

McKnight, David W. ..1972-73-74

McKnight, John (c)1933-34-35

McInnis, Carter 1997

McKnight, Larry 1970-71

McClain, C.M..................1910

McLaws, W.H. 1916

McLee, Kevin (c) ...1975-76-77

McManus, Fred...........1949-50

McMichael, Edward Howard 1916-17-18

McMichael, Randy M. 1999

McMickens, Donnie...1978-79-80

McPhee, Richard....1941-42-46

McPipkin, Jim 1971-72-73

McPipkin, Joe 1972

McPipkin, Paul 1969-71

McShea, Pat...........1978-79-80

McSwain, Keith 1983

McTigue, Robert E. 1926-27

McWhorter, Fonville 1907

McWhorter, J. Vason 1903

McWhorter, J. Vason, Jr. (c)......1930-31-32

McWhorter, Mac (c) ..1971-72-73

McWhorter, R.B.(m).........1899

McWhorter, Robert Ligon ("Bob")...................1910-13

McWhorter, Thurmond ..1919-20

McWhorter, William H. ..1965-66

Meadows, Jonathan A. (c) 1993-94-95-96

Meatheringham, Michael 1955-56-57

Meeks, Calvin 1943

Merola, Michael (c).....1949-50

Messer, Matt...................1993

Messer, Paul J..............1984-85

Methvin, Eugene 1954

Michael, Max, Jr. (m) 1934

Middlebrooks, G. Percy ..1895-96

Middleton, Keith ...1978-79-80

Milam, Ed 1973

Miles, Robert 1978-79-80

Millen, William Alexander (c) ..1991-92

Miller, Brandon Raymon .1996-97-98-99

Miller, Fred............1930-31-32

Miller, James (a) 1941-42-45

Miller, Jesse 1999

Miller, Mark..........1978-79-80

Miller, Rob (t) 1992

Miller, Shawn (m) 1997

Miller, Thomas.................1957

Miller, Wallace (m)...........1903

Miller, Warner Barker ("Chip").1974-75

Miller, Wallace, Jr. 1937

Millican, Brett W....1997-98-99

Mills, C.G......................1907

Mills, Doug (m) 1973-74

Milner, Thomas..........1935-37

Milo, Jim....................1977-78

Mims, William.......1937-38-39

Minish, Bryan Shelnut......1996

Minot, Al 1933-34-35

Mitchell, Danny (m) ...1966-67

Mitchell, Emmett 1995

Mitchell, Frank R.(m).......1897

Mitchell, George...............1954

Mitchell, G. William ..1982-83-84-85

Mitchell, LaBrone........1998-99

Mitchell, Mark.......1974-75-76

Mitchell, Shannon Lamont (c)..1990-91-92-93

Mixon, Billy...........1948-49-50

Monahan, Johnny 1901-02

Monk, Marion S..........1900-01

Montgomery, Adam (t).....1994

Montgomery, Jack 1969-70

Montgomery, Keith 1982-83

Montgomery, Lee..............1963

Montgomery, Willie, Jr. ...1991-92-93-94

Monti, Angelo, Jr. 1955-56

Moody, John Walker (m)..1995

Moody, Steve (m)........1974-76

Moore, Brian Kelly .1990, 1992

Moore, Edwin M.........1982-83

Moore, G.A. 1903-04

Moore, Jonathan Threatt .1895-97

Moore, Kirby (c)....1965-66-67

Moore, Ricky (m)........1974-75

Moore, Steven George .1990-91

Moore, Virlyn B. 1903-04

Moore, W.W. 1916-17-18

Moore, Andrew Cecil, Jr..1923-24-25

Moorehead, Leroy..1932-33-35

Moran, Tommy 1931

Moreno, H.C.(m)........1893-94

Morgan, Matt (m)............1997

Morgan, Stephen L (m) 1988

Morocco, Anthony.1949-50-51

Morris, Fred...............1894-95

Morris, J. Robert 1925-26-27

Morris, Bobby G. 1950-51

Morris, Warren Joel (t) 1988

Morrison, Tim ..1977-78-79-80

Morton, George D.(c) 1924-25-26

Moseley, Reid, Jr. ...1943-44-45-46

Mosher, Stu 1965-66-67

Moss, Gary 1983-85-86

Mosteller, James.....1954-55-56

Mott, Kennon...................1919

Mott, Norman 1930-31-32

Mrvos, Samuel.......1951-52-53

Mulherin, William 1953-55

Mull, Curtiss Michael 1987-88-89

Mullis, Mitch....................1979

Mulvehill, Richard.............1922

Munn, Edmund K............1919

Murphey, Eugene F. 1893

Murray, Jesse...............1976-77

Murray, W. Mercer...........1921

Muschamp, William Larry (c) ..1991-92-93-94

N

Nall, Hugh 1977-78-79-80

Nally, Rufus B. 1892-93-94-95-96

Napier, James..............1907-09

Nash, Thomas C. 1909

Nash, Tom.............1969-70-71

Nash, Tom A..........1925-26-27

Neathery, Milton 1976

Nelson, Curtis.................1939

Nelson, Tom 1923-24-25

Nestorak, Stan..................1947

Neuhaus, Steve 1965-66

Neville, Walter E. .1915-16-17-18

Newkirk, Duncan.............1964

Newsome, Erle T.........1907-08

Newton, Lee (m) 1940

Nix, Sidney J...............1901-02

Nix, Tommy 1980

Nolan, Mario N. 1993

Norley, Walt 1983

Norris, Carnie ..1979-80-81-82

Norris, Ulysses 1976-77-78

Northcutt, John R. 1909

Nowell, Robin, Jr. (c) 1940

Nowicki, George....1962-63-64

Nunley, Glen 1956-58

Nunn, George A. 1905

Nunnally, Jerry............1941-42

Nutt, Fred, Jr. 1953-54

O

O'Malley, Joseph (c)...1952-53-54

O'Neal, Gregory..........1992-93

Oakes, Mike 1970

Oberdorfer, Donald.....1919-20

Ogletree, Carl..................1946

O'Keefe, Michael Francis .1993

O'Leary, William T. 1984-85

Oliver, W. Maxwell, Jr. 1923

Opper, Charles 1932-33-34

Orgel, Frank 1959-60

Orr, James, Jr. 1955-56-57

Orrick, Chuck (t) 1979

Orris, Norman 1952

Osbolt, Terry...............1966-68

Osborn, Cassius (c) ...1984-85-86-87

Osborne, John P. 1993

Outlar, Barry 1970

Owens, James Eddie ..1992-93-94-95

P

Paddock, David F.(c)..1912-13-14-1915

Page, Ralph 1973

Paine, Thad A. 1916-17-18

Paine, Trav 1968-69

Painter, David W...1980-81-82-83

Palmer, Henry G. 1927-28

Palmer, Jason Glover...1992-93

Paris, Thomas 1929

Paris, Thomas Hanie, Jr...1958-59-60

Parker, Ernest Earl, Jr. 1992

Parker, Thaddeus Terrell .1997-98-99

Parkman, G. Kanon.........1991, 1993-94-95

Parks, Justin B................1999
Parks, Tim 1978-79-80
Parrish, Joel 1974-75-76
Parrish, Joseph S. 1909-11
Pascale, Donald................1977
Pass, Patrick Deandrea 1996-97-98
Passavant, Oscar W...........1905
Passmore, Homer 1940
Pate, Brady B. 1997-98-99
Patel, Harris (t)...............1997
Patterson, James 1929-30-31
Patton, Charlie (m) 1933
Patton, George (c)..1964-65-66
Paul, Jerry 1973-74
Paulk, Jeffrey A. 1980-81-82
Payne, Billy 1966-67-68
Payne, Jimmy ..1978-79-80-81-82
Payne, Porter....1946-47-48-49
Peacock, Albert 1914
Peacock, David R. (c).1910-11-12
Peacock, Howell B. 1908-09
Pearce, C.C., Jr. 1921
Peeples, Terry 1970
Pellock, Brett J. 1993-94
Pennington, Huey........1966-67
Pennington, Penny 1968
Pennington, Durward, Jr. 1959-60-61
Perhach, Andrew..1944-45-46-47
Perkins, John 1953
Perkinson, Tom 1933
Perl, Al...........................1944
Perno, Lou (t)........1978-79-80
Perry, Bill..........................1943
Perry, Lamar, Jr................1993
Perry, Victor A. 1984-85-86
Peterson, Joseph Todd (c).........1991-92
Petree, Russell Reyno, Jr..1915-16-17-18
Petrisko, Paul 1976-77-78
Petty, Hinton (m) 1988
Pew, Authur, Jr.(c) 1916-17-18-19-21
Phelps, Morris..................1941
Phillips, Barry 1946-47-48
Phillips, Benjamin Carlson 1943-44-45
Phillips, Courtland 1999
Phillips, Harry (at,t)....1965-66
Phillips, Jermaine........1998-99
Phillips, Richard ("Dickie").......1964-65-66
Philpot, William K. 1923
Pickett, Jason Marc...........1992
Pickett, Les (t) 1991
Pierce, Brooke 1942
Pilcher, George............1971-72
Pilgrim, Harold 1954-56
Pillsbury, Kenneth .1964-65-66

Pittman, Marvin, Jr...........1940
Pitts, Suquorey ("Nicky") .1989
Plant, Frank 1945
Pledger, Charles Henderson 1991-92-93
Polak, Joe 1942
Pollard, Al 1974-75-76
Pomperoy, Edgar Erastus (m) ...1895-98
Ponder, Ernest.................1978
Pope, Clarence 1973
Pope, Thomas ..1945-47-48-49
Porter, John Hart..............1908
Porterfield, Donald 1962-63-64
Poschner, George...1940-41-42
Posey, Wyatt 1939-40-41
Poss, Dexter C. 1950-51-52
Poss, Robert 1942
Poss, Bob, Jr. 1969-70-71
Post, Dan M. 1922
Poulos, Jimmy 1971-72-73
Powell, David James ..1994-95-96
Powell, John William.1913-14-15
Powell, Tom N. 1911-12
Power, John William 1993
Powers, Henry 1939-41
Price, Fred O. 1894-95-96
Price, George W................1897
Price, Kirk 1973-76
Prince, Carmon 1976-77-78-79
Principe, Rocco 1949-50-51
Prosperi, Raymond 1948-49-50
Pullen, Todd (m) 1983
Purcell, Jones 1913
Putnal, Rex 1970-71-72
Putnam, I.M. 1900
Pyburn, Jeff 1976-77-78-79

R

Raber, Mike.................1975-76
Raber, Richard 1949-50-51
Rabon, Christopher Matthew ...1995-96-97
Radar, Jason R. 1999
Radloff, Wayne R..1979-80-81-82 (c)
Ragan, James J.(m) 1905
Ragsdale, Randolph 1951-52
Rajecki, Peter 1968-69-70
Rakestraw, Larry 1961-62-63
Ramsey, Carter, Jr. 1958-59
Randall, L.C. 1921-22-23-24
Ransom, Eugene M. 1905-06
Ransom, Kojara Lamont ...1995
Raoul, Loring 1904
Rauch, John(a) .1945-46-47-48
Ray, James.............1970-71-72
Reed, Robert 1953
Reid, Andy 1973-74-75
Reid, Bernie (c)......1944-47-48
Reid, Floyd.......1945-47-48-49
Reider, Ric 1973-74

Register, Bradley Clay 1997-98-99
Render, Antonio 1981
Reynolds, James Thomas 1917-18-19-21
Reynolds, Owen Gaston (c)......1916-17-18-19-1921
Reynolds, Timothy B. 1983
Rholetter, David 1966-68
Richards, Leander 1937
Richardson, Dick..............1942
Richardson, Jake ..1982-83-84-85
Richardson, Sam L.1921-22-23
Richardson, William H....1952-53
Richwine, Sam (t)..............1947
Richter, Frank........1964-65-66
Ricketts, Richard (m) 1990
Ricks, Adam (t) 1997
Ridgway, Jennifer (t).........1997
Ridlehuber, Preston ...1963-64-65
Ridley, Frank M., Jr. (c)...1900-02
Rigdon, John 1916-17-18-19
Rinard, Patrick John.........1989
Ringwall, Richard 1952
Riofski, Frank 1942
Rissmiller, Raymond ..1962-63-64
Rissmiller, Scott Clifton...1990-91-92
Ritchie, Andrew J. (c).......1899
Ritchie, Horace Bonar 1902-03-04
Ritchie, William R. 1898
Robbins, Gordon 1973-74
Roberson, Terry Clayton ..1987
Roberts, Jack 1929-30-31
Roberts, James 1950-51-52
Roberts, James M. (m)......1927
Roberts, Joe Wayne 1952
Roberts, Laneair (a) ...1954-55-56
Roberts, William 1963
Roberts, James, Jr. 1958
Roberts, Steven Wade 1991-92-93-94
Robertson, Julius T...........1999
Robich, Rich Christopher..1997-98
Robson, E.J. 1909
Robeson, L.S. 1905
Robich, Richard 1998
Robinson, Cory 1997-98-99
Robinson, Dennard 1968
Robinson, Erik William...1994-95
Robinson, Matt....1974-75-76
Robinson, Mike 1973-74
Robinson, Mixon (c)..1969-70-71
Robinson, Rex ..1977-78-79-80

Robinson, Will (t) 1994
Rocco, Patsy................1949-50
Roddenbery, Andy .1935-36-37
Rodrique, Patrick...1966-67-68
Rogers, Daniel Steve ..1991-92-93
Rogers, Danny..1976-77-78-79
Rogers, Ernest P. 1924-25-26
Rogers, Ronnie 1967-69-70
Rogers, Steve 1977
Roland, Billy 1957-58-59
Ros, Frank (c)........1978-79-80
Rose, Frank D. 1919
Rose, Robert 1929-30-31
Rosenberg, Buzy ...1970-71-72
Rosenberg, William Thomas.....1989-90- 91-93
Ross, James Tyson (m)......1995
Ross, Seth (m) 1997-98-99
Rossiter, Joseph A............1904
Rothe, E.S. 1919
Rothstein, Bennie ..1927-28-29
Rouse, Walter D. 1993-94
Ruark, Walter (a) ...1940-41-42
Rucker, Lamar..................1900
Ruff, Calvin 1983-84-85-86
Russaw, Carver T. 1987
Runyon, Thomas...............1962
Russell, Erk (h) 1981
Russell, Jay 1978-79-80
Russell, John ("Rusty")....1973-74-75
Russell, Phillip........1967-68-69
Rutland, James William (c).......1943-44

S

Sadler, Hazen Heyward, Jr........1989-90-91
Sadowski, Robert Troy 1985-86-87-88
Sage, Dan Y. (c).1904-05, 1906
Salerno, Frank V. ...1950-51-52 (a)
Salisbury, Robert....1937-38-39
Sam, David (m) 1977-78-79
Sampson, Bill 1967
Sanchez, Jeff R. 1982-84
Sancken, George A.1910-11-12
Sanders, Carl E. 1945
Sanders, Jeff...........1974-75-76
Sanders, Robert 1945
Sanderson, Fred 1971
Sanderson, Ryan H..........1993, 1995-96
Sanks, Jasper...............1998-99
Sapp, Theron (c)....1956-57-58
Saunders, Tom 1974-75
Saussy, Stuart Hunter 1991
Saye, David............1968-69-70
Saye, Jake 1960-61-62
Saye, William 1953-54-55
Schoenbaum, Brian S. 1999
Schopen, Joseph...............1955

Schultez, Kenneth.......1956-57
Schwak, David (c) .1973-74-75
Scichilone, Joseph .1950-51-52
Scott, Danny ...1968-69-70 (m)
Scott, Chris...............1993 (m)
Scott, Jake..................1967-68
Scott, Lindsay (c) .1978-79-80-81
Scott, Robert B. 1907
Scott, Ros (m) ..1988-89-90-91
Scott, Terry............1961-62-63
Seaborn, Louis........1917-1918
Sealy, James.....................1958
Sedlock, Robert..................1957
Sellers, Terry..........1965-66-67
Sellers, Weyman (c)...1945-46-47-48
Seymour, Richard (c) .1997-98-99
Shackelford, George O. 1893
Shamblin, Jackson 1959-60
Shannon, Emory.....1898-1900
Sharp, Randy (t)..............1974
Shaw, David (t) 1975-76
Shaw, Ken...............1968-69-70
Shea, Donald (a) 1953-54-55
Sheffield, Charles (m).......1964
Sherlock, Cecil Wyman...1925-26
Sherrer, Bobby 1952
Shi, Allen...............1933-34-35
Shimkus, Dennis..............1960
Shirer, Jimmy 1969-70-71
Shiver, Ivy, III..............1949-50
Shiver, Ivy M., Jr. (c)...1926-27
Short, George 1956
Sidberry H. William 1913
Sills, Bruce..................1997-98
Simcox, Horace................1899
Simmons, Dwayne Darnell (c)..1990-91
Simmons, Melvin .1980-81-82-83
Simmons, Patrick Dewayne 1988
Simon, Matthew ...1978-79-80-81
Simons, Walter.................1943
Simonton, Abner..............1939
Simpson, H. Lee ("Tripp") 1981
Simpson, Marisa 1994-95-96
Sims, Alandus D. ...1994-95-96
Sims, Kenneth ..1982-83-84-85
Singletary, Wilson Eugene 1944
Singleton, Robert 1997
Sinkwich, Frank (c)...1940-41-42
Sipe, Robert Fred, III .1994-95-96-97
Skipworth, George 1944
Skipworth, James (c)...1939-40
Slater, J.F. 1909-1910
Slaughter, William N........1959

Sleek, Steve (c) 1970-71-72
Smaha, Jiggy 1967
Small, Antoine LeVarr1995-96-97-98
Smart, Kirby P. (c) 1995-96-97-98
Smiley, Julian 1969-70
Smiley, Ronnie 1972
Smith, Allen N...............1925-26
Smith, Andre 1983-84
Smith, Benjamin J. (c)1987-88-89
Smith, Brian Stantley ..1995-96
Smith, Charles H. (a).1943-44-45-46
Smith, Danny....................1970
Smith, Derrick Antwon...1992-93-94-95
Smith, Don 1957
Smith, Henry Eugene 1925-26-27
Smith, J.H. 1928
Smith, Jeffrey Alan 1986
Smith, Jim 1963-65
Smith, John......................1972
Smith, John Roy 1913
Smith, Marcus.L...........1995-96
Smith, Marion................1901-02
Smith, Marvin H. 1965
Smith, Matt Jarmaine ..1995-96
Smith, Mike (t).................1988
Smith, Miles Jason .1985-86-87
Smith, Patrick........1959-60-61
Smith, Paul 1943
Smith, Quinton 1957
Smith, Reginald1994-95-96-97
Smith, R. Kyle (c) ..1905-06-07
Smith, Ronny Wendell 1985-86-88
Smith, Royce (c) 1969-70-71
Smith, Talbot F. 1893
Smith, Terin 1998-99
Smith, Vern 1972-73-74
Smith, Vernon, Jr. ..1929-30-31
Smoak, Tommy...........1971-72
Smart, Kirby.....1995-96-97-98
Snell, Jerry......................1964
Snellings, Paul Malcolm (c) 1995-96-97-98
Snider, Billy......................1952
Snider, Leonard...........1894-95
Soberdash, Donald (c) 1957-58-59
Sowell, Bryan (t) 1994
Spadafino, Leonard 1954-55
Spain, Frank 1894
Spain, J.W. 1894-96
Spangler, Thomas E..........1982
Spencer, Bill (t)......1976-77-78
Spicer, James P..................1921
Spivey, Dan............1972-73-74
Spooner, Johnny 1956
St. John, Herbert ..1944-45-46-47

Stafford, Bradford Kinard .1976
Stanfill, Bill (c).......1966-67-68
Stapleton, Charles 1974
Stargell, Guy 1980
Stargill, Reggie 1997-98-99
Stark, Troy Alan1992-93-94-95
Starnes, Mark (t) 1985
Staton, James Bradley.......1995
Steele, Michael D. 1982
Steele, Michael James..1989-90
Steele, Richard.......1949-50-51
Steely, Harold..............1964-65
Stegeman, John 1939
Steiner, Godfrey 1945
Stelling, H. Cree 1927-28-29
Stephens, Jock Alonzo......1992
Stephens, Kim T. (c) ..1984-85-86-87
Stevens, Harry 1936-38
Stewart, Jason (m)............1994
Stewart, Kirby L...........1984-85
Stewart, Mark (c)...1966-67-68
Stewart, Ronnie 1977-78-80-81
Stickel, Robert (m)...........1999
Stiles, George 1892
Stinchcomb, Matthew Douglas (c) 1995-96-97-98
Stinchcomb, Jonathan 1999
Stinson, Les 1973-74
Stoinoff, James M. 1930
Stone, Craig (m) 1980-82
Story, Al 1991
Storm, Matt 1993-94
Straub, Karen ....1997 (t)
Strickland, Allan (m)........1946
Strickland, Allan (m) ..1973-74
Striplin, Mike...............1974-75
Strong, Mack Carlington (c) 1989-90- 91-92
Strother, Clinton, Jr. 1942
Stroud, Marcus 1997-98-99
Stroud, Travis Mandell 1994-95-96-97
Strozier, Wilbur (c)....1983-84-85-86
Strumke, William.............1956
Stubbs, Herbert William (c) 1893-94-95
Styles, Randy (t) 1980-81-82
Styles, Ricky (t)...........1975-76
Sullivan, Arthur R..1903-04-05
Sullivan, Phil 1969-70-71
Sullivan, Wendell........1930-31
Swan, Jack W.(c) ..1989-90-91-92
Swanson, Ben...................1900
Swindle, Buck 1968-69-70
Swinford, Gene......1970-71-72
Swinford, Wayne ...1962-63-64
Swoopes, Ronnie (c)..1974-75-76-77

T

Talley, Gregory Tyson (c) .1988-89-90-91
Talton, Chadwick Travis..1997-98-99
Tang, William 1983-85
Tanner, Fred A. 1919-20-21-22
Tanner, Hampton ..1948-49-50
Tanner, Jody ....1983 (m)
Tanner, Charles Mabry, Jr. 1916 (m)
Tardits, Richard 1985-86-87-88
Tarkenton, Francis.1958-59-60 (c)
Tarleton, Wendell ..1954-55-56
Tarpley, Ted ....1990 (m)
Tarrer, Harold 1966-67-68
Tassapoulas, Spero 1929-30
Tate, C.B....................1951 (m)
Tate, E.B...........1915-16-17-18
Tate, Lars J. 1984-85-86-87
Taylor, Bob 1963-64-65
Taylor, Michael Renai, Jr. 1994-95-96
Taylor, N. James 1920-22-23
Taylor, Nathaniel ..1979-80-81-82
Taylor, Paul Edward...1992-93-94-95
Taylor, Spafford...........1947-48
Taylor, Steve 1972-73-74
Taylor, Wayne........1959-60-61
Teasley, Joe 1995
Tedder, Stan 1975
Teel, Kerry 1968
Tellis, LeMonte Donzell ..1987-88-90-91
Tener, Matthew R. 1988
Tereshinski, Joe 1942-45-46
Tereshinski, Joe Peter.1974-75-76
Tereshinski, Wally.......1976-77
Terry, Christopher Alexander ...1995-96-97-98 (c)
Terry, Gordon ...1976-77-78-79 (c)
Terry, John 1946
Tholetter, David 1967
Thomas, Carroll 1937-38
Thomas, Jeffrey Carl ..1991-92-93-94
Thomas, John...................1974
Thomas, John 1986-87-88
Thomason, James D...1922-23-24
Thompson, Albert.......1949-50
Thompson, Andy (m) 1999
Thompson, Billy Joe ..1957-58-59
Thompson, Brad 1974-75
Thompson, Charlie E.1912-13-14-15
Thompson, Homer...........1910
Thompson, Horace Van....1989
Thompson, Ralph.1921-22-24-25 (c)

Thompson, Ralph Cecil-1990-91, 1993

Thompson, Robert.1975-76-77

Thompson, Thomas, Jr.....1960 (m)

Thornhill, Thomas 1959

Thornton, Michael Leon .1992-93

Thrash, Tom A....1913-14-15-16 (c) 17-18

Thrasher, Babe 1898

Thurman, Allen................1906

Thurson, Thomas N. .1980-81-82-83 (c)

Tichenor, W.R. 1897

Tidmore, Ronnie 1966-67

Tidmore, Steve 1967

Tilliski, John 1948-49-50

Tinsley, Elijah Pope, Jr.....1935-36-37

Toburen, David (t) 1990

Todd, Jr., James 1940-41-42

Tolbert, Brandon Scott 1994-95-96-97

Tomberlin, Donald 1960

Toodle, Melvin Gene..1993-94-95-96 (c)

Tootle, Marvin 1965-66

Towns, Forest 1936-37

Towns, Robert 1957-58-59

Townsend, E.C. 1931

Townsend, Glenn .1976-77 (m)

Traylor, I. Bothwell ....1935 (m)

Traylor, Joseph A. (t)

Treadaway, Charlie 1934-35

Tremble, Greg Deshawn..1992-93

Tremblay, Sean K.............1995

Trippi, Charles .1942-45-46 (c)

Trousdale, Louis C. (m)....1941

Troutman, Walter........1936-37

Tsiklistas, Tony .1980-81-82 (t)

Tuburen, David (t) 1989

Tuck, Reuben M. 1909

Tucker, Doug....................1967

Tucker, Mayo 1969-70-71

Turbyville, Charlie ......1933 (c)

Turner, C. Lewis 1906

Turner, Paul 1913

Turner, Richard Thomas ...1990

Turner, William R. 1901-02

Twitty, W.C. 1903

U

Uga I ....1956-66 (h)

Uga II ....1966-72 (h)

Uga III..................1973-80 (h)

Uga IV..................1981-89 (h)

Uga V ....1990-99 (h)

Ullrich, Andy 1975

Usry, Mike.......................1998

V

Van Buren, Robert 1954

Van Giesen, George 1925-26

Vandiver, J.H. ...1919-20-21-22

Vandiver, Sanford, Jr. ..1936-37

Vann, Kenneth.......1960-61-62

Varble, Brad.............1984 (m)

Varnado, Gerald 1964-65-66

Veal, Gene 1978

Veazy, Charlton.............1953 (t)

Vella, Leonard 1960-61

Vickers, Jimmy .1957-58-59 (a)

Vickery, Farrar.................1942

Vincent, Kevin Mark 1987

Vinesett, Travis ......1956-57 (a)

Vollrath, Charles Gordon .1992

Von Harten, Raymond Alan......1990

W

Waddell, R. Spencer ..1932 (m)

Wade, Todd....................1986

Wadley, Bubba 1974

Wadley, L.R. 1904

Wagnon, Henry 1933-34-35

Wainwright, Robert S.......1988

Walden, H.S. 1897

Walden, P.H. ....1898 (c)

Walden, Robert 1958-59-60-61

Walker, Herschel ...1980-81-82 (c)

Walker, James.............1959 (t)

Walker, Joseph ....1986 (m)

Walker, Reginald 1986

Wallace, Michael A..........1989

Wallace, Thomas M. ...1991-92

Walsh, William, Jr.......1950-51

Walston, Robert1947-48-49-50

Wansley, Timothy L. ...1998-99

Ward, Damon Leon.....1991-92

Ward, Hines 1994-95-96-97

Ward, Kelly ....1992-93 (t)

Ware, Clay Alan 1991

Ware, Larry Lanard....1988-89-90-91 (c)

Warner, James Edward....1991-92-93-94

Warner, Kirk 1986-87-88-89

Warthen, Ralph................1979

Washington, Andre Bernard.....1990

Washington, Gene 1973-74-75-76

Waters, Gregory Henry ...1983-84-85(a)

Watkins, Herbert 1976-77

Watkins, Newton 1892-94

Watkins, William 1956

Watson, Dennis 1969-70-71

Watson, Steve...................1971

Watson, Young L.........1896-97

Watson, A.D., III 1961

Watt, Josh 1975

Watts, Frank Alan 1994-95

Waugh, Armin 1929-30

Weaver, Michael L. 1981-82-83-84

Weaver, Eddie, Jr..1978-79-80-81

Webster, Terrie Lee 1985-86-87-88

Weeks, David West 1992-93-94-95

Weir, John Benson, Jr. 1908

Welch, Clarence 1941

Wells, Don Ray................1944

Welton, Chris 1978-79-80

West, David A. 1990

West, John.............1932-33-34

West, Larry 1972-73-74

West, Robert.....1950-51-52 (c)

Westmoreland, Ralph 1961

Wheatley, J.D. 1905

Wheeler, Charles R. 1965-66

Wheeler, Matthew Todd..1985-86-87-88 (c)

Whelchel, Hugh C.....1919-20-21-22(c)

Whiddon, Clinton ("Ken") 1965-66

Whire, Joseph 1931

White, Gene 1951-52-53

White, George 1966-67-68

White, J. Harry.................1956

White, Steve 1970-71-72

White, John Walter1953-54-55

Whitehead, J. Comer.1935 (m)

Whitehead, James 1962

Whitmire, Brook 1989

Whittemore, Charles .1968-69-70

Whitton, George 1956-58

Whitworth, Keith.............1973

Wiehrs, Charles F. 1923-24

Wiggins, Jermaine.......1997-98

Wilfong, Walter 1938-39

Wilhite, Charles 1938

Wilkins, Roy 1953-54-55-56

Williams, Bennie Bernard1990-91-92-1993 (c)

Williams, Charles H. 1921

Williams, Dale 1979-80-81

Williams, Dave E..1995-96-97-98

Williams, E. Scott.1981-82-83-84 (c)

Williams, Garland.......1942-46

Williams, Greg.......1976-77-78

Williams, Gregory Alan...1985-86-87

Williams, Henry..........1984-85

Williams, James ....1942 (m)

Williams, Kelvin 1998-99

Williams, Langdale 1959-60-61

Williams, Marcus .1993-94-95-96

Williams, Rayfield..1974-75-76

Williams, Ronald..............1952

Williams, Todd D. 1982-83-84-86

Williams, James, Jr.....1952-53-54-55

Williamson, Wallace ..1960-61-62

Willingham, Broadus E. ...1908

Willingham, Durward1932 (m)

Willingham, N. 1902

Willis, Gary 1994

Willis, Michael W. 1984-85

Wilson, Barry 1962-63-65

Wilson, Chad Larry ...1990-91-92-93

Wilson, Christopher Lee .1989-90- 91-92

Wilson, Duane ("Bubba")1973-74

Wilson, Gene E. 1956-57

Wilson, Jim..................1963-64

Wilson, Mark.........1974-75-76

Wilson, Mike 1974-75-76

Wilson, Robert............1974-75

Wilson, Steve.........1973-74-75

Wilson, Troutman......1933 (m)

Wimberly, Bruce 1952-53

Wimberly, William H., Jr. .1987 (m)

Wingate, Harry L..1915-16-17-18

Winsett, Gerald 1963

Winship, Blanton 1892

Wisdom, Chip 1969-70-71

Wisham, James M. 1982-83

Witherspoon, Will 1998-99

Witt, Tom 1939-40

Woerner, Scott..1977-78-79-80

Wolfe, David 1972

Wolford, Randolph Glenn 1989-91

Wolfson, Louis 1931

Womack, James1977-78-79-80

Wood, Jimmy Haralson, Sr. 1968-69-70

Wood, Jimmy Haralson, Jr........1996

Wood, Sam W. ....1925 (m)

Wood, William ("Butch") 1973-74

Woodall, Luke.................1926

Woodall, Woody 1967-68

Woodruff, George C. .1907-08-10-1911 (c), 1912

Woodruff, Harry Ernest ..1903-04

Woodruff, Joseph Grady...1912

Woods, Billy 1975-76-77

Woodward, Brigham..1961-62-63

Woodward, Steve...1966-67-68

Worley, Timothy 1985-86-88

Worrell, Billy 1960

Wray, C.B. 1905

Wright, Graham ....1936 (m)

Wright, Hank....1979-81-82 (t)

Wright, Louis M. 1901

Georgia Scores

1892: 1-1-0
Coach: Dr. Charles Herty; Captain: A.O. Halsey, HB

Date	Result		Opponent	Record
J. 30	hW	50-0	Mercer (Athens)	1-0
F. 20	aL	0-10	Auburn (Atlanta)	1-1

1893: 2-2-1
Coach: Ernest Brown; Captain: George Butler, QB

Date	Result		Opponent	Record
N. 4	hL	6-28	Georgia Tech (Athens)	0-1
N. 1	hL	10-35	Vanderbilt (Nashville)	0-2
N. 30	hT	0-0	Savannah AC (Savannah)	0-2-1
D. 1	aW	24-0	Augusta AC (Augusta)	1-2-1
D. 9	aW	22-8	Furman (Augusta)	2-2-1

1894: 5-1-0
Coach: Robert Winston; Captain: George Butler, QB

Date	Result		Opponent	Record
O. 29	hL	8-12	Sewanee (Athens)	0-1
N. 3	aW	40-0	S.C. State (Columbia)	1-1
N. 10	aW	10-0	Wofford (Spartanburg)	2-1
N. 17	aW	66-0	Augusta AC (Augusta)	3-1
N. 24	aW	10-8	Auburn (Atlanta)	4-1
N. 29	aW	22-0	Savannah AC (Savannah)	5-1

1895: 3-4-0
Coach: Glenn Warner; Captain: H.W. Stubbs, FB

Date	Result		Opponent	Record
O. 19	hW	34-0	Wofford (Athens)	1-0
O. 26	aL	0-6	North Carolina (Atlanta)	1-1
O. 31	aL	6-10	North Carolina (Atlanta)	1-2
N. 2	aW	30-6	Alabama (Columbus)	2-2
N. 9	aW	22-0	Sewanee (Atlanta)	3-2
N. 23	aL	0-6	Vanderbilt (Nashville)	3-3
N. 28	aL	6-16	Auburn (Atlanta)	3-4

1896: 4-0-0
Coach: Glenn Warner; Captain: R.B. Nally, HB

Date	Result		Opponent	Record
O. 24	aW	26-0	Wofford (Spartanburg)	1-0
O. 31	aW	24-16	North Carolina (Atlanta)	2-0
N. 9	hW	26-0	Sewanee (Athens)	3-0
N. 26	aW	12-6	Auburn (Atlanta)	4-0

1897: 2-1-0
Coach: Charles McCarthy; Captain: William B. Kent, T

Date	Result		Opponent	Record
O. 9	hW	24-0	Clemson (Athens)	1-0
O. 23	hW	28-0	Georgia Tech (Athens)	2-0
O. 30	aL	4-17	Virginia (Atlanta)	2-1

1898: 4-2-0
Coach: Charles McCarthy; Captain: H.S. Walden, T

Date	Result		Opponent	Record
O. 8	hW	11-0	Clemson (Athens)	1-0
O. 15	hW	14-0	Atlanta AC (Athens)	2-0
O. 22	hW	15-0	Georgia Tech (Athens)	3-0
O. 29	aW	4-0	Vanderbilt (Atlanta)	4-0
N. 12	aL	0-44	North Carolina (Macon)	4-1
N. 24	aL	17-18	Auburn (Atlanta)	4-2

1899: 2-3-1
Coach: Gordon Saussy; Captain: W.A. Ritchie, T

Date	Result		Opponent	Record
O. 27	hW	11-0	Clemson (Athens)	1-0
O. 21	aL	0-12	Sewanee (Atlanta)	1-1
O. 28	hW	33-0	Georgia Tech (Athens)	2-1
N. 11	aL	0-5	Tennessee (Knoxville)	2-2
N. 18	aT	0-0	Auburn (Atlanta)	2-2-1
N. 30	aL	0-5	North Carolina (Atlanta)	2-3-1

1900: 2-4-0
Coach: E.E. Jones; Captain: F.K. McCutcheon, QB

Date	Result		Opponent	Record
O. 13	aW	12-0	Georgia Tech (Atlanta)	1-0
O. 20	hW	5-0	South Carolina (Athens)	2-0
O. 27	aL	6-21	Sewanee (Atlanta)	2-1
N. 10	hL	5-39	Clemson (Athens)	2-2
N. 17	aL	0-55	North Carolina (Raleigh)	2-3
N. 29	aL	0-44	Auburn (Atlanta)	2-4

1901: 1-5-2
Coach: Billy Reynolds; Captain: F.M. Ridley, E

Date	Result		Opponent	Record
O. 12	aW	10-5	South Carolina (Augusta)	1-0
O. 19	aL	0-47	Vanderbilt (Nashville)	1-1
O. 21	aL	0-47	Sewanee (Sewanee)	1-2
O. 26	hL	5-29	Clemson (Athens)	1-3
N. 2	aL	0-27	North Carolina (Atlanta)	1-4
N. 9	aT	0-0	Alabama (Montgomery)	1-4-1
N. 16	hL	6-16	Davidson (Athens)	1-5-1
N.28	aT	0-0	Auburn (Atlanta)	1-5-2

1902: 4-2-1
Coach: Billy Reynolds; Captain: F.M. Ridley, E

Date	Result		Opponent	Record
O. 18	hW	11-0	Furman (Athens)	1-0
O. 25	aT	0-0	Georgia Tech (Atlanta)	1-0-1
N. 1	aW	5-0	Alabama (Birmingham)	2-0-1
N. 7	hW	20-0	Davidson (Athens)	3-0-1
N. 8	aL	0-36	Clemson (Clemson)	3-1-1
N. 11	aL	0-11	Sewanee (Atlanta)	3-2-1
N. 27	aW	12-5	Auburn (Atlanta)	4-2-1

1903: 3-4-0
Coach: M.M. Dickinson; Captain: Harold Ketron, C

Date	Result		Opponent	Record
O. 10	hL	0-29	Clemson (Athens)	0-1
O. 17	hL	0-17	South Carolina (Athens)	0-2
O. 24	aW	38-0	Georgia Tech (Atlanta)	1-2
O. 31	hL	0-33	Vanderbilt (Athens)	1-3
N. 7	aW	5-0	Tennessee (Knoxville)	2-3
N. 14	aL	0-6	Savannah (Savannah)	2-4
N. 26	aW	22-13	Auburn (Atlanta)	3-4

1904: 1-5-0
Coach: Charles A. Barnard; Captain: H.I. Killorain, FB

Date	Result		Opponent	Record
O. 15	aW	52-0	Florida (Macon)	1-0
O. 22	aL	0-10	Clemson (Clemson)	1-1
O. 26	aL	0-2	South Carolina (Columbia)	1-2
N. 5	aL	5-16	Alabama (Tuscaloosa)	1-3
N. 12	aL	6-23	Georgia Tech (Atlanta)	1-4
N. 24	aL	5-17	Auburn (Macon)	1-5

1905: 1-5-0
Coach: M.M. Dickinson; Captain: Dan Sage, HB

Date	Result		Opponent	Record
O. 2	hL	10-35	Clemson (Athens)	0-1
O. 3	hL	10-39	Cumberland (Athens)	0-2
N. 4	aL	0-36	Alabama (Birmingham)	0-3
N. 11	hW	16-12	Dahlonega (Athens)	1-3
N. 18	aL	0-46	Georgia Tech (Atlanta)	1-4
N. 30	aL	0-29	Auburn (Macon)	1-5

1906: 2-4-1
Coach: W.S. Whitney; Captain: J.D. Lowndes, QB

Date	Result		Opponent	Record
O. 13	hL	0-15	Davidson (Athens)	0-1
O. 20	aL	0-6	Clemson (Clemson)	0-2
N. 3	aW	55-0	Mercer (Mackon)	1-2
N. 10	hL	0-17	Georgia Tech (Athens)	1-3
N. 21	hT	0-0	Tennessee (Athens)	1-3-1
N. 29	hW	4-0	Auburn (Athens)	2-3-1
D. 2	aL	0-12	Savannah AC (Savannah)	2-4-1

1907: 4-3-1
Coach: W.S. Whitney; Captain Kyle Smith, HB

Date	Result		Opponent	Record
O. 5	hW	57-0	Dahlonega (Athens)	1-0
O. 12	hL	0-15	Tennessee (Athens)	1-1
O. 19	aW	26-6	Mercer (Macon)	2-1
O. 26	aT	0-0	Alabama (Montgomery)	2-1-1
N. 2	aL	6-10	Georgia Tech (Atlanta)	2-2-1
N. 7	aW	8-0	Clemson (Augusta)	3-2-1
N. 11	hL	0-16	Sewanee (Athens)	3-3-1
N. 28	aW	6-0	Auburn (Macon)	4-3-1

1908: 5-2-1
Coach: Branch Bocock; Captain: Herman DeLaPerriere, G

Date	Result		Opponent	Record
O. 3	hW	16-0	Dahlonega (Athens)	1-0
O. 17	hW	29-6	South Carolina (Athens)	2-0
O. 24	aL	0-10	Tennessee (Knoxville)	2-1
O. 31	hW	10-0	Mercer (Athens)	3-1
N. 5	aW	8-0	Clemson (Augusta)	4-1
N. 14	aT	6-6	Alabama (Birmingham)	4-1-1
N. 21	hW	2-0	Davidson (Athens)	5-1-1
N. 26	aL	0-23	Auburn (Montgomery)	5-2-1

1909: 1-4-2
Coach: Jay Coulter; Captain: Hugh Bostwich, FB

Date	Result		Opponent	Record
O. 9	aT	0-0	Citadel (Charleston)	0-0-1
O. 16	hT	0-0	Davidson (Athens)	0-0-2
O. 23	aW	3-0	Tennessee (Knoxville)	1-0-2
O. 30	aL	0-14	Alabama (Atlanta)	1-1-2
N. 11	aL	0-5	Clemson (Augusta)	1-2-2
N. 20	aL	6-12	Georgia Tech (Atlanta)	1-3-2
N. 26	aL	5-16	Auburn (Montgomery)	1-4-2

1910: 6-2-1
Coach: W.A. Cunningham; Captain: Omer W. Franklin, G-T

Date	Result		Opponent	Record
O. 1	hW	101-0	Locust Grove (Athens)	1-0
O. 8	hW	79-0	Gordon (Athens)	2-0
O. 15	aW	22-0	Alabama (Birmingham)	3-0
O. 22	hW	35-5	Tennessee (Athens)	4-0
O. 29	hW	21-0	Mercer (Athens)	5-0
N. 5	aL	12-15	Sewanee (Sewanee)	5-1
N. 10	aT	0-0	Clemson (Augusta)	5-1-1
N. 19	aW	11-6	Georgia Tech (Atlanta)	6-1-1
N. 24	aL	0-26	Auburn (Savannah)	6-2-1

1911: 7-1-1
Coach: W.A. Cunningham; Captain: George Woodruff, QB

Date	Result		Opponent	Record
S. 30	hW	51-0	Alabama Pres. (Athens)	1-0
O. 7	hW	38-0	South Carolina (Athens)	2-0
O. 14	aW	11-3	Alabama (Birmingham)	3-0
O. 21	hW	12-3	Sewanee (Athens)	4-0
O. 28	hW	8-5	Mercer (Athens)	5-0
N. 4	aL	0-17	Vanderbilt (Nashville)	5-1
N. 9	aW	22-0	Clemson (Augusta)	6-1
N. 18	aW	5-0	Georgia Tech (Atlanta)	7-1
N. 23	aT	0-0	Auburn (Savannah)	7-1-1

1912: 6-1-1
Coach: W.A. Cunningham; Captain: D.R. Peacock, G

Date	Result		Opponent	Record
O. 5	hW	33-0	Chattanooga (Athens)	1-0
O. 12	hW	33-0	Citadel (Athens)	2-0
O. 19	aL	0-46	Vanderbilt (Atlanta)	2-1
O. 26	aW	13-9	Alabama (Columbus)	3-1
N. 2	hT	13-13	Sewanee (Athens)	3-1-1
N. 9	aW	27-6	Clemson (Augusta)	4-1-1
N. 16	aW	20-0	Georgia Tech (Atlanta)	5-1-1
N. 28	hW	12-6	Auburn (Athens)	6-1-1

1913: 6-2-0

Coach: W.A. Cunningham; Captain: Bob McWhorter, HB

Date	Result	Opponent	Record
O. 4	hW108-0	Alabama Presb. (Athens)	1-0
O. 11	hW 51-0	Dahlonega (Athens)	2-0
O. 18	aW 20-0	Alabama (Birmingham)	3-0
O. 25	aL 6-13	Virginia (Atlanta)	3-1
N. 1	hW 19-6	North Carolina (Athens)	4-1
N. 6	aW 18-15	Clemson (Augusta)	5-1
N. 15	aW 14-0	Georgia Tech (Atlanta)	6-1
N. 22	aL 7-21	Auburn (Atlanta)	6-2

1914: 3-5-1

Coach: W.A. Cunningham; Captain: Dave Paddock, QB

Date	Result	Opponent	Record
S. 26	hW 81-0	Dahlonega (Athens)	1-0
O. 3	hW 13-0	Citadel (Athens)	2-0
O. 10	aW 7-6	Sewanee (Sewanee)	3-0
O. 17	aL 6-41	North Carolina (Atlanta)	3-1
O. 24	aL 0-28	Virginia (Charlottesville)	3-2
O. 31	hL 0-9	Mississippi A&M (Athens)	3-3
N. 7	hL 13-35	Clemson (Athens)	3-4
N. 14	aL 0-7	Georgia Tech (Atlanta)	3-5
N. 21	aT 0-0	Auburn (Atlanta)	3-5-1

1915: 5-2-2

Coach: W.A. Cunningham; Captain: J.G. Henderson, C

Date	Result	Opponent	Record
S. 28	hW 79-0	Newberry (Athens)	1-0
O. 1	hW 64-0	Dahlonega (Athens)	2-0
O. 9	aT 6-6	Chattanooga (Chattanooga)	2-0-1
O. 16	aW 39-0	Citadel (Charleston)	3-0-1
O. 23	hL 7-9	Virginia (Athens)	3-1-1
O. 30	hL 0-12	Auburn (Athens)	3-2-1
N. 1	aW 37-0	Florida (Jacksonville)	4-2-1
N. 13	aT 0-0	Georgia Tech (Atlanta)	4-2-2
N. 25	hW 13-0	Clemson (Athens)	5-2-2

1916: 6-3-0

Coach: W.A. Cunningham; Captain: T.A. Thrash, T

Date	Result	Opponent	Record
S. 30	hW 6-0	Citadel (Athens)	1-0
O. 7	aW 26-0	Clemson (Anderson)	2-0
O. 14	hW 21-0	Florida (Athens)	3-0
O. 21	aW 13-7	Virginia (Charlottesville)	4-0
O. 28	aL 3-27	Navy (Annapolis)	4-1
N. 4	aL 0-3	Auburn (Columbus)	4-2
N. 11	hW 49-0	Furman (Athens)	5-2
N. 18	hL 0-21	Georgia Tech (Athens)	5-3
N. 30	aW 3-0	Alabama (Birmingham)	6-3

1917-1918: NO GAMES

1919: 4-2-3

Coach: W.A. Cunningham; Captain: Artie Pew, T

Date	Result	Opponent	Record
O. 4	hW 28-0	Citadel (Athens)	1-0
O. 11	hW 14-0	South Carolina (Athens)	2-0
O. 18	hW 13-0	Sewanee (Athens)	3-0
O. 25	aW 16-0	Florida (Tampa)	4-0
N. 1	aL 0-7	Auburn (Columbus)	4-1
N. 7	hT 7-7	Virginia (Athens)	4-1-1
N. 15	aT 7-7	Tulane (Augusta)	4-1-2
N. 22	aL 0-6	Alabama (Atlanta)	4-2-2
N. 27	hT 0-0	Clemson (Athens)	4-2-3

1920: 8-0-1

Coach: H.J. Stegeman; Captain: A.M. Day, C

Date	Result	Opponent	Record
O. 2	hW 40-0	Citadel (Athens)	1-0
O. 9	aW 37-0	South Carolina (Columbia)	2-0
O. 13	aW 7-0	Furman (Greenville)	3-0
O. 23	aW 27-3	Oglethorpe (Atlanta)	4-0
O. 30	aW 7-0	Auburn (Columbus)	5-0
N. 6	aT 0-0	Virginia (Charlottesville)	5-0-1
N. 13	hW 56-0	Florida (Athens)	6-0-1
N. 20	aW 21-14	Alabama (Atlanta)	7-0-1
N. 25	hw 55-0	Clemson (Athens)	8-0-1

1921: 7-2-1

Coach: H.J. Stegeman; Captain: Owen Reynolds, E

Date	Result	Opponent	Record
O. 1	hW 28-0	Mercer (Athens)	1-0
O. 8	hW 27-7	Furman (Athens)	2-0
O. 15	aL 7-10	Harvard (Cambridge)	2-1
O. 22	hW 14-0	Oglethorpe (Athens)	3-1
O. 29	aW 7-0	Auburn (Columbus)	4-1
N. 6	hW 21-0	Virginia (Athens)	5-1
N. 13	aT 7-7	Vanderbilt (Nashville)	5-1-1
N. 20	aW 22-0	Alabama (Atlanta)	6-1-1
N. 25	hW 28-0	Clemson (Athens)	7-1-1
N. 27	aL 0-7	Dartmouth (Atlanta)	7-2-1

1922: 5-4-1

Coach: H.J. Stegeman; Captain: Hugh Whelchel, G

Date	Result	Opponent	Record
S. 23	hW 82-13	Newberry (Athens)	1-0
S. 30	hW 41-0	Mercer (Athens)	2-0
O. 7	aL 0-20	Chicago (Chicago)	2-1
O 14	aW 7-0	Furman (Greenville)	3-1
O. 21	hW 7-3	Tennessee (Athens)	4-1
O. 28	hW 26-6	Oglethorpe (Athens)	5-1
N. 4	aL 3-7	Auburn (Columbus)	5-2
N. 11	aT 6-6	Virginia (Charlottesville)	5-2-1
N. 18	hL 0-12	Vanderbilt (Athens)	5-3-1
N. 25	aL 6-10	Alabama (Montgomery)	5-4-1

1923: 5-3-1
Coach: George Woodruff; Captain: Joe Bennett, T

Date	Result		Opponent	Record
S. 29	hW	7-0	Mercer (Athens)	1-0
O. 6	hW	20-6	Oglethorpe (Athens)	2-0
O. 13	aL	0-40	Yale (New Haven)	2-1
O. 20	aW	17-0	Tennessee (Knoxville)	3-1
N. 3	aW	7-0	Auburn (Columbus)	4-1
N. 10	hW	13-0	Virginia (Athens)	5-1
N. 17	aL	7-35	Vanderbilt (Nashville)	5-2
N 24	aL	0-36	Alabama (Montgomery)	5-3
D. 1	hT	3-3	Centre (Athens)	5-3-1

1924: 7-3-0
Coach: George Woodruff; Captain: John Fletcher, E

Date	Result		Opponent	Record
S. 27	hW	26-7	Mercer (Athens)	1-0
O. 4	hW	18-0	South Carolina (Athens)	2-0
O. 11	aL	6-7	Yale (New Haven)	2-1
O. 18	aW	22-0	Furman (Augusta)	3-1
O. 25	aW	3-0	Vanderbilt (Nashville)	4-1
N. 1	hW	33-0	Tennessee (Athens)	5-1
N. 8	aW	7-0	Virginia (Charlottesville)	6-1
N. 15	aW	6-0	Auburn (Columbus)	7-1
N. 27	aL	0-33	Alabama (Birmingham)	7-2
N. 29	aL	7-14	Centre (Danville)	7-3

1925: 4-5-0
Coach: George Woodruff; Captain Ralph Thompson, E

Date	Result		Opponent	Record
S. 26	aW	32-0	Mercer (Macon)	1-0
O. 3	hL	6-7	Virginia (Athens)	1-1
O. 10	aL	7-35	Yale (New Haven)	1-2
O. 17	aW	21-0	Furman (Augusta)	2-2
O 24	hW	26-7	Vanderbilt (Athens)	3-2
O. 31	aL	7-12	Tennessee (Knoxville)	3-3
N. 7	aW	34-0	Auburn (Columbus)	4-3
N. 14	aL	0-3	Georgia Tech (Atlanta)	4-4
N. 26	aL	0-27	Alabama (Birmingham)	4-5

1926: 5-4-0
Coach: George Woodruff; Captain: George Morton, HB

Date	Result		Opponent	Record
S. 25	hW	20-0	Mercer (Athens)	1-0
O. 2	aW	21-0	Virginia (Charlottesville)	2-0
O. 9	aL	0-10	Yale (New Haven)	2-1
O. 16	hL	7-14	Furman (Athens)	2-2
O. 23	aL	13-14	Vanderbilt (Nashville)	2-3
O. 30	hW	32-9	Florida (Athens)	3-3
N. 6	aW	16-0	Auburn (Columbus)	4-3
N. 13	aW	14-13	Georgia Tech (Atlanta)	5-3
N. 25	aL	6-33	Alabama (Birmingham)	5-4

1927: 9-1-0
Coach: George Woodruff; Captain: Chick Shiver, E

Date	Result		Opponent	Record
O. 1	hW	32-0	Virginia (Athens)	1-0
O. 8	aW	14-10	Yale (New Haven)	2-0
O. 15	hW	32-0	Furman (Athens)	3-0
O. 22	aW	33-0	Auburn (Columbus)	4-0
O. 29	aW	31-0	Tulane (New Orleans)	5-0
N. 5	aW	28-0	Florida (Jacksonville)	6-0
N. 12	hW	32-0	Clemson (Athens)	7-0
N. 19	hW	26-7	Mercer (Athens)	8-0
N. 24	aW	20-6	Alabama (Birmingham)	9-0
D. 3	aL	0-12	Georgia Tech (Atlanta)	9-1

1928: 4-5-0
Coach: Harry Mehre; Captain: Glenn Lautzenhiser, T

Date	Result		Opponent	Record
O. 6	hW	52-0	Mercer (Athens)	1-0
O. 13	aL	6-21	Yale (New Haven)	1-1
O. 20	hW	7-0	Furman (Athens)	2-1
O. 27	hW	20-14	Tulane (Athens)	3-1
N. 3	aW	13-0	Auburn (Columbus)	4-1
N. 10	aL	6-26	Florida (Savannah)	4-2
N. 17	hL	12-13	LSU (Athens)	4-3
N. 29	aL	0-19	Alabama (Birmingham)	4-4
D. 8	aL	6-20	Georgia Tech (Atlanta)	4-5

1929: 6-4-0
Coach: Harry Mehre; Captain: Joe Boland, C

Date	Result		Opponent	Record
S. 28	hL	6-13	Oglethorpe (Athens)	0-1
O. 5	hW	27-0	Furman (Athens)	1-1
O. 12	hW	15-0	Yale (Athens)	2-1
O. 19	aW	19-12	N. Carolina (Chapel Hill)	3-1
O. 26	aL	6-18	Florida (Jacksonville)	3-2
N. 2	aL	15-21	Tulane (Columbus)	3-3
N. 9	aL	19-27	NYU (New York)	3-4
N. 16	hW	24-0	Auburn (Athens)	4-4
N. 28	aW	12-0	Alabama (Birmingham)	5-4
D. 7	hW	12-6	Georgia Tech	6-4

1930: 7-2-1
Coach: Harry Mehre; Captain: Herbert Maffett, E

Date	Result		Opponent	Record
S. 27	hW	31-6	Oglethorpe (Athens)	1-0
O. 4	hW	51-0	Mercer (Athens)	2-0
O. 11	aW	18-14	Yale (New Haven)	3-0
O. 18	hW	26-0	North Carolina (Athens)	4-0
O. 25	aW	39-7	Auburn (Columbus)	5-0
N. 1	aT	0-0	Florida (Savannah)	5-0-1
N. 8	aW	7-6	NYU (New York)	6-0-1
N. 15	aL	0-25	Tulane (New Orleans)	6-1-1
N. 27	aL	0-13	Alabama (Birmingham)	6-2-1
D. 6	aW	13-0	Georgia Tech (Atlanta)	7-2-1

1931: 8-2-0
Coach: Harry Mehre; Captain: Austin Downs, QB

Date	Result		Opponent	Record
O. 3	hW	40-0	VPI (Athens)	1-0
O. 10	aW	26-7	Yale (New Haven)	2-0
O. 17	aW	32-6	North Carolina (Chapel Hill)	3-0
O. 24	hW	9-0	Vanderbilt (Athens)	4-0
O. 31	aW	33-6	Florida (Gainesville)	5-0
N. 7	aW	7-6	NYU (New York)	6-0
N. 14	hL	7-20	Tulane (Athens)	6-1
N. 21	aW	12-6	Auburn (Columbus)	7-1
N. 18	hW	35-6	Georgia Tech (Athens)	8-1
D 12	aL	0-60	Southern Cal(Los Angeles)	8-2

1932: 2-5-2
Coach: Harry Mehre; Captain: Vason McWhorter, C

Date	Result		Opponent	Record
O. 1	hL	6-7	VPI (Athens)	0-1
O. 8	aL	25-34	Tulane (New Orleans)	0-2
O. 15	hT	6-6	North Carolina (Athens)	0-2-1
O. 22	aL	6-12	Vanderbilt (Nashville)	0-3-1
O. 29	hW	33-12	Florida (Athens)	1-3-1
N. 5	aL	7-13	NYU (New York)	1-4-1
N. 11	aW	32-18	Clemson (Clemson)	2-4-1
N. 19	aL	7-14	Auburn (Columbus)	2-5-1
N. 26	aT	0-0	Georgia Tech (Atlanta)	2-5-2

1933: 8-2-0
Coach: Harry Mehre; Captain: Graham Batchelor, E

Date	Result		Opponent	Record
S. 30	hW	20-10	N.C. State (Athens)	1-0
O. 7	hW	26-13	Tulane (Athens)	2-0
O. 14	aW	30-0	N. Carolina (Chapel Hill)	3-0
O. 20	aW	13-12	Mercer (Macon)	4-0
O. 28	hW	25-0	NYU (Athens)	5-0
N. 14	aW	14-0	Florida (Jacksonville)	6-0
N. 11	aW	7-0	Yale (New Haven)	7-0
N. 18	aL	6-14	Auburn (Columbus)	7-1
N. 25	aW	7-6	Georgia Tech (Atlanta)	8-1
D. 2	aL	0-31	Southern Cal(Los Angeles)	8-2

1934: 7-3-0
Coach: Harry Mehre; Captain: Charlie Tubyville, E

Date	Result		Opponent	Record
S. 29	hW	42-0	Stetson (Athens)	1-0
O. 6	aW	7-2	Furman (Greenville)	2-0
O. 13	hL	0-14	North Carolina (Athens)	2-1
O. 20	aL	6-7	Tulane (New Orleans)	2-2
O. 27	aL	6-26	Alabama (Birmingham)	2-3
N. 3	aW	14-0	Florida (Jacksonville)	3-3
N. 10	aW	14-7	Yale (New Haven)	4-3
N. 17	hW	27-0	N.C. State	5-3
N. 24	aW	18-0	Auburn (Columbus)	6-3
D. 1	hW	7-0	Georgia Tech (Athens)	7-3

1935: 6-4-0
Coach: Harry Mehre; Captain: John McKnight, C; John Bond, HB

Date	Result		Opponent	Record
S. 28	hW	31-0	Mercer (Athens)	1-0
O. 5	aW	40-0	Chattanooga (Chattanooga)	2-0
O. 12	hW	31-7	Furman (Athens)	3-0
O. 19	aW	13-0	N.C. State (Raleigh)	4-0
O. 26	hL	7-17	Alabama (Athens)	4-1
N. 2	aW	7-0	Florida (Jacksonville)	5-1
N. 9	aW	26-13	Tulane (New Orleans)	6-1
N. 16	hL	0-13	LSU (Athens)	6-2
N. 23	aL	7-19	Auburn (Columbus)	6-3
N. 30	aL	7-19	Georgia Tech (Atlanta)	6-4

1936: 5-4-1
Coach: Harry Mehre; Captains: J.C. Hall, G; Harry Harman, G

Date	Result		Opponent	Record
S. 26	hW	15-6	Mercer (Athens)	1-0
O. 3	hW	13-0	Furman (Athens)	2-0
O. 10	aL	7-47	LSU (Baton Rouge)	2-1
O. 17	hL	6-13	Rice (Athens)	2-2
O. 24	aL	13-20	Auburn (Columbus)	2-3
O. 31	hL	0-46	Tennessee (Athens)	2-4
N. 7	aW	26-8	Florida (Jacksonville)	3-4
N. 14	aW	12-6	Tulane (New Orleans)	4-4
N. 21	aT	7-7	Fordham (New York)	4-4-1
N. 28	hW	16-6	Georgia Tech (Athens)	5-4-1

1937: 6-3-2
Coach: Harry Mehre; Captain: Bill Hartman, FB

Date	Result		Opponent	Record
S. 25	hW	60-0	Oglethorpe (Athens)	1-0
O. 2	aW	13-7	South Carolina (Columbia)	2-0
O. 9	hW	14-0	Clemson (Athens)	3-0
O. 16	aL	6-7	Holy Cross (Boston)	3-1
O. 23	hW	19-0	Mercer (Athens)	4-1
O. 30	aL	0-32	Tennessee (Knoxville)	4-2
N. 6	aL	0-6	Florida (Jacksonville)	4-3
N. 13	hW	7-6	Tulane (Athens)	5-3
N. 20	aT	0-0	Auburn (Columbus)	5-3-1
N. 27	aT	6-6	Georgia Tech (Atlanta)	5-3-2
D. 10	aW	26-8	Miami (Miami)	6-3-2

1938: 5-4-1
Coach: Joel Hunt; Captain: Quinton Lumpkin, C

Date	Result		Opponent	Record
S. 27	hW	20-0	Citadel (Athens)	1-0
O. 3	aW	7-6	South Carolina (Columbia)	2-0
O. 9	hW	38-7	Furman (Athens)	3-0
O. 17	hW	28-19	Mercer (Athens)	4-0
O. 26	aL	6-29	Holy Cross (Worcester)	4-1
N. 6	aW	19-6	Florida (Jacksonville)	5-1
N. 13	aL	6-28	Tulane (New Orleans)	5-2
N. 20	aL	14-23	Auburn (Columbus)	5-3
N. 27	hT	0-0	Georgia Tech (Athens)	5-3-1
D. 3	aL	7-13	Miami (Miami)	5-4-1

1939: 5-6-0

Coach: Wallace Butts; Captain: Vassa Kate, HB

Date	Result		Opponent	Record
S. 30	hW	26-0	Citadel (Athens)	1-0
O. 7	aL	0-20	Furman (Greenville)	1-1
O. 14	hL	0-13	Holy Cross (Athens)	1-2
O. 21	aL	6-13	Kentucky (Louisville)	1-3
O. 28	aL	13-14	NYU (New York)	1-4
N. 4	hW	16-9	Mercer (Athens)	2-4
N. 11	aW	6-2	Florida (Jacksonville)	3-4
N. 18	hW	33-7	South Carolina (Athens)	4-4
N. 25	aL	0-7	Auburn (Columbus)	4-5
D. 2	aL	0-13	Georgia Tech (Atlanta)	4-6
D. 8	aW	13-0	Miami (Miami)	5-6

1940: 5-4-1

Coach: Wallace Butts; Captain: James Skipworth, E

Date	Result		Opponent	Record
S. 27	aW	53-0	Oglethorpe (Atlanta)	1-0
O. 5	aW	33-2	South Carolina (Columbia)	2-0
O. 12	hL	14-28	Ole Miss (Athens)	2-1
O. 19	aL	13-19	Columbia (New York)	2-2
O. 25	hT	7-7	Kentucky (Athens)	2-2-1
N. 2	aW	14-13	Auburn (Columbus)	3-2-1
N. 9	aL	13-18	Florida (Jacksonville)	3-3-1
N. 16	aL	13-21	Tulane (New Orleans)	3-4-1
N. 30	hW	21-19	Georgia Tech (Athens)	4-4-1
D. 6	aW	28-7	Miami (Miami)	5-4-1

1941: 9-1-1

Coach: Wallace Butts; Captain: Heyward Allen, HB

Date	Result		Opponent	Record
S. 27	aW	81-0	Mercer (Macon)	1-0
O. 4	hW	34-6	South Carolina (Athens)	2-0
O. 10	hT	14-14	Ole Miss (Athens)	2-0-1
O. 18	aW	7-3	Columbia (New York)	3-0-1
O. 25	aL	14-27	Alabama (Birmingham)	3-1-1
N. 1	aW	7-0	Auburn (Columbus)	4-1-1
N. 8	aW	19-3	Florida (Jacksonville)	5-1-1
N. 15	hW	47-6	Centre (Athens)	6-1-1
N. 22	hW	35-0	Dartmouth (Athens)	7-1-1
N. 29	aW	21-0	Georgia Tech (Atlanta)	8-1-1
J. 1,42	aW	40-26	TCU (Orange Bowl, Miami)	9-1-1

1942: 11-1-0

Coach: Wallace Butts; Captain: Frank Sinkwich, HB & FB

Date	Result		Opponent	Record
S. 19	aW	7-6	Kentucky (Louisville)	1-0
S. 25	aW	14-0	Jacksonville NAS (Macon)	2-0
O. 3	hW	40-7	Furman (Athens)	3-0
O. 10	aW	48-13	Ole Miss (Memphis)	4-0
O. 17	hW	40-0	Tulane (Athens)	5-0
O. 24	aW	35-13	Cincinnati (Cincinnati)	6-0
O. 31	aW	21-10	Alabama (Atlanta)	7-0
N. 7	aW	75-0	Florida (Jacksonville)	8-0
N. 14	aW	40-0	Chattanooga (Chattanooga)	9-0
N. 21	aL	13-27	Auburn (Columbus)	9-1
N. 28	hW	34-0	Georgia Tech (Athens)	10-1
J. 1/43	aW	9-0	UCLA (Rose Bowl, Pasadena)	11-1

1943: 6-4-0

Coach: Wallace Butts; Captain Mike Castronis, G

Date	Result		Opponent	Record
S. 17	hW	25-7	Presbyterian (Athens)	1-0
S. 25	aL	27-34	LSU (Baton Rouge)	1-1
O. 1	hW	67-0	Tennessee Tech (Athens)	2-1
O. 8	hw	7-0	Wake Forest (Athens)	3-1
O. 10	aL	7-18	Daniel Field (Augusta)	3-2
O. 23	aL	6-27	LSU (Columbus)	3-3
O. 29	hW	39-0	Howard (Athens)	4-3
N. 5	hW	40-12	Presbyterian (Athens)	5-3
N. 13	aW	46-7	VMI (Atlanta)	6-3
N. 27	aL	0-48	Georgia Tech (Atlanta)	6-4

1944: 7-3-0

Coach: Wallace Butts; Captain: Billy Rutland, HB

Date	Result		Opponent	Record
S. 29	hL	7-14	Wake Forest (Athens)	0-1
O. 6	hW	67-0	Presbyterian (Athens)	1-1
O. 13	hW	13-12	Kentucky (Athens)	2-1
O. 20	hW	57-6	Daniel Field (Athens)	3-1
O. 28	aL	7-15	LSU (Atlanta)	3-2
N. 4	aW	14-7	Alabama (Birmingham)	4-2
N. 11	aW	38-12	Florida (Jacksonville)	5-2
N. 18	aW	49-13	Auburn (Columbus)	6-2
N. 24	hW	21-7	Clemson (Athens)	7-2
D. 2	hL	0-44	Georgia Tech (Athens)	7-3

1945: 9-2-0

Coach: Wallace Butts; Captain: Charles Eaves, G

Date	Result		Opponent	Record
S. 22	hW	49-0	Murray State (Athens)	1-0
S. 29	hW	21-0	Clemson (Athens)	2-0
O. 5	aW	27-21	Miami (Miami)	3-0
O. 13	aW	48-6	Kentucky (Lexington)	4-0
O. 20	hL	0-32	LSU (Athens)	4-1
O. 27	aL	14-28	Alabama (Birmingham)	4-2
N. 4	aW	34-7	Chattanooga (Chattanooga)	5-2
N. 11	aW	34-0	Florida (Jacksonville)	6-2
N. 17	aW	35-0	Auburn (Columbus)	7-2
D. 1	aW	33-0	Georgia Tech (Atlanta)	8-2
J. 1/46	aw	20-6	Tulsa (Oil Bowl, Houston)	9-2

1946: 11-0-0

Coach: Wallace Butts; Captain: Charles Trippi, HB

Date	Result		Opponent	Record
S. 27	hW	35-12	Clemson (Athens)	1-0
O. 4	aW	35-7	Temple (Philadelphia)	2-0
O. 11	hW	28-13	Kentucky (Athens)	3-0
O. 19	hW	33-13	Oklahoma A&M (Athens)	4-0
O. 26	aW	70-7	Furman (Greenville)	5-0
N. 2	hW	14-0	Alabama (Athens)	6-0
N. 9	aW	33-14	Florida (Jacksonville)	7-0
N. 16	aW	41-0	Auburn (Columbus)	8-0
N. 23	aW	48-27	Chattanooga (Chattanooga)	9-0
N. 30	hW	35-7	Georgia Tech (Athens)	10-0
J. 1/47	aW	20-10	North Carolina (Sugar Bowl, New Orleans)	11-0

1947: 7-4-1
Coach: Wallace Butts; Captain: Dan Edwards, E

Date	Result	Opponent	Record
S. 19	hW 13-7	Furman (Athens)	1-0
S. 27	aL 7-14	N. Carolina (Chapel Hill)	1-1
O. 4	hW 35-19	LSU (Athens)	2-1
O. 11	aL 0-26	Kentucky (Lexington)	2-2
O. 18	aW 20-7	Oklahoma A&M (Stillwater)	3-2
O. 25	hL 7-17	Alabama (Athens)	3-3
O. 31	hW 21-6	Clemson (Athens)	4-3
N. 8	aW 34-6	Florida (Jacksonville)	5-3
N. 15	aW 28-6	Auburn (Columbus)	6-3
N. 22	aW 27-0	Chattanooga (Chattanooga)	7-3
N. 29	aL 0-7	Georgia Tech (Atlanta)	7-4
J. 1/48	aT 20-20	Maryland (Gator Bowl, Jkv)	7-4-1

1948: 9-2-0
Coach: Wallace Butts: Captains: Weyman Sellers, E;
Bernie Reid, G

Date	Result	Opponent	Record
S. 25	hW 14-7	Chattanooga (Athens)	1-0
O. 2	hL 14-21	North Carolina (Athens)	1-1
O. 9	hW35 12	Kentucky (Athens)	2-1
O. 16	aW 22-0	LSU (Baton Rouge)	3-1
O. 22	aW 42-21	Miami (Miami)	4-1
O. 30	aW 35-0	Alabama (Birmingham)	5-1
N. 6	aW 20-12	Florida (Jacksonville)	6-1
N. 13	aW 42-14	Auburn (Columbus)	7-1
N. 20	hW 33-0	Furman (Athens)	8-1
N. 27	hW 21-13	Georgia Tech (Athens)	9-1
J. 1/49	aL 28-41	Texas (Orange Bowl, Miami)	9-2

1949: 4-6-1
Coach: Wallace Butts; Captain: Porter Payne, G

Date	Result	Opponent	Record
S. 16	hW 25-0	Furman (Athens)	1-0
S. 23	hW 42-6	Chattanooga (Athens)	2-0
O. 1	aL 14-21	N. Carolina (Chapel Hill)	2-1
O. 8	aL 0-25	Kentucky (Lexington)	2-2
O. 14	hW 7-0	LSU (Athens)	3-2
O. 21	aL 9-13	Miami (Miami)	3-3
O. 29	hL 7-14	Alabama (Athens)	3-4
N. 5	aL 7-28	Florida (Jacksonville)	3-5
N. 12	hW 40-0	Duquesne (Athens)	4-5
N. 19	aT 20-20	Auburn (Columbus)	4-5-1
N. 26	aL 6-7	Georgia Tech (Atlanta)	4-6-1

1950: 6-3-3
Coach: Wallace Butts; Captain: Mike Merola, E

Date	Result	Opponent	Record
S. 23	hW 27-7	Maryland (Athens)	1-0
S. 29	aT 7-7	St. Mary's (San Francisco)	1-0-1
O. 7	hT 0-0	North Carolina (Athens)	1-0-2
O. 14	hW 27-0	Miss State (Athens)	2-0-2
O. 21	aT 13-13	LSU (Baton Rouge)	2-0-3
O. 27	aW 19-7	Boston College (Boston)	3-0-3
N. 5	aL 7-14	Alabama (Birmingham)	3-1-3
N. 11	aW 6-0	Florida (Jacksonville)	4-1-3
N. 18	aW 12-10	Auburn (Columbus)	5-1-3
N. 25	hW 40-0	Furman (Athens)	6-1-3
D. 2	hL 0-7	Georgia Tech (Athens)	6-2-3
D. 9	aL 20-40	Texas A&M (Presidtl. Cup)	6-3-3

1951: 5-5-0
Coach: Wallace Butts; Captain: Claude Hipps, HB

Date	Result	Opponent	Record
S. 22	hW 33-0	G. Washington (Athens)	1-0
S. 29	aW 28-16	N. Carolina (Chapel Hill)	2-0
O. 6	aL 0-6	Miss. State (Starkville)	2-1
O. 13	hL 7-43	Maryland (Athens)	2-2
O. 20	hL 0-7	LSU (Athens)	2-3
O. 27	hW 35-28	Boston College (Athens)	3-3
N. 3	hL 14-16	Alabama (Athens)	3-4
N. 10	aW 7-6	Florida (Jacksonville)	4-4
N. 17	aW 46-14	Auburn (Columbus)	5-4
D. 1	aL 6-48	Georgia Tech (Atlanta)	5-5

1952: 7-4-0
Coach: Wallace Butts; Captain: Robert West, E

Date	Result	Opponent	Record
S. 20	aW 19-7	Vanderbilt (Nashville)	1-0
S. 27	aW 21-16	Tulane (New Orleans)	2-0
O. 4	hW 49-0	North Carolina (Athens)	3-0
O. 11	hL 0-37	Maryland (Athens)	3-1
O. 18	aW 27-14	LSU (Baton Rouge)	4-1
O. 25	aL 0-30	Florida (Jacksonville)	4-2
N. 1	aL 19-34	Alabama (Birmingham)	4-3
N. 8	aW 34-27	Pennsylvania (Philadelphia)	5-3
N. 15	aW 13-7	Auburn (Columbus)	6-3
N. 29	hL 9-23	Georgia Tech (Athens)	6-4
D. 5	aW 35-13	Miamia (Miami)	7-4

1953: 3-8-0
Coach: Wallace Butts; Captain: Zeke Bratkowski, QB

Date	Result	Opponent	Record
S. 19	aW 32-19	Villanova (Philadelphia)	1-0
S. 26	hW 16-14	Tulane (Athens)	2-0
O. 3	aL 12-14	Texas A&M (Dallas)	2-1
O. 10	aL 13-40	Maryland (College Park)	2-2
O. 17	hL 6-14	LSU (Athens)	2-3
O. 24	hW 27-14	North Carolina (Athens)	3-3
O. 31	hL 12-33	Alabama (Athens)	3-4
N. 7	aL 7-21	Florida (Jacksonville)	3-5
N. 14	aL 18-39	Auburn (Columbus)	3-6
N. 21	aL 0-14	Miss. Southern (Jackson)	3-7
N. 28	aL 12-28	Georgia Tech (Atlanta)	3-8

1954: 6-3-1
Coach: Wallace Butts; Captain: Joe O'Malley, E

Date	Result	Opponent	Record
S. 18	aW 14-0	Florida St. (Tallahassee)	1-0
S. 25	hW 14-7	Clemson (Athens)	2-0
O. 2	hL 0-6	Texas A&M (Athens)	2-1
O. 9	aW 21-7	N. Carolina (Chapel Hill)	3-1
O. 16	hW 16-14	Vanderbilt (Athens)	4-1
O. 23	aW 7-0	Tulane (New Orleans)	5-1
O. 30	aT 0-0	Alabama (Birmingham)	5-1-1
N. 6	aW 14-13	Florida (Jacksonville)	6-1-1
N. 13	aL 0-35	Auburn (Columbus)	6-2-1
N. 27	hL 3-7	Georgia Tech (Athens)	6-3-1

1955: 4-6-0

Coach: Wallace Butts; Captain: Bobby Garrard, FB

Date	Result		Opponent	Record
S. 17	aL	13-26	Ole Miss (Atlanta)	0-1
S. 24	hW	14-13	Vanderbilt (Athens)	1-1
O. 1	aL	7-26	Clemson (Clemson)	1-2
O. 8	hW	28-7	North Carolina (Athens)	2-2
O. 15	aW	47-14	Florida St. (Tallahassee)	3-2
O. 22	hL	0-14	Tulane (Athens)	3-3
O. 29	hW	35-14	Alabama (Athens)	4-3
N. 5	aL	13-19	Florida (Jacksonville)	4-4
N. 12	aL	13-16	Auburn (Columbus)	4-5
N. 26	aL	3-21	Georgia Tech (Atlanta)	4-6

1956: 3-6-1

Coach: Wallace Butts; Captain: Knox Culpepper, Sr., FB

Date	Result		Opponent	Record
S. 22	aL	0-14	Vanderbilt (Nashville)	0-1
S. 29	hW	3-0	Florida St. (Athens)	1-1
O. 6	hL	7-19	Miss. State (Athens)	1-2
O. 13	aW	26-12	N. Carolina (Chapel Hill)	2-2
O. 19	aT	7-7	Miami (Miami)	2-2-1
O. 27	hL	7-14	Kentucky (Athens)	2-3-1
N. 3	aW	16-13	Alabama (Birmingham)	3-3-1
N. 10	aL	0-28	Florida (Jacksonville)	3-4-1
N. 17	aL	0-20	Auburn (Columbus)	3-5-1
D. 1	hL	0-35	Georgia Tech (Athens)	3-6-1

1957: 3-7-0

Coach: Wallace Butts: Captain: J.B. Davis, HB

Date	Result		Opponent	Record
S. 21	aL	7-26	Texas (Atlanta)	0-1
S. 28	hL	6-9	Vanderbilt (Athens)	0-2
O. 5	aL	0-26	Michigan (Ann Arbor)	0-3
O. 11	aW	13-6	Tulane (New Orleans)	1-3
O. 19	aL	14-27	Navy (Norfolk)	1-4
O. 26	aW	33-14	Kentucky (Lexington)	2-4
N. 2	hL	13-14	Alabama (Athens)	2-5
N. 9	aL	0-22	Florida (Jacksonville)	2-6
N. 16	aL	0-6	Auburn (Columbus)	2-7
N. 30	aW	7-9	Georgia Tech (Atlanta)	3-7

1958: 4-6-0

Coach: Wallace Butts; Captain: Theron Sapp, FB

Date	Result		Opponent	Record
S. 20	aL	8-13	Texas (Austin)	0-1
S. 27	aL	14-21	Vanderbilt (Nashville)	0-2
O. 4	hL	14-24	S. Carolina (Athens)	0-3
O. 11	aW	28-13	Florida (Jacksonville)	1-3
O. 25	hW	28-0	Kentucky (Athens)	2-3
N. 1	aL	0-12	Alabama (Tuscaloosa)	2-4
N. 8	aL	6-7	Florida (Jacksonville)	2-5
N. 15	aL	6-21	Auburn (Columbus)	2-6
N. 22	hW	76-0	The Citadel (Athens)	3-6
N. 29	hW	16-3	Georgia Tech (Athens)	4-6

1959: 10-1-0

Coach: Wallace Butts; Captain: Don Soberdash, HB

Date	Result		Opponent	Record
S. 19	hW	17-3	Alabama (Athens)	1-0
S. 26	hW	21-6	Vanderbilt (Athens)	2-0
O. 3	aL	14-30	S. Carolina (Columbia)	2-1
O. 10	hW	35-6	H. Simmons (Athens)	3-1
O. 17	aW	15-0	Miss State (Atlanta)	4-1
O. 24	aW	14-7	Kentucky (Lexington)	5-1
O. 31	hW	42-0	Florida St. (Athens)	6-1
N. 7	aW	21-10	Florida (Jacksonville)	7-1
N. 14	hW	14-13	Auburn (Athens)	8-1
N. 28	aW	21-14	Georgia Tech (Atlanta)	9-1
J. 1/60	aW	14-0	Missouri (Orange Bowl)	10-1

1960: 6-4-0

Coach: Wallace Butts; Captain: Francis Tarkenton, QB

Date	Result		Opponent	Record
S. 17	aL	6-21	Alabama (Birmingham)	0-1
S. 24	aW	18-7	Vanderbilt (Nashville)	1-1
O. 1	hW	38-6	South Carolina (Athens)	2-1
O. 7	aL	3-10	U. of South. Cal. (L.A.)	2-2
O. 15	hW	20-17	Mississippi St. (Athens)	3-2
O. 22	aW	17-13	Kentucky (Lexington)	4-2
O. 29	hW	45-7	Tulsa (Athens)	5-2
N. 5	aL	14-22	Florida (Jacksonville)	5-3
N. 12	aL	6-9	Auburn (Auburn)	5-4
N. 26	hW	7-6	Georgia Tech (Athens)	6-4

1961: 3-7-0

Coach: Johnny Griffith; Captain: Pete Case, LT

Date	Result		Opponent	Record
S. 23	hL	6-32	Alabama (Athens)	0-1
S. 30	hL	0-21	Vanderbilt (Athens)	0-2
O. 7	hW	17-14	South Carolina (Athens)	1-2
O. 14	aL	0-3	Florida St. (Tallahassee)	1-3
O. 21	aW	10-7	Miss. State (Atlanta)	2-3
O. 28	hW	16-15	Kentucky (Athens)	3-3
N. 3	aL	7-32	Miami (Miami)	3-4
N. 11	aL	14-21	Florida (Jacksonville)	3-5
N. 18	hL	7-10	Auburn (Athens)	3-6
D. 2	aL	7-22	Georgia Tech (Atlanta)	3-7

1962: 3-4-3

Coach: Johnny Griffith; Captain: Ray Clark, E

Date	Result		Opponent	Record
S. 22	aL	0-35	Alabama (Birmingham)	0-1
S. 29	aW	10-0	Vanderbilt (Nashville)	1-1
O. 6	aT	7-7	South Carolina (Columbia)	1-1-1
O. 13	aW	24-16	Clemson (Clemson)	2-1-1
O. 20	hL	0-18	Florida State (Athens)	2-2-1
O. 27	hT	7-7	Kentucky (Athens)	2-2-2
N. 3	hT	10-10	N.C. State (Athens)	2-2-3
N. 10	aL	15-23	Florida (Jacksonville)	2-3-3
N. 17	aW	30-21	Auburn (Auburn)	3-3-3
D. 1	hL	6-37	Georgia Tech (Athens)	3-4-3

1963: 4-5-1
Coach: Johnny Griffith; Captain: Billy Knowles, HB

Date	Result		Opponent	Record
S. 21	hL	7-32	Alabama (Athens)	0-1
S. 28	hW	20-0	Vanderbilt (Athens)	1-1
O. 5	hW	27-7	South Carolina (Athens)	2-1
O. 12	aT	7-7	Clemson (Clemson)	2-1-1
O. 18	aW	31-14	Miami (Miami)	3-1-1
O. 26	aW	17-14	Kentucky (Lexington)	4-1-1
N. 2	aL	7-28	N. Carolina (Chapel Hill)	4-2-1
N. 9	aL	14-21	Florida (Jacksonville)	4-3-1
N. 16	hL	0-14	Auburn (Athens)	4-4-1
N. 30	aL	3-14	Georgia Tech (Atlanta)	4-5-1

1964: 7-3-1
Coach: Vince Dooley; Captain: Barry Wilson, DE

Date	Result		Opponent	Record
S. 19	aL	3-31	Alabama (Tuscaloosa)	0-1
S. 26	aW	7-0	Vanderbilt (Nashville)	1-1
O. 3	aT	7-7	South Carolina (Columbia)	1-1-1
O. 10	hW	19-7	Clemson (Athens)	2-1-1
O. 17	hL	14-17	Florida St. (Athens)	2-2-1
O. 24	hW	21-7	Kentucky (Athens)	3-2-1
O. 31	hW	24-8	North Carolina (Athens)	4-2-1
N. 7	aW	14-7	Florida (Jacksonville)	5-2-1
N. 14	aL	7-14	Auburn (Auburn)	5-3-1
N. 28	hW	7-0	Georgia Tech (Athens)	6-3-1
D. 26	aW	7-0	Texas Tech (Sun Bowl)	7-3-1

1965: 6-4-0
Coach: Vince Dooley; Captain: Doug McFalls, DB

Date	Result		Opponent	Record
S. 18	hW	18-17	Alabama (Athens)	1-0
S. 25	hW	24-10	Vanderbilt (Athens)	2-0
O. 2	aW	15-7	Michigan (Ann Arbor)	3-0
O. 9	hW	23-9	Clemson (Athens)	4-0
O. 16	aL	3-10	Florida St. (Tallahassee)	4-1
O. 23	aL	10-28	Kentucky (Lexington)	4-2
O. 30	aW	47-35	N. Carolina (Chapel Hill)	5-2
N. 6	aL	10-14	Florida (Jacksonville)	5-3
N. 13	hL	19-21	Auburn (Athens)	5-4
N. 27	aW	17-7	Georgia Tech (Atlanta)	6-4

1966: 10-1-0
Coach: Vince Dooley; Captain: George Patton, T

Date	Result		Opponent	Record
S. 17	aW	20-17	Miss. State (Jackson)	1-0
S. 24	aW	43-7	VMI (Roanoke)	2-0
O. 1	aW	7-0	South Carolina (Columbia)	3-0
O. 8	hW	9-3	Ole Miss (Athens)	4-0
O. 14	aL	6-7	Miami (Miami)	4-1
O. 22	hW	27-15	Kentucky (Athens)	5-1
O. 29	hW	28-3	North Carolina (Athens)	6-1
N. 5	aW	27-10	Florida (Jacksonville)	7-1
N. 12	aW	21-13	Auburn (Auburn)	8-1
N. 26	hW	23-14	Georgia Tech (Athens)	9-1
D. 31	aW	24-9	SMU (Cotton Bowl, Dallas)	10-1

1967: 7-4-0
Coach: Vince Dooley; Captain: Kirby Moore, QB

Date	Result		Opponent	Record
S. 23	hW	30-0	Miss. State (Athens)	1-0
S. 30	aW	24-17	Clemson (Clemson)	2-0
O. 7	hW	21-0	South Carolina (Athens)	3-0
O. 14	aL	20-29	Ole Miss (Jackson)	3-1
O. 21	aW	56-6	VMI (Athens)	4-1
O. 28	aW	31-7	Kentucky (Lexington)	5-1
N. 4	aL	14-15	Houston (Houston)	5-2
N. 11	aL	16-17	Florida (Jacksonville)	5-3
N. 18	hW	17-0	Auburn (Athens)	6-3
N. 25	aW	21-14	Georgia Tech (Atlanta)	7-3
D. 16	aL	7-14	N.C. State (Liberty Bowl)	7-4

1968: 8-1-2
Coach: Vince Dooley; Captain: Bill Stanfill, T

Date	Result		Opponent	Record
S. 14	aT	17-17	Tennessee (Knoxville)	0-0-1
S. 28	hW	31-13	Clemson (Athens)	1-0-1
O. 5	aW	21-20	South Carolina (Columbia)	2-0-1
O. 12	hW	21-7	Ole Miss (Athens)	3-0-1
O. 19	hW	32-6	Vanderbilt (Athens)	4-0-1
O. 26	aW	35-14	Kentucky (Lexington)	5-0-1
N. 2	hT	10-10	Houston (Athens)	5-0-2
N. 9	aW	51-0	Florida (Jacksonville)	6-0-2
N. 16	aW	17-3	Auburn (Auburn)	7-0-2
N. 30	hW	47-8	Georgia Tech (Athens)	8-0-2
J. 1/69	aL	2-16	Arkansas (Sugar Bowl)	8-1-2

1969: 5-5-1
Coach: Vince Dooley; Captain: Steve Greer, DG

Date	Result		Opponent	Record
S. 20	hW	35-0	Tulane (Athens)	1-0
S. 27	aW	30-0	Clemson (Clemson)	2-0
O. 4	hW	41-16	South Carolina (Athens)	3-0
O. 11	aL	17-25	Ole Miss (Jackson)	3-1
O. 18	aW	40-8	Vanderbilt (Nashville)	4-1
O. 25	hW	30-0	Kentucky (Athens)	5-1
N. 1	hL	3-17	Tennessee (Athens)	5-2
N. 8	aT	13-13	Florida (Jacksonville)	5-2-1
N. 15	hL	3-16	Auburn (Athens)	5-3-1
N. 29	aL	0-6	Georgia Tech (Atlanta)	5-4-1
D. 20	aL	6-45	Nebraska (Sun Bowl, El P.)	5-5-1

1970: 5-5-0
Coach: Vince Dooley; Captain: Tommy Lyons, C

Date	Result		Opponent	Record
S. 19	aL	14-17	Tulane (New Orleans)	0-1
S. 26	hW	38-0	Clemson (Athens)	1-1
O. 3	aL	6-7	Mississippi St. (Jackson)	1-2
O. 10	hL	21-31	Ole Miss (Athens)	1-3
O. 17	hW	37-3	Vanderbilt (Athens)	2-3
O. 24	aW	19-3	Kentucky (Lexington)	3-3
O. 31	hW	52-34	South Carolina (Athens)	4-3
N. 7	aL	17-24	Florida (Jacksonville)	4-4
N. 14	aW	31-17	Auburn (Auburn)	5-4
N. 28	hL	7-17	Georgia Tech (Athens)	5-5

1971: 11-1-0

Coach: Vince Dooley; Captain: Royce Smith, OG

Date	Result		Opponent	Record
S. 11	hW	56-25	Oregon St. (Athens)	1-0
S. 18	hW	17-7	Tulane (Athens)	2-0
S. 25	aW	28-0	Clemson (Clemson)	3-0
O. 2	hW	35-7	Miss. State (Athens)	4-0
O. 9	aW	38-7	Ole Miss (Jackson)	5-0
O. 16	aW	24-0	Vanderbilt (Nashville)	6-0
O. 23	hW	34-0	Kentucky (Athens)	7-0
O. 30	aW	24-0	South Carolina (Columbia)	8-0
N. 6	aW	49-7	Florida (Jacksonville)	9-0
N. 13	hL	20-35	Auburn (Athens)	9-1
N. 25	aW	28-24	Georgia Tech (Atlanta)	10-1
D. 31	aW	7-3	N. Carolina (Gator Bowl)	11-1

1972: 7-4-0

Coach: Vince Dooley; Captain: Robert Honeycutt, FB

Date	Result		Opponent	Record
S. 16	hW	24-14	Baylor (Athens)	1-0
S. 23	aL	13-24	Tulane (New Orleans)	1-1
S. 30	hW	28-22	N.C. State (Athens)	2-1
O. 7	hL	7-25	Alabama (Athens)	2-2
O. 14	aW	14-13	Ole Miss (Jackson)	3-2
O. 21	hW	28-3	Vanderbilt (Athens)	4-2
O. 28	aW	13-7	Kentucky (Lexington)	5-2
N. 4	hL	0-14	Tennessee (Athens)	5-3
N. 11	aW	10-7	Florida (Jacksonville)	6-3
N. 18	aL	10-27	Auburn (Auburn)	6-4
N. 2	hW	27-7	Georgia Tech (Athens)	7-4

1973: 7-4-1

Coach: Vince Dooley; Captain: Bob Burns, FB

Date	Result		Opponent	Record
S. 15	hT	7-7	Pittsburgh (Athens)	0-0-1
S. 22	hW	31-14	Clemson (Athens)	1-0-1
S. 29	hW	31-12	N.C. State (Athens)	2-0-1
O. 6	aL	14-28	Alabama (Tuscaloosa)	2-1-1
O. 13	hW	20-0	Ole Miss (Athens)	3-1-1
O. 20	aL	14-18	Vanderbilt (Nashville)	3-2-1
O. 27	hL	7-12	Kentucky (Athens)	3-3-1
N. 3	aW	35-31	Tennessee (Knoxville)	4-3-1
N. 10	aL	10-11	Florida (Jacksonville)	4-4-1
N. 17	hW	28-14	Auburn (Athens)	5-4-1
D. 1	aW	10-3	Georgia Tech (Atlanta)	6-4-1
D. 28	aW	17-16	Maryland (Peach Bowl)	7-4-1

1974: 6-6-0

Coach: Vince Dooley; Captain: Keith Harris, LB

Date	Result		Opponent	Record
S. 14	hW	48-35	Oregon State (Athens)	1-0
S. 21	aL	14-38	Miss. State (Jackson)	1-1
S. 28	hW	52-14	South Carolina (Athens)	2-1
O. 5	aL	24-28	Clemson (Clemson)	2-2
O. 12	hW	49-0	Ole Miss (Athens)	3-2
O. 19	hW	38-31	Vanderbilt (Athens)	4-2
O. 26	aW	24-20	Kentucky (Lexington)	5-2
N. 2	hL	24-31	Houston (Athens)	5-3
N. 9	aW	17-16	Florida (Jacksonville)	6-3
N. 16	aL	13-17	Auburn (Auburn)	6-4
N. 30	hL	14-34	Georgia Tech (Athens)	6-5
D. 20	aL	10-21	Miami OH (Tangerine Bowl)	6-6

1975: 9-3-0

Coach: Vince Dooley; Captain: Glynn Harrison, RB

Date	Result		Opponent	Record
S. 6	hL	9-19	Pittsburgh (Athens)	0-1
S. 20	hW	28-6	Miss. State (Athens)	1-1
S. 27	aW	28-20	South Carolina (Columbia)	2-1
O. 4	hW	35-7	Clemson (Athens)	3-1
O. 11	aL	13-28	Ole Miss (Oxford)	3-2
O. 18	aW	47-3	Vanderbilt (Nashville)	4-2
O. 25	hW	21-13	Kentucky (Athens)	5-2
N. 1	hW	28-24	Richmond (Athens)	6-2
N. 8	aW	10-7	Florida (Jacksonville)	7-2
N. 15	hW	28-13	Auburn (Athens)	8-2
N. 27	aW	42-26	Georgia Tech (Atlanta)	9-2
J. 1/76	aL	10-31	Arkansas (Cotton Bowl)	9-3

1976: 10-2-0

Coach: Vince Dooley; Captain: Ray Goff, QB

Date	Result		Opponent	Record
S. 11	hW	36-24	California (Athens)	1-0
S. 18	aW	41-0	Clemson (Clemson)	2-0
S. 25	hW	20-12	South Carolina (Athens)	3-0
O. 2	hW	21-0	Alabama (Athens)	4-0
O. 9	aL	17-21	Ole Miss (Oxford)	4-1
O. 16	hW	45-0	Vanderbilt (Athens)	5-1
O. 23	aW	31-7	Kentucky (Lexington)	6-1
O. 30	hW	31-17	Cincinnati (Athens)	7-1
N. 6	aW	41-27	Florida (Jacksonville)	8-1
N. 13	aW	28-0	Auburn (Auburn)	9-1
N. 27	hW	13-10	Georgia Tech (Athens)	10-1
J. 1/77	aL	3-27	Pittsburgh (Sugar Bowl)	10-2

1977: 5-6-1

Coach: Vince Dooley; Captain: Ben Zambiasi, LB

Date	Result		Opponent	Record
S. 10	hW	27-16	Oregon (Athens)	1-0
S. 17	hL	6-7	Clemson (Athens)	1-1
S. 24	aW	15-13	South Carolina (Columbia)	2-1
O. 1	aL	10-18	Alabama (Tuscaloosa)	2-2
O. 8	hW	14-13	Ole Miss (Athens)	3-2
O. 15	aW	24-13	Vanderbilt (Nashville)	4-2
O. 22	hL	0-33	Kentucky (Athens)	4-3
O. 29	hW	23-7	Richmond (Athens)	5-3
N. 5	aL	17-22	Florida (Jacksonville)	5-4
N. 12	hL	14-33	Auburn (Athens)	5-5
N. 26	aL	7-16	Georgia Tech (Atlanta)	5-6

1978: 9-2-1

Coach: Vince Dooley; Captain: Willie McClendon, TB

Date	Result		Opponent	Record
S. 16	hW	16-14	Baylor (Athens)	1-0
S. 23	hW	12-0	Clemson (Athens)	2-0
S. 30	aL	10-27	South Carolina (Columbia)	2-1
O. 7	hW	42-3	Ole Miss (Athens)	3-1
O. 14	aW	24-17	LSU (Baton Rouge)	4-1
O. 21	hW	31-10	Vanderbilt (Athens)	5-1
O. 28	aW	17-16	Kentucky (Lexington)	6-1
N. 4	hW	41-3	VMI (Athens)	7-1
N. 11	aW	24-22	Florida (Jacksonville)	8-1
N. 18	aT	22-22	Auburn (Auburn)	8-1-1
D. 2	hW	29-28	Georgia Tech (Athens)	9-1-1
D. 31	aL	22-25	Sanford (Bluebonnet Bowl)	9-2-1

1979: 6-5-0

Coach: Vince Dooley; Captain: Gordon Terry, DE

Date	Result		Opponent	Record
S. 15	hL	21-22	Wake Forest (Athens)	0-1
S. 22	aL	7-12	Clemson (Clemson)	0-2
S. 29	hL	20-27	South Carolina (Athens)	0-3
O. 6	aW	24-21	Ole Miss (Oxford)	1-3
O. 13	hW	21-14	LSU (Athens)	2-3
O. 20	aW	31-10	Vanderbilt (Nashville)	3-3
O. 27	hW	20-6	Kentucky (Athens)	4-3
N. 3	hL	0-31	Virginia (Athens)	4-4
N. 10	aW	33-10	Florida (Jacksonville)	5-4
N. 17	hL	13-33	Auburn (Athens)	5-5
N. 24	aW	16-3	Georgia Tech (Atlanta)	6-5

1980: 12-0

Coach: Vince Dooley; Captain: Frank Ros, LB

Date	Result		Opponent	Record
S. 6	aW	16-15	Tennessee (Knoxville)	1-0
S. 13	hW	42-0	Texas A&M (Athens)	2-0
S. 20	hW	20-16	Clemson (Athens)	3-0
S. 27	hW	34-3	TCU (Athens)	4-0
O. 11	hW	28-21	Ole Miss (Athens)	5-0
O. 18	hW	41-0	Vanderbilt (Athens)	6-0
O. 25	aW	27-0	Kentucky (Lexington)	7-0
N. 1	hW	13-10	South Carolina (Athens)	8-0
N. 8	aW	26-21	Florida (Jacksonville)	9-0
N. 15	aW	31-21	Auburn (Auburn)	10-0
N. 29	hW	38-20	Georgia Tech (Athens)	11-0
J 1/81	aW	17-10	Notre Dame (Sugar Bowl)	12-0

1981: 10-2

Coach: Vince Dooley; Captain: Buck Belue, QB

Date	Result		Opponent	Record
S. 5	hW	44-0	Tennessee (Athens)	1-0
S. 12	hW	27-13	California (Athens)	2-0
S. 19	aL	3-13	Clemson (Clemson)	2-1
S. 26	hW	24-0	South Carolina (Athens)	3-1
O. 10	aW	37-7	Ole Miss (Oxford)	4-1
O. 17	aW	53-21	Vanderbilt (Nashville)	5-1
O. 24	hW	21-0	Kentucky (Athens)	6-1
O. 31	hW	49-3	Temple (Athens)	7-1
N. 7	aW	26-21	Florida (Jacksonville)	8-1
N. 14	hW	24-13	Auburn (Athens)	9-1
D. 5	aW	44-7	Georgia Tech (Atlanta)	10-1
J. 1/82	aL	20-24	Pittsburgh (Sugar Bowl)	10-2

1982: 11-1

Coach: Vince Dooley; Captain: Wayne Radloff, C

Date	Result		Opponent	Record
S. 6	hW	13-7	Clemson (Athens)	1-0
S. 11	hW	17-14	Brigham Young (Athens)	2-0
S. 25	aW	34-18	South Carolina (Columbia)	3-0
O. 2	aW	29-22	Miss. State (Starkville)	4-0
O. 9	hW	33-10	Ole Miss (Athens)	5-0
O. 16	hW	27-13	Vanderbilt (Athens)	6-0
O. 23	aW	27-14	Kentucky (Lexington)	7-0
O. 30	hW	34-3	Memphis State (Athens)	8-0
N. 6	aW	44-0	Florida (Jacksonville)	9-0
N. 13	aW	19-14	Auburn (Auburn)	10-0
N. 27	hW	38-18	Georgia Tech (Athens)	11-0
J. 1/83	aL	23-27	Penn State (Sugar Bowl)	11-1

1983: 10-1-1

Coach: Vince Dooley; Captain: Freddie Gilbert, DE

Date	Result		Opponent	Record
S. 3	hW	19-8	UCLA (Athens)	1-0
S. 17	aT	16-16	Clemson (Clemson)	1-0-1
S. 24	hW	31-13	South Carolina (Athens)	2-0-1
O. 1	hW	20-7	Miss. State (Athens)	3-0-1
O. 8	aW	36-11	Ole Miss (Oxford)	4-0-1
O. 15	aW	20-13	Vanderbilt (Nashville)	5-0-1
O. 22	hW	47-21	Kentucky (Athens)	6-0-1
O. 29	hW	31-14	Temple (Athens)	7-0-1
N. 5	aW	10-9	Florida (Jacksonville)	8-0-1
N. 12	hL	7-13	Auburn (Athens)	8-1-1
N. 26	aW	27-24	Georgia Tech (Atlanta)	9-1-1
J. 2/84	aW	10-9	Texas (Cotton Bowl)	10-1-1

1984: 7-4-1

Coach: Vince Dooley; Captain: Knox Culpepper, LB

Date	Result		Opponent	Record
S. 8	hW	26-19	Southern Miss. (Athens)	1-0
S. 22	hW	26-23	Clemson (Athens)	2-0
S. 29	aL	10-17	South Carolina (Columbia)	2-1
O. 6	aW	24-14	Alabama (Birmingham)	3-1
O. 13	hW	18-12	Ole Miss (Athens)	4-1
O. 20	hW	62-35	Vanderbilt (Athens)	5-1
O. 27	aW	37-7	Kentucky (Lexington)	6-1
N. 3	hW	13-3	Memphis State (Athens)	7-1
N. 10	aL	0-27	Florida (Jacksonville)	7-2
N. 17	aL	12-21	Auburn (Auburn)	7-3
D. 1	hL	18-35	Georgia Tech (Athens)	7-4
D. 22	aT	17-17	Florida St. (Citrus Bowl)	7-4-1

1985: 7-3-2

Coach: Vince Dooley; Captain: Peter Anderson, C

Date	Result		Opponent	Record
S. 2	hL	16-20	Alabama (Athens)	0-1
S. 14	hW	17-14	Baylor (Athens)	1-1
S. 21	aW	20-13	Clemson (Clemson)	2-1
S. 28	hW	35-21	South Carolina (Athens)	3-1
O. 12	aW	49-21	Ole Miss (Jackson)	4-1
O. 19	aT	13-13	Vanderbilt (Nashville)	4-1-1
O. 26	hW	26-6	Kentucky (Athens)	5-1-1
N. 2	hW	58-3	Tulane (Athens)	6-1-1
N. 9	aW	24-3	Florida (Jacksonville)	7-1-1
N. 16	hL	10-24	Auburn (Athens)	7-2-1
N. 30	aL	16-20	Georgia Tech (Atlanta)	7-3-1
D. 28	aT	13-13	Arizona (Sun Bowl)	7-3-2

1986: 8-4

Coach: Vince Dooley; Captain: John Little, SAF

Date	Result		Opponent	Record
S. 13	hW	31-7	Duke (Athens)	1-0
S. 20	hL	28-31	Clemson (Athens)	1-1
S. 27	aW	31-26	South Carolina (Columbia)	2-1
O. 4	hW	14-10	Ole Miss (Athens)	3-1
O. 11	aL	14-23	LSU (Baton Rouge)	3-2
O. 18	hW	38-16	Vanderbilt (Athens)	4-2
O. 25	aW	31-9	Kentucky (Lexington)	5-2
N. 1	hW	28-13	Richmond (Athens)	6-2
N. 8	aL	19-31	Florida (Jacksonville)	6-3
N. 15	aW	20-16	Auburn (Auburn)	7-3
N. 29	hW	31-24	Georgia Tech (Athens)	8-3
D. 23	aL	24-27	Boston Col. (Hall/Fame B.)	8-4

1987: 9-3-0

Coach: Vince Dooley; Captain: Kim Stephens, OG

Date	Result	Opponent	Record
S. 5	hW 30-22	Virginia (Athens)	1-0
S. 12	hW 41-7	Oregon State (Athens)	2-0
S. 19	aL 20-21	Clemson (Clemson)	2-1
S. 26	hW 13-6	South Carolina (Athens)	3-1
O. 3	aW 31-14	Ole Miss (Oxford)	4-1
O. 10	hL 23-26	LSU (Athens)	4-2
O. 17	aW 52-24	Vanderbilt (Nashville)	5-2
O. 24	hW 17-14	Kentucky (Athens)	6-2
N. 7	aW 23-10	Florida (Jacksonville)	7-2
N. 14	hL 11-27	Auburn (Athens)	7-3
N. 28	aW 30-16	Georgia Tech (Atlanta)	8-3
D. 29	aW 20-17	Arkansas (Liberty Bowl)	9-3

1988: 9-3-0

Coach: Vince Dooley; Captain: Todd Wheeler, C

Date	Result	Opponent	Record
S. 3	hW 28-17	Tennessee (Athens)	1-0
S. 10	hW 38-10	TCU (Athens)	2-0
S. 17	aW 42-35	Miss. State (Starkville)	3-0
S. 24	aL 10-23	South Carolina (Columbia)	3-1
O. 1	hW 36-12	Ole Miss (Athens)	4-1
O. 8	hW 41-22	Vanderbilt (Athens)	5-1
O. 22	aL 10-16	Kentucky (Lexington)	5-2
O. 29	hW 59-24	Wm.& Mary (Athens)	6-2
N. 5	aW 26-3	Florida (Jacksonville)	7-2
N. 12	aL 10-20	Auburn (Auburn)	7-3
N. 26	hW 24-3	Georgia Tech (Athens)	8-3
J. 1/89	aW 34-27	Michigan St. (Mazda Gator Bowl)	9-3

1989: 6-6-0

Coach: Ray Goff; Captain: Ben Smith, FS

Date	Result	Opponent	Record
S. 16	hW 15-3	Baylor (Athens)	1-0
S. 23	hW 23-6	Miss. State (Athens)	2-0
S. 30	hL 20-24	South Carolina (Athens)	2-1
O. 7	aL 14-17	Tennessee (Knoxville)	2-2
O. 14	aL 13-17	Ole Miss (Oxford)	2-3
O. 21	aW 35-16	Vanderbilt (Nashville)	3-3
O. 28	hW 34-23	Kentucky (Athens)	4-3
N. 4	hW 37-10	Temple (Athens)	5-3
N. 11	aW 17-10	Florida (Jacksonville)	6-3
N. 18	hL 3-20	Auburn (Athens)	6-4
D. 2	aL 22-33	Georgia Tech (Atlanta)	6-5
D. 30	aL 18-19	Syracuse (Peach Bowl)	6-6

1990: 4-7

Coach: Ray Goff; Captain: Brian Cleveland, FB

Date	Result	Opponent	Record
S. 8	aL 13-18	LSU (Baton Rouge)	0-1
S. 15	hW 18-17	Southern Miss.	1-1
S. 22	hW 17-16	Alabama (Athens)	2-1
S. 29	hW 19-15	East Carolina (Athens)	3-1
O. 6	aL 3-34	Clemson (Clemson)	3-2
O. 13	hL 12-28	Ole Miss (Athens)	3-3
O. 20	hW 39-28	Vanderbilt (Athens)	4-3
O. 27	aL 24-26	Kentucky (Lexington)	4-4
N. 10	aL 7-38	Florida (Jacksonville)	4-5
N. 17	aL 10-33	Auburn (Auburn)	4-6
D. 1	hL 23-40	Georgia Tech (Athens)	4-7

1991: 9-3

Coach: Ray Goff; Captain: Greg Talley, QB

Date	Result	Opponent	Record
A. 31	hW 48-0	W. Carolina (Athens)	1-0
S. 7	hW 31-10	LSU (Athens)	2-0
S. 21	aL 0-10	Alabama (Tuscaloosa)	2-1
S. 28	hW 27-14	Cal State Full. (Athens)	3-1
O. 5	hW 27-12	Clemson (Athens)	4-1
O. 12	aW 37-17	Mississippi (Oxford)	5-1
O. 19	aL 25-27	Vanderbilt (Nashville)	5-2
O. 26	hW 49-27	Kentucky (Athens)	6-2
N. 9	aL 13-45	Florida (Jacksonville)	6-3
N. 16	hW 37-27	Auburn (Athens)	7-3
N. 30	aW 18-15	Georgia Tech (Atlanta)	8-3
D. 29	aW 24-15	Arkansas (Ind. Bowl)	9-3

1992: 10-2

Coach: Ray Goff; Captain: Alec Millen, OT

Date	Result	Opponent	Record
S. 5	aW 28-6	South Carolina (Columbia)	1-0
S. 12	hL 31-34	Tennessee (Athens)	1-1
S. 19	hW 56-0	Cal. St. Full. (Athens)	2-1
S. 26	hW 37-11	Mississippi (Athens)	3-1
O. 3	aW 27-3	Arkansas (Fayetteville)	4-1
O. 10	hW 34-7	Georgia Southern (Athens)	5-1
O. 17	hW 30-20	Vanderbilt (Athens)	6-1
O. 24	aW 40-7	Kentucky (Lexington)	7-1
O. 31	aL 24-26	Florida (Jacksonville)	7-2
N. 14	aW 14-10	Auburn (Auburn)	8-2
N. 28	hW 31-17	Georgia Tech (Athens)	9-2
J. 1/93	aW 21-14	Ohio State (Citrus Bowl)	10-2

1993: 5-6-0

Coach: Ray Goff; Captain: Eric Zeier, QB

Date	Result	Opponent	Record
S. 4	hL 21-23	South Carolina (Athens)	0-1
S. 11	aL 6-38	Tennessee (Knoxville)	0-2
S. 18	hW 52-37	Texas Tech. (Athens)	1-2
S. 25	aL 14-31	Ole Miss (Oxford)	1-3
O. 2	hL 10-20	Arkansas (Athens)	1-4
O. 9	hW 54-24	Southern Miss. (Athens)	2-4
O. 16	aW 41-3	Vanderbilt (Nashville)	3-4
O. 23	hW 33-28	Kentucky (Athens)	4-4
O. 30	aL 26-33	Florida (Jacksonville)	4-5
N. 13	hL 28-42	Auburn (Auburn)	4-6
N. 25	aW 43-10	Georgia Tech (Atlanta)	5-6

1994: 6-4-1

Coach: Ray Goff; Captain: Eric Zeier, QB

Date	Result	Opponent	Record
S. 3	aW 24-21	South Carolina (Columbia)	1-0
S. 10	hL 23-41	Tennessee (Athens)	1-1
S. 17	hW 70-6	N.E. Louisiana (Athens)	2-1
S. 24	hW 17-14	Ole Miss (Athens)	3-1
O. 1	aL 28-29	Alabama (Tuscaloosa)	3-2
O. 8	hW 40-14	Clemson (Athens)	4-2
O. 15	hL 30-43	Vanderbilt (Athens)	4-3
O. 22	aW 34-30	Kentucky (Lexington)	5-3
O. 29	aL 14-52	Florida (Gainesville)	5-4
N. 12	aT 23-23	Auburn (Auburn)	5-4-1
N. 25	hW 48-10	Georgia Tech (Athens)	6-4-1

1995: 6-6
Coach: Ray Goff; Captain: Whit Marshall, MLB

Date	Result		Opponent	Record
S. 2	hW	42-23	South Carolina (Athens)	1-0
S. 9	aL	27-30	Tennessee (Knoxville)	1-1
S. 16	hW	40-13	N.M. State (Athens)	2-1
S. 23	aL	10-18	Ole Miss (Oxford)	2-2
S. 30	hL	0-31	Alabama (Athens)	2-3
O. 7	aW	19-17	Clemson (Clemson)	3-3
O. 14	aW	17-6	Vanderbilt (Nashville)	4-3
O. 21	hW	12-3	Kentucky (Athens)	5-3
O. 28	hL	17-52	Florida (Athens)	5-4
N. 11	hL	31-37	Auburn (Athens)	5-5
N. 23	aW	18-17	Georgia Tech (Atlanta)	6-5
D. 30	aL	27-34	Virginia (Peach Bowl)	6-6

1996: 5-6
Coach: Jim Donnan; Captains: Mike Bobo, QB, Robert Edwards, TB, Jason Ferguson, DT, Corey Johnson, FS, Adam Meadows, OT, Gene Toodle, BK

Date	Result		Opponent	Record
A. 31	hL	7-11	Southern Miss. (Athens)	0-1
S. 14	aL	14-23	South Carolina (Columbia)	0-2
S. 21	hW	15-12	Texas Tech. (Athens)	1-2
O. 5	aW	38-19	Miss. State (Starkville)	2-2
O. 12	hL	17-29	Tennessee (Athens)	2-3
O. 19	hW	13-2	Vanderbilt (Athens)	3-3
O. 26	aL	17-24	Kentucky (Lexington)	3-4
N. 2	aL	7-47	Florida (Jacksonville)	3-5
N. 16	aW	56-49	Auburn (OT) (Auburn)	4-5
N. 23	hL	27-31	Ole Miss (Athens)	4-6
N. 30	hW	19-10	Georgia Tech (Athens)	5-6

1997: 10-2
Coach: Jim Donnan; Captains: Hines Ward, Brandon Tolbert, Mike Bobo, Greg Bright

Date	Result		Opponent	Record
A. 30	hW	38-7	Arkansas St. (Athens)	1-0
S. 13	hW	31-15	South Carolina (Athens)	2-0
S. 20	hW	42-3	N.E. Louisiana (Athens)	3-0
O. 4	hW	47-0	Miss. State (Athens)	4-0
O. 11	aL	13-38	Tennessee (Knoxville)	4-1
O. 18	aW	34-13	Vanderbilt (Nashville)	5-1
O. 25	hW	23-13	Kentucky (Athens)	6-1
N. 1	aW	37-17	Florida (Jacksonville)	7-1
N. 15	hL	34-45	Auburn (Athens)	7-2
N. 22	aW	21-14	Ole Miss (Oxford)	8-2
N. 19	aW	27-24	Georgia Tech (Atlanta)	9-2
J. 1/98	aW	33-6	Wisconsin (Outback Bowl)	0-2

1998: 9-3
Coach: Jim Donnan; Captains: "Champ" Bailey, Matt Stinchcomb, Olandis Gray, Chris Terry, Paul Snellings, Kirby Smart

Date	Result		Opponent	Record
S. 5	hW	56-3	Kent State (Athens)	1-0
S. 12	aW	17-3	South Carolina (Columbia)	2-0
S. 19	hW	16-9	Wyoming (Athens)	3-0
O. 3	aW	28-27	LSU (Baton Rouge)	4-0
O. 10	hL	3-22	Tennessee (Athens)	4-1
O. 17	hW	31-6	Vanderbilt (Athens)	5-1
O. 24	aW	28-26	Kentucky (Lexington)	6-1
O. 31	aL	7-38	Florida (Jacksonville)	6-2
N. 14	aW	28-17	Auburn (Auburn)	7-2
N. 21	hW	24-17	Ole Miss (Athens)	8-2
N. 28	hL	19-21	Georgia Tech (Athens)	8-3
D. 31	aW	35-33	Virginia (Peach Bowl)	9-3

1999: 7-4
Coach: Jim Donnan; Captains: Quincy Carter, Steve Herndon, Orantes Grant, Richard Seymour

Date	Result		Opponent	Record
S. 4	hW	38-7	Utah St. (Athens)	1-0
S. 11	hW	24-9	South Carolina (Athens)	2-0
S. 25	hW	24-23	Central Florida (Athens)	3-0
O. 2	hW	23-22	LSU (Athens)	4-0
O. 9	aL	20-37	Tennessee (Knoxville)	4-1
O. 16	aW	27-17	Vanderbilt (Nashville)	5-1
O. 23	hW	49-34	Kentucky (Athens)	6-1
O. 30	aL	14-30	Florida (Jacksonville)	6-2
N. 13	hL	21-38	Auburn (Athens)	6-3
N. 20	aW	20-17	Ole Miss (Oxford)	7-3
N. 27	aW	51-48	Georgia Tech (Atlanta)	8-3
J. 1/00	aW	28-25	Purdue (OT) (Outback Bowl)	9-3